INSIDE THE PERFORMANCE WORKSHOP

Inside The Performance Workshop: A Sourcebook for Rasaboxes and Other Exercises is the first full-length volume dedicated to the history, theory, practice, and application of a suite of performer training exercises developed by Richard Schechner and elaborated on by the editors and contributors of this book. This work began in the 1960s with The Performance Group and has continued to evolve.

Rasaboxes—a featured set of exercises—is an interdisciplinary approach for training emotional expressivity through the use of breath, body, voice, movement, and sensation. It brings together:

- the concept of *rasa* from classical Indian performance theory and practice
- research on emotion from neuroscience and psychology
- experimental and experiential performance practices
- theories of ritual, play, and performance

This book combines both practical "how-to" guidance and applications from diverse contexts including undergraduate and graduate actor training, television acting, K-12 education, devising, and drama therapy. The book serves as an introduction to the work as well as an essential resource for experienced practitioners.

Rachel Bowditch, PhD, is Professor of Theatre in the School of Music, Dance, and Theatre at Arizona State University, USA, and a theatre director. Bowditch is author of *On the Edge of Utopia: Performance and Ritual at Burning Man*, *Performing Utopia*, and *Physical Dramaturgy: Perspectives from the Field*.

Paula Murray Cole, MFA, LMT, is Associate Professor of acting, voice, movement, and the Alexander Technique in the School of Music, Theatre and Dance at Ithaca College, USA. Cole acted in Schechner's productions and has taught and developed Rasaboxes and The Performance Workshop (TPW) since 1999.

Michele Minnick, PhD, CMA, is an independent artist, scholar, and educator, whose current work focuses on the intersections of performance, somatic practice, social justice, and climate change. She is a core creator with Submersive Productions in Baltimore, MD, and the founder of Vital Matters.

For workshops and more information, you can reach us at www.rasaboxes.com.

Inside The Performance Workshop

A Sourcebook for Rasaboxes and Other Exercises

Edited by

**RACHEL BOWDITCH
PAULA MURRAY COLE
MICHELE MINNICK**

Routledge
Taylor & Francis Group
LONDON AND NEW YORK

Cover image: Participants doing chorus work in vira rasabox, TPW at NYU.
Photo courtesy of Ryan Jensen Photography, 2004

First published 2023
by Routledge
4 Park Square, Milton Park, Abingdon, Oxon OX14 4RN

and by Routledge
605 Third Avenue, New York, NY 10158

Routledge is an imprint of the Taylor & Francis Group, an informa business

© 2023 selection and editorial matter, Rachel Bowditch, Paula Murray Cole, and Michele Minnick; individual chapters, the contributors

The right of Rachel Bowditch, Paula Murray Cole, and Michele Minnick to be identified as the authors of the editorial material, and of the authors for their individual chapters, has been asserted in accordance with sections 77 and 78 of the Copyright, Designs and Patents Act 1988.

All rights reserved. No part of this book may be reprinted or reproduced or utilised in any form or by any electronic, mechanical, or other means, now known or hereafter invented, including photocopying and recording, or in any information storage or retrieval system, without permission in writing from the publishers.

Trademark notice: Product or corporate names may be trademarks or registered trademarks, and are used only for identification and explanation without intent to infringe.

British Library Cataloguing-in-Publication Data
A catalogue record for this book is available from the British Library

Library of Congress Cataloging-in-Publication Data
Names: Bowditch, Rachel, editor.
Title: Inside the performance workshop : a sourcebook for rasaboxes and other exercises / edited by Rachel Bowditch, Paula Murray Cole and Michele Minnick.
Description: 1st edition. | New York : Routledge, 2023. | Includes bibliographical references and index.
Identifiers: LCCN 2022055442 (print) | LCCN 2022055443 (ebook) | ISBN 9781138680012 (hardback) | ISBN 9781138680029 (paperback) | ISBN 9781315563619 (ebook)
Subjects: LCSH: Movement (Acting) | Acting—Problems, exercises, etc.
Classification: LCC PN2071.M6 I525 2023 (print) | LCC PN2071.M6 (ebook) | DDC 792.028—dc23/eng/20230223
LC record available at https://lccn.loc.gov/2022055442
LC ebook record available at https://lccn.loc.gov/2022055443

ISBN: 978-1-138-68001-2 (hbk)
ISBN: 978-1-138-68002-9 (pbk)
ISBN: 978-1-315-56361-9 (ebk)

DOI: 10.4324/9781315563619

Typeset in Sabon
by Apex CoVantage, LLC

Dedicated to Richard Schechner
and to practitioners of the work—past, present, and future.

BRIEF CONTENTS

List of Figures xiii

List of Contributors xv

Acknowledgments xix

Crossing the Line: Why The Performance Workshop? 1

PART I   HISTORY AND THEORY

1. **Richard Schechner and Origins of The Performance Workshop** 10
2. **What is Rasa?** 46
3. **Rasaesthetics** 55

PART II   PRACTICE

4. **Inside the Performance Workshop** 82

PART III   FACILITATING THE PERFORMANCE WORKSHOP

5. **Principles of the Performance Workshop: An Interview with Richard Schechner** 190
6. **The Unavoidable Guru: Roles of the Performance Workshop Leader** 197

PART IV   NOTES FROM THE FIELD

7. **Freeing Emotional Expression in Young Performers: Rasaboxes in K–12 Context** 212
8. **Psychophysical Preparation for Rasaboxes with Strasberg and Stanislavsky** 225
9. **Adapting Rasaboxes to Rasa≈Therapy: Clinical Applications in Drama Therapy** 235

- 10 Rasaboxes, Drama Therapy, and Stability through Dynamic Change: A Case Study 244
- 11 Rasaboxes in the Training of Drama Therapists 251
- 12 Dancing on the Tongue 258
- 13 Lights, Camera, Action! Rasaboxes Training and Coaching for Brazilian Telenovelas 263
- 14 Character Building Through Rasaboxes: Staging *Electra* at Teatro Prometeo 269
- 15 Experimenting with the Clown in Rasaboxes 275
- 16 Dramaturgy of the Emotions: The Performance Workshop and Rasaboxes in Directing *Machinal* 280

Index 295

CONTENTS

List of Figures xiii

List of Contributors xv

Acknowledgments xix

Crossing the Line: Why The Performance Workshop? 1
Michele Minnick, Paula Murray Cole, and Rachel Bowditch
with Cobina Gillitt

PART I HISTORY AND THEORY

1 Richard Schechner and Origins of The Performance Workshop 10
Cobina Gillitt and Michele Minnick

2 What Is Rasa? 46
Shanti Pillai

3 Rasaesthetics 55
Richard Schechner

PART II PRACTICE

4 Inside The Performance Workshop 82
Paula Murray Cole, Michele Minnick, and Rachel Bowditch

Fundamental Principles and Practices 82
    Four Phases of Performer Training 83
    Presence and Absence 83
    Consent and Boundary Checks 83
    Feedback and Discussion Circles 84
    Time in TPW 85

Navigation Guide 87
    A Note About Language 87
    A Note About Order 87

Instructions 87
Experience 87
Discussion 88

Rules for Play 88

Beginnings 89
Set Up 89
Entering the Space 89
Crossing the Line 90
Names 92
Performative Introductions 93
Greetings 93

Warm-Ups: Physical and Vocal Training 94
Yoga Asanas and Breath Work 94
  Yoga Asanas 95
  Breath Work 98
Panting and Sounding with Resonators 100

Group Sound Work 102
Open Sound 102
Aiming and Passing Sound 103
One Sound 104
One Sound One Movement 106

Crossings 108
Crossings I: Encounters 108
Crossings II: Display 112
Crossings III: Desires 114

Performance of Self and Persona 116
Song of Self 117
Object Exercise 121
Animal Exercise 122
Group Performances 124

Creating Performance Worlds 125
Crossings IV: Slow Motion 125
Crossings V: Slow Motion Transformation 128

Rasaboxes 136
Overview 136
Why Rasa? 137
Orange Exercise: Rasa, Literally 139
Setting Up the Rasaboxes Grid 141
Introducing Each Rasa 142
Writing and Drawing in Rasaboxes 142

Embodying Rasas 143
Around the World I 144
Sculpting in Partners 145
Showing and Regarding 147

Making a Breath Phrase 148
Shanta Rasabox: First Taste 150
Shopping for Rasas 150
Relating in Rasaboxes for Two Players 152
Transitions in Rasaboxes 154
Sound Sensation in Rasaboxes 156
Around the World II 158
Relating with Shanta 160
Scaling Intensity 161
Text in the Rasaboxes: Monologues 164
Chorus Work in Rasaboxes 167
Chorus with Text 168
Relating with Text: Scene Work 169
Mixing Rasas 171
Layering Rasas 173
Rasawalk: Site-Specific Explorations 177

Cool Downs 179

Closings 181
The Banquet 181
Uncrossing the Line 183

Structure and Practice of TPW 184
Sample Outline for Three-Week Workshop 184

PART III FACILITATING THE PERFORMANCE WORKSHOP

5 Principles of The Performance Workshop: An Interview with Richard Schechner 190
With Paula Murray Cole, Michele Minnick, and Rachel Bowditch

6 The Unavoidable Guru: Roles of The Performance Workshop Leader 197
Scott Wallin

PART IV NOTES FROM THE FIELD

7 Freeing Emotional Expression in Young Performers: Rasaboxes in K–12 Context 212
Elise Forier Edie

Rasaboxes with Middle and High School Students 213

Using Rasaboxes with Kindergarten Through 5th Grade Students 219

8 **Psychophysical Preparation for Rasaboxes with Strasberg and Stanislavsky** 225
Ursula Neuerburg

9 **Adapting Rasaboxes to Rasa≈Therapy: Clinical Applications in Drama Therapy** 235
Andrew M. Gaines

10 **Rasaboxes, Drama Therapy, and Stability Through Dynamic Change: A Case Study** 244
Dana Arie

11 **Rasaboxes in the Training of Drama Therapists** 251
Nisha Sajnani

12 **Dancing on the Tongue** 258
Erin B. Mee

13 **Lights, Camera, Action! Rasaboxes Training and Coaching for Brazilian Telenovelas** 263
Fernanda Guimarães
Translated by Michele Minnick

14 **Character Building Through Rasaboxes: Staging *Electra* at Teatro Prometeo** 269
Fernando Calzadilla

15 **Experimenting with the Clown in Rasaboxes** 275
Ana Achcar
Translated by Michele Minnick

16 **Dramaturgy of the Emotions: The Performance Workshop and Rasaboxes in Directing *Machinal*** 280
Rachel Bowditch

Index 295

FIGURES

0.0　Participant in Rasaboxes workshop led by Richard Schechner in Norway, 2013. 1
0.1　Sketch of performers doing Rasaboxes by Joan Schirle. 9
1.1　Audience interaction and environmental staging of TPG's *Commune,* directed by Richard Schechner, 1970. The Performing Garage, NYC. 16
1.2　William Finley as Dionysus and William Shephard as Pentheus in *Dionysus in 69* directed by Richard Schechner, 1968. The Performing Garage, NYC. 21
1.3　Schechner looking at a photo of Krishnamacharya in his 1971 journal. 25
1.4　TPG'S *Mother Courage* directed by Richard Schechner, in Lucknow, India, 1976. 27
1.5　An early draft of the "Magnitudes of Performance" chart in Richard Schechner's 1980–1981 journal. 34
1.6　Rebecca Wilenski and Jeff Ricketts in *Faust/gastronome*, directed by Richard Schechner, 1993. 37
1.7　*Three Sisters* directed by Richard Schechner, La MaMa Annex, NYC, 1997. 38
1.8　*YokastaS Redux* by Richard Schechner and Saviana Stanescu, directed by Richard Schechner at La Mama Annex, NYC, 2005. 39
1.9　*Imagining O*, directed by Richard Schechner and Benjamin Mosse. Montclair State University, NJ, 2014. 39
4.1　Sketch of performers doing Rasaboxes by Joan Schirle. 81
4.2　Rolls of masking tape. 89
4.3　Yoga drawings by Fernando Calzadilla. 96
4.4　Yoga drawings by Fernando Calzadilla. 97
4.5　Students in a Feedback and Discussion Circle. 105
4.6　After Animal Exercise. 124
4.7　Crossing the line in Slow Motion. 125
4.8　Slow Motion Crossing diagram. 126
4.9　Shay Webster in Slow Motion Crossing. 127
4.10　Slow Motion Transformation diagram. 131
4.11　Dressing corners. 132
4.12　Slow Motion Transformation: at the Crossing Line. 132
4.13　Slow Motion Transformation encounter. 134
4.14　Aerial view of rasaboxes grid. 136
4.15　Michele Minnick drawing in the rasaboxes. 143
4.16　Drawing in raudra rasabox from workshop led by Richard Schechner. 144
4.17　TPW participant in hasya rasabox. 145

4.18 Performer in bhayanaka rasabox. 146
4.19 Participants relating in the rasaboxes. 153
4.20 Performer in bibhatsa rasabox. 157
4.21 Alyssa Duerksen exploring karuna with body, paint, and canvas. 160
4.22 Michele Minnick in adbhuta rasabox. 164
4.23 Drawing in shringara rasabox in workshop with Richard Schechner. 165
4.24 Participants doing chorus work in vira rasabox. 168
4.25 Paula Murray Cole in shringara rasabox. 175
4.26 Matt Watkins rasawalking on Moonstone Beach, CA. 177
4.27 Performers in shavasana. 179
5.1 Sketch of performers doing Rasaboxes by Joan Schirle. 189
5.2 Richard Schechner with an early sketch of Rasaboxes from his 1993 journal. 191
6.1 Discussion circle with participants in workshop with Richard Schechner. 198
7.1 Sketch of performer doing Rasaboxes by Joan Schirle. 211
13.1 Close-Up Rasaboxes exercise during rehearsals for TV Record's telenovela, "The Ten Commandments." 266
14.1 Rehearsal for *Electra* directed by Fernando Calzadilla at Teatro Prometeo. 270
15.1 Patrícia Ubeda doing clown work in karuna rasabox. 276
16.1 *Machinal* by Sophie Treadwell directed by Rachel Bowditch. 281
16.2 Slow Motion Transformation diagram for *Machinal* directed by Rachel Bowditch. 287
16.3 *The House of the Spirits* by Caridad Svich directed by Rachel Bowditch. 290

CONTRIBUTORS

Ana Achcar is Associate Professor of Performing Arts, Federal University of the State of Rio de Janeiro, *UNIRIO*, teaching in the Pos-graduação and Graduate Programs in the Theater School. She coordinates the interdisciplinary program for training, social action, and research, *Enfermaria do Riso*, which trains theatre students to perform as clowns in hospitals. She also heads the Mask Study Group/*Núcleo do Ator*—*UNIRIO*. She has published various articles on mask and clown work.

Dana Arie is a drama therapist located in Israel and is a graduate of the William Esper Studio, NYU Drama Therapy program, and the Neuroscience and Psychobiology graduate program at Tel Aviv University. Arie was first exposed to Rasaboxes during her drama therapy training and continued to incorporate it into her clinical work, in both individual and group therapy with different populations—from adults with chronic psychiatric disorders to autistic children and adolescents. Her research and interest in neuroscience focus on the embodiment of emotions and the connection between somatic, emotional, and cognitive experiences.

Rachel Bowditch, PhD (NYU Performance Studies), is a theatre director and Professor of Theatre in the School of Music, Dance, and Theatre in the Herberger Institute for Design and the Arts at Arizona State University. She attended Ecole de Jacques Lecoq in Paris in 1998 and is a core teacher of TPW and Rasaboxes. Bowditch acted in Schechner's productions of *YokastaS* (2005 and 2007) with East Coast Artists. She has taught and developed Rasaboxes and The Performance Workshop (TPW) since 2003. Her books include *On the Edge of Utopia: Performance and Ritual at Burning Man* (2010), *Performing Utopia* (University of Chicago Press/Seagull Books, 2018), and *Physical Dramaturgy: Perspectives from the Field* (Routledge, 2018).

Fernando Calzadilla, PhD (NYU Performance Studies), is a visual artist, theater designer, dramaturg, performance scholar, and a core teacher of TPW and Rasaboxes. He has been awarded 14 times for best set, costumes, and lighting designer. He has performed and exhibited in Caracas, São Paulo, New York, and Miami art galleries. His work has received support from the Knight Foundation, the Shubert Foundation, and the National Endowment for the Arts. Calzadilla was a Fulbright Specialist 2017–2020 in theater and was Guest Artist at the Directors Lab West 2017. Between 2007 and 2017, he was Resident Artist for Miami Theater Center, where he co-authored three original plays and four adaptations. He designed sets, lights, and costumes for all of them.

Paula Murray Cole is Associate Professor in the School of Music, Theatre, and Dance at Ithaca College, a teacher of the Alexander Technique, and a licensed massage therapist. Cole acted in Schechner's *Three Sisters* and *Hamlet* with East Coast Artists. Her professional work centers on the development and dissemination of

Rasaboxes and The Performance Workshop (TPW). She has taught and/or presented this work at colleges, universities, conferences, and independent arts organizations nationally and internationally since 1999. In 2009, Cole produced the only documentary video recording of Schechner teaching the whole of TPW, *Crossing the Line: Inside Richard Schechner's Performance Workshop*.

Elise Forier Edie is a playwright, author, and children's theater practitioner based in Los Angeles. Her award-winning solo show, *The Pink Unicorn*, has been performed throughout the US and Canada. Her newest play, *American Pain*, debuted at the United Solo Theater Festival in 2021. She is Chair of Arts and Performance at West Los Angeles College, where she teaches classes in cinema, acting, playwriting, and dramatic literature.

Andrew M. Gaines, PhD, RDT-BCT, LCAT, is Head of Theatre Arts and Communication at Grays Harbor College and a licensed creative arts therapist and board-certified trainer of drama therapists as well as a director, playwright, and actor. Andrew created the award-winning *Kindergarten Truck*, a mobile, immersive, community-engaged, drama therapy-inspired performance that toured nationwide. His Rasaboxes training began in 2004, and he has led workshops for NYU Drama Therapy, Pratt Institute, CUNY, North American Drama Therapy Association, Expressive Arts Summit, ManKind Project, and the Theatre and Performance Research Association. His research and publications investigate how performance builds empathy and visibility for those who have been historically marginalized and disenfranchised.

Cobina Gillitt, PhD, translator, freelance dramaturg, scholar, and performer, did her graduate work in performance studies at NYU under Richard Schechner's mentorship. Her translations of Indonesian plays have been published in several anthologies, while her scholarly work on Indonesian theatre has appeared in *Performing Indonesia* (Smithsonian Institution, 2016), *Antigone on the Contemporary World Stage* (OUP, 2011), and *The Senses in Performance* (Routledge, 2006), as well as in *The Drama Review* and other academic journals. She has held faculty appointments in the Department of Drama, Tisch School of the Arts, NYU, and in Theatre and Performance, SUNY Purchase. Since 1988, she has performed across Indonesia and internationally as a member of Jakarta-based Teater Mandiri.

Fernanda Guimarães has taught and coached acting since 2003 and developed Rasaboxes as preparation for actors in theatre, television, and in workshops in Rio de Janeiro and elsewhere in Brazil, focusing on televisual language, including Acting Workshops for Record TV; Wolf Maya School for Actors; and Acting Workshops for the Cesgranrio Foundation. She presented the monograph "Rasaboxes in Movement Preparation for Actors in Teledramaturgy: A Workshop Proposal," as her final project at Faculdade Angel Vianna School of Dance (2010). In 2022, her year-long study focusing on neuroscience and behavior at the Pontifical Catholic University of Rio included Rasaboxes in her research project, "The Neurosciences Applied to the Body–Mind–Brain–Emotion of the Actor."

Erin B. Mee, PhD, is Associate Arts Professor in Undergraduate Drama at Tisch School of the Arts, NYU. She is the author of *Theatre of Roots: Redirecting the Modern Indian Stage* (Seagull Books, 2008), co-editor of *Antigone on the Contemporary World Stage* (OUP, 2011), and *Modern Asian Theatre and Performance 1900–2000* (Methuen, 2014), and editor of *Drama Contemporary: India* (JHUP, 2005). Her articles on rasa have been published in *Natarang, Performance Research, Sangeet Natak, Critical Stages, Reti, Saperi, Linguaggi: Italian Journal of Cognitive Sciences*, and in five book collections published by Routledge, Methuen, Common Ground, and McFarland. She is the founding co-artistic director of This Is Not A Theatre Company.

Michele Minnick, PhD, CMA, is a performance maker and producer, somatic movement educator, independent scholar, and teaching artist. She has taught, presented, and applied TPW and Rasaboxes internationally since 1998 and applied the work to the creation of performance in professional and educational settings in the US and Brazil. Minnick was a member of East Coast Artists from 1994 to 2005, translating and performing in Schechner's production of *Three Sisters* (1995–1997) and performing in *Hamlet* (1999). In 2023, she launched Vital Matters, an interdisciplinary, arts-based laboratory for change motivated by the climate crisis and social injustice. Minnick is a Core Creator with Submersive Productions in Baltimore, where she uses Rasaboxes as a core pedagogy with K-12 students through Arts for Learning Maryland.

Ursula Neuerburg, PhD, educated in Berlin and New York, is Associate Professor of Theater at Concordia University, Montreal. She connects her commitment to ecology, de-colonization, history, and feminism with her work in somatic engagement, a CATR working group, as member of the Seedings Collective (Rwanda, Israel, Germany), and through the performance of space and place, particularly in the meeting of indigenous and non-indigenous world views. As a performer/director she was a founding member of two companies, TZF in Berlin and East Coast Artists, NY. She is a core teacher of Rasaboxes and volunteers regularly at Bread & Puppet Theater. She has published widely in English and German.

Shanti Pillai, PhD, is Assistant Professor of Theatre at Williams College. Her writing has appeared in *The Drama Review, Conversations Across the Field of Dance Studies, Theatre Topics, Women and Performance*, and *Dance Research Journal*. In 2017, she received a Fulbright-Nehru Fellowship for research on women artists and contemporary performance in India. She is a bharatanatyam dancer trained by the great T. Balasaraswati's senior disciples, Nandini Ramani and Priyamvada Sankar. From 2005 to 2014 she collaborated with dancers and actors in Cuba to create original works. In 2016, she co-founded Third Space Performance Lab with actor Marc Gomes to explore collaborative art making and Indian performance principles.

Nisha Sajnani, PhD, RDT-BCT, is the Director of the Program in Drama Therapy and Theatre & Health Lab and founding Co-Director of the Arts + Health at NYU. In her capacity as Chair of the NYU Creative Arts Therapies Consortium, she leads a World Health Organization commission to map the evidence for the physical, mental, and social health benefits of the arts and arts therapies. An award-winning author, educator, and advocate, her body of work explores the unique ways in which aesthetic experience can inspire care, equity, and collective human flourishing across the lifespan.

Richard Schechner, an NYU University Professor Emeritus, is a founder of performance studies, a performance theorist, theater director, author, and editor of *TDR* and the Enactments book series. Founder of The Performance Group and East Coast Artists, his productions include *Dionysus in 69*, *Commune*, *The Tooth of Crime*, *Mother Courage and Her Children*, *Seneca's Oedipus*, *Faust/gastronome*, *Three Sisters*, *The Cherry Orchard*, *Hamlet*, *The Oresteia*, *YokastaS*, *Ma Rainey's Black Bottom*, *Swimming to Spalding*, and *Imagining O*. His books include *Public Domain*, *Environmental Theater*, *Between Theater and Anthropology*, *Performance Theory*, *The Future of Ritual*, *Performance Studies: An Introduction*, and *Performed Imaginaries*. He has been awarded three honorary doctorates and numerous fellowships.

Scott Wallin, PhD, MSW, is on the faculty at the University of California, Berkeley, where he has taught a variety of courses in writing and research, theater, and acting, and directed a number of theater productions. He previously taught in the interdisciplinary arts at Stanford University. As a clinical case manager and therapist, he has worked extensively with people who are homeless and within the criminal justice system in San Francisco and New York. He has had the privilege to live and study in Europe, travel extensively throughout Central America, and serve as a Peace Corps Volunteer in the Caribbean. He is a core TPW and Rasaboxes facilitator.

ACKNOWLEDGMENTS

Since this is a book about practice, we have to thank not only the people who have made the book possible, but also those who have enabled us to sustain the practice of developing this work in a variety of contexts. First of all, we would like to thank our teacher and mentor, Richard Schechner, for sharing his decades of performance knowledge with us and for his trust and support in translating this embodied tradition into a two-dimensional written document. His ongoing friendship and guidance have been invaluable. Thank you to our contributors for their dedication and continued commitment to the development of this work; thanks to the students who participated in the filming of The Performance Workshop in 2009, and to Matt Bockleman of Fly-Eye Films, with Corey Silver of Silver Sound, for filming it and producing the 30-minute documentary *Crossing the Line*. Gratitude to Nicole Potter, who published our first Rasaboxes essay in *Movement for Actors*, our Routledge editors Claire Margerison, Ben Piggott, Laura Soppelsa, Kate Edwards, Steph Hines, and Nick Craggs for their unbelievable patience and support throughout this process, Apex for their diligent work in production and to Mariellen Sanford for her editorial suggestions on early versions of the manuscript. Thank you to Jeff Casazza, Annette Thornton, Scott Wallin, Cobina Gillitt, Freddy Villano, and Tom Fish for their copy editing, perspective, and insights; to the Association for Theatre Movement Educators and the Association for Theatre in Higher Education for providing a national platform to share the work; to Dr. Martin Blaser for recognizing the potential of Rasaboxes to contribute to the education and wellness of physicians; to Noel Rodriguez, students, and faculty of the Department of Performance Studies at New York University, Joan Schirle and Dell'Arte International School of Physical Theatre, Jaroslaw Fret and the Grotowski Institute in Wroclaw, Poland, and Janice Orlandi for providing a venue and a platform for sharing the development of the work over the years; and to Paul Ekman and Leeny Sack for the invaluable research and ideas that have supported the development of this pedagogy.

Rachel Bowditch: my mentors Kevin Burns, Phil Soltanoff, RoseLee Goldberg, Gautam Dasgupta; my colleagues and students at the School of Music, Dance, and Theatre in the Herberger Institute for Design and the Arts at Arizona State University, who have been partners in the development and evolution of Rasaboxes through classwork and productions; the Creighton Medical School in Arizona for incorporating Rasaboxes into their medical humanities training for first-year medical students; and especially to my mom, my daughter Sophie, Moon, Bruce, Mark, Scott Hannon, Scott B., and all my friends, whose encouragement, love, and support have been a beacon of strength throughout this process.

Paula Murray Cole: my friends and family for the years of support—Freddy Villano, Nancy and Stephen Cole, Leslie Dixon, Sharon Byrd, and Rachel Hogancamp—all past and present students and colleagues at Ithaca College, especially Susannah Berryman and Norm Johnson, who developed and applied the work;

the Phoenix Players Theatre Group, Auburn, NY; Elise Forier Edie for bringing the work to CWU; Casey Sams and Jed Diamond at UT Knoxville; Sheri Sanders and Rock the Audition; Lindsay Gilmour and Durga Bor, who co-produced the Rasa Symposium (2012); Lawrence J. McCrea, scholar of Sanskrit and rasa theory; performers Alyssa Duerksen, Hannah Dubner, Andrew Karl; Michael Kushner, Joshua Johnson, Marla Montgomery, and Ryan Jensen for their photography and videography of the work.

Michele Minnick: Arts for Learning Maryland for welcoming an adaptation of Rasaboxes as a tool for artistic, social, and emotional learning; in Brazil—Regina Miranda, Joana Ribeiro, Zeca Ligeiro, Marisa Naspolini, Ana Bevilaqua, Adriana Bonfatti, Henrique Fontes, and Reiner Tenente; Harrison Long and students at Kennesaw State University Department of Theatre and Performance Studies; Robin Quick and the faculty and students at Towson University; the 2016 NYU cohort for the workshop and the photos; Shobha Sobramanian and her Jayamangalam; my colleagues at Submersive Productions; my friends and family, who have supported me through "the book" for all these years; and to Jennifer Fleming for helping me work through the many layers of the process.

And finally, to all our students, who are our best teachers, and who help us deepen the work.

Crossing the Line
Why The Performance Workshop?

MICHELE MINNICK, PAULA MURRAY COLE, AND RACHEL BOWDITCH, WITH COBINA GILLITT

FIGURE 0.0 Participant in Rasaboxes workshop led by Richard Schechner in Norway, 2013.

Source: Photo courtesy of Richard Schechner.

Welcome to The Performance Workshop (TPW).

We have spoken those words at the beginning of workshops for over two decades now. Over the past six years, the editors of and contributors to this book have faced the strange and wonderful process of putting these words, and everything that follows, into print. It is always a challenge to translate embodied practice into the written word, producing the inevitable impression that once published, what was once alive and fluid is now frozen and fixed. This book invites you to peer into the world of TPW, and some of what has contributed to its development which, up to now has been a present tense, body to body, oral tradition, passed on through multiple generations in the privacy of intimate, vibrant theatre and studio spaces. For those of us who have nurtured this tradition, the book is not a stopping point, but rather a transition. Writing it down has allowed us to reflect on how we have shaped and shared this work thus far, while at the same time serving as a jumping off point to its many possible futures.

Created by director, educator, theorist, and editor Richard Schechner (b. 1934), the origins of this approach to performer training and group collaboration extend back to the 1950s, even before his work with The Performance Group (TPG). Schechner continued to develop the training as an independent workshop, at first in the 1980s and 1990s in the Department of Performance Studies in the Tisch School of the Arts at New York University (NYU), where he was a professor from 1967 to 2017, and with members of East Coast Artists (ECA), a theatre company he has led since 1992. Shortly after Rasaboxes was introduced to TPW's extensive catalog of exercises in the mid-1990s, Schechner began to pass on the teaching of the work to ECA members and others who, in turn, have continued to teach and develop its pedagogy while maintaining a strong connection to its core practices and foundational principles.

This volume includes key elements of the historical development of TPW, the theoretical foundations that support the work, a detailed inside view of its pedagogy, and examples of how the work has been applied in a variety of contexts. It is neither a teacher's manual nor a critical analysis; rather, it is a *sourcebook*, a companion to the living practice that is TPW itself. TPW is an important part of Schechner's legacy, a unique hybrid of embodied practices inspired by his experiences during the civil rights movement in the 1960s, his experimentation in environmental theatre, physical performance training he learned and adapted from Jerzy Grotowski and others, his work with performers and other collaborators in TPG, and an exploration into and adaptation of rasa theory from the *Natyashastra*, a classical Indian manual of performance. The development of TPW can also be seen as a practical reflection of much of what Schechner has contributed to the academic field of performance studies since its inception as an academic discipline. This sourcebook addresses all of this and more. But the book is not the work. It does not replace training with experienced practitioners. To fully engage with TPW or Rasaboxes—certainly as a practitioner, but even as a theorist or scholar—one must meet oneself within the context of the work itself, in an embodied fashion—not as an observer, but as a participant, from the *inside*. That is when the context, how-tos, and reflections about the work we offer here will gain their full meaning and usefulness. This book is intended for several overlapping groups of people: performance practitioners, scholars, teachers, and others interested in getting to know TPW as a significant contribution to 20th- and 21st-century performer training. Perhaps most importantly, it is for current and future teachers of the work—a resource that holds what is (currently) most fundamental to its continued practice.

Many are familiar with Schechner's theatrical productions—which have taken place across four continents over seven decades—or may have read some of his prolific collection of books and essays, or attended any number of his presentations at conferences and various events. Others around the world have experienced some version of Rasaboxes, which, among the essential exercises/practices of TPW, is the most widely taught and developed. Few of these individuals may be aware of TPW's deep and broad investigations into self, group, and performance-making that grew from a practical need: to innovate performer training in support of the experimental directing and devising work of TPG. This book continues Schechner's long-term interest in/commitment to the development of new traditions in performer training as taken up and continued by his collaborators and those they have taught. Articles by Schechner (2001, revised and updated for this volume), Minnick and Cole (2002), and several of our contributors have helped to introduce Rasaboxes to a broader audience. However, Rasaboxes is only one element within the complex set of exercises, experiences, and explorations that comprise TPW. This is the first publication to present TPW as a whole, along with many newer Rasaboxes exercises.

This book represents a particular lineage of teaching of TPW and Rasaboxes that traces back to first wave teachers (or facilitators—we use the two words interchangeably) and members of ECA: Ursula Neuerburg (Montreal, CA), Paula Murray Cole (Ithaca, NY), and Michele Minnick (Baltimore, MD), and follows on with second wave teachers Rachel Bowditch (Phoenix, AZ), Fernando Calzadilla (Valencia, Spain), Marcia Moraes (Berlin and Rio de Janeiro), and Scott Wallin (Berkeley, CA). At the time of this writing, these seven core facilitators represent a lineage that includes values, exercises, and applications we have developed together and independently of each other. In the tradition forged at NYU and represented by this book, no TPW teacher completes their teacher training without first experiencing TPW as a participant, then as a participant-observer, then as an assistant teacher, before co-teaching with experienced workshop leaders and then teaching the work independently. The larger national and international TPW network includes teachers who have trained extensively with us and developed their own practice in Rasaboxes but have not yet experienced TPW. It includes apprentices or teachers-in-training, and practitioners who have stayed in touch with us over the years.

The largest communities who engage with the specific TPW and Rasaboxes lineage represented here are in the US and Brazil, which has become an important site for its development since Minnick taught the first Rasaboxes workshop in Rio de Janeiro in 2003. The proliferation of Rasaboxes throughout Brazil, in practice as well as in writing through numerous publications and graduate theses, is one example of the spiraling spread of this work and the feedback loop between generations of practitioners. The resonance with viral spreading is apt—the work spreads easily in a way that is difficult to manage or control as it is highly contagious. Because its focus is a visceral sharing of emotions (which are contagious), and because of how enjoyable it is to play with them, Rasaboxes in particular seems to have this effect of spreading out in all directions from any point of contact. Schechner prefers it that way. Other teachers and practitioners of this work, many of whom learned from Schechner, have developed their own derivations of Rasaboxes or other exercises, such as Sun Huizhu (William Sun) and his colleagues at the Shanghai Theatre Academy in China. The fact is, we have no idea how many people are out there doing something they call "Rasaboxes," or "rasa boxes," or "Rasa Box." We certainly cannot represent in these pages the many people around the world who have taken up this work and are creating their own lineages and pedagogies. As we continue to build community through and around the work, we look forward to meeting more practitioners and teachers who have brought their own distinctive backgrounds to it. At the same time, we hope this book makes accessible to a wider audience the principles by which we have been practicing and training the next generation of TPW and Rasaboxes teachers. It also can help to anchor current and future practitioners with key concepts and best practices to engage with as the work continues to spread, grow, and change.

The process for becoming core facilitators of TPW has been both unconventional and highly traditional. Current core teachers learned this work the old-fashioned way—by apprenticeship. We encountered the training because we were working with Schechner, either as a member of ECA or as a graduate student in the Department of Performance Studies at NYU, or both. After participating in TPW multiple times, he gave us his blessing to teach the work. There was no structured mentoring process for the first wave/generation; no pedagogical materials other than his teaching of TPW itself, the many conversations we had with him over the years, and Schechner's publications about performance. Then, with one another, we learned to teach teachers of TPW. We have offered workshops, integrated the work into our graduate and undergraduate teaching programs, and presented it at conferences and festivals around the globe. We have used it to direct and devise numerous productions, in both professional and educational contexts. The work has flourished with the support of individuals and their institutions, who have believed in and supported its development.

The editors of this book were born and grew up during the era in which Schechner first developed his approach to performer training. We are white, privileged, American women—cisgendered, straight and queer, and in our forties and fifties. We all have worked extensively with both graduate and undergraduate performance students and are all directors of both plays and devised work. Unlike Schechner, we are performers and acting teachers trained in other forms of expressive and somatic movement modalities, including the Laban/Bartenieff approach, Viewpoints and Suzuki, the Alexander Technique, Lecoq, and Body–Mind Centering®, among others. This gives us both the concern and the know-how for working with the nuances of the actor's process. We have trained with and been directed by Schechner in theatre productions from the mid-1990s to the 2000s. Neuerburg, Bowditch, Calzadilla, Wallin, Cole, and Minnick studied with Schechner in the Department of Performance Studies at NYU. Along with somatic, anti-racist, and consent-based practices, these experiences continue to shape our conception, implementation, and practice of this work in diverse communities.

We have written this book, and invited others to contribute, because each of us, in our own way, has been changed by encountering ourselves, the group, and Schechner in The Performance Workshop. Although we work with many modalities in our own teaching and directing, we have not known anything like The Performance Workshop, which functions as a kind of total training, an immersive ensemble and world-building experience. Nor have we encountered anything that liberates the performer's creative being and agency in quite the way TPW does. We have written this book for the same reason we have been dedicated to teaching and developing the work for over 20 years—we want to share its transformational possibilities with you.

How to Read This Book

There is no right way to use this sourcebook. It can be read sequentially, or not. You may find that chapters in Part I make more sense after you have read all or parts of Part II, for example. Instructions for exercises have been formatted in an easy-to-follow, numbered format. Text boxes throughout the book contain several different kinds of information for the reader: sometimes they highlight a principle or practice within the work, or provide background information on a theory or historical movement, or offer additional exercises. Schechner's books, *Between Theater and Anthropology* (1985), *Performance Theory* (1988), and *Environmental Theater* (1994 [1973]) continue to serve as key resources for teachers and practitioners, and we strongly urge those interested in diving deeper into the work to use these books as supplements to this sourcebook. In particular, we recommend the reader consult Schechner's *Performance Studies, An Introduction* (2020), which is a useful companion to this book. We reference it particularly in Chapters 1 and 4 for its concise descriptions of topics related to performance studies, but also its positioning of performance practices and concepts within wider historical, political, and cultural contexts. The Sanskrit words related to Rasaboxes practice are transliterated without diacriticals, just as we use them in TPW itself. There are many systems of transliteration. We are using spellings of the words shringara, shanta and *Natyashastra*, with an "h" to approximate the "sh" sound in these words.

Regardless of the shape the training takes in the future, most next-generation TPW teachers will be the first to not have had any direct connection with Schechner. Many may not know his work or the field of performance studies. In Part I, performance scholars and practitioners who have worked closely with Schechner present historical and theoretical background for TPW. Chapter 1, "Richard Schechner and Origins of The Performance Workshop," is co-authored by Cobina Gillitt and Michele Minnick. Gillitt took TPW with Schechner in 1991 and completed her Ph.D. in Performance Studies under Schechner's mentorship. She has incorporated the work into her teachings on Asian and intercultural performance. Chapter 1 provides context for the work by focusing on the nexus between Schechner's life experiences and key tenets of TPW as they have interfaced with contemporaneous social movements, politics, and aesthetic and cultural theories. This chapter highlights pivotal points of contact and influence between these different aspects of his thought and practice. Chapter 1 also shares some of the history of how we and other core facilitators learned and developed TPW and Rasaboxes.

The second two chapters of Part I focus on theory and practice derived or adapted from the classical Indian theory of *rasa*. In Chapter 2, TPW and Rasaboxes practitioner Shanti Pillai, who worked with Schechner while pursuing her doctoral degree at NYU, addresses the cultural context for rasa theory and reflects on Schechner's deep appreciation for Indian performance. "What Is Rasa?" stands on its own and functions as a prequel for Chapter 3, "Rasaesthetics," an updated version of Schechner's 2001 essay. Pillai outlines rasa as a theory and methodology of emotion and transcendence as elucidated in the *Natyashastra* and as embodied in Indian performance. In "Rasaesthetics," Schechner compares Aristotelian and rasic models of performance, explains how a synthesis of neuroscientific workings of the enteric nervous system with rasa theory led to the development of

Rasaboxes, and proposes rasaesthetics as an approach to the making and study of a wide range of performance forms.

Part II, Chapter 4, *Inside The Performance Workshop*, is the heart of the book. It takes the reader through fundamental exercises of TPW, elaborating key principles and guidelines for engaging with this unique performative world built through training, workshop, rehearsal, performance, and cool downs. It includes a glimpse of the yoga used in TPW and instructions for breath and sound (vocal) work and extended group improvisations, such as Crossings and Rasaboxes, and invitations for solo and group performance work.

The two chapters in Part III, *Facilitating The Performance Workshop*, are included as resources for those interested in the teaching of TPW. In his 2016 interview, "Principles of The Performance Workshop," Schechner answers questions about rules, expectations, and process. He summarizes core tenets of this practice drawn from his 60 years of facilitating the work. Scott Wallin's chapter, "The Unavoidable Guru," describes and theorizes his first experience of the Workshop and his attempts to continue the work with his cohort. Reflections on their failure to do so in the absence of a strong leader steer him to examine the paradoxes inherent in the role of a TPW facilitator.

Part IV, *Notes from the Field*, is a collection of short chapters contributed by practitioners and facilitators in a range of fields from drama therapy to clowning, from the preparation of actors on a Brazilian telenovela to K–12 education, as well as directing, devising, and immersive theatre. In "Freeing Emotional Expression in Young Performers: Rasaboxes in K–12 Context," Elise Forier Edie demonstrates the power of Rasaboxes as an educational tool for young people from elementary through high school. Drawing on her own and other teaching artists' experience, she shares classroom and rehearsal examples, tips, and techniques. In "Psychophysical Preparation for the Rasaboxes with Strasberg and Stanislavsky," Ursula Neuerburg offers a view into the possibilities of combining Rasaboxes with Stanislavsky-based acting methods as part of a semester-long class. Using chair relaxation and sense-memory exercises combined with work on the Rasaboxes grid, Neuerburg proposes the grid as a rich field for exploring the subconscious, while also providing a safety net for the performer.

Since the late 1990s, Rasaboxes has developed a presence in drama therapy and the training of drama therapists. Andrew M. Gaines' "Adapting Rasaboxes to Rasa≈Therapy: Clinical Applications in Drama Therapy" offers an overview of some of the ways rasa and Rasaboxes have been deployed in the field. Gaines describes the adaptations of its structure required by clinical environments. In "Rasaboxes, Drama Therapy, and Stability Through Dynamic Change: A Case Study," Dana Arie focuses on her use of Rasaboxes with a single client. She describes a process of moving from emotions in the body to emotions in story, supporting her client in developing adaptive reactions to unstable environments. In "Rasaboxes in the Training of Drama Therapists," Director of the NYU Drama Therapy Program, Nisha Sajnani, presents Rasaboxes as a model for performing sustained care in the training of drama therapists. Sajnani illustrates ways in which Rasaboxes can expand one's capacities to symbolize inner experience, cultivate a contemplative stance, be present with others in times of suffering, and attune to and transition from the emotional demands of working in managed care settings.

Next, we offer five chapters illustrating how TPW and Rasaboxes have been used in the realms of acting, directing, devising and immersive performance. In "Dancing on the Tongue," Erin B. Mee asks "What does it mean to 'taste' theatre?" Using examples from This Is Not A Theatre Company's *A Serious Banquet* (2014), *Versailles* (2015), and Impractical Theatre's *Three Sisters* (2014), Mee explains how rasa theory allows us to understand—more fully than other aesthetic theories—the pleasures of immersive and participatory performance. Brazilian acting teacher and coach Fernanda Guimarães takes us inside the Rio de Janeiro-based television studio in her chapter, "Lights, Camera, Action! Rasaboxes Training and Coaching for Brazilian Telenovelas." She offers insights into why and how the quick changes and deep psychophysical preparation of Rasaboxes help telenovela and other TV actors to work efficiently and safely on set. She shares exercises that engage with personal material and that prepare actors for the close-up.

In "Character Building Through Rasaboxes: Staging *Electra* at Teatro Prometeo," Fernando Calzadilla discusses his process of training actors, workshopping, and staging *Electra* at Teatro Prometeo in Miami in 2013. He emphasizes the use of other TPW exercises as support for Rasaboxes in building each character for this highly physical devised piece. In "Experimenting with the Clown in Rasaboxes," Ana Achcar shares her process of training first-year students by using Rasaboxes to get to the heart of the comic body in her medical clown training program at UNIRIO in Rio de Janeiro, Brazil. In the final chapter, "Dramaturgy of the Emotions: The Performance Workshop and Rasaboxes in Directing *Machinal*," Rachel Bowditch details a rehearsal process at Arizona State University in 2007 that combined TPW's Slow Motion Transformation exercises, Rasaboxes, and work drawn from the Lecoq pedagogy.

Crossing the Line

At the very heart of TPW is a deceptively simple idea—"crossing the line." We use masking tape to create literal lines on the floor, designating distinct areas for being, doing, and watching. Whole worlds, relationships, and stories emerge from the simple action of crossing the line, walking across the space, and turning to face someone. "Crossing the line" has many implications—breaking taboos, going too far, or at least pushing the boundaries of what we are willing to do, to explore, and to be seen doing. Generally, when you have "crossed a line," something has irrevocably changed. Sometimes opening an inner world of experience, and sometimes emphasizing extreme theatricality and fully embodied expression, the lines crossed are performative boundaries enabling both superficial and deep play. The pedagogical methods of TPW enable teachers to invite and facilitate these crossings in ways that are at times everyday, at times extraordinary, sometimes scary, often fun.

This work was born of the liberatory social and aesthetic impulses of the 1960s and 1970s. Those movements, and the various forms of reckoning that appear now to many as new, are not. Since we have known it, this work has embraced and celebrated difference of all kinds. However, the primary pedagogical leadership has remained in the hands of a small group of mostly white practitioners.

The resilience and longevity of TPW's approach lies in the incredible breadth of what it can hold, and still there are questions to ask ourselves moving forward. Here are a few:

- What are our own inherent biases, not only those inherent to our identities, but also as longtime practitioners of the work? What are the power dynamics, embedded in the structure of the work, that we and future practitioners and teachers might need or wish to examine more closely?
- What will existing and new practitioners bring to this work, with their own experiences and identities, fields of expertise, and cultural backgrounds that might shape it in new ways?
- What can be gained by exploring the limits and possibilities of adapting this work for online contexts? On the other hand, how does the deep, embodied, juicy set of practices fill a deep need to engage with one another in person in our changing world?
- How can the "intercultural" aspects of this practice, especially of Rasaboxes, continue to be a source of productive dialogue and the building of new relationships?

Finally, this book is an invitation. Schechner's retirement from NYU in 2017 coincided with the end of TPW's long run in the Department of Performance Studies, last taught in the summer of 2016. New partnerships with performance makers and practitioners, teachers, and institutions around the world will ensure that this unique and vital approach to ensemble and performer training continues to nourish and inspire future generations of artists and teachers. Above all, it is important to us that the work be accessible. This book is one step in that direction. We hope the book, in combination with the practical work of TPW and Rasaboxes, provides grounding and provokes questions that inspire innovation. You are the future of this work.

Now, we invite you to step up to the line of tape on the floor, with your toes right up against it but not touching.

> Look out into the space on the other side.
> What do you imagine?
> What do you desire?
> What will you do?
> When you are ready, cross the line.

Works Cited

Minnick, Michele, and Paula Murray Cole. "The Actor as Athlete of the Emotions: The Rasaboxes Exercise." In *Movement for Actors*, edited by Nicole Potter, Mary Fleischer, and Barbara Adrian, 2nd Rev. ed. New York: Allworth Press, 2017 [2002], pp. 285–97.

Schechner, Richard. *Between Theater and Anthropology*. Philadelphia: University of Pennsylvania Press, 1985.

———. *Performance Theory*. London and New York: Routledge, 1988 [1977].

———. *Environmental Theater*, 2nd ed. New York: Applause, 1994 [1973].

———. "Rasaesthetics." *TDR (1988–)*, vol. 45, no. 3, 2001, pp. 27–50.

———. *Performance Studies: An Introduction*, 4th ed. London and New York: Routledge, 2020.

PART I
History and Theory

FIGURE 0.1 Sketch of performers doing Rasaboxes by Joan Schirle. Dell'Arte International School of Physical Theatre, 2005.

Source: Courtesy of Paula Murray Cole.

CHAPTER 1

Richard Schechner and Origins of The Performance Workshop

COBINA GILLITT AND MICHELE MINNICK

Richard Schechner's hybrid career combines the identities of scholar, teacher, editor, and director, all of which are integrated in overlapping and dynamic ways. One could argue that Schechner's most important and lasting contribution to performance practice and theory is the impact he has had on the many students who have directly benefited from his teachings and mentorship. While The Performance Workshop (TPW), particularly Rasaboxes, has been expanded by successive generations of practitioners beyond its original pedagogy as developed by Schechner, teachers of the work find tremendous value in grounding their practice in an understanding of the history, experiences, and theories that inspired Schechner's focus on performer training. This chapter offers an overview of key influences in Schechner's life, theatrical practice, and scholarship that have directly contributed to TPW. At its most basic level, TPW grows from his ever active, curious, and critical mind, his desire to provoke, his belief that the best creativity arises from places of discomfort, and his proclivity to be an instigator, one who disrupts—often theatrically or performatively—the system or institution in which he is operating. His experiences and interests are broad and multivarious; they are not a reflection of a linear journey with a fixed goal.

Schechner is an unabashed cultural gourmand; he is interested in tasting, partaking, and ingesting as much as he is interested in shaking things up. His combined contributions and innovations are like a *masala*, a mix of Indian spices that brings together contrasting flavors and textures better savored together than separately. Schechner's openness to new experiences has enabled him to innovate using an expansive menu of materials, while his desire to dismantle conventions (of thought and practice) has also made him controversial at times. This chapter is offered not as an exhaustive history, accounting, or elaboration of what went into the development of TPW, nor does it address critical responses to Schechner's work. Rather, it is intended to provide a taste of the vast array of ingredients that have contributed to his unique approach to performer training. We have provided text boxes, endnotes, and resources for further reading for those who may not be familiar with specific topics. In particular, you will see many references to *Performance Studies: an Introduction* 4th Edition (Schechner 2020), which provides comprehensive and accessible resources for further exploration into many of the topics you will encounter here.

Setting the Table
Discomfort, Disruption, Resistance

Richard Schechner does not shy away from the complex, the difficult, the sacred, or the controversial. Much of his approach is unique to his personality, while much can be attributed to social and political upheavals taking place during his formative years. What interests him is opening and expanding ideas about performance and culture through dialogue, confrontation, analysis, theory-making, invention, hybridization, encounter, and enactment. According to Schechner, cultures are not bound by international borders, but leak and spread around the world through both benevolent and oppressive means: exploration and diaspora, but also forced trafficking, conquest, and colonialism. His interest in intercultural exchange and hybridization is a recognition that for "as long as we can look in human history, peoples have been deeply, continuously unashamedly intercultural,"[1] and that in fact,

> Borrowing is natural to our species . . . What is borrowed is swiftly transformed into native material—at the very same time borrowing re-makes native culture . . . Syncretism and the making of new cultural stuff is the norm of human history.
>
> (1982b, 3)

Beginning in the 1970s, Schechner's focus on interculturalism and syncretism was "as a contrast to 'internationalism,' " the word that was more commonly used at the time (1996, 42). His point has been that international exchanges through the arts based on political boundaries and tied to a sense of nationalism are not as important, interesting, or valid as the exchange of cultures between individual artists not defined solely by their country of origin.[2]

Interestingly, Schechner's early life wasn't syncretic or intercultural. He had a comfortable childhood, spending his early years in the Jewish Weequahic section of Newark, NJ when the city was still characterized by distinct ethnic neighborhoods—Jewish, Greek, Portuguese, Italian, and Black. As a child, he had very little contact with others outside of his insular middle class Jewish circle of friends and family. Although his family synagogue, founded by his great-grandfather, was by then in a Black neighborhood, he remembers having only one close friend who was not part of his Jewish community (Nesmith 2022). The different groups lived side by side but didn't intermingle. His father worked in the family insurance and real estate business and, as he grew older, he remembers recognizing the unjust disparity between his family's living conditions and the dilapidated housing in the Black neighborhoods where his father was the landlord's agent of several buildings. This nascent realization opened the path to his future dedication to activism, and artistic and scholarly pursuits.

The first area he explored seriously was writing—scholarly, but also fiction, poetry, and journalism, which led him to his first real reckoning with racial injustice on a larger scale. He majored in English at Cornell University from 1952–1956. While at Cornell working on the student newspaper, *The Cornell Daily Sun*, Schechner wrote several articles on the 1954 Brown v. Board of Education case while it was being argued before the Supreme Court. Wanting to understand the issues driving the case, Schechner contacted Thurgood Marshall, the head of the NAACP Legal Defense and Educational Fund and chief attorney for the plaintiff. Marshall invited him to his office on 125th Street in Harlem for an interview. In a meeting that lasted several hours, Marshall gave Schechner a lesson on the history of segregation in America by eviscerating the notion, upheld in the landmark 1896 case of Plessy v. Ferguson, that segregation was constitutional under the doctrine of "separate but equal." Marshall opened Schechner's eyes to the entrenched systemic nature of the racial and social inequalities shaping American life and institutions. The idea that separate was not and could never be equal was a profound revelation (Schechner 2012a).

Schechner's second passion, theatre, and particularly directing, was sparked and fueled during three summers in Provincetown, MA, just before and just after earning his Masters in English at the University of Iowa. During those years, Provincetown was a haven for eclectic artists and free thinkers. At the end of the first summer in 1957, he founded the East End Players (EEP) with a staged reading of his original one act play *Lot's Daughters*. He returned the following summer as co-artistic director of EEP (with Karl Harshbarger), and again in 1961 for the final year of EEP. Two of his productions during the summer of 1961 are early examples of what Schechner would later call "environmental theater," referring to his directorial work characterized by unconventional use of space that specifically encourages audience/performer interaction. He staged Sophocles' *Philoctetes* on the beach in Wellfleet (a few miles south of Provincetown) with Odysseus and Neoptolemus arriving by boat to encounter Philoctetes on the beach. For his production of Ibsen's *When We Dead Awaken*, the interior of the Provincetown Town Hall was completely reconfigured. In the final scene, Rubek climbed high into the rafters.

When he left Provincetown in November 1958, Schechner had returned to New Jersey and, despite his dedication to non-violent activism, volunteered for the draft.[3] He explains,

> By then I knew I wanted to be a college professor and I wanted to do theatre. I knew that I had to go on and get a Ph.D. I also knew I had lived a very insulated life. My life experiences were Ivy League college, summer theatre in Provincetown, that kind of thing. I said, how am I ever really going to meet people who are really not like me?"
>
> (Nesmith 2022)

The conversation Schechner had with Thurgood Marshall while an undergraduate at Cornell ignited in him a strong commitment to the civil rights movement, but it also seeded the notion that the only way to truly understand those for whom the civil rights movement was advocating was through lived experience. Schechner has often articulated the value of being with and moving through difference without trying to assimilate or eliminate conflict or disparity. "I'm interested in the dialogue," he claims. "I'm not interested in the illusion that I can be somebody I'm not or understand another culture 'in its own terms.' I think that's fancy language but it doesn't really mean very much" (2012a). Rather than follow the expected path of becoming an officer in the army, Schechner enlisted.

Schechner served for two years in the U.S. Army, stationed first at Fort Polk in Leesville, Louisiana and then at Fort Hood in Texas. During his service, he united his interest in theatre with his anti-establishment views, directing Gore Vidal's 1957 anti-military, anti-Red scare satire, *Visit to a Small Planet*, which did not endear him to his military superiors. He also wrote his first scholarly essay while serving, "The Bacchae: A City Sacrificed to a Jealous God," that would be published in the *Tulane Drama Review* in 1961. Schechner's leftist opinions and actions while in the army resulted in an investigation leading to the opening of FBI, CIA, and Army Intelligence dossiers on him.[4]

He later reflected in 1973, "[M]oving South when I was drafted in 1958 was the most important single event in my artistic life" (1994, 65). In his performance work, Schechner has explored the embodied practices of experimental theatre, protest theatre, and intercultural exchange, a journey he began while he was stationed in the Jim Crow South. Upon his discharge from the army in 1960, Schechner chose to remain in the South and pursue his doctorate in Theatre at Tulane University in New Orleans under the mentorship of Professor Robert W. Corrigan, who was also the editor of the *Tulane Drama Review (TDR)*.[5] In the spring of 1962, Tulane offered Schechner Corrigan's job when he accepted a new position at Carnegie Tech in Pittsburgh. Schechner completed his dissertation on Eugène Ionesco in the late spring of 1962 and became an assistant professor in Tulane's Theatre Department. As *TDR*'s new editor, Schechner transformed the journal into a vanguard publication for new currents and trends in performance scholarship. He did this in part by radically broadening its focus from mostly European and North American theatre to an international-intercultural one, over the years paying attention to an increasingly wide variety of performance genres: dance, experimental performance (including what is now called performance art), ritual, anthropology, sports, performance of everyday life, and, in due time, multimedia.

First Course
Activism and Environmental Theatre

While beginning his academic career at Tulane, Schechner became more deeply committed to the growing Black-led civil rights movement that had been becoming more active in New Orleans by the mid-1960s. Like many artists and activists at the time, he merged his art with his activism. He drew on his interest in performance theory by blurring the boundaries between performance as protest and protest as performance. Invited by the founders of the Free Southern Theater (FST)—Gilbert Moses, John O'Neal, and Doris Derby—Schechner became one of the three producing directors when FST's headquarters shifted from Tougaloo College in Jackson, Mississippi, to New Orleans. Racially integrated at the time of its founding in late 1963, the FST's mission was aligned with the Movement (as the Black freedom struggle was called). FST's stated vision was to "stimulate creative and reflective thought" in the deep South "by the establishment of a legitimate theater" and "to strengthen communication" between Blacks in the South (Dorsey 2014). As a producing member of the theatre's board of directors, Schechner worked closely in developing FST's first touring season as part of the 1964 Freedom Summer. The FST mounted three plays that toured rural Mississippi, Alabama, and Louisiana: Samuel Beckett's *Waiting for Godot*, Martin Duberman's documentary, *In White America*,[6] and Ossie Davis' *Purlie Victorious*, which Schechner directed. These plays, produced, directed, and performed by an integrated company in the deep south challenged racist and "accepted" ways of thinking and behaving. Performances were held in churches, yards, small theatres, and schools. The FST was enthusiastically received by audiences, but their performances also resulted in racist threats against FST members and sponsors. As the Black Nationalism movement gained momentum, the question of the FST's identity as an integrated theatre was raised. In 1966, a decision was reached that FST should be an all-Black company and focus on community building between Black audiences and artists. Schechner resigned from his artistic and producing role, but remained on the board of directors.[7]

The year before resigning from his active role with FST, Schechner and two Tulane faculty colleagues, painter Franklin Adams and composer Paul Epstein, had formed the New Orleans Group (NOG) at the same time *TDR* put out a special issue on Happenings (see Happenings, p. 15).[8] Inspired by what was occurring in the art-and-performance world, in April 1966, NOG produced *4/66*, an intermedia, Happening-like event. Performed mostly by non-actors and including audience participation, *4/66* featured chance games and other actions that were "loosely connected in a progression leading to the selection of a hero/victim spectator who was stripped and bathed in a sudsy bath, the bottom of which was mud—so that the white, warm, sensuous, softness gave way to the gritty heavy brown mudness" (Schechner 1994, 67).

4/66 was Schechner's first opportunity to work collaboratively with two artists outside of the discipline of theatre. Because his contract with Tulane did not include directing campus productions, and because he, Adams, and Epstein wanted a non-theatre venue, *4/66* was staged in a large open space. The spectators moved their chairs changing their perspective throughout the performance. What excited Schechner about *4/66* was that the "piece had no plot, but instead was held together by a progression of actual events. Like a game, what went on in *4/66* had no one-to-one relation to life outside the room" (67). There was no characterization, no back story. Any meaning to be found in *4/66* "was metaphoric, structural, by analogy; or in the events themselves which were not secondary, not reflections, not mimetic, but actual" (67). Working with "actuals"–doings or behaviors that do not represent anything other than themselves—is an important element of TPW. In exercises such as Crossings (see p. 108), TPW performers learn to let go of the trappings of realistic acting in order to focus on simply "showing doing."[9]

4/66 lay the ground for Schechner to direct his first all-out consciously so-named, environmental theatre production: Eugene Ionesco's *Victims of Duty* in May 1967 with NOG. This production went further than the explorations of site-specific staging with EEP; it exemplified a more radical move toward audience

Happenings

American painter and pioneering performance artist Allan Kaprow (1927–2006) coined the term 'Happenings' to describe experiments that blurred the boundaries between art and life, marking a sensory and perceptual awakening that engaged performers and spectators together within a shared environment. Happenings abandoned narrative structure and were typically arranged in a series of scored, sequential, and/or simultaneous actions determined in advance, sometimes through chance techniques. The first Happening was Kaprow's *18 Happenings in 6 Parts*, presented at the Reuben Gallery in 1959. Spectators moved through a three-room environment with transparent walls, engaging in a series of actions based on the random selection of instructional cards, while witnessing the actions performed by other spectators and actors. For Kaprow, Happenings were "unrehearsed and performed by nonprofessionals, once only" using themes, materials, and inspiration coming from life, not other artworks (Kaprow and Kelly 2003 [1966], 63). Each participant became a necessary part of and simultaneously a spectator for a non-dramatic performance.

participation by narrowing and even eliminating the space between performers and spectators. Schechner coined the term "environmental theater" based on Kaprow's analysis of how the history of western painting showed a progression from figuration, to collage, to environment—designing the whole space, not hanging works on walls (Kaprow 1965). He first used "environmental theater" in print in his 1968, "6 Axioms for Environmental Theater" (Schechner 1968, 41–64). The axioms are a helpful guide for understanding some of the underlying principles of TPW:

1. The theatrical event is a set of related transactions
2. All the space is used for performance; all the space is used for audience
3. The theatrical event can take place either in a totally transformed space or in "found space"
4. Focus is flexible and variable
5. All production elements speak in their own language
6. The text need be neither the starting point nor the goal of a production. There may be no text at all[10] (Schechner 1968)

The "6 Axioms" do not address performer training per se, but the essay outlines an intermixing of aesthetic, political, and everyday behaviors that suggest some of the new demands that environmental theatre made on actors (see Figure 1.1). In the essay, Schechner describes the guerrilla theatre protests he staged in 1967 against the Vietnam War in New York's Times Square and the Port Authority Bus Terminal as examples of environmental theatre. In his introduction to the 1994 revised edition of his 1973 *Environmental Theater*, Schechner reflects:

FIGURE 1.1 Audience interaction and environmental staging of TPG's *Commune*, directed by Richard Schechner, 1970. The Performing Garage, NYC.

Source: Photo courtesy of Richard Schechner.

Neither ecological nor performance environments are passive. They are interactants in events organically taking place throughout vivified spaces. A performance environment is a "position" in the political sense, a "body of knowledge" in the scholarly sense, a "real place" in the theatrical sense. Thus, to stage a performance "environmentally" means more than simply to move it off the proscenium or out of the arena. An environmental performance is one in which all the elements or parts making up the performance are recognized as alive. To "be alive" is to change, develop, transform; to have needs and desires; even, potentially, to acquire, express, and use consciousness.

(Schechner 1994)

The performer is perhaps the most "alive" interactant in this configuration. The question becomes, what is required to prepare and train performers to participate in these "vivified spaces" in which the hermetic seals of traditional theatrical spaces and social agreements are removed? The Method, based on Stanislavsky's System of actor training, was then, and still is, the core of most undergraduate and graduate acting programs in the U.S. Because it focuses on realism and the actor's ability to disappear into a role within the context of a highly controlled theatrical environment, the Method was not up to the task of preparing actors for such a range of performance environments and circumstances. Schechner wanted to find new ways of training actors, not only to meet the demands of his own work as a director, but also because of the many innovations in form and the blurring of boundaries that were taking place around him, including Happenings and early performance art, the culture of political protest, post-modern dance, and experimental music. The American experimental performance scene during the 1960s and 1970s—in New York and California especially—not only redefined the relationship of actors and directors to texts, but also marked a turn toward the actor as a primary creator on a par with the playwright, choreographer, composer, and director. This connection between personal experience and political action, and the blurring of the boundaries separating life and art reflected new theories about the nature of the self and of human behavior more generally. Artists of all kinds, including performers, directly participated in political actions during the 1960s and 1970s. In turn, they brought their politically awakened selves into their art, using their individual, social, and political positions to engage audiences as participants in works that questioned not only theatre practice, but the very foundations of society. For Schechner and others, actors granted this level of agency in the creative process became "performers," co-creators of productions rather than merely interpreters of existing plays. Characteristically, Schechner's concept of "performer" has been influenced by an eclectic range of ideas beyond theatre, including the work of sociologist Erving Goffman, whose *The Presentation of Self in Everyday Life* (1959) introduced the notion of the "performance" of social roles into the social sciences (see "Performing in Everyday Life" in Schechner 2020, 104–8). We discuss other major influences below.

Second Course

A Broad Spectrum Approach: From Drama to Performance

In 1966, Schechner published "Approaches to Theory/Criticism" in TDR, in which he challenges scholars to move away from a narrow, conventional study of drama and theatre and toward a more broadly based inquiry into "the formal relations between play, games, sports, theatre, and ritual" (1966, 34). This call mirrored Schechner's theatrical practice at the time with FST and NOG and helps explain his approach to theatre making and performer training moving forward. His vision for a "broad spectrum approach" upset some western arts-focused and text-based academics who saw Schechner more as another iconoclast smashing their class and cultural traditions than as a serious theorist. There was worry that his call would undermine the status of theatre studies departments that had fought so hard for legitimacy within the academy. However, Schechner's "performance theory," a term he began using in the mid-1970s to describe his and allied ways of thinking, took hold especially among younger scholars and artists. The full impact of Schechner's theoretical approach wasn't felt widely in academia until 1992 when he delivered a keynote at the 1992 Association for Theatre in Higher Education (ATHE) Conference. There he (in)famously rocked the world of academic theatre by calling for a paradigm shift from drama to performance. He asserted that "[t]heatre departments should become 'performance departments'" and focus more on a "broad spectrum" because:

> Performance is about more than the enactment of Eurocentric drama. Performance engages intellectual, social, cultural, historical, and artistic life in a broad sense. Performance combines theory and practice. Performance studied and practiced interculturally can be at the core of a "well-rounded education." That is because performed acts, whether actual or virtual, more than the written word, connect and negotiate the many cultural, personal, group, regional, and world systems comprising today's realities. Performance, of course, includes "the arts" but goes beyond them. Performance is a broad spectrum of entertainments, arts, rituals, politics, economics, and person-to-person interactions. This broad spectrum enacted multiculturally and interculturally can do much to enhance human life.
>
> (1992, 9)

In the spring of 1967, the year after he published "Approaches," Schechner and five of his colleagues resigned from Tulane after an irreconcilable dispute with the administration. In 1965, Robert W. Corrigan helped found and was the inaugural dean of New York University's School of the Arts (later Tisch School of the Arts). Corrigan offered Schechner a professorship in the School's Department of Graduate Drama. Schechner brought the *Tulane Drama Review (TDR)* with him and renamed it *The Drama Review*. From the mid-60s through the 1970s, Schechner and his NYU colleagues developed what was to become "performance studies," and in 1981, the Department of Graduate Drama officially became the world's first performance studies department. At around the same time, rising out of its long tradition of rhetoric, debate, and public speaking, Northwestern University also moved toward what would become the second performance studies department in the U.S.

Third Course

Performer Training in Context: NYU, Grotowski, and The Performance Group

A major influence on Schechner's approach to theatre-making and actor training was the Polish director, Jerzy Grotowski, who was also a pioneer of environmental staging. Grotowski had been deeply influenced by Stanislavsky, whose work laid the ground for explorations of the "psychophysical" (see Neuerburg, pp. 227–228). During the 1960s and 1970s, avant-garde theatre groups, including Grotowski's Polish Laboratory Theatre, and in the U.S. The Living Theatre, The Open Theatre, The Performance Group, and others, started to explore the psychophysical training of the actor not only as a question of technique for "building a role," but as liberatory practice for individuals and groups and the generation of original material. Although not a focus of Schechner's "6 Axioms," the centrality of the body as a creative source and the expressive center of theatre is featured in *Environmental Theater* and is a core principle of TPW.

Grotowski had been gaining prominence in Europe since the late 1950s. His company, The Theatre of 13 Rows, later The Polish Laboratory Theatre of Opole and then Wroclaw, modeled a new approach to the psychophysical training of the actor by emphasizing the relationship between the actor's interior process and the spectator, rather than the play text as the most essential element of theatre. During Grotowski's "theatre of productions" phase (1959–69), performer training was the main focus of his theatre company's work together. Schechner, who had been publishing articles by and about Grotowski in *TDR* since 1964,[11] was so intrigued that he met Grotowski in Montreal in the spring of 1967 and helped arrange for the Polish director to lead a workshop at NYU's School of the Arts November 6–30, 1967. Grotowski was assisted by his close collaborator, actor Ryszard Cieslak. Several NYU faculty observed the workshop, while Schechner participated fully, along with graduate student actors-in-training.

Jerzy Grotowski

Jerzy Grotowski (1933–99) was a theatre director and founder of the Polish Laboratory Theatre (1958–84) and after that, the Workcenter of Jerzy Grotowski and Thomas Richards in Pontedera, Italy. Grotowski's work unfolded through a set of overlapping periods, from the Theatre of Productions (1959–69), to Paratheatre (1969–78), Theatre of Sources (1976–82), Objective Drama (1983–86), and Art as Vehicle (1986–99). During the Theatre of Productions phase, Grotowski explored environmental theatre staging, scenic and textual montage, and performer training. During this period, he developed his concept of the "Poor Theater," that advocated eradicating all that is superfluous to the core of the theatrical experience (elaborate sets and lighting) while focusing on the actors as the principal source of the performance and emphasizing the actor-spectator relationship. From the 1950s to the mid-1960s, The Polish Laboratory Theatre practiced a set of psychophysical exercises, known as *plastiques*. These exercises were not designed to build a collection of skills, as one would normally understand the goal of actor training. Rather, Grotowski worked with performers on eradicating blocks arising from social and cultural norms in order to release natural impulses. After his Theatre of Productions phase, Grotowski stopped showing works to the public, concentrating instead on the actor's work on the self, doing away with social masks and conditioning, and delving deeply into discovering the sources of performance in both contemporary and ancient rituals.

Grotowski and Cieslak's intense workshop at NYU met for five hours a day, four days a week, for four weeks. The two demonstrated and taught the *plastiques* and other aspects of their rigorous psychophysical approach to actor training. Immediately after the 1967 workshop, drawing on what he learned from Grotowski, and combining it with his work with EEP and NOG, Schechner led a workshop at the Tompkins Square Community Center on New York's Lower East Side. The workshop initially had about thirty participants. Because of Schechner's "no absences" policy, within two weeks, the number stabilized at about a dozen (in practice, the rule meant a person could miss one session, but no more; this remained his policy throughout his teaching of TPW and was adapted by subsequent generations of teachers). With the workshop participants, he shared his adaptation of Grotowski's plastiques, which he called "association exercises," so named because the performer was instructed to let associations—fantasies, impulses, memories—guide the tempo, intensity, and amplitude of the movements and sounds. Schechner emphasized other core principles he learned in Grotowski's NYU workshop, including the importance of continuous training, the notion that the personal process of the performer is made evident in the performance, and the concept of the *secure partner*—the idea that the performer is always in contact with, communicating with, someone or something absolutely trusted (Schechner 2016).[12] For Schechner, trust was established most importantly by the reliable presence of all involved. After the Tompkins Square group stabilized, this deeply committed group cohered into The Performance Group (TPG), which was formally named as such by Schechner early in 1968. Schechner led the group until 1980.[13] The first TPG production was *Dionysus in 69*, which opened June 8, 1968 at The Performing Garage, a converted metal-stamping shop purchased by the company in the winter of 1968.[14] Like Grotowski, Schechner's leadership of TPG made continuous training and generating performance material for productions through rigorous workshops the primary undertaking of the company.

Schechner explains:

> When I was doing The Performance Group, we did a whole lot of training. The notion is the sort of iceberg effect, you don't show the training, but it's underneath. You do more training than you do workshopping, and you do more workshopping than you do rehearsals, and you do more rehearsals than you do performances. Performances are the tip of the iceberg.
>
> (Schechner 2016)

Early versions of some TPW exercises and many of the principles of the work are in Schechner's *Environmental Theater* (Schechner 1973, revised 1994). In chapters such as "Participation," "Space," "Performer," and "Nakedness," Schechner makes the case for training and workshops to serve as psychophysical-aesthetic exploration while also preparing performers for specific productions. He focuses on training that promotes a disciplined and creative culture of the group. In "Performer," Schechner lays out his belief in the importance of embodied tradition:

> [P]resence is the fundamental aspect of training. I believe in apprenticeship: conscious observation and imitation, seasoned with critical questioning and experimentation. Presence is possible only in safe places, in moments of trust when ego-boundaries dissolve, or at least thin out. Training is the struggle to make places safe, to encourage trust in the middle of a social system that breeds danger and apprehension.
>
> (1994, 128)

The Performing Garage at 33 Wooster Street in Soho, not far from NYU's campus, is where TPG developed its performer training and presented performances. Schechner and the company were also frequently invited to give workshops at

CHAPTER 1 ▶ Richard Schechner and Origins of The Performance 21

colleges throughout the country and overseas. These workshops—both at the Garage and elsewhere—were the foundations for the emerging pedagogy of TPW.

TPG's first production, *Dionysus in 69*, juxtaposed intense psychophysical acting with a more intimate style in which actors addressed the audience in everyday speech (see Figure 1.2). Drawing on his two essays on Euripides' *The Bacchae*, the 1961 "*The Bacchae:* A City Sacrificed to a Jealous God" and the 1967 "In Warm Blood: *The Bacchae*," Schechner and TPG intermixed *The Bacchae* with autobiographical texts from TPG actors and original writing by Schechner and the company. The production broke from the conventional staging of dramatic texts in several ways. It was staged environmentally—in a space totally designed by Jerry Rojo, Michael Kirby, and Schechner. Spectators sat on carpets and on platforms and towers of varying heights. The performers shared the space with the spectators; there was a good deal of audience participation, some of it highly personal, even intimate. The actors played their dramatic roles but infused them with language and allusions to their "real lives" outside the theatre, including using their own names as well as their character names. Two scenes—the birth ritual and the death ritual—were often performed naked. After Dionysus is born, he invites spectators to join him in dancing. This dance led to the enactment to some degree of the orgies on Mount Cithaeron described by Euripides. Sometimes spectators took off some or all their clothes; sometimes they fondled and kissed each other and the performers. The invitations the group made to the audience led to spectators devising ways they could become a part of the performance. Although

FIGURE 1.2 William Finley as Dionysus and William Shephard as Pentheus in *Dionysus in 69*, directed by Richard Schechner, 1968. The Performing Garage, NYC.

Source: Photo courtesy of Richard Schechner.

unprepared for such participatory involvement by experiences attending conventional theatre productions, audiences at the time were likely primed for such invitations by late 1960's culture of sexual freedom and public manifestations both social and political from the Freedom Movement to Woodstock to anti-Vietnam War protests. Many audience members returned repeatedly, and even devised ways of "saving" young King Pentheus from his tragic fate. Some spectators became so actively involved that they believed themselves to be part of The Performance Group, which they imagined to be a commune. Audience involvement in *Dionysus in 69* was one of Schechner's most extreme explorations with TPG of the possibilities of a theatre that dismantled the expected structures of aesthetic and social norms. In the "Participation" chapter of *Environmental Theater*, Schechner puts it this way:

> What happens to a performance when the usual agreements between performer and spectator are broken? What happens when performers and spectators actually make contact? When they talk to each other and touch? Crossing the boundaries between theatre and politics, art and life, performance event, social event, stage, and auditorium? Audience participation expands the field of what a performance is, because audience participation takes place precisely at the point where the performance breaks down and becomes a social event. In other words, participation is incompatible with the idea of a self-contained, autonomous, beginning-middle-and-end artwork.
>
> (1994, 40)

Schechner and TPG's performers did not always agree about how to handle the moments in which a theatrical event became a social one, or about the outcome of a drama that depended partly upon the audience's participation. Sometimes, the audience even attempted to take control of the drama. Schechner describes an example of this when a "a bunch of students from Queens College kidnapped Pentheus, preventing his sacrifice to Dionysus" (41). William Shephard, who was playing Pentheus, went limp and refused to go on, saying "I was taken out of it and that's that" (41). When confronted, the students admitted to coming to the performance with the kidnap planned in advance. After Shephard refused to continue, Schechner asked for a volunteer from the audience to play the role of Pentheus. A sixteen year-old, who had seen the play five times, agreed to step in. Schechner and the performers instructed him on the actions and physical tasks he needed to perform while he improvised the lines he had essentially memorized.

Schechner describes the confusion and disagreement this experience caused amongst the members of TPG. Part of their confusion mirrored audiences': was this a theatre company, offering a unique aesthetic experience, or a commune that was inventing new rules about both social and theatrical life? The group subsequently underwent weekly encounter therapy sessions led by a professional therapist in order to resolve these questions. However, no unanimous conclusions were reached and as Schechner noted, "[b]y the time *Dionysus in 69* closed at the end of July 1969, most of the performers had had it with participation" (44). Later productions would rely on more structured scenarios and fewer opportunities for audience participation.[15] It is important to keep in mind TPG was working in the late 1960s and 1970s, before AIDS, before third wave feminism, #MeToo, the Covid-19 pandemic, and within a different culture of consent than currently exists.[16] Many forms of what is now known as immersive theatre or performance draw upon environmental theatre as a source of inspiration. Many foreground an interactive use of space and interdependent relationship between performers and spectators, although not all invite the kinds of participation Schechner describes.[17] TPW provides theatre makers an opportunity to continually revisit and rework the basic questions proposed by "6 Axioms," making them relevant and actionable in contemporary performance practice.

Fourth Course
Asian Encounters

Schechner's ideas about theatre, ritual, play—the broad spectrum—were enriched and expanded by his research in Asia. Since his first trip from October 1971 through March 1972 to India and many other Asian nations, Schechner has deeply engaged with Asian artists, scholars, and others during his subsequent travels. When he founded TPG, he had no formal knowledge of Asian performance or theory. Until his 1971 trip to Asia, he had only experienced Asian performance when performances came to New York and circuitously through Grotowski, whose exercises had been developed with input from the Kathakali Kalamandalam via Eugenio Barba (b. 1936), co-founder of the Odin Teatret in Holstebro, Denmark, and from 1962–65 an assistant to Grotowski. The exercises Barba brought back from the Kalamandalam were incorporated into Grotowski's performer training. Grotowski and Cieslak taught these to the 1967 NYU workshop. Schechner then adapted them for use by The Performance Group—before his first direct experiences in India. As Schechner explains it:

> I didn't know much about Asian performances until the 1970s. When I was doing *Dionysus in 69*, which was in 1968, I was already thirty-four years old. At the end of one of the performances, a man came up to me and said, "Very interesting, very interesting. You must have been to Asia. I see lots of Asian influence." And I said, "No, I've never been to Asia." And he said, "Well, I think you should go. I think you'll find it interesting." And I, being me, said, "Well, I think you should send me then."
>
> (Schechner 2012a)

The man was Porter McCray, the executive director of the JDR 3rd Fund (a non-profit organization funded by John D. Rockefeller the 3rd to promote cultural exchanges in the arts between the U.S. and Asia, now the Asian Cultural Council). The "Asia" McCray saw in *Dionysus in 69* was a theatrical event that took "place on several planes—physically, psychologically, wholly" (Schechner 1970, 579). One element of Asian influence undoubtedly was the "birth ritual" and its reverse, the "death ritual," famous scenes from *Dionysus in 69* modeled after an Asmat birth ritual (from the Indonesian province of Papua, known as West Irian until 1973), something Schechner had seen in *The Sky Above and the Mud Below*, the 1961 award-winning French documentary film directed by Pierre Dominique Gaisseau.

However, it was his distaste for and rejection of the proscenium stage and his development of environmental theatre, characterized by the elimination of the fourth wall, organic whole-space staging, audience participation, and an overall theatricality that characterizes so many Asian theatre traditions, that had likely led McCray to assume Schechner had been to Asia and inspired by Asian performance. Schechner's rethinking of the performative circumstances encoded in dominant western theatrical practice while working with EEP, FST, NOG, and participating in street demonstrations made him particularly receptive to the modes of practice offered by Asian theatre.

Since first traveling to Asia, Schechner's relationship with Asian performance genres, theory, and especially Asian artists and scholars has deeply influenced his vision of performance studies and his approach to performer training. He thinks of himself not as "an Asian scholar so much as an intercultural scholar," whose work focuses heavily on Asian performance forms, history, and social structures (Schechner 2012a). This despite the fact that he neither speaks nor reads any Asian language, nor is proficient at performing any Asian forms of theatre or dance—although he has never shied away from experiencing the training firsthand to get a sense of what it is like to practice an embodied technique.

Schechner's first trip to Asia started after TPG toured their production of *Commune* to Paris and Wroclaw, Poland in the fall of 1971. Schechner and his former wife and company member Joan MacIntosh set off for a six-month tour of several Asian countries. They spent the first four months in India and then divided two months among Sri Lanka, Singapore, Malaysia, Thailand, Indonesia, Papua-New Guinea, Australia, the Philippines, Hong Kong, Taiwan, Korea, and Japan. In India, they met and exchanged ideas with countless performing artists and experienced local, regional, traditional, and modern theatre, dance, and music performances in Bengal, Tamil Nadu, Kerala, Punjab, Kashmir, Maharashtra, and Gujarat. Schechner's encounters with Asia, and India in particular, not only confirmed and reinforced his own ideas and practice but also had an impact on local theatre people, an important representation of the kind of cultural feedback loops Schechner's work engenders. For example, while in Kolkata (formerly Calcutta), he met Indian playwright, city planner, and social activist Badal Sircar (1925–2011).[18] Schechner and Sircar hit it off. The Indian playwright-director wanted to learn environmental theatre techniques from The Performance Group. Schechner invited Sircar to take part in TPG's 1972 summer workshop at the University of British Columbia. It was after his work with TPG that Sircar left the proscenium stage and took his Satabdi Theatre into Kolkata's streets. As Schechner explains, "Badal's use of the ideas and exercises he observed that summer completed a very interesting circle because I had learned the core of those exercises from Grotowski who had taken them, or adapted at least some of them, from kathakali. Then I taught them to Sircar who brought them back to Kolkata" (Schechner 2012a). This circular flow inhabits much of Schechner's practice and scholarship.

The 1971 trip was also Schechner's introduction to the practice of yoga, which revolutionized his personal life as well as his professional practice and approach to performer training. At that time, yoga was not the ubiquitous or commercial

FIGURE 1.3 Schechner looking at a photo of Krishnamacharya in his 1971 journal.

Source: Photo courtesy of Rachel Bowditch.

presence it is in American culture today. Schechner spent six weeks in Chennai (formerly Madras) observing training and performances at Kalakshetra while studying yoga in private lessons—as is the tradition—with the famed yoga master, Tirumalai Krishnamacharya (see Figure 1.3).[19] The esteemed teacher gave him permission to share what he had learned during the four weeks of daily lessons. Schechner brought this yoga to TPG, where it became a core practice for training and warmups. Participants of TPW, members of East Coast Artists—Schechner's second New York company founded in 1992, and other groups he has worked with have learned what Krishnamacharya taught him. Unlike many of his contemporaries, Schechner did not adapt the yoga or its principles but taught the sequence of asanas as he had learned it. For Schechner, the significance of yoga as a foundational practice goes beyond its use as performer training. He credits his own vigor, mental clarity, and physical fitness—still evident in his late 80s—to his yoga practice. Of yoga's continued presence in TPW, Schechner says:

> The yoga changed my life. So why not share it? And I do believe, and I say it to people in the workshop: "If you get nothing else from this workshop except how to breathe, and how to do this yoga you will have done good things for yourself in your life. The rest is icing. This is cake. So, I can promise that it will lead you someplace. The rest of my exercises may or may not lead you someplace. But if you go *ha ha ha ha* with the resonators [forceful panting] a few times a week and you do this yoga a few times a week, your life will be changed for the better. I know that.

(Schechner 2016)

Tirumalai Krishnamacharya

Tirumalai Krishnamacharya (1888–1989) was a yoga master considered by many to be the father of modern yoga practice. Two of his best known students, responsible for bringing yoga to rest of the world's attention, were B.K.S. Iyengar (1918–2014), author of *Light on Yoga: Yoga Dipika* (2017), and Patabi Jois (1915–2009) author of *Yoga Mala: The Seminal Treatise and Guide from the Living Master of Ashtanga Yoga* (2010). For more on Krishnamacharya, see Desikachar (2005), Mohan (2010).

Schechner's research in Asia enabled him to explore in new ways fundamental questions such as how "audiences relate, how long performances last, whether people should partake of food at the same time as they partake of the performance, whether the identity of the performer is out in front and displayed as well as the identity of the character, and how these elements play back and forth with each other" (1996, 44). In 1976, at the start of his second trip to Asia, he and TPG toured Bertolt Brecht's *Mother Courage and Her Children*. Moving this complex environmental theatre production around north India generated multiple important shifts in Schechner's life and thinking. In India, his staging of *Courage* for The Performing Garage was adapted to found spaces: the Modern School gymnasium in Delhi; a courtyard in Mumbai; a car garage in Lucknow (see Figure 1.4); a large open space in Kolkata, under two trees in Singjole.[20] Although there was some backlash in India from critics who felt Schechner and TPG were misrepresenting Brecht, the production was also praised and had a lasting effect on experimental theatre practice and thoughts about Brecht in India. After the tour, TPG members agreed to take almost a year off to reconsider both their individual lives and the life of the Group, which had been dealing with conflict since before the India trip.

Schechner then spent some weeks experiencing performances in various parts of India. He settled for the summer in a small cottage near the Kerala Kalamandalam where he underwent basic kathakali training with preteens, some barely eight years old, just entering the kathakali world. He also watched rehearsals of the most accomplished performers. In a chapter from his book *Between Theatre and Anthropology* (1985) entitled "Performer Training Interculturally," Schechner reflects, "What impressed me most about the methods at the Kalamandalam was the insistence—not spoken or theorized but omnipresent nevertheless—that the body comes first, that performance knowledge enters a person by means of rigorous, continuous, rhythmical bodywork" (1985, 229). Throughout the chapter, Schechner explores the relationship between tradition and experimentation, ritual and play. These aspects of performer training have been key pillars for the development and continued practice of TPW.

FIGURE 1.4 TPG'S *Mother Courage* directed by Richard Schechner, in Lucknow, India, 1976. Joan MacIntosh (Mother Courage) confronted by the Sergeant (James Griffiths). In the background, Eilif (Jim Clayburgh), one of Courage's two sons.

Source: Photo courtesy of Richard Schechner.

In his spare time at the Kalamandalam, Schechner read for the first time parts of Manomohan Ghosh's 1967 English translation of the 2000-year-old Sanskrit performing arts "manual," the *Natyashastra* (NS) as well as scholarly studies of it. The NS quickly became a key text for Schechner because it introduced him to the concept of *rasa*:

> I was particularly struck by Chapter 6: the rasa chapter. Being interested in food, but also learning from Grotowski and my own studies about non-proscenium performance, performance where it's not about telling a story, it's not about enacting a character, this notion of performing the emotions—and that these emotions are liquid and flavorful, sensuous and experiential—it just so strongly reverberated with me.
>
> (Schechner 2012a)

These reverberations had a lasting effect on his scholarship and practice, most directly serving as a theoretical basis for Rasaboxes, which he introduced to East Coast Artists performers in 1994, and then taught regularly in performance workshops beginning in 1996. The NS also was one of the sources for Schechner's essay, "Rasaesthetics," first published in 2001.[21]

Maya-Lila

"*Maya-lila* is an Indian philosophical concept that perceives life as a game, a sport, a drama that defines existence as play where boundaries separating 'real' and 'illusion,' 'true' and 'false,' are continuously shifting and are wholly permeable."

(Schechner 2020, 194)

During his 1976 visit to India, Schechner also witnessed for the first time several days of the 31-day-long Ramlila of Ramnagar (a town of about 50,000). Ramlila, literally Rama's Play (*lila*), refers to the thousands of re-enactments of the life of Rama, the hero of the Sanskrit epic, *Ramayana*, attributed to the sage Valmiki who lived about 2,000 years ago. However, the version of Rama's story performed in Ramlila is the *Ramcharitmanas* of Tulsidas (1632–1623) composed in the late 16th century (European calendar). The Ramlila is performed during annual festivals not only in India, but globally within the vast Hindu Indian diaspora. Most Ramlilas last only a few days, whereas the 31-day Ramlila of Ramnagar, sponsored and overseen by the Maharaja of Banaras, is the longest and most fully realized theatrically.

During the Ramnagar Ramlila, the story of Rama, his birth and banishment from Ayodhya along with his wife Sita and brother Lakshmana, Sita's abduction by Ravana (a ten-headed demon king), Rama's war against Ravana, and the recovery of Sita, aided by the monkey god Hanuman and the bear general Jambavan and their troops of animal warriors is enacted in detail. Also every verse of the *Ramcharitmanas* is chanted by a chorus of 12 Hindu priests. The outdoor performance takes place in different locations and in the streets and paths of Ramnagar. As the performance moves, its audience follows. On some days, there are 80,000 spectators; on others, less than 1,000. The performers are all local people, some having played the same roles for decades. Unlike the majority of the performers, the five pre-adolescents boys who are "swarups," or shapes of the gods, are presumed to be the gods while they perform in the Ramlila. They are selected by the Maharaja and trained by theatrically skilled priests, called *vyas*. The audiences participate in a number of ways. They bring offerings to the gods; they worship the gods at the close of each night's lila; they sing in praise of Rama and Sita; they shout in greeting whenever the Maharaja appears for the first time in each performance, believing him to be the representative of the god Shiva paying honor to the god Rama.

Of course, such a performance would attract Schechner.[22] He has said that the Ramlila "is probably the best single performance I've ever encountered because its scope is enormous and yet it is intimate at the same time [. . .] It has everything [. . .] It is so popular and so beautiful, so well produced, so devotional, so ritual, and so overtly theatrical all at the same time" (Schechner 2012a). The Ramlila of Ramnagar's spatial and temporal scope over miles and weeks has within it all the complexities and contradictions that drive Schechner to map, diagram, and analyze every aspect of it from the sacred to the secular, the historical to the political, the literary to the performative, the ritual to the civic. Maya-lila, so clearly evident in the Ramlila, has deeply influenced Schechner's ideas about play and performance (see Maya-Lila, p. 28).[23]

The Main Course
Ritual, Play, Performance, and Performance Studies: Hybridity in Action

Schechner's travels in India and elsewhere, and his direct in-depth engagement with the Ramlila, enhanced his theories of ritual and play, which form the backbone of his approach to performance studies and structure much of what happens in TPW. Schechner introduces ritual and play as follows:

> Ritual and play underlie all performances and performance-making. Ritual and play have biological roots in nonhuman animals. People perform rituals both sacred and secular from before birth to after death; people play throughout their lives. Rituals also help people (and animals) deal with transitions, relationships, hierarchies, and desires that trouble, exceed, or violate the norms of daily life. Play gives people a chance to temporarily experience the taboo, the excessive, and the risky. You may never be Oedipus or Cleopatra, but you can perform them "in play."
>
> (Schechner 2020, 122)

In the context of TPW, ritual and play are important because they are designated (mutually agreed upon) safe spaces to experience and experiment with extra-daily behaviors or with being someone else. Ritual and play enable individuals, groups, and whole cultures to create alternate or doubled realities, which may transform them temporarily or permanently.

Perhaps the most central term from ritual theory for TPW (also central to the field of performance studies) is *liminality*, a key spatial, temporal, conceptual feature of ritual, play, and performance that effects material change, or transformations, such as in rites of passage. Schechner first learned about the liminal from Victor Turner, a colleague and close friend he met in 1976, who theorized liminality (see Victor Turner and Spontaneous Communitas, p. 30). Turner developed ideas first presented by ethnographer-folklorist Arnold van Gennep (1873–1957), in his 1909 *Rites of Passage* (2019). "Liminal" refers to the architectural feature of a threshold, or *limen*, a part of a building's structure that is neither in one room nor another, but in-between. A rite of passage—a bar mitzvah, a wedding, a funeral, and so on—changes who a person is. The bar mitzvah confers onto a boy a new status as a man, the wedding transforms single individuals into a married couple, a funeral ushers the dead from the world of the living to whatever comes next. During the liminal phase of a rite of passage, the person or persons enter(s) "a time-place where they are not-this-or-that, neither here nor there," a betwixt and between time during the ritual ceremony after the transformation has started but before it has been completed (Schechner 2020, 145). It is during this in-between time, the liminal phase, that the initiates are "inscribed with their new identities, given new things to do, initiated into their new status" (145). The rituals of theatre cannot claim such transformational power as rites of passage, but still take on a liminal quality:

> In ritual and aesthetic performances, the narrow space of the limen is expanded into a wide space both actually and conceptually. What usually is a brief and small "go-between" is enlarged. But even as it is enlarged it keeps its qualities as passageway and for-the-time-being. [. . .] The front of the frame of the proscenium stage [. . .] is a limen "betwixt and between" the imaginary worlds performed onstage and the experiences of the spectators in the "house." [. . .] An empty stage [or workshop or rehearsal room] is liminal, open to all possibilities: a space that by means of performing could become anywhere anytime.
>
> (145–48)

Many of the structuring elements in TPW not only involve demarcating spaces for specific extra-daily activities to take place, but also making clear distinctions between the liminal workshop world and the everyday world surrounding it.

Schechner's work in ritual studies and his collaborations with Turner led to a deep friendship that lasted until Turner's death in 1983. They enriched each other's work, cross-pollinating performance studies and anthropology. Schechner's *Between Theater and Anthropology* (1985) has a foreword written by Turner; Turner's book *From Ritual to Theatre: The Human Seriousness of Play* (1982) takes its title from Schechner's essay "From Ritual to Theatre and Back" (1974). Their theories of liminality mutually inform one another. Turner theorizes on differences between the liminal and the *liminoid*, a term he coined to refer to modern and postmodern rituals that, as Schechner puts it, "transport," rather than "transform," such as games and theatre. The activities of TPW exist mostly in the liminoid realm, although one could argue that for some participants an *inner* transformation results from participation in them.

Victor Turner and Spontaneous Communitas

A Scottish-born anthropologist best known for his theory of "social drama"—an adaptation of the Aristotelian model of tragedy—as the underlying process of ritual, Victor Turner (1920–1983) co-planned the 1981–82 "World Conference on Ritual, Drama, and Spectacle" with Schechner. Though later criticized for applying a western theory of drama to diverse non-western ritual processes, Turner's theories of structure and anti-structure, liminal and liminoid are foundational to performance studies. One of the most important aspects of liminality is the possibility of *communitas*. As Turner explains,

> Communitas, which takes place in the liminal period of a rite or ritual, is a "moment in and out of time," and in and out of secular social structure, which reveals, however fleetingly, some recognition [. . .] of a generalized social bond that has ceased to be

and has simultaneously yet to be fragmented into a multiplicity of structural ties. [. . .] The first is of society as a structured, differentiated, and often hierarchical system of politico-legal-economic positions with many types of evaluation, separating men in terms of "more" or "less." The second [. . .] is of society as an unstructured or rudimentarily structured and relatively undifferentiated comitatus, community, or even communion of equal individuals who submit together to the general authority of the ritual elders.

(Turner 1969, 96)

Communitas is an affective and energetic *result* of liminal practices, including sometimes exercises in The Performance Workshop. It is a feeling, and like many feelings, cannot be planned or depended upon. When it happens, however, it can be a tremendous source of "good vibes," a sense of connection between the people present, or between the people present and the rest of humanity. Most importantly, it creates a space of creativity and potentiality for the making of meaningful performance.

TPW is a world of serious play, a temporary world within which other smaller, more temporary worlds are created, dismantled, and reformulated. The structures and rules for the overall container of the workshop are introduced at the start of the workshop. Rules for each exercise are articulated as each is introduced. This enables participants to make clear decisions about their participation in each activity. Should the rules of play be transgressed in a significant way, the play world may change, or even collapse and need to be reconstituted with different rules (as happened during the performance of *Dionysus in 69* when Pentheus was kidnapped by the college students in the audience). The setting up of clear spatial and temporal boundaries confers upon the group an agreement about when and what can happen "inside" and what can happen "outside" those boundaries. The more rigorously the boundaries are held, the further and more safely we can go into our play, and the more risks we are willing to take. Schechner states,

> Play is hard to define. It is a mood, an activity, a spontaneous eruption. Sometimes it is rule-bound, sometimes free. It is pervasive. Everyone plays and most people enjoy watching others play—either formally in sports, theatre, on television, in films; or casually, at parties, while working, on the street, on playgrounds. Play can subvert the powers that be, as in parody or carnival, or it can be cruel, amoral power, what Shakespeare's Gloucester meant when he cried out, "As flies to wanton boys, are we to the gods, | They kill us for their sport (King Lear, 4, 1:38–39)."
>
> (Schechner 2020, 166)

Johan Huizinga's theories of play have had a significant impact on Schechner, the field of performance studies in general, and are particularly relevant to the play world of TPW. In his 1938 *Homo Ludens: A Study of the Play-element in Culture*, Huizinga claims that play is both older than culture (animals play), and a founding attribute of human culture and civilization.

Play Theory: Johan Huizinga

Johan Huizinga (1872–1945) was a Dutch historian and one of the founders of modern cultural history who brought a vast knowledge of history, literature, and cultural forms to his theory of play. Previous theories of play had assigned evolutionary, educational, or other "purpose" in the activity of play, whereas Huizinga insists that what is unique and most valuable about play is its freedom from purpose or productivity external to itself. The main characteristics of play, according to Huizinga, are that:

1. Play is voluntary (non-coercive).
2. Play is an extra-daily activity (distinct from ordinary life) that exists in a pretend world into which players are transported while remaining aware it is pretend.
3. This pretend world creates its own rules that are agreed upon and followed by all the players. It contains within it a unique and distinct sense of order.
4. Play exists for its own sake—nothing is materially gained from play except for the joy of playing.
5. Playing by the rules and adhering to the boundaries created by the pretend world are key to maintaining its integrity and success as pure play. The key is that pure play "resists any attempt to reduce it to other terms."
6. Play creates community and a sense of shared secrets between players over time. When the rules of the pretend world are transmitted to others, it becomes tradition. (Huizinga 1998, 1–13)

While TPW accommodates a diverse range of perspectives, its core principles remain grounded in the interplay between ritual and play that underpins many of Schechner's theories of performance. Both ritual and play only exist through embodied practice, and together form an important conceptual and practical bridge between Schechner's scholarship and training pedagogy.

Schechner's willingness to cross boundaries takes shape as intellectual play, a tendency that continues to move through performance studies. From the mid 1970s, at NYU Schechner taught an ongoing course, "Performance Theory," that each semester involved a different set of guests who lectured and then held a one-day seminar with graduate students. The guests included several artists and theorists mentioned in this chapter, such as Jerzy Grotowski, Victor Turner, Erving Goffman, Allan Kaprow, Spalding Gray, and many more from diverse fields. Each semester concentrated on a different subject: Performing the Self, Play, Shamanism, Cultural and Intercultural Performance, Experimental Performance. Soon it became clear that "drama" was not what was being taught, so the department name was changed to Performance Studies. In this transformation, Schechner was allied with his colleagues Professors Michael Kirby, a visual artist, performance artist, and scholar of Happenings and performance art and Brooks McNamara, a scholar of popular entertainments and commercial theatre. Schechner and the others envisioned the Department of Performance Studies as fostering "research on the how of performance—asking not 'what does it mean?' but 'what does it do?'" ("Performance Studies: History of PS"). In 1980, anthropologist Barbara Kirshenblatt-Gimblett was hired to chair the department. Because of its ever-evolving interdisciplinarity and resistance to singular methodologies she has called performance studies "a provisional coalescence on the move, [. . .] more than the sum of its inclusions" (Schechner 2020, 27). Since its inception, the field has expanded to include dance studies, feminist and queer theory, post-colonial studies, critical race theory, and the development of digital and other non-live forms of performance, incorporating new points of view, objects of study, and methodologies.[24]

One of Schechner's important contributions to the development of the discipline, and a move that has been central to performance studies' expansive approach, has been to broaden its outlook from that which 'is' performance to what can be studied 'as' performance. According to Schechner,

> Something "is" a performance when historical and social context, convention, usage, and tradition say it is. [. . .] One cannot determine what "is" a performance without specifying cultural circumstances. There is nothing inherent in an action in itself that makes it a performance or disqualifies it from being a performance.
>
> (2020, 12)

By this logic, any action or behavior can be looked at or studied 'as' a performance and be theorized through the *lens* of performance. In "Magnitudes of Performance," Schechner lays out performance as a "figure for all genres" (Schechner 2003 [1988], 291). The essay includes a Time/Space/Event chart (292–95), first diagrammed in his personal 1980–81 notebook (see Figure 1.5). His explanation of this chart further elucidates what the broad spectrum approach to performance could include:

> I wanted to take an intergeneric, intercultural perspective and see what the "limits" of performance were. I tried to think of performances of different magnitudes from the very longest lasting months or even years, to split second events; from the largest spanning millions of miles, to the smallest "brain events" of conceptual art-performances making no spatial claims at all [. . .] What [the chart] expresses is my triune thesis: 1) there is a unifiable realm of performance that includes ritual, theater, dance, music, sports, play, social drama, and various popular entertainments; 2) certain patterns can be detected among these examples; 3) from these patterns theorists can develop consistent broad-based models that respect the immediacy, ephemerality, peculiarity, and ever-changingness of individual performances, runs, and genres.
>
> (2003 [1988], 296)

In other words, Schechner's "broad spectrum" finds the universals of performance across a tremendous array of activities, while paying close attention to the particular, historically, and culturally-bound instances of any individual enactment.

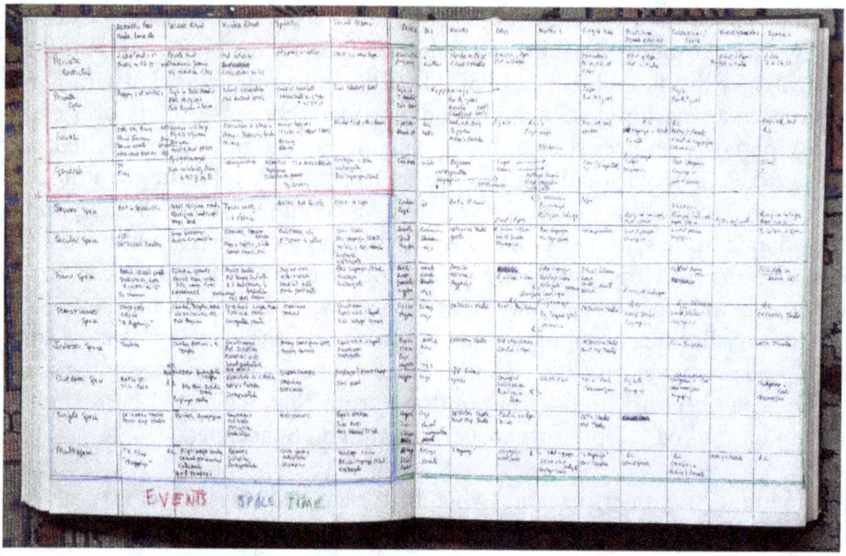

FIGURE 1.5 An early draft of the "Magnitudes of Performance" chart in Richard Schechner's 1980–1981 journal.

Source: Photo courtesy of Michael Kushner Photography, 2016.

Just as performance studies takes up the "limits of performance," TPW explores and expands the parallel limits of embodied practice. The ritual, play, and performance scaffolding of the Workshop originally devised by Schechner, and recreated by each group, engender a temporary TPW world whose unique performative circumstances invite new experiments and investigations.

The Self and Solo Performance: Spalding Gray and Leeny Sack

If ritual and play are the structural backbone of TPW, a primary tension of the Workshop is between group formation and unity on the one hand and the liberation of individual creative impulses and expression on the other. This ever-shifting dynamic reflects a historical and cultural tension at play in the theatre and performance scene as it shifted from the group theatres of the 1960s and 70s, and the emerging voices of solo artists—both theatrical soloists and performance artists, some of whom have backgrounds in the visual arts.

Two solo performers of note emerged directly out of The Performance Group: Spalding Gray (1941–2004), and Leeny Sack (b. 1951). Gray, who joined The Performance Group in 1969, and continued with The Wooster Group after Schechner's departure, is best known for his monologues. Gray's performance style, as seen in solo works such as Swimming to Cambodia (1983–85), which was later made into a film (1987), began to develop earlier with his TPG work. Gray was featured in several productions directed by Schechner, including playing Spalding in Commune (1970–72), Hoss in Sam Shepard's The Tooth of Crime (1972–74), and Swiss Cheese in Mother Courage 1975–77). During the run of Courage, Gray and several TPG colleagues directed by Elizabeth LeCompte devised a trilogy of autobiographical works, Three Places in Rhode Island (1975–1978). Gray credits his work in Schechner's productions as laying the groundwork for the move towards autobiography and performer-generated material because "Schechner emphasized the performer, making him more than, or as important as, the text. This made him very unpopular with critics and playwrights, but he was a liberator from assembly-line acting techniques" (Schechner 1982a, 45). In Commune (1970), Schechner instructed performers to tell personal stories to specific members of the audience, which led Gray to develop his autobiographical style and a performance persona that both was and was not Spalding Gray.

Leeny Sack joined TPG in 1973, after dropping out of Juilliard and studying with members of Grotowski's company. She performed Kattrin in Mother Courage and Her Children (1976) both in New York and India, several roles in The Tooth of Crime, and Manto in Seneca's Oedipus, all directed by Schechner. She worked with Gray on Sakonnet Point (the first of the Rhode Island trilogy). While part of TPG, Sack began developing The Survivor and the Translator: A solo theatre work about not having experienced the Holocaust (1980). The child of Holocaust survivors, Sack used found texts from multiple sources and testimony from her maternal grandmother who had been imprisoned in multiple concentration camps. Unlike Gray's solo works, Survivor was highly physical, theatricalizing the disjointed, trauma-based narratives of her family's experiences, and her own. When TPG transitioned to The Wooster Group, Sack left the group to focus on solo performance work and teaching. Sack's unique and sustained approach to somatic practice and performance-making, "The Performative Self," is the subject of Minnick's doctoral dissertation (2016) and has contributed to Minnick and Cole's teaching of TPW.

TPW encourages performers to explore different aspects of self and different ways of performing them. Song of Self (see pp. 117–120) and other exercises are used both as a way of exploring self through performance and as a way of generating material that can be incorporated into group performances as the Workshop progresses. Schechner's development of the "solo" aspect of TPW, came from his work with TPG and was informed by artists who in the 1980s and 90s found diverse and innovative ways of exploring identity, culture, politics and the body.[25]

Dessert, Coffee, Digestifs
Legacy and Pedagogy of TPW since 1999

While many of TPW's exercises have roots in Schechner's work with TPG, and were further shaped in early independent workshops, Rasaboxes was developed with his second New York Company, East Coast Artists (ECA) and during TPW summer courses at NYU in the early- to mid-1990s. This book includes a revised edition of Schechner's essay, "Rasaesthetics," in which he introduces Rasaboxes and explains the theory and reasoning behind the training. Rasaboxes and all other fundamental exercises of TPW are discussed at length in Chapters 4 and 5 of this book, with detailed instructions and reflections on exercises developed by Schechner and the editors. Shanti Pillai's essay "What is Rasa?" delves into the multiple meanings and applications of rasa in the Indian context. Here, we provide a brief look at the development of TPW and Rasaboxes since the 1990s, in order to contextualize the transformation of the work from a practice sustained primarily by Schechner, into a legacy and transmissible pedagogy.

Schechner had been offering TPW as a summer course in NYU's Department of Performance Studies for several years by the time he began working with ECA. Teaching the workshop as something separate from directing productions allowed Schechner to explore performance pedagogy as pure process and to expand his role as workshop facilitator. In this context, without the pressures of directing or having to lead the work in a particular direction to a public showing, he could follow his curiosity and his impulses more freely, allowing the Workshop to focus more on the desires and creativity of the participants than on realizing his directorial vision.

In 1992, Schechner gathered a group to develop a production for a *Faust* festival in Italy to which he had been invited. He brought together performers with whom he had worked in the past as well as former and current students in the Department of Performance Studies, and some from the NYU Graduate Department of Drama. Together with members of this group, he founded East Coast Artists, of which he remains artistic director. Although the production, *Faust/gastronome*, never went to Italy, it played successfully in New York at La MaMa, ETC in 1993 and on tour in the U.K. in 1994. Composed as a hybrid of versions of the *Faust* story by Goethe and Marlowe, interwoven with original texts by Schechner and ECA members, *Faust/gastronome* was a feast for the senses in which Faust (Jeff Ricketts) cooked an enormous pot of marinara sauce onstage into which he was eventually thrown by a troupe of devils led by Mephistopheles (Rebecca Wilenski—later, Ortese) (see Figure 1.6). ECA continues to serve as Schechner's artistic home. Since 2009, Schechner has shared the leadership of ECA with theatre director Benjamin Mosse and general manager Sarah Lucie. This chapter does not provide a detailed history of the company, but rather, focuses on key moments and key players relating to performer training, TPW, and Rasaboxes.

ECA members were generally an older and more professionally experienced than the people who formed TPG. Several ECA members were already trained in various forms of intense psychophysical performer techniques. Schechner had worked with Wilenski in 1981 at the University of Wisconsin-Madison on *Richard's Lear* (Schechner's hybrid of *Richard III* and *King Lear*). The *Richard's Lear* actors were trained in TPW and in the Kerala martial art kalarippayattu by Phillip Zarrilli (1947–2020), Professor of Theatre, Folklore, and South Asian Studies at the University of Wisconsin-Madison. By 1981, Zarrilli was already internationally known for his intense psychophysical actor training method based on his many years of study and practice of yoga and martial arts in India and China.[26] Wilenski

FIGURE 1.6 Rebecca Wilenski and Jeff Ricketts in *Faust/gastronome,* directed by Richard Schechner, 1993.

Source: Photo courtesy of Richard Schechner.

brought this intercultural approach, aligned with Schechner's, to early ECA training and productions. Ursula Neuerburg who took TPW in 1991 with Schechner at NYU while completing her Masters in Performance Studies, had extensive physical theatre training and performance experience in Berlin. Vernice Miller trained with members of Odin Teatret. Maria Vail-Guevara, who directed ECA's second production, *AmeriKa* (1994), based on the Franz Kafka novel, completed her MFA in Graduate Acting at NYU—as did Frank Wood, Marissa Copeland, Dan Berkey, and Shaula Chambliss. This core group also included Jeff Ricketts who trained at Southern Methodist University and Ralph Denzer, Neuerburg's then husband and musical director for *Faust/gastronome's* and subsequent ECA productions. ECA established a rigorous schedule of training that integrated yoga, physical and vocal exercises from Schechner's TPW, and vocal training based on Kristin Linklater's approach (see pp. 100–101). Singing and other musical skills, an important part of TPW, were bolstered by Wilenski's participation. Minnick was the last and one of the youngest to join, at first in 1994 to stage manage *AmeriKa* and a *Faust/gastronome* remount, and then to translate and perform Anfisa in Russian in Schechner's ECA production of Chekhov's *Three Sisters* in 1995. It was between the workshop production of *Three Sisters* in 1995 and its completion in 1997 (see Figure 1.7), that Minnick experienced TPW for the first time. She participated in the workshop for three summers before joining Cole and Schechner in 1999 as one of the workshop facilitators.

Many ECA actors came and went over the years. Some worked on several productions sequentially, while others participated more sporadically. The actors

FIGURE 1.7 Frank Wood as Vershinin and Marissa Copeland as Masha in *Three Sisters*, directed by Richard Schechner. Act Three, set in a Russian gulag, 1997. La Mama Annex, NYC.

Source: Photo courtesy of Richard Schechner.

in these ECA productions were not required to be "performers" in the same expansive sense discussed earlier, although they were expected to sing, to dance, sometimes to work on film, and to occasionally directly address the audience. The experimentation of ECA productions before 2014 was not through environmental staging, which, without a permanent rehearsal and performance space such as The Performing Garage, was not feasible. Instead, Schechner focused on using many sources, texts, styles, and genres to create hybrid projects. However, in 2014, *Imagining O*, conceived by Schechner and codirected by Benjamin Mosse, was staged environmentally at Montclair State University, NJ, in multiple spaces and included audience participation (see Figure 1.9). All productions directed by Schechner used TPW exercises, including yoga, Panting with Resonators, Crossings, and sometimes Rasaboxes—led by Schechner and/or other company members. Schechner also invented exercises to explore specific themes, relationships, and moments of what he was directing. However, members of ECA did not experience a sustained Workshop "world," or the broad set of possibilities for performance that characterize the full spectrum of performer training offered by TPW. Some members of the company, who took TPW at NYU, became instrumental in furthering the development of the work. Several of them—Neuerburg, Paula Murray Cole, who joined ECA to play Natasha for the remount of *Three Sisters* (1997), and played Ofelia in *Hamlet* (1999) at the Performing Garage (see pp. 174–176), Rachel Bowditch, (who joined the company in 2003 as a performer in *YokastaS* and *YokastaS Redux* (2005)—went on to careers as professors where they have embedded the work in

CHAPTER 1 ▶ Richard Schechner and Origins of The Performance 39

FIGURE 1.8 (Left to right) Daphne Gaines, Rachel Bowditch, Phyllis Jackson, Christopher Healey, and Jennifer Lim in *YokastaS Redux* by Richard Schechner and Saviana Stanescu, directed by Richard Schechner. La Mama Annex, NYC, 2005.

Source: Photo courtesy of Richard Schechner.

FIGURE 1.9 *Imagining O*, directed by Richard Schechner and Benjamin Mosse. Montclair State University, NJ, 2014.

Source: Photo courtesy of Richard Schechner.

theatre programs. Minnick has taught and developed the work internationally as an independent artist and scholar, and as adjunct and visiting professor at various universities.

Schechner used to say at the end of every workshop he taught at NYU, "Everything you've learned here is now yours. Take it. Do your own thing with it. Make it better." Many people have taken him at his word. They apply and modify the work in their productions, their teaching, and their therapeutic practice. ECA members and others who have taken the work, not only as something useful to apply, but as a legacy whose roots are worth sustaining, elaborated a pedagogy for teaching teachers. So far there have been two generations of teachers of TPW and Rasaboxes who have studied with, and/or worked with Schechner artistically. They have dedicated themselves both to carrying on his legacy and to developing the work in their own directions. They each have the requisite experience to teach The Performance Workshop, including Rasaboxes, as well as independent Rasaboxes workshops. The first generation includes Neuerburg, who participated in Schechner's first Rasaboxes exercise during a *Three Sisters* workshop held with ECA in 1994, already with the now familiar grid structure and the Sanskrit names for the rasas. He introduced a further development of the exercise to TPW in 1996. Some of the first participants in Rasaboxes exercises outside of ECA were students at the University of California Santa Cruz, where Neuerburg taught from 1996 to 1999, and students at Swarthmore College, where she taught from 1999 to 2005. Neuerburg has been at Concordia University in Montreal since 2006, where she regularly teaches Rasaboxes in coursework and integrates it with other acting techniques (see Neuerburg, pp. 225–234).[27]

Cole and Minnick taught TPW at NYU starting in 1999, creating a stable base for the training of a new generation of teachers. Schechner continued to attend TPW and teach a "master class" once a week at the beginning of this transition. He eventually dropped out as it was contrary to the ethos of the work itself to show up only occasionally. He did continue to come as a "guest" to answer questions about the work or to lead an exercise. For the most part, Schechner let the next generations develop their approach to teaching TPW through trial and error supplemented by conversations with him outside of workshop hours. The second generation of teachers, which includes Bowditch and Fernando Calzadilla (who have PhD's in Performance Studies from NYU), Marcia Moraes (who participated in one of Minnick's early workshops at UNIRIO in Rio de Janeiro, Brazil in 2003) and Scott Wallin (who completed his M.A. in Performance Studies at NYU—see Wallin, pp. 197–210), all completed their training under the direct mentorship of Cole and Minnick, primarily by repeatedly attending the summer workshop at NYU as guests. The transition from Schechner as the workshop leader to two women, co-facilitators at least thirty years his junior, changed the dynamic of TPW significantly. At the same time, it created an opportunity for Minnick and Cole, and subsequently other teachers, to tease out the underlying logic and principles of the work.

This book is a result of that process, which has unfolded over many years. As these teachers have developed the work since 1999, they have continued to integrate TPW and Rasaboxes exercises more deeply with one another, to expand the repertory of exercises, and to experiment with combining this work with other techniques. As they introduced TPW and Rasaboxes exercises into rehearsal for an assortment of different kinds of productions, they discovered new avenues of exploration. Several teachers have explored applications of the work beyond theatre and performance, such as in the training of physicians, work with drama therapy, or use of rasa and Rasaboxes principles in somatic movement therapy. You can read several examples of applications of TPW and Rasaboxes in Part IV of this book.

Schechner retired from teaching at NYU in 2017, but continues as editor of *TDR*. He also writes, publishes, and lectures internationally. When COVID struck, he suspended his most recent directing project, a devised work called *Dark Yes*.[28] The inheritors of TPW continue Schechner's tradition of ending each workshop with a banquet prepared by and for the participants (see Banquet, pp. 181–183). TPW and its practitioners continue to be nourished by the history and theory briefly accounted for here. Keep in mind this is just a taste of what has gone into the complex masala of TPW. We invite you to explore and learn more about any of the flavors or dishes included in this chapter, to learn more about their origins and elaborations, and to find new meanings and make novel combinations.

Notes

1 For more on Schechner's argument for culture of choice and interculturalism see Schechner 1982b, 1991, 1996, 2020.
2 When speaking about culture, Schechner addresses the power differential implied by this "borrowing," but this acknowledgment does not excuse any generational, gendered, or racial blindness, or unwillingness to address some of the more subtle areas of concern that might be raised.
3 Volunteering for the draft meant that a young man (women were not being drafted) instructed his draft board to draft him immediately for two years of service instead of waiting to be called up for the draft which meant a minimum of three years of service. Schechner volunteered in order to serve with enlisted men rather than in an elite position as an officer (see Nesmith 2022).
4 Using the FOIA, Schechner has seen heavily redacted copies of the FBI files. What's there from the other agencies is still not available for "security" reasons.
5 In 1955 while on faculty at Carlton College in Northfield, Minnesota, Robert W. Corrigan founded *The Carlton Drama Bulletin*, later called *Carlton Drama Review*. Corrigan brought the journal with him to Tulane in 1957, renaming it *The Tulane Drama Review (TDR)*. Schechner took over as *TDR*'s editor in 1962. Schechner brought *TDR* with him to NYU in 1967, renaming it *The Drama Review*. He continued as editor until 1969 and then again from 1985 to the present. In the intervening years, *TDR* was edited for two years by Erika Munk and for 15 years by Michael Kirby. Schechner was Guest Editor for the 1973 Social Science issue and for the 1982 Intercultural issue.
6 *In White America* by Martin Duberman is a 1963 documentary made from historical records recounting the history of Blacks in the USA. The play won the Off-Broadway Drama Desk Award.
7 For more on the FST's work until 1969, see *The Free Southern Theater by The Free Southern Theater: A Documentary of the South's Radical Black Theater, with Journals, Letters, Poetry Essays and a Play Written By Those Who Built It* (Dent et al. 1969).
8 The Happenings issue of *TDR* (vol 10, no. 2, 1965) was guest edited by Michael Kirby. It is a thorough survey of Happenings and associated events. The issue includes an

interview with John Cage conducted by Kirby and Schechner and several items by Allan Kaprow.
9   Schechner explains that all existence is "being," being in action is "doing," performing is "showing doing," and performance studies is "explaining showing doing." See "What is Performance," in Schechner 2020, 4.
10 A slightly revised version of the original 1968 essay was published in the 1994 edition of *Environmental Theater*. The first edition of *Environmental Theater* appeared in 1973. Note: The editors of this book spell "theatre" with "re" at the end (rather than "er") but we have kept the different spelling and numbering conventions used in each published version of Schechner's essays.
11 For some publications in English in *TDR* about or by Grotowski see Grotowski and Schechner 1964; Grotowski et al. 1968; Schechner 1970. See also, *Towards a Poor Theater* (Grotowski 1968). For a more comprehensive book, see Schechner and Wolford 1997.
12 The secure partner is being both another and oneself simultaneously—a sense of the double as it were. For more on this, see Forsythe 1978; Grotowski 1968; Schechner and Wolford 1997.
13 Schechner formed The Wooster Group, Inc. early in 1968—it was TPG's legal name. After Schechner left TPG in 1980, Elizabeth LeCompte, who had assistant directed and performed in a number of TPG productions, as well as directing original works with Spalding Gray and others, became artistic director and changed the group's name to The Wooster Group, so the corporate and operating name were one and the same.
14 So named by Schechner because when he first saw the space, a garbage truck was parked inside; and also because the front door is a large up-and-down sliding metal door like those on some garages.
15 For detailed description of the different types of audience participation during *Dionysus in 69* see Schechner 1970; 1994, 40–45.
16 See "Consent" in pp. 83–84.
17 For more on 20th century experimental and avant-garde theatre, including immersive theatre, see Innes 1993; Shank 1982.
18 For more on Badal Sircar, The Third Theatre, and Schechner's influences, see Mitra 2004.
19 Kalakshetra was, and remains, a center for training in Bharatnatyam dance and Ghandavaveda music. For more information see www.kalakshetra.in.
20 For more on the critical reception of *Mother Courage* in India, see Harding and Rosenthal 2011, 50–58.
21 See Chapters 2 and 3 for more on rasa and Rasaboxes, and Chapter 4, pp. 136–179 for an extensive collection of Rasaboxes exercises.
22 The Ramlila of Ramnagar has fascinated Schechner so much that he has returned many times to Ramnagar, most recently in 2013. He has attended all 31 days twice. With the Maharaja's permission, Schechner has photographed and filmed Ramlila. His Ramlila Collection at NYU is the world's largest with over 8,000 photographs, films, and sound recordings.
23 For more on the Ramlila of Ramnagar, see Schechner and Hess 1977; Schechner 1993, 131–83; Schechner 2012b; 2015, 81–138.
24 See Schechner 2015, 50–52 for the development of the discipline in the Performance Studies, NYU. Performance studies is more broadly addressed in other sections of Schechner 2020; Citron et al. 2014; Harding and Rosenthal 2011; Bell 2008; Madison and Hamera 2006; Jackson 2004.

25 The bibliography on solo performance and performance art is vast. Some key references include Goldberg 2001; Champagne 1990 (which includes *The Survivor* and *The Translator*); Hughes and Román 1998.
26 For more on Phillip Zarrilli's own work on performer training, see Zarrilli 2002; 2019.
27 Cole and Minnick exchanged ideas about Rasaboxes work with Neuerburg at an interdisciplinary Rasa Symposium organized by Cole at Ithaca College in 2012 and when the first six core TPW and Rasaboxes teachers gathered in Montreal in 2013 in conjunction with the annual Association for Theatre in Higher Education (ATHE) conference.
28 *Dark Yes* combines elements from Joseph Conrad's *Heart of Darkness* with James Joyce's *Ulysses*, while also drawing on other texts and the experiences of the performers and other members of the creative team.

Works Cited

Artaud, Antonin. "Theatre and Cruelty." In *The Twentieth-Century Performance Reader*, edited by Teresa Brayshaw and Noel Witts. London and New York: Routledge, 2014, pp. 31–34.
Barba, Eugenio. *A Dictionary of Theatre Anthropology: The Secret Art of the Performer.* Trans. Richard Fowler, 2nd ed. London and New York: Routledge, 2005.
———. "Words or Presence." In *The Twentieth-Century Performance Reader*, edited by Teresa Brayshaw and Noel Witts. London and New York: Routledge, 2014, pp. 46–52.
Bell, Elizabeth. *Theories of Performance*. Los Angeles: Sage Publications, 2008.
Brayshaw, Teresa, and Noel Witts, eds. *The Twentieth-Century Performance Reader*, 3rd ed. London and New York: Routledge, 2014.
Brecht, Bertolt. "Short Description of a New Technique of Acting Which Produces an Alienation Effect." In *The Twentieth-Century Performance Reader*, edited by Teresa Brayshaw and Noel Witts. London and New York: Routledge, 2014, pp. 101–12.
Champagne, Lenora, ed. *Out from Under: Texts by Women Performance Artists.* New York: Theatre Communications Group, 1990.
Citron, Atay, Sharon Aronson-Lehavi, and David Zerbib, eds. *Performance Studies in Motion: International Perspectives and Practices in the Twenty-First Century*. London: Bloomsbury, 2014.
Dent, Thomas C., Richard Schechner, and Gilbert Moses, eds. *The Free Southern Theater, by the Free Southern Theater: a Documentary of the South's Radical Black Theater, with Journals, Letters, Poetry, Essays, and a Play Written by Those who Built it*. Indianapolis: Bobbs-Merrill Co., 1969.
Desikachar, Kausthub. *The Yoga of the Yogi: The Legacy of T. Krishnamacharya*. New York: North Point Press, 2005.
Dorsey, Chianta. "The Free Southern Theater: Foundations of a Southern Black Arts Movement." Amistad Research Center, 2014. https://artsandculture.google.com/story/the-free-southern-theater-amistad-research-center/-AVx0M-5vTtQIg?hl=en. Accessed 13 October 2022.
Forsythe, Eric. "Conversations With Ludwik Flaszen." *Educational Theatre Journal*, vol. 30, no. 3, 1978, pp. 301–28.
Gillitt, Cobina. "Richard Schechner." *Asian Theatre Journal*, vol. 30, no. 2, 2013, pp. 276–94.
Goffman, Erving. *The Presentation of Self in Everyday Life*. New York: Doubleday, 1959.
Goldberg, Rose Lee. *Performance Art: From Futurism to the Present*. London: Thames & Hudson, 2001 [1979].

Grotowski, Jerzy. *Towards a Poor Theatre*. New York: Simon and Schuster, 1968.
———. "Statement of Principles." In *The Twentieth-Century Performance Reader*, edited by Teresa Brayshaw and Noel Witts. London and New York: Routledge, 2014, pp. 241–52.
Grotowski, Jerzy, and Richard Schechner. "'Doctor Faustus' in Poland." *The Tulane Drama Review*, vol. 8, no. 4, 1964, pp. 120–33.
Grotowski, Jerzy, Richard Schechner, and Jacques Chwat. "Interview with Grotowski." *The Drama Review: TDR*, vol. 13, no. 1, 1968, pp. 29–45.
Harding, James Martin, and Cindy Rosenthal, eds. *The Rise of Performance Studies: Rethinking Richard Schechner's Broad Spectrum*. Basingstoke: Palgrave Macmillan, 2011.
Hughes, Holly, and David Román, eds. *O Solo Homo: The New Queer Performance*. New York: Grove Press, 1998.
Huizinga, Johan. *Homo Ludens: A Study of the Play-Element in Culture*. London and New York: Routledge, 1998.
Innes, Christopher D. *Avant Garde Theatre 1892–1992*. London and New York: Routledge, 1993.
Iyengar, B. K. S. *Light on Yoga: Yoga Dipika*. Uttar Pradesh: HarperCollins Publishers, India, 2017
Jackson, Shannon. *Professing Performance: Theatre in the Academy from Philology to Performativity*. New York: Cambridge University Press, 2004.
Jois, K. Pattabhi. *Yoga Mala: The Seminal Treatise and Guide from the Living Master of Ashtanga Yoga*. New York: North Point Press, 2010.
Kaprow, Allan. *Assemblages, Environments, and Happenings*. New York: Abrams, 1965.
Kaprow, Allan, and Jeff Kelly. *Essays on the Blurring of Art and Life*. Berkeley, Los Angeles, and London: University of California Press, 2003 [1966].
Madison, D. Soyini, and Judith Hamera, eds. *The Sage Handbook of Performance Studies*. Thousand Oaks: Sage Publications, 2006.
Manomohan, Ghosh, ed. *The Natyasastra—A Treatise on Hindu Dramaturgy and Histrionics Ascribed to Bharata-Muni*, vol. I, Chapters I–XXVII. Calcutta: Royal Asiatic Society, 1950.
Minnick, Michele. "Breathing Worlds: Somatic Practice, Performance and the Self in the Life/Art Work of Leeny Sack." Dissertation, New York University. UMI, 2016.
Mitra, Shayoni. "Badal Sircar: Scripting a Movement." *TDR (1988–)*, vol. 48, no. 3, 2004, pp. 59–78.
Mohan, A. G., and Ganesh Mohan. *Krishnamacharya: His Life and Teachings*. Boston and London: Shambala, 2010.
Nesmith, Nathaniel G. "From Newark to New Orleans: Richard Schechner's Backstory." *American Theatre*, March 2022. www.americantheatre.org/2022/03/21/from-newark-to-new-orleans-richard-schechners-backstory/. Accessed 30 September 2022.
"Performance Studies: History of PS." Tisch School of the Arts, NYU. https://tisch.nyu.edu/performance-studies/degree-programs/history-of-performance-studies-. Accessed 11 October 2022.
Schechner, Richard. "The Bacchae: A City Sacrificed to a Jealous God." *Tulane Drama Review*, vol. 5, no. 4, 1961, pp. 24–134.
———. "Approaches to Theory/Criticism." *The Drama Review*, vol. 10, no. 4, 1966, pp. 20–53.
———. "6 Axioms for Environmental Theatre." *The Drama Review: TDR*, vol. 12, no. 3, 1968, pp. 41–61.
———. "In Warm Blood." In *Public Domain*. Indianapolis: Bobbs-Merrill Co., 1969, pp. 93–107.
———. "Commentary on Mandel's 'Reactionary Notes on the Experimental Theatre'." *The Massachusetts Review*, vol. 11, no. 3, 1970, pp. 578–83.

———. *Environmental Theater*. New York: Hawthorn Books, 1973.
———. "From Ritual to Theatre and Back." *Theatre Journal*, vol. 26, no. 4, 1974, pp. 455–81.
———. *The End of Humanism: Writings on Performance*. New York: PAJ Publications, 1982a.
———. "Intercultural Performance: An Introduction." *The Drama Review: TDR*, vol. 26, no. 2 (T94) Summer 1982b, pp. 3–4.
———. *Between Theater and Anthropology*. Philadelphia: University of Pennsylvania Press, 1985.
———. "Intercultural Themes." In *Interculturalism and Performance*, edited by Bonnie Marranca and Guatam Dasgupta, vol. 11–12. New York: PAJ Publications, 1991, pp. 308–17.
———. "A New Paradigm for Theatre in the Academy." *TDR (1988–)*, vol. 36, no. 4, 1992, pp. 7–10.
———. *The Future of Ritual*. London and New York: Routledge, 1993.
———. *Environmental Theater: An Expanded New Edition Including 'Six Axioms for Environmental Theater'*, rev. ed. New York: Applause, 1994.
———. "Six Axioms for Environmental Theater." In *Environmental Theatre: An Expanded New Edition Including 'Six Axioms For Environmental Theatre'*, rev. ed. New York: Applause, 1994 [1973], pp. xix–xlv.
———. "Interculturalism and the Culture of Choice: Richard Schechner Interviewed by Patrice Pavis." In *The Intercultural Performance Reader*, edited by Patrice Pavis. London and New York: Routledge, 1996, pp. 41–50.
———. "Magnitudes of Performance." In *Performance Theory*, rev. and expanded ed. London and New York: Routledge, 2003 [1988], pp. 290–332.
———. "Interview with Cobina Gillitt." 24 May 2012a, New York.
———. "Who Is Rama?" In *Religion, Theatre, and Performance*, edited by Lance Gharavi. London and New York: Routledge, 2012b, pp. 185–91.
———. *Performed Imaginaries*. London and New York: Routledge, 2015.
———. "Interview with Rachel Bowditch, Paula Murray Cole, and Michele Minnick." 26 June 2016, New York.
———. *Performance Studies: An Introduction*, 4th ed. London and New York: Routledge, 2020.
Schechner, Richard, and Linda Hess. "The Ramlila of Ramnagar [India]." *The Drama Review: TDR*, vol. 21, no. 3, 1977, pp. 51–82.
Schechner, Richard, and Lisa Wolford, eds. *The Grotowski Sourcebook*. London and New York: Routledge, 1997.
Shank, Theodore. *American Alternative Theatre*. New York: Grove Press, 1982.
Turner, Victor. *The Ritual Process: Structure and Anti-structure*. London: Routledge and Kegan Paul, 1969.
———. *Dramas, Fields, and Metaphors: Symbolic Action in Human Society*. Ithaca: Cornell University Press, 1974.
———. *From Ritual to Theatre: The Human Seriousness of Play*. New York: PAJ Publications, 1982.
Van Gennep, Arnold. *The Rites of Passage*. Trans. Monika B. Vizedom and Gabrielle L. Caffee, 2nd ed. Chicago: University of Chicago Press, 2019.
Zarrilli, Phillip. *Acting (Re) Considered*. London and New York: Routledge, 2002.
Zarrilli, Phillip, T. Sasitharan, and Anuradha Kapur, eds. *Intercultural Acting and Performer Training*. London and New York: Routledge, 2019.

CHAPTER 2

What Is Rasa?

SHANTI PILLAI

Richard Schechner's Rasaboxes is a testament to the power of *rasa*, the concept that is India's original contribution to the world of performance and aesthetics. The exercise constitutes a particular translation of an already multivalent theory into terms and techniques meant to serve theatrical practices very different from those associated with rasa's origins. As Schechner points out, Rasaboxes "comes from" rather than operates as an "example of" rasa theory (see Chapter 3, p. 73). By extension, one cannot really understand rasa's ideational or pragmatic origins by doing the exercises, but one can understand a great deal more about Rasaboxes by gaining familiarity with rasa's roots and current manifestations.

In India, rasa is a concept that crisscrosses religious ceremonies and a range of artistic practices, including theatre, dance, music, painting, and poetry. Its relevance is perhaps most assiduously articulated with respect to the performing arts. Like many Indian concepts, its meaning varies in historical periods and according to various commentators and practitioners up to the present.[1] Its explanation and practical applications can be found in ancient textual sources as well as in its current embodied iterations in performance.

Discussions about rasa, whether in scholarly circles or popular forums such as the numerous internet websites dedicated to Indian dance, often reference the ancient Sanskrit manual on performance, the *Natyashastra*, as the ultimate authoritative rendering of rasa's definition and connotations. However, limiting one's understanding of the subject to text-based epistemologies can be misleading. First of all, rasa's dimensions can be understood through direct observation of what traditional Indian performers across an array of genres are actually *doing*. Positing the *Natyasastra* as the most salient source of information affirms an assumption about the superiority of Sanskrit text over other forms of expression, a perspective that has long operated as a dominant trope within the field of South Asian studies. Secondly, to observe how performance principles incarnate across multiple performance forms would be closer to Schechner's process of encountering rasa. He traveled for four months in India between 1971 and 1972 and saw many kinds of performance. He supplemented his understanding of rasa by reading the *Natyashastra* several years later, during a summer's stay in Kerala in 1976 (Schechner 2016).

Having acknowledged this, I will defy my own caveat—harmonious contradiction being a hallmark of Indian modes of thought (Ramanujan 1989). I will start by outlining the *Natyashastra*'s indications on the subject by way of establishing a working definition from which to contextualize rasa's other manifestations. This is necessary because it is the first written documentation that delineates rasa in detail. This rich performance manual is traced to between the 2nd century BCE and 4th century CE, although exact dating is not possible. What is certain is that the text encapsulates a performance philosophy and set of practices that long predate its inscription and would have comprised the wisdom of numerous voices in the context of the oral culture of the ancient Sanskrit world. It is important to note that while the word *natya* refers to practices that in western terms would fall into the distinct classifications of dance, theatre, and music, the Indian tradition does not make these differentiations of genre, and indeed many performance forms include elements of all three (Richmond et al. 1993; Vatsyayan 1968, 1983).

The attributed author of the *Natyashastra*, Bharata-muni ("muni" designating a sage, sometimes denoting someone sworn to silence), is not a historical figure but rather a mythological personage who first received the art of performance from none other than the creator, Brahma. In the first chapter of the *Natyashastra*, Bharata tells the story of how this came about and in so doing affirms the sacred, existential importance of performance.[2] He relates that in an era in which beings had lost all civility, the gods came to Brahma and requested something that would both instruct and be a pleasing diversion. They acknowledged that while truths could be known through the Vedic scriptures, lower castes were prevented from listening to them. To solve the dilemma, Brahma created the art of drama as a fifth Veda, selecting components from the other four Vedas.[3]

Brahma summoned Bharata and bequeathed to him this knowledge. Bharata then set about training his 100 sons and eventually conducted a grand debut performance depicting a mighty battle in which the gods emerged victorious over the demons. So incensed were the demons sitting in the audience that they disrupted the show, prompting Brahma to create rites for protecting all performances. When asked why they had spoiled the event, the demons complained that it was unfair to have been depicted in an unfavorable light. Brahma, creator and father of all, pacified them, explaining that natya is for everyone and that even the gods can be portrayed in various ways.

From this episode, it is clear that performance is an exalted activity from which anyone can receive both pleasure and truth. Brahma further clarifies that each individual will receive a performance according to their tastes and ability to do so. Performance is serious business and links the collective and the personal on a path toward the highest forms of knowledge. Of such primacy is the subject that the *Natyashastra* is related in the form of a dialogue between the expert Bharata and a group of sages curious about the art.

The *Natyasastra* outlines in detail virtually all of the facets of stagecraft. Included are theatrical architecture, the structure of plays, stock characters, the appropriate costumes for specific kinds of characters, as well as their accompanying makeup, wigs, beards, gestural language, movements of the eyes, music, and so on. In his essay on "Rasaesthetics," Schechner compares this focus on theatrical techniques with Aristotle's discussion of drama in the *Poetics* (see Chapter 3, pp. 55–57). The Greek text does not take performance mechanics as its central concern and instead focuses largely on the structure of dramatic plot.[4]

Rasa is covered in chapters six and seven of the *Natyashastra*. The importance of rasa is underscored by the fact that Bharata develops the theory *before* going on to detail the nuances of the performer's labor. In order to understand Bharata's discussion of rasa in these chapters, one must know that the term in Sanskrit denotes juice, flavor, or essence:

> But what is this thing called rasa? Here is the reply. Because it is enjoyably tasted, it is called rasa. How does the enjoyment come? Persons who eat prepared food mixed with different condiments and sauces, if they are sensitive, enjoy the different tastes and then feel pleasure; likewise, sensitive spectators, after enjoying the various emotions expressed by the actors through words, gestures, and feelings, feel pleasure. This feeling by the spectators is here explained as rasas of natya.
>
> (Bharata-muni 1996, 55)

The objective of performance is to inspire in spectators the same experience they have when enjoying good food: it is sensuous, intimate, and involves the savoring of a deeply personal moment. It also entails a dynamic connection between what is outside and what is inside and, like digestion, involves a generative process of transformation. As articulated by poet Rabindranath Tagore:

> Our emotions are the gastric juices, which transform this world of appearance into the more intimate world of sentiments. On the other hand, this outer world has its own juices, having their various qualities which excite our emotional activities. This is called in our Sanskrit rhetoric rasa, which signifies outer juices having their response in the inner juices of our emotions. And a poem, according to it, is a sentence or sentences containing juices, which stimulate the juices of emotion. It brings to us ideas, vitalized by feelings, ready to be made into the life-stuff of our nature.
>
> (1961, 18)

The food metaphor should not be underestimated. In India, flavor is not only a central preoccupation of everyday life but also strictly theorized in relation to medicine and religious practice. In the context of ritual, the offering of food is a central performative act in which the preservation of the body directly relates to cosmic sustenance (Schwartz 2004, 7–8). Food served to the deity for relishing returns to the givers, who eat it after the ritual and thereby synchronize their own physicality with the body of the divine.

Rasa operates in the singular, designating the apex of performance's potential, as well as in the plural to delineate the particular heightened, aesthetic experiences of emotion that compose that potential. Bharata outlines eight rasas that correlate to eight *sthayi bhavas*, translated as permanent or inward-residing emotions:

TABLE 2.1 Rasas and corresponding sthayi bhavas.

Rasa	Sthayi Bhava
shringara (eroticism, pleasure)	rati (love)
hasya (humor)	hasya (laughter)
karuna (pity)	shoka (grief)
raudra (anger)	krodha (anger/wrath)
vira (heroism)	utsaha (vigor)
bhayanaka (fear)	bhaya (fear)
bibhatsa (disgust)	jugupsa (aversion)
adbhuta (wonderment)	vismaya (surprise)

Rasa designates the experience of the sthayi bhava. As Schechner puts it, "the sweetness in a ripe plum is its sthayi bhava, the experience of tasting the sweet is rasa" (Schechner, this volume, p. 61). These sthayi bhavas correspond with specific colors, deities, and melodies used in the visual arts and performance to both represent and invoke sentiments.

Acting, or *abhinaya*, consists in communicating *bhava* (emotion or sentiment), and particularly the sthayi bhavas so that rasa can be experienced. At times in the *Natyasastra* and in common usage today, the terms "bhava" and "rasa" seem interchangeable. Bhava is created through a kind of alchemy of elements: *vibhava* references the underlying causes or determinants of emotional situations, and *anubhava* is used to indicate the physical results that become the indicators of feelings in performance. While the principal bhavas are the sthayi bhavas, they are enhanced by 33 transient emotions called *vyabhichari* bhavas: despondency, weakness, apprehension, envy, intoxication, weariness, indolence, depression, anxiety, distraction, recollection, contentment, shame, inconstancy, joy, agitation, stupor, arrogance, despair, impatience, sleep, epilepsy, dreaming, awakening, indignation, dissimulation, cruelty, assurance, sickness, insanity, death, fright, and deliberation (Rangacharya 1996, 364). The list might seem confusing, as one might not define sleep and disease as emotional or mental states. Also important to note is that many of the vyabhichari bhavas are common to several of the sthayi bhavas. Things are complicated further by Bharata's specification of eight *sattvika* states: paralysis, perspiration, horripilation, change of voice, trembling, change of color, weeping, and fainting. These translate roughly as "involuntary states," although Bharata does not clearly distinguish them from the other anubhavas.

Thus, there are 49 different feelings in all that contribute to rasa, the sthayi bhavas being like a "king" and the others like his retinue of "attendants" (Bharata-muni 1967, 122). This vast repertoire of bhava allows a performance to present the spectator with various emotional experiences to savor in the same way that a meal should delight the partaker with multiple flavors. The relationship of bhava to rasa mirrors other Indian concepts that posit freedom in terms of a release from the particularities and relational values of place, time, personality, and social role. As argued by Ramanujan, "In the realm of feeling, bhavas are private, contingent, context-roused sentiments.... But rasa is generalized, it is an essence" (1989, 54).

The experience of rasa belongs to the realm of *alaukika*, the extraordinary. This is the thesis of Abhinavagupta, a Kashmiri worshipper of Shiva who produced an extensive commentary on the *Natyashastra* during the 10th century (2006). Rasa, he asserted, is wholly distinct from the emotions of everyday life. It is the abstract essence of emotion that allows a spectator to identify with a character portrayed whose psychology and situation may differ sharply from their own.[5] The tasting of rasa would seem to be profoundly spiritual in this view.

In correspondence with his prioritization of transcendence, Abhinavagupta references a ninth rasa: *shanta*, defined as peace or tranquility. Shanta exists as a kind of blissful repose to which one might arrive after a thorough experience of all emotional states. Schechner uses the analogy of white light, claiming shanta as "the transcendent rasa that, when accomplished, absorbs and eliminates all the others" (see Chapter 3, p. 61). Since Abhinavagupta, shanta has generally been accepted as part of the rasic experience, although it does not correspond to any of the sthayi bhavas and is difficult to depict.[6]

Abhinavagupta's assertions about rasa as a universal, impersonal experience of an expansive consciousness is echoed by numerous other thinkers whose concerns are not strictly with the performing arts. It resonates deeply with those who associate rasa with *bhakti*, a spiritual orientation in which a devotee develops a deeply personal, loving attachment to a particular deity and through that relationship can attain salvation from the cycle of birth and death regardless of their caste. Foremost of the bhakti theorists is Rupa Gosvami, a 16th-century poet and playwright who defined *bhaktirasa* as the highest form of rasa and an experience to be found in the heavens in the transcendent play of Lord Krishna (see Buchta and Schweig 2010, 625–26). The same idea can be found centuries later in the recent, secular musings of Vikram Chandra on the nature of poetry and computer coding (2014). Chandra discusses rasa, analyzing Abhinavagupta at length, to redefine beauty and style and expand the assumed parameters of the sublime.

In Bharata's conception, rasa is the central organizing principle of natya. As explained by Venkatarama Raghavan, "Characters, story or plot take a secondary place; in fact, the story is in place not as a story but as a medium of rasa" (1993, 14). At odds with Aristotle's mandate for the unity of time, space, and action, rasa requires a unity of emotion. Actual plot elements are of less importance than their effects on characters (73).

All of a performer's work is directed toward the portrayal of bhavas to lay the ground for rasa. "In this regard, the theory of sentiment is a practical guide to a performer in developing his or her craft, as well as being a useful tool in realizing the maximum potential of the art" (Richmond 1993, 82). The four vectors of performance—*angika* (movements of the body), *vachika* (vocal communication), *aharya* (costume, props, and sets), and *sattvika abhinaya* (a total inner involvement that gives nuance and power to acting)—all serve as vehicles for rasa.

The spectator also plays a crucial role in rasa. Chapter 27 of the *Natyashastra* deals with the success of a production. Here, Bharata specifies the requirements for the ideal spectator. Bharata understands that people have different tastes and that in any audience there will be varying levels of understanding, yet there is still the possibility of an ideal spectator. The greatest appreciation of performance requires expertise in music and the other components of performance, as well as an ability to feel what the characters feel. This responsive person is known as a *rasika*. The experience of rasa thus requires both cultivation and innate qualities.

Performance scholar Farley Richmond makes a comparison between rasa and French haute cuisine as an experience that is strictly for experts. He affirms how in partaking of such a feast,

> the meal is savored by a connoisseur who recognizes the difference between haute cuisine prepared by an expert chef, served in a quiet dining room of a four star restaurant on a quiet summer evening with friends, and meat and potatoes dished up by a harried cook in a steamy kitchen on a Saturday night.
>
> (1993, 80–81)

Although theatre, like food, may be for everyone, not all who attend will be rasikas. The question as to whether only the rasika experiences rasa, or whether it is an experience also available to the performer, is not entirely clear from Bharata's specifications. Abhinavagupta believed that only the audience experiences rasa. Art historian Ananda Coomaraswamy, in an in-depth reflection on passages from the *Sahitya Darpana*, a 14th-century tome on aesthetics, seems to concur. He highlights that the sthayi bhava "is brought to life as rasa because of the spectator's own capacity for tasting" (1994, 50). His analysis leaves room for the possibility of performer involvement, however, in the assertion that a performer "may obtain aesthetic experience from the spectacle of his own performance" (51). Renowned dance scholar Kapila Vatsyayan agrees:

> The representation of the emotions of the hero is to be entirely independent of the actor's or dancer's own feelings. Hence, he or she can enjoy the transcendental flavor, the rasa, in the same impersonal way as the audience. The work of art and also the artist and the actor thus become participants in a ritual where the work of art is the *yantra*—the device through which the *sadhaka* (artist) sees the vision of the Absolute as much as the audience to whom the work of art is presented.
>
> (1968, 10)

This sense of the performer's ability to partake in rasa seems to shape Schechner's thoughts on the topic as well when he makes the argument that the Indian performer engages in a "self-regarding" that constitutes a reception of their own performance (see Chapter 3, p. 74). At the same time, Schechner indicates that in abhinaya, the acting through which a performer conveys rasa to the spectators, one may or may not create feelings in oneself.

Although the *Natyasastra* is a rich guide for both performers and spectators, it does not function as a manual to which all practitioners refer. In fact, most classical and folk performers and their audiences throughout the centuries might not actually have read it or any of its commentators, a fact that continues to be true today. Thus, rasa has always lived primarily in the various interpretations that performers give to it and in the cultural frameworks that shape the ways in which both performers and audiences have given meaning and importance to their interrelated labors of production and reception.[7]

In some performance instruction today, particularly of classical forms, emotional communication is trained explicitly through specific techniques. For example, a *kathakali*[8] artist learns the control of minute muscles of the eyes and face that correspond to particular bhavas. An *odissi*[9] dancer, through years of watching their own teacher perform, will acquire a tool kit of gestures and scenarios to portray the sentiments of a heroine who pines for her lover. In the modern era, it is not uncommon to see showcases of the emotional capabilities of performers. For example, there are lecture demonstrations in which a *kudiyattam*[10] artist goes through the nine rasas, delighting audiences with the clarity of depiction and the deftness of transitions from one rasa to the next. Another variant are the group choreographies of *bharatanatyam* in which multiple dancing bodies morph through a sequence of nine tableaux vivants of mythological scenes that exemplify the rasas. On the other hand, some training only implicitly imparts the tools for bhava. For example, some bharatanatyam teachers do not instruct emotions per se, but rather allow the bhavas to assume form organically as students gain the skills of storytelling.

The centrality of emotional communication is not a feature solely of traditional forms of performance. Contemporary artists interested in investigating the possibilities for an Indian language of theatre rooted in Indian source material rather than mimicry of western dramatic literature and stage conventions interpret rasa for their own purposes. The artist who has most extensively investigated the physiological underpinnings of the communication of emotion as part of the formulation of a technique for modern actors is director and playwright Veenapani Chawla. After years of instruction in and experimentation with kudiyattam, Chawla and her actors arrived at a precise system of breath patterns, tongue placements, and the management of rhythm and energy in the body that provide the actor with concrete tools for performance (Gokhale 2014).

Schechner's Rasaboxes also aims to provide tools. The exercises cultivate actors' psychophysical capabilities, assisting them in an artistic process rooted in exploration—a process that need not be limited to application in conventional forms of performance. Rasa provides the inspiration for these exercises because Schechner saw it as the key to unlocking the kind of feeling and knowing he saw in gifted Indian performers and their audiences.

I remember one afternoon in the mid-1990s when I sat in Schechner's seminar on Indian performance at New York University and listened to him relate being in the audience for a 1971 performance by the late bharatanatyam dancer T. Balasaraswati, at a winter concert series in Madras. Bala, as she was affectionately known, was from a long, hereditary lineage of temple and court dancers and musicians known as *devadasis*. She was also a genius, particularly known in India and abroad for her abhinaya. Schechner saw her perform her signature piece, *Krishna Ni Bengane Baro*, a composition in which Krishna's mother scolds her little son for eating sand. When she obliges him to open his mouth, she is confronted with a dazzling and terrifying view of all of creation and is thrust into a cosmic consciousness. When he closes his mouth, he once more looks like her naughty little boy, as she forgets the panorama of transcendence and enters once more into the world of everyday perception. As Schechner described his own astonishment at the vivid and playful way that Bala showed this favorite scene with little more than a tapping of her foot, a wagging of her finger, and her dancing eyes, his voice faltered and his eyes filled with tears. That a mother could be so transported to another reality by the cosmic play of her little child mirrored how the great bharatanatyam artist had mesmerized an audience.

This vignette of seeing my teacher so moved by a performance he had seen decades earlier has remained with me. I often recount it to my students, and when I do, I feel a lump in my own throat. Seeing his tears that day, I understood that in Indian performance Schechner saw the potential for a singular poignancy and power. I believe that this potential for transcendent knowledge and pleasure is what he wanted for his own actors and their audiences when he created the Rasaboxes.

Notes

1. At the start of his comprehensive examination of rasa in relation to broader discussions on aesthetics from various historical periods, Sanskrit scholar and intellectual historian Sheldon Pollock argues that although storytelling is a cross-cultural practice, "few people have meditated as deeply and systematically on the questions it raises as thinkers in India, who over a period of 1,500 years, between the third and the eighteenth centuries, carried on an intense conversation about the emotional world of the story and its complex relationships to the world of the audience" (2016, 1).
2. For an analysis of the first chapter of the *Natyashastra*, see Byrski (1974).
3. There are not recent, complete translations of the *Natyashastra* from Sanskrit to English. I cross-referenced two frequently used versions in preparing this chapter: Bharata-muni, translated by Ghosh (1967); Rangacharya (1996).
4. For extensive comparison of ancient Greek and Indian concepts of theatre, see Bharat Gupt (1994).
5. For a detailed discussion of Abhinavagupta's views on performance, see Ganser (2022).
6. There is some dispute among scholars about whether Abhinavagupta was the first to introduce shanta into the conversation about rasa. See Chapter 3, p. 56.
7. For discussion from disciplines as wide-ranging as cognitive science and performance studies on the relationship between rasa theory and embodied practice, see Nair (2015).
8. For discussion of kathakali acting technique, see Raina (2015); Zarrilli (2000).
9. For a description of Odissi technique and a history of the dance see Banerji (2019).
10. For a description of kudiyattam acting technique see Madhavan (2012).

Works Cited

Abhinavagupta. "Abhinavbharati." In *Natyasastra of Bharatamuni: Sanskrit, Romanized Text with Commentary of Abhinavbharati*, English Translation, Notes and Index, edited by Pushpendar Kumar and translated by Manomohan Ghosh. New Delhi: New Bharatiya Book Corporation, 2006.

Banerji, Anurima. *Dancing Odissi: Paratopic Performances of Gender and State*. London, New York and Calcutta: Seagull Books, 2019.

Bharata-muni. *The Natyasastra*. Translated and edited by Manomohan Ghosh. Calcutta: Manisha Granthalaya, 1967.

———. *The Natyasastra*. Translated and edited by Adya Rangacharya. New Delhi: Munshiram Manoharlal Publishers Pvt. Ltd, 1996.

Buchta, David, and Graham M. Schweig. "Rasa Theory." In *Brill's Encyclopedia of Hinduism, Volume 2*, edited by Knut A. Jacobsen. Leiden, The Netherlands: Brill, 2010, pp. 623–29.

Byrski, M. Christopher. *Concept of Ancient Indian Theatre*. New Delhi: Munshiram Manoharlal Publishers Pvt. Ltd, 1974.

Chandra, Vikram. *Geek Sublime: The Beauty of Code, the Code of Beauty*. Saint Paul, MN: Graywolf Press, 2014.

Coomaraswamy, Ananda K. *The Transformation of Nature in Art*. New Delhi: Munshiram Manoharlal Publishers Pvt. Ltd, 1994.

Ganser, Elisa. *Theatre and Its Other: Abhinavagupta on Dance and Dramatic Acting*. Leiden: Brill, 2022.

Gokhale, Shanta, ed. *The Theatre of Veenapani Chawla: Theory, Practice, and Performance*. New Delhi: Oxford University Press, 2014.

Gupta, Bharat. *Dramatic Concepts Greek and Indian: A Study of the Poetics and the Natyasastra*. New Delhi: D.K. Printworld, 1994.

Madhavan, Arya. "Eyescape: Aesthetics of 'Seeing' in 'Kudiyattam'." *Asian Theatre Journal*, vol. 29, no. 2, 2012, pp. 550–70.

Nair, Sreenath, ed. *The Natyasastra and the Body in Performance: Essays on Indian Theories of Dance and Drama*. Jefferson, NC: McFarland & Company, Inc, 2015.

Pollock, Sheldon. *A Rasa Reader: Classical Indian Aesthetics*. New York: Columbia University Press, 2016.

Raghavan, V. *Sanskrit Drama: Its Aesthetics and Production*. Madras: Paprinpack, 1993.

Raina, Arjun. "The Art of Creating a Kathakali Performer's 'Presence.'" *Theatre, Dance and Performance Training*, vol. 6, no. 3, 2015, pp. 323–38.

Ramanujan, A. K. "Is There an Indian Way of Thinking? An Informal Essay." *Contributions to Indian Sociology*, vol. 23, no. 1, 1989, pp. 41–58.

Rangacharya, Adya. "Thoughts on the Theory of Rasa." In *The Natyasastra: English Translation with Critical Notes*, translated by Adya Rangacharya. New Delhi: Munshiram Manoharlal Publishers Pvt. Ltd, 1996, pp. 356–67.

Richmond, Farley P. "Characteristics of Sanskrit Theatre and Drama." In *Indian Theatre: Traditions of Performance*, edited by Farley P. Richmond, Darius L. Swann, and Phillip B. Zarrilli. New Delhi: Motilal Banarsidass Publishers, 1993, pp. 33–85.

Schechner, Richard. "Rasaesthetics." *TDR*, vol. 45, no. 3, 2001, pp. 27–50.

———. Email correspondence with author. 21 September 2016.

Schwartz, Susan. *Rasa: Performing the Divine in India*. New York: Columbia University Press, 2004.

Tagore, Rabindranath. *On Art and Aesthetics: A Selection of Lectures, Essays and Letters*. Calcutta: Orient Longmans, 1961.

Vatsyayan, Kapila. *Classical Indian Dance in Literature and the Arts*. New Delhi: Sangeet Natak Akademi, 1968.

———. *The Square and the Circle of the Indian Arts*. New Delhi: Roli Books International, 1983.

Zarrilli, Phillip B. *Kathakali Dance-Drama: Where Gods and Demons Come to Play*. London and New York: Routledge, 2000.

CHAPTER 3

Rasaesthetics[1]

RICHARD SCHECHNER

Where in the body is theatricality located? What is its place? Traditionally in western theatre, the eyes and to some degree the ears are the loci of theatricality. By etymology and by practice, a theatre is a place of/for seeing. Seeing requires distance; engenders focus or differentiation; encourages analysis, a logical assessment of components; privileges meaning, theme, narration. Modern science depends on instruments of observation, of ocularity: telescopes and microscopes. Theories derived from observations made by means of ocular instruments define the time–space continuum. From clusters of galaxies on the one hand to infinitesimal subatomic particles/energies on the other, we know the universe by seeing it.

But in other cultural traditions, there are other locations for theatricality. One of these is the mouth, or better said, the snout-to-belly-to-bowel. The mouth-to-belly-to-bowel is the where of tasting, digesting, and excreting. The performance of the mouth-to-belly-to bowel is an ongoing interlinked muscular, cellular, and neurological process of testing-tasting, separating nourishment from waste, distributing nourishment throughout the body, and eliminating waste. The snout-to-belly-to-bowel is the where of intimacy, sharing of bodily substances, mixing the inside and the outside, emotional experiences, and gut feelings. A good meal with good company is a pleasure; so are foreplay and lovemaking; so is a good shit.

The *Poetics* and the *Natyashastra*

Aristotle's *Poetics* and Bharata-muni's *Natyashastra* (*NS*), a Sanskrit manual of performance and performance theory, occupy parallel positions in European and Indian performance theory (and, by extension, throughout the many areas and cultures where European-derived or Indian-derived performing arts are practiced). Both ancient texts continue to be actively interpreted and debated, theoretically and in practice. Both are at or near the "origins" of their respective performance traditions; both have evoked after-texts or counter-texts aimed at enhancing, revising, and/or refuting their basic principles.

But similar as they are in some ways, the two texts differ profoundly. Aristotle was an historical figure (384–322 BCE), the author of many key philosophical texts affecting, even determining, western thought in various fields as wide-ranging as the physical sciences, politics, social thought, aesthetics, and theology. The Macedonian-Greek philosopher's writings have been actively debated for nearly two-and-a-half millennia. He specialized in dividing knowledge into knowable

DOI: 10.4324/9781315563619-5

portions; he formulated the syllogism. Bharata-muni is a mythic-historical figure, the name of the author or compiler of a very detailed compendium concerning the religious-mythic origins and practices of *natya*, a Sanskrit word not easily translatable, but reducible to dance–theatre–music. The precise date of the NS remains in question—scholars have placed it anywhere from the 6th century BCE to the 2nd century CE. Exactly how much of the NS was the work of one person and how much the lore of many will probably never be known. Bharata is almost certainly a pseudonym for a collective oral tradition; he is named as the author of only one treatise, the NS.

Furthermore, the NS is a *shastra*, a sacred text, authorized, if not directly authored, by the gods, full of myth, detailed instructions for performers, directors, and theatre architects—and performance theory. The *Poetics* is secular, focused on the structure of drama, and dependent on the logical thinking that its author helped invent. The *Poetics* is also laconic, running about 30 pages in English translation; some believe it to be lecture notes compiled by Aristotle's students after his death rather than the philosopher's own finished work. In contrast, the NS is an extended disquisition, 345 pages in the Rangacharya translation; it is Bharata's answer to sages who ask him to explain natya. Bharata begins with the story of how natya came about, what its proper subjects are, and for whom it was made.[2] Then he goes on to detail everything from theatre architecture to how to perform the various emotions to the structure of dramas, and more.

Some centuries after it was completed, the NS was "lost"—fragmented, submerged, misplaced, and unread. It comes to modern Indians not directly and not as a single text. The NS comes down in performance practices and as a series of interpretations. The most important interpreter of the NS is the 10th-century Kashmiri Saivite, Abhinavagupta, though earlier interpreters such as Udbhata, Bhatta Lollata, Srisankuka, Bhatta Nayaka, and Bhatta Tauta are known, mainly from references in Abhinavagupta's commentary. As for the NS "itself," according to Kapila Vatsyayan, "not many texts have been systematically collated and edited and published. Hundreds . . . lie as manuscripts in public or private collections, in India and abroad, and an equal or larger number are in fragments" (1996, 115). There are several "complete" NS editions in Sanskrit, Hindi, and English. None are definitive.[3]

This fragmentation ought not to be read as neglect. The NS tradition is active, oral, and corporeal. It is present in performers, their teachers, and their performances. We must distinguish the NS as a text (a work brought to light in modern times first by western orientalists) from its vital presence in actual performances, where it has been absorbed into and forms the core of a multiplicity of genres such as kutiyattam, kathak, kathakali, odissi, kuchipudi, mohiniyattam, manipuri, sattriya, and bharatanatyam, which, taken together, comprise Indian classic theatre–dance. The NS is much more powerful as a set of embodied ideas and practices than as a written text. Unlike the *Poetics*, the NS is performed more than read.

Thus, the NS and the *Poetics* are different in style, intent, and historical circumstance. The *Poetics*, written nearly a century after Greek tragedy's heyday, constitutes only a small portion of Aristotle's enormous output. The *Poetics* lacks descriptions of actual performances; it is mostly about drama, not theatre, focusing on one play, Sophocles' *Oedipus Tyrannus*, which Aristotle offers as a model for the right way to write plays. Framed as "rational" and "historical," the *Poetics* is not regarded as sacred, although it has been, and remains, remarkably influential. On the other hand, the *NS* is a hybrid of myth, performance theory, and down-to-earth performance knowledge, far-ranging and detailed.

The greatest difference between the *Poetics* and the *NS* is that the Indian book deals in detail with performance: emotional expression as conveyed by specific gestures and movements, role and character types, theater architecture, music, and types of drama. The *NS*'s consideration of drama (chapters 20–21) is not the core of the shastra. In fact, drama in itself—a written narrative text—is not a core idea of the *NS* or the traditions that look to the *NS*. Many Indian artists subscribe to the ideal of a performance that integrates drama, dance, and music. Traditional genres accomplish this integration in ways that do not privilege plot (as Aristotle advised) over dance, gesture, and music. And then there is *rasa*.

Rasa, First Take

Chapter 6 of the *NS* deals specifically with the eight rasas, though rasa theory permeates the entire shastra. To bluntly summarize: the eight rasas—or flavors, tastes, juices—are: *shringara* (love), *bhayanaka* (fear), *karuna* (sadness), *hasya* (humor), *raudra* (anger), *vira* (courage), *bibhatsa* (disgust), and *adbhuta* (wonder). Of rasa, the *NS* says,

> There is no natya without rasa. Rasa is the cumulative result of *vibhava* [causes], *anubhava* [possible reactions], and *vyabhicari bhava* [short-lived feelings]. For example, just as when various condiments and sauces and herbs and other materials are mixed, a taste is experienced, or when the mixing of materials like molasses with other materials produces six kinds of taste, so also along with the different bhavas [emotions] the sthayi bhava becomes a rasa.
>
> But what is this thing called rasa? Here is the reply. Because it is enjoyably tasted, it is called rasa. How does the enjoyment come? Persons who eat prepared food mixed with different condiments and sauces, if they are sensitive, enjoy the different tastes and then feel pleasure; likewise, sensitive spectators, after enjoying the various emotions expressed by the actors through words, gestures, and feelings feel pleasure. This feeling by the spectators is here explained as the rasas of natya.
>
> (Bharata-muni 1996, 54–55)[4]

There is a lot going on here. What is important for my theory of rasaesthetics is the relationship between bhava and rasa.

Sthayi bhavas are "permanent" emotions—stable, abiding, indwelling; but also in themselves empty categories actualized only when expressed via anubhavas and vyabhicari bhavas. These expressions create rasa. The sthayi bhavas are not experienced directly; they are (pick your concept) unconscious, latent, potential. In daily life, they are expressed/experienced as feelings; in performance they are prepared/

presented/represented by *abhinaya*, acting. Both performers and spectators experience the sthayi bhavas as rasa. In "Emotion in Motion: The *Nātyashāstra*, Darwin, and Affect Theory," Vinay Dharwadker puts it this way:

> Bharata suggests that these *sthāyī bhāvas* are major or dominant emotions; commentators have interpreted them also as general or permanent dispositions that are latent in the human psyche and become manifest to a subject's consciousness when they are actualized phenomenologically. The *Nātyashāstra*'s boldest implication is that the *sthāyī bhāvas* comprise an individual subject's fundamental modes of existence in the world—that a self exists only in one or another of these long-lasting states at any given time, persists over time in a succession of such states, and has no other mode of existence. [. . .] A *sthāyī bhāva* is characterized as persistent and pervasive, but it always retains a constitutive temporality, a discernible beginning, middle, and end. In fact, the temporal dimension of an emotional state that persists in the subject provides a poet, dancer, or an actor with the basic structural principle of plot and narrative whenever he or she seeks to represent feelings and emotions aesthetically in a text or performance. A state of being that stays in place for a long time, however, does not amount to emotional stasis; the protracted removal of any *sthāyī bhāva* is actually a turbulent phase in which many short-lived sensations, feelings, and emotions come and go constantly over an established undertone.
>
> (2015, 1384)

Rasa is experiencing this turbulence as a flavor or mix of flavors. After stating that Bharata metaphorizes the aesthetic experience as *āsvāda*, "tasting and savoring in the act of ingestion" (Bharata-muni 1996, 32–38), Dharwadker defines rasa:

> [A] *rasa* is neither a substance nor a quality inherent in an artwork; as elusive and insubstantial as the underlying emotional state whose flavor it extracts, concentrates, and conveys, it becomes manifest only in the active experiencing of *rasa-āsvāda*, which is nothing but the temporality of poesis-semiosis-aesthesis in dynamic process. As the philosopher-critic Abhinavagupta put it around 1000 CE, a *rasa* is not an object of cognition: we do not and cannot know a rasa because we can only savor it, and we can savor it only while experiencing an artwork—it is never an object that can be separated from an act of reading, listening, or viewing.
>
> (2015, 1388)

Bharata says the rasic experience is cognate with the pleasure and process of eating, the work of the digestive system. Why this is important to rasaesthetics will be made clear later when I discuss the enteric nervous system, the "brain in the belly." Rasa is savoring the flavors, textures, smells, and sounds of food. Rasa is the experience of perceiving food, bringing it within reach, smelling, touching, and taking it into the mouth and then chewing, mixing, and swallowing it. The eyes, nose, ears, and mouth participate in the food, join with it. You see the food, hear it sizzle or boil, absorb its odors, feel its texture as you bite and chew. The mouth waters in anticipation. Smell and taste dissolve into each other. The hands convey the food to the mouth—either directly as in the traditional Indian way, eating with the right hand and fingers, or indirectly by means of utensils (a latecomer everywhere). The whole snout is engaged. The snout concentrates all the senses. The lower part of the face opens as the mouth; in the center of the face, the nose; above, the eyes; and to the sides, the ears. Negative rasa experience is also possible, of course: disgusting smells, looks, and flavors ("disgust" literally means *bad tasting*); the taste of some medicines and poisons.

Rasa also means *juice*, the stuff that conveys the flavor, the medium of tasting. The juices of eating originate both in the food and from the body. Saliva not only moistens food but also distributes flavors. Rasa is sensuous, proximate, experiential. Rasa is aromatic. Rasa fills space, joining the outside to the inside. Food is actively taken into the body, becomes part of the body, works from the inside. What was outside is transformed into what is inside. Rasa is savoring—not only food, but emotions and feelings. Even negative emotions and feelings, which, paradoxically, are pleasurably experienced by means of art. An aesthetic founded on rasa is fundamentally different than one founded on the *theatron*, the rationally ordered, analytically distanced panoptic.

Etymologies and Distanced Knowing

The word "theatre" is cognate with "theorem," "theory," "theorist," and such—from the Greek *theatron*, itself from *thea*, "a sight," and from *theasthai*, "to view," related to *thauma*, "a thing compelling the gaze, a wonder, and *theorein*, "to look at" (Partridge 1966, 710). "Theorein" is related to *theorema*, "spectacle" and/or "speculation" (Shipley 1984, 69). These words are thought to be related to the Indo-European root *dheu* or *dhau*, "to look at" (Partridge 1966, 710). The Indo-European root of "Thespis"—the legendary founder of Greek theatre—is *seku*, a "remark" or "saying," but with the implication of a divine vision; and from seku derive such English words as "see," "sight," and "say" (Shipley 1984, 353). Greek theatre, then, and all European-types of theatre derived from it, are places of/for seeing and saying. What marks this kind of theatre (and after it, film, TV, and to a large degree the internet) is its specularity, its strategies of gazing.

These etymologies trace the tight bond linking Greek theatre, European epistemology, and seeing. This binding of knowing to seeing is the root master narrative of western thought. If the humans in Plato's cave were ignorant, it was because all they could see of "truth" were shadows cast on the wall. True reality was so much brighter even than the sun that no human eye could look at it directly. The truth, Plato said, could be known through dialectics. Since the Renaissance, scientists have tried to "see truth" by devising finer and finer instruments of observation. A single net holds Plato's allegory, Galileo's observations, the Hubble and James Webb interstellar space telescopes, electron microscopes, and the Large Hadron Collider particle accelerator.

Where does seeing take place? Only at a distance from what is being seen. There is both a logical and a practical distance needed to keep what is observed separate from the observing instrument (and/or observer). "Objectivity" is understandable as the desire to keep things at enough distance from the observer for whatever is observed to "take shape": to see things "in perspective," to "focus on" them. The "indeterminacy principle" linking the instrument of observation to what is observed does not dissolve the distance between observer–observed so much as assert that whatever is observed is affected by the means of observing. What *moves* the quantum particle is the light that is needed to observe it.

At a more everyday level, an object brought close to the observing eye goes out of focus, blurs, loses its visual shape. And, of course, one mustn't put things into one's eyes. Poking out the eyes is a terrible thing both legendarily (Oedipus, Gloucester, et al.) and actually. On the positive side, an infant learns early to see something, reach for it, grasp it, and bring it to the mouth. For the infant, the mouth precedes the eyes as the end-point for exploring the outer world and relating it to the inner world. The "transitional object" (see Winnicott 1971) is how the infant first experiences the sameness–difference between the world outside herself and the world inside herself: from the nipple-breast, to the fingers (thumb especially), to the grasped-tasted-chewed whatever, to the security blanket, to favored objects. Even before birth, as in-utero photographs show, the pre-born sucks her/his fingers and toes. Can we doubt that the pre-born enjoys this activity? Nor is the mouth a singular conduit connected solely to the brain (as the eye is via the optic nerve). The mouth opens to the nasal cavity and the whole digestive system; the mouth—including lips and tongue—intimately engages the senses of touch, taste, and smell. The ocular system is extraordinarily focused, while the snout system is wide open, combining rather than separating.

The Greek theatre that Aristotle based his theories on was fundamentally a seeing place. Architecturally, as is evident from what is left of the Theatre of Dionysus on the hillside of the Akropolis, the almost wholly intact theater at Epidaurus, and from other sites and restorations, the Greek theater was immense but tightly focused. Most scholars place the number in the audience at the ancient Greek festivals at between 14,000 and 17,000. And although Aristotle favored written drama over theatre, the actual experience of being in a classical Greek theater strongly includes the spectacle—dancing, singing/chanting, and declaiming through masks that amplified sound. The Greek theatre was also ferociously competitive. For the Greeks, the *agon* (direct confrontation, contest) was the model, motor, source, and energy of creation; a model of becoming.[5] Whatever Aristotle may have proscribed, the living heart of Greek tragedy was not plot as such, but a particular kind of storytelling that depended on the agon and the lyrical chorus: the struggle between individuals alternating with the feelings and opinions of the collective. By means of performing the tragedies, the Greeks sorted winners from losers. The judges—and those judging the judges, the spectators—had to see clearly, basing their judgments on "objectivity." Of course, there were probably all kinds of politicking and pressures. Maybe even bribes and cheating. But, as in today's spectator sports (with or without instant replays), clarity in presentation and reception was absolutely essential. A principal goal of the festivals of theatre was to determine winners and losers— in both the narratives and the competitions among poets and actors.

Rasic Performance Is Different

Separating winners from losers is not the goal of rasic performance. The goal of rasic performance is to explore and extend pleasure—as in a banquet of many courses or a long deferred "almost" sexual orgasm. A rasic performance accomplishes its goal in a process analogous to cooking: by combining distinct items in a specific way (recipe) in order to transform them into a coherent whole (the meal) that delivers to the partakers intense and/or favorite flavors. (I prefer "partaker" over "spectator," which privileges the eye, or "audience," which privileges the ear.) Sometimes these flavors are new, sometimes familiar—that is, sometimes avant-garde, sometimes traditional. Rasic performance's paradigmatic action is a sharing among performers and partakers. A rasic performance is more a banquet than a day in court. As the NS puts it: "Those who are connoisseurs of tastes enjoy the taste of food prepared from (or containing) different stuff; likewise, intelligent, healthy persons enjoy various *sthayi bhavas* related to the acting of emotions" (Bharata-muni 1996, 55).

Rasa is experiencing the sthayi bhavas. To put it another way, the sweetness in a ripe plum is its sthayi bhava; the experience of tasting the sweet is rasa. The means of bringing the taste across—preparing it, presenting it—is abhinaya. Every emotion is a sthayi bhava. Acting is the art of preparing and presenting the sthayi bhavas so that *both* the performer and the partaker can "taste" the emotions as feelings, as rasas.

In chapters 6 and 7, the NS gives the eight rasas and their corresponding sthayi bhavas:

Rasa	Sthayi Bhava	English
shringara	rati	desire, love
hasya	hasa	humor, laughter
karuna	soka	pity, grief
raudra	krodha	Anger
vira	utsaha	energy, vigor, courage
bhayanaka	bhaya	fear, shame
bibhatsa	jugupsa	disgust
adbhuta	vismaya	surprise, wonder

Abhinavagupta added a ninth rasa, shanta, "peace" or "bliss." From Abhinavagupta's time onward, many Indians speak of the nine rasas. But shanta does not correspond to any particular sthayi bhava. Rather, like white light, shanta is the perfect balance/mix of them all; or shanta may be regarded as the transcendent rasa that, when accomplished, absorbs and eliminates all the others. A perfect performance, should one occur, would not transmit or express shanta (as it could transmit or express any of the other rasas), but allow shanta to be experienced as the culminating outcome of a perfect performance. Shanta would be experienced simultaneously and absolutely by both performers and partakers.

It is not my aim in this chapter to investigate the many connections between the sthayi bhavas and the rasas. It is enough to note that "emotions" in the Indian aesthetic performance system, far from being personal—based on individual experience or locked up and only accessible by means of an "emotional memory" exercise or a "private moment" (per Stanislavsky and his disciples)—are in the public or social sphere.

In the rasic system, there are "artistically performed emotions" that comprise a distinct kind of behavior (different, perhaps, for each performance genre). These performed emotions are separate from the "feelings"—the interior, subjective experience of any given performer during a particular performance. There is no necessary and ineluctable chain linking these performed emotions with the emotions of everyday life. In the rasic system, it is only the emotions in the arts, not in ordinary life, that are knowable, manageable, and transmittable in roughly the same way that the flavors and presentation of a meal are manageable by following recipes and the conventions of presenting the meal.

In his 1773 *Paradoxe sur le Comedien* (badly translated as *The Paradox of Acting*), Denis Diderot argues that acting is artifice; that actors do not feel what they represent. Diderot's opinion seems in accord with the rasic system, the "prepared meal" of theatre. But actors themselves disagree on this matter. When I spoke to kathakali actors, some told me they felt the emotions they performed; others did not. Actors I've worked with, trained in western systems, say the same thing. Some actors experience strong feelings but not the feelings of the character. For example, Ryszard Cieslak—a great actor who worked very closely with Jerzy Grotowski—while performing the Prince in *The Constant Prince* screamed and groaned as if suffering greatly, as the character does. When asked what he was experiencing, Cieslak reported that he was re-experiencing a moment of intense sexual pleasure. From actors I've spoken to and worked with, I conclude that feeling the emotions is not necessary, though it is not a bad thing, either. In some instances, it happens; in others, it does not. Whether it happens or not to any particular performer on any particular occasion does not necessarily make the performance better or worse. What is relevant is making certain that the partakers receive the rasas appropriate to the emotions being performed; that these rasas are specific and controlled. The emotions, the sthayi bhava, are objective; the feelings (what an individual performer or partaker experiences) are subjective. What is shared are the rasas of a single or combination of emotions. In order for rasas to be shared, performers must enact the abhinaya of a particular emotion or concatenation of emotions according to the traditions of a specific genre of performance. The feelings aroused may be personal, intimate, and indescribable; but the emotions enacted are consciously constructed and objectively managed.

According to Stanislavsky–Strasberg[6] American acting, one does not directly play an emotion. One plays the "emotional memory," the "given circumstances," the "objectives," the "through-line of action," the "magic if." If this is done right, "real" feelings will be experienced and "natural" emotions will be displayed. But according to my interpretation of the *NS* rasic system, one can work directly on the emotions, mixing them according to "recipes" known to the great acting *gurus* (which means, simply, "teachers")—or even by devising new recipes. From a Stanislavsky–Strasberg vantage, such direct work on the emotions will result in false or mechanical acting. But anyone who has seen performers thoroughly trained in the *NS* rasic system knows these performers are every bit as convincing as performers trained in the Stanislavsky–Strasberg system.

In my work from the early 1990s onward, I have integrated Rasaboxes into my performer workshop/performer training process. Rasaboxes is a technique I devised assisted by several of my East Coast Artists[7] colleagues. Rasaboxes is my adaptation of the Sanskrit performance theory rasic system of emotions adapted to the needs of contemporary performers.

If to perform rasically is to offer feelings to partakers in the same way that a chef offers a meal to diners, then the effectiveness of the performance depends very much on an active response from the partakers. The *NS* emphatically insists that natya appeal to people of all stations in life, but affect different people differently.[8] At the same time, the more knowledgeable the partakers, the better their experience. To respond to the fullest, partakers need to be connoisseurs of whatever performance genre they are taking in—just as wine tasters need to know vintages, bottling procedures, and ways of sampling in order to fully appreciate a wine. There is a sliding scale of how much one needs to know. In the rasic system, each person enjoys according to her abilities; the higher the level of knowledge, the greater the enjoyment (or disappointment, if the performance is not up to standards). All performers know this. The best performers save their best performances for the most discerning partakers, and those who know the most expect the best. Japanese *noh* actors study the audience immediately before entering the stage and then adjust their performances to the particular partakers on hand. In India, the active response of the partakers is expected. At dance or music concerts people quietly beat out the *tal*, or rhythm, sing under their breath, and sometimes move their hands in harmony with the *mudras* or hand-gesture system. At the Ramlila of Ramnagar, many persons carry texts of Tulsidas' *Ramcaritmanas*, following along, even singing, as the Ramayanis chant. The same is true of sports or pop music connoisseurs around the world. In sports, the "home team advantage" is a direct measurement of how the active participation of the crowd can impact the level of performance. Audiences at pop concerts often sing and dance to the music.

Oral Pleasures, Rasically

Fundamentally, the attainment of pleasure and satisfaction in a rasic performance is oral—through the snout, by combining various flavors and tastes; and the satisfaction is visceral, in the belly. How can this be when Indian theatre, dance, and music—like western performing arts—are presented visually and sonically? To understand why, one must appreciate the importance of participatory festivity to Indian performing arts. Indian theatre is not based on the agon, on determining winners and losers, either within the dramas (where often, everyone wins) or in terms of competition among dramatists and actors. In ancient India, there were no judges formally ensconced on marble benches prominently in view, as there were in the Greek theatre of Dionysus. In ancient India, there was no attempt to measure/quantify the performance experience, to separate performers from judges and other spectators, to bring performance under the theatron's aegis of visuality. Instead, there was—and still is—collaboration between performers and partakers, artists and patrons. Festive performances are integral to weddings and other happy celebrations. The Hindu (and related) religions combine worshipping, singing and dancing, and feasting. The *murtis*—gods sculpted from stone, metal, or earth—are washed, dressed, and fed. *Prasad*, the food brought to the temple by worshippers, is offered to the gods, blessed, and returned to the givers for them to savor—food that is both sweet and sacred.[9] Generally, the separation of work from play and the sacred from the profane is more a western than Indian phenomenon. In fact, in India the gods' lives on earth are often described as *lila*, play, as in Ramlila or Raslila. There was no anti-theatrical prejudice or Puritanism in India until Islam and then the English arrived. Far from it: the arts were infused with intense sexual pleasure, which was often an essential component of the religious experience. The dancing in the temples, the erotic temple sculptures, the *Kamasutra*, and much more attest to this convergence of pleasure, worship, and arts.

India today is less open to the rasic mix of art, worship, pleasure, and feasting than before the advent of the Mughals and the British. But imagining performances from the period of Sanskrit drama (4th–11th centuries CE), as indicated by sculptings and paintings at such sites as Khajuraho, Konark, the shore temple of Mamallapuram, or the "theatre caves" of Ajanta, can bring us closer to the kind of experience I am talking about.

> The Ajanta style approaches as near as it is likely for an artist to get to a felicitous rendering of tactile sensations normally experienced subconsciously. These are felt rather than seen when the eye is subordinate to a total receptivity of all the senses. . . . The seated queen with the floating hand is drawn so that we obtain information which cannot be had by looking at her from a single, fixed viewpoint. . . . [T]he logic of this style demands that movements and gestures can only be described in terms of the area or space in which they occur; we cannot identify a figure except by comparing its position with others around it. . . . It could be said that the Ajanta artist is concerned with the order of sensuousness, as distinct from the order of reason.
>
> (Lannoy 1971, 48–49)

Richard Lannoy argues that the caves were exquisitely suited as participatory theatres, and that this was no accident.

> The structure and ornamentation of the caves were deliberately designed to induce total participation during ritual circumambulation. The acoustics of one Ajanta *vihara*, or assembly hall (Cave VI), are such that any sound continues to echo round the walls. This whole structure seems to have been tuned like a drum.
>
> (43)

This tuning was not fortuitous. The Ajanta caves are human-made, carved out of solid rock. Lannoy continues:

> In both cases [the caves, the theatre] total participation of the viewer was ensured by a skillful combination of sensory experience. The "wrap-around" effect [of] the caves was conveyed on the stage by adapting the technically brilliant virtuosity of Vedic incantation and phonetic science to the needs of the world's most richly textured style of poetic drama.
>
> (54)

What the NS supplies are the concrete details—and a theory underlying the practice—of a style that at its core is theatrical, not literary; rasa-driven, not plot-driven. Indian classical theatre and dance do not emphasize clear beginnings, middles, and ends but favor open narratives, a menu of many delectable story parts and detailed enacted descriptions—offshoots, sidetracks, pleasurable digressions—not all of which can be savored at a single time. Performances often were staged in phases, over periods of days or weeks. The performances were part of multifaceted celebrations that also featured audience participation in the accompanying feasting and worshipping. Taken as a whole, this forms an integral performance complex that can be experienced in events such as Ramlila with its immersive environmental theatre staging, or Raslila with its dancing, and during bhajan-singing/dancing.[10]

There are phases of these performances where partakers stand back to watch and/or listen and other phases where they participate. It's not all one way or the other. There is a lot of movement—actual and conceptual—from one kind of involvement to another. This blending of theatre, dance, music, eating, and religious devotion is for many participants a full and satisfyingly pleasurable, often spiritual, experience that cannot be reduced to any single category—religious, aesthetic, personal, or gustatory. This kind of event yields experiences that dissolve differences, if only for a little while. The experience is hard to measure from the inside or observe from the outside because the inside swallows the outside. If you are inside, there is no you to observe from the outside. This all-is-inside theatricality most clearly distinguishes rasaesthetics from orthodox western aesthetics. The rasic experience obliterates objectivity, which is the key to western aesthetic judgment from the ancients to the Renaissance and modern western theatrical aesthetics. This aesthetics is derived from the ancient Greek theatre, modified in Rome, reinterpreted in the Renaissance, and expressed in modernity as drama-based proscenium or frontal-stage theater. Some postmodern performances—environmental theatre, immersive theatre, certain kinds of performance art—are more in harmony with rasaesthetics, the "in the gut" formulation, than with classical-to-modern western aesthetics.

The Enteric Nervous System

In the gut. Take a step into neurobiology. According to studies published in the 1990s, there is a brain in the belly, literally. The basic research in this area has been conducted by Michael D. Gershon (see his *The Second Brain* 1998), whose work was summarized in the *New York Times* by Sandra Blakeslee:

> The gut's brain, known as the enteric nervous system [ENS], is located in sheaths of tissue lining the esophagus, stomach, small intestine, and colon. Considered a single entity, it is a network of neurons, neurotransmitters, and proteins that zap messages between neurons, support cells like those found in the brain proper and a complex circuitry that enables it to act independently, learn, remember, and, as the saying goes, produce gut feelings.
>
> (1996, C1)

The ENS derives from the "neural crest," a bunch of related cells that forms in mammals and birds early in embryo genesis. "One section turns into the central nervous system. Another piece migrates to become the enteric nervous system. Only later are the two nervous systems connected via a cable called the vagus nerve" (C3). According to Gershon and his co-researchers:

> The ENS resembles the brain and differs both physiologically and structurally from any other region of the PNS [peripheral nervous system].[11] . . . [B]oth the avian and mammalian bowel are colonized by émigrés from the sacral as well as the vagal level of the neural crest. . . . The PNS contains more neurons than the spinal cord and, in contrast to other regions of the PNS, the ENS is capable of mediating reflex activity in the absence of central neural input. In fact, most of the neurons of the ENS are not directly innervated by a preganglionic input from the brain or spinal cord. The functional independence of the ENS is mirrored in its chemistry and structure.
>
> (Gershon et al. 1993, 199)

Again, Blakeslee:

> Until relatively recently, people thought that the gut's muscles and sensory nerves were wired directly to the brain and that the brain controlled the gut through two pathways that increased or decreased rates of activity. . . . The gut was simply a tube with simple reflexes. Trouble is, no one bothered to count the nerve fibers in the gut. When they did . . ., they were surprised to find that the gut contains 100 million neurons—more than the spinal cord has. Yet the vagus nerve only sends a couple of thousand nerve fibers to the gut.
>
> (1996, C3)

What this means is that the gut—esophagus, stomach, intestines, and bowels—has its own nervous system. This system does not replace or preempt the brain. Rather, it operates alongside the brain, or—evolutionarily speaking—"before" or "underneath" the brain. Again, Gershon:

> The enteric nervous system is . . . a remnant of our evolutionary past that has been retained. [It] has been present in each of our predecessors through the millions of years of evolutionary history that separate us from the first animal with

a backbone.... [T]he enteric nervous system is a vibrant, modern data-processing center that enables us to accomplish some very important and unpleasant tasks with no mental effort. When the gut rises to the level of conscious perception, in the form of, for example, heartburn, cramps, diarrhea, or constipation, no one is enthused. Few things are more distressing than an inefficient gut with feelings.

(Gershon 1998, xiv)

Indeed, what about emotions and feelings? In December 2000, I emailed Gershon about rasaesthetics and the ENS. He replied:

Thank you for your letter. You touch a bit of a raw nerve. You are certainly correct in that we in the West who consider ourselves "hard" scientists have not taken Eastern thought very seriously. The problem with a great deal of Eastern thought is that it is not based on documentable observation. You cannot quantify ideas about strong feelings or deep power. We therefore, either ignore Eastern ideas about the navel, or take them as metaphors, which are not very different from our own metaphors about "gut feelings". On the other hand, I have recently become aware of quantifiable research that establishes, without question, that vagus nerve stimulation can be used to treat epilepsy and depression. Vagus nerve stimulation also improves learning and memory. Vagus nerve stimulation is something physicians do and is not natural,[12] but 90% of the vagus carries ascending information from the gut to the brain. It is thus possible that vagus nerve stimulation mimics natural stimulation of the vagus nerve by the "second brain." This relationship is particularly important in relation to the human condition of autism. Autism affects the gut as well as the brain. It is thus conceivable that autism could be the result in whole or in part of a disturbed communication between the two brains. In short, I now take the possibility that the gut affects emotions very seriously. This seems much more likely to me now than it did when I wrote my book. A dialogue between us might be of mutual interest.

Unfortunately, the dialogue did not progress beyond these emails. Related to Gershon's work, and building on it, is the research of Emeran Mayer, professor of physiology, psychiatry, and behavioral sciences at UCLA, quoted here in an article by Adam Hadhazy on "how the gut's 'second brain' influences mood and well-being." Mayer explicitly connects the ENS to human emotions:

The [ENS] system is way too complicated to have evolved only to make sure things move out of your colon," says Mayer.... "A big part of our emotions are probably influenced by the nerves in our gut," Mayer says.... Although gastrointestinal (GI) turmoil can sour one's moods, everyday emotional well-being may rely on messages from the brain below to the brain above. For example, electrical stimulation of the vagus nerve—a useful treatment for depression— may mimic these signals, Gershon says.... Down the road, the blossoming field of neurogastroenterology will likely offer some new insight into the workings of the second brain—and its impact on the body and mind.... Mayer is doing work on how the trillions of bacteria in the gut "communicate" with enteric nervous system cells (which they greatly outnumber). His work with the gut's nervous system has led him to think that in coming years psychiatry will need to expand to treat the second brain in addition to the one atop the shoulders.

(Hadhazy 2010)

Let us suppose, in light of ENS research, that when someone says "I have a gut feeling," she actually is experiencing an emotion, a neural response, but not one that is head–brain centered. Let us suppose that her emotion is located in, or emanating from, the "second brain," the brain in the belly. Can such emotions be trained? That is, what are the systems converting gut feelings into expressible feelings? Gershon is interested primarily in the therapeutic value of vagus nerve stimulation, of causing or evoking feelings in autistics who suffer from lack of affect or lack of range of affect. My practice shows that the gut feeling of an aroused sthayi bhava, when expressed artistically, as learned coded behavior can be shared as one or more rasas.

The presence and location of the ENS confirms a basic principle of Asian medicine, meditation, and martial arts: that the region in the gut between the navel and the pubic bone is the center/source of readiness, balance, and reception; the place where action and meditation—seeming opposites but actual twins—are centered. A related place is the base of the spine, the resting place of kundalini, an energy that can be aroused and transmitted up the spinal column. Gaining an awareness of and control over the gut and lower spine is crucial to anyone learning various Asian performance practices, martial arts, or meditations.

For many years, Phillip Zarrilli researched as both a scholar and a practitioner the relationship between what in the Keralan martial art *kalaripayattu* (which Zarrilli mastered) is called the *nabhi mula* (root of the navel) and performer training, psychophysical centering, and ayurvedic medicine. According to Zarrilli:

> When impulses originate from the *nabhi mula* [. . .] they] are "grounded," "centered," "integrated," "filled out," "dynamic." The *nabhi mula* of kalaripayattu is identical to the *svadhisthanam* of classical yoga. Its location is two finger widths above the anus and two finger widths below the root of the navel. It is at this center that both breath and impetus for movement into and out of forms originate.
>
> (1990, 136)

Zarrilli emphasizes that the nabhi mula is important psychophysically, as the source of feeling-and-movement, a kind of "gripping" (*piduttam*) or firmness of body, spirit, and feelings that affects the whole human being. The Chinese notion of *ch'i* and the Japanese *ki* (activating force) are closely related to the nabhi mula and the sense of piduttam. In noh theatre, the *tanden*, located in the belly two inches below the navel, is the radiating energy center.

> The actor is engaged in his total being in a psychophysical process where his internal energy, aroused in his vital center below the navel, then directed into and through the embodied forms of external gesture (body and voice) is of course fundamentally the same [in noh] as the interior process of the kathakali

actor. This despite the fact that the exterior manifestation of the interior process is different.

(Zarrilli 1990, 143)

I could cite many more examples. But it all comes down to what Zarrilli so accurately summarizes:

> In all such precise psychophysical moments, the "character" is being created—not in the personality of the actor but as an embodied and projected/energized/living form between actor and audience. These Asian forms assume no "suspension of disbelief," rather the actor and spectator co-create the figure embodied in the actor as "other." The "power of presence" manifest in this stage other, while embodied in this particular actor in this particular moment, is not limited to that ego. That dynamic figure exists between audience and actor, transcending both, pointing beyond itself.
>
> (144)

The rasic system of response does not preclude the eye and ear during actual performances, but during training especially, it works *directly and strongly* on the ENS, which, under different names, has been very important and well theorized in various Asian systems of theatre–dance–music, medicine, and the martial arts. These three domains are tightly related in Asian cultures. Thus, when I say the rasic aesthetic experience is fundamentally different than the eye-dominant system prevalent in the West, I am not talking metaphorically.

Rasaboxes

But if not metaphorically, how? Let me answer that first in terms of training, then in terms of public performances. Since the early 1990s, I and several of my colleagues have been developing Rasaboxes.[13] Rasaboxes has evolved over the decades of its existence, and it continues to develop. What I describe in the following is my way of doing Rasaboxes. There are some basic parameters, rules and principles, that all the teachers of Rasaboxes share. But there is no definitive way to do the exercise. It develops organically in each workshop and from workshop to workshop. Rasaboxes is part of The Performance Workshop, a set of exercises that taken together comprise an approach to performer training. Rasaboxes is a practice based on expressing the key ideas in this chapter. Rasaboxes assumes that emotions are both socially constructed and deeply embedded in each person's sub/unconscious while feelings are individually, consciously, and subjectively experienced.

Introducing Rasaboxes takes at least 10–12 hours over several sessions. The introduction is just that, a beginning. Rasaboxes is open-ended: once you start, there is no limit to where you can go—to where it can take you. Rasaboxes is the culmination of exercises I've developed and taught for decades.[14] Rasaboxes unfolds in an orderly progression of steps:

1. A grid of nine rectangular boxes is laid out on the floor, which is covered by sturdy white paper or some other surface that one can draw on. All rectangles

TABLE 3.1 Rasaboxes grid.

RAUDRA	BIBHATSA	BHAYANAKA
KARUNA	SHANTA empty	SHRINGARA
HASYA	VIRA	ADBHUTA

are the same, about 6' × 5'—large enough for one or two people to stand, sit, or lie down in at the same time. In chalk or crayon, inside each rectangle write in Romanized Sanskrit the name of one rasa. Which rasa goes where is determined by chance. The center box is left empty (see Table 3.1). The workshop leader "defines" each rasa (such definitions are huge over-simplifications, prompts for starting the exercise). For example, *raudra* means angry, rage, roaring; *bibhatsa* means disgusting, foul tasting/smelling, spitting, vomiting; *karuna* means sadness, grief, weeping, pathos; *shringara* means love, affection, lust; *vira* means courage, determination, valor; *adbhuta* means wonderful, amazing, astonishing; *bhayanaka* means fear, cowering, horrifying; *hasya* means funny, laughing, mocking. Name the center box "*shanta*," but do not write it in the box or define it. If someone asks about it, say "We'll deal with shanta later. For now, don't go into it, always leave it empty."

2. Participants draw and/or write the rasas. That is, each person interprets the Sanskrit word, associates feelings and ideas to it. Emphasize that these "definitions" and associations are not for all time, but just for now. Emphasize also that people can draw specific things or abstract configurations. People can write words. In moving from one box to another, people must either "walk the line" between the boxes or step outside the grid entirely and walk around to a different box. There is no order of progression from box to box. A person may return to a box as often as she likes. Be careful not to overwrite someone else's contribution. Take as much time as necessary. When a person is finished, she or he steps outside the grid. This phase of the exercise is over when everyone is outside the rasaboxes. It is important not to rush. Sometimes this phase of the exercise takes hours.

3. When everyone is standing around the edges of the grid, people take in what has been drawn/written. Participants walk around the edges. They read to

themselves and out loud what is written. They describe what is drawn. But they can't ask questions. Nor can anything be explained. Things are what they are.

4. Pause. Silence. The leader emphasizes that the group—and all the individuals in the group—need to take the time necessary, but how long that is cannot be known in advance. The pause in silence is a moving away from clock time to event time or Rasaboxes time.

5. Someone enters a box. The person takes/makes a pose of that rasa. No sound. For example, a pose of shringara or karuna or whatever. The person can do as few as a single rasa or as many as eight rasas. The ninth box at the center is not entered. A person can move from box to box either around the outside or on the lines. These transitions are neutral. Of course, no movement can be neutral or blank, but one does the best one can to be uninflected in moving around the edge or along the lines. When a person steps into a box, she must take/make a rasic pose. Even if she accidentally steps into a box. This phase continues until everyone has had at least two chances to enter and pose within the rasaboxes.

6. Same as 5, but now poses are supplemented by breath and then sounds.

   In steps 5 and 6, there is no thinking. Just take/make a pose and/or a sound. Don't prepare; just do. Move quickly from one rasabox to the next. Don't worry how "pretty," "true," or "original" the pose/sound is. Once outside the boxes, reflect on how you composed your rasa and what it felt like to be in a composed rasa. In other words, begin exploring the distinction between feelings and how you publicly express those feelings. Don't worry which came first. It is a chicken-and-egg question with no correct answer. In fact, the first poses/sounds often are clichés—well-known expressions that fit the rasas as they are usually understood: big laughs for hasya, clenched fists for raudra, weeping for karuna, gagging for bibhatsa, and so on. The distance between stereotype and archetype is not great. Sooner or later, the social stereotype/archetype will be augmented by gestures and sounds that are more intimate, personal, quirky, unexpected. The road from outer to inner = the road from inner to outer.

7. Move more rapidly from one box to the next. Quick changes, no time for thinking in advance.

   Here we are beginning to grapple with Antonin Artaud's call for actors to become "athletes of the heart."[15] Actual athletic competitions come to mind. A basketball player sits on the sideline, quiet, a towel draped over his shoulder. But when called on to enter the game, he explodes with energy, performs at a high level of skill, and is entirely focused on his task. A whistle blows, and the athlete relaxes. Then when the time out is over, he jumps back into the game. One of the goals of Rasaboxes exercises is to prepare actors to move with the same swift mastery from one emotion to another, in a random or almost random sequence, with no preparation between emotional displays, and with full commitment to each emotion. What happens at the level of emotions and feelings is left indeterminate; as with the performers in India (and elsewhere), some doers of Rasaboxes exercises will "feel" it—others will not.

Did David Garrick (1717–1779) Do Rasaboxes?

Diderot in *The Paradox of Acting* described the great 18th-century English actor David Garrick who, astonishingly, seems to be doing Rasaboxes:

> Garrick will put his head between two folding doors, and in the course of five or six seconds his expression will change successively from wild delight to temperate pleasure, from this to tranquility, from tranquility to surprise, from surprise to blank astonishment, from that to sorrow, from sorrow to the air of one overwhelmed, from that to fright, from fright to horror, from horror to despair, and thence he will go up again to the point from which he started.
>
> ([1773] 1883, 38)

Diderot argues that Garrick's genius is in his mastery of technique, not his experience of feeling what the technique enacts: "Can his [Garrick's] soul have experienced all these feelings, and played this kind of scale in concert with his face? I don't believe it; nor do you" ([1773] 1883, 38).

Who is to say?

---

8. Next comes relating. Two persons enter, each one in their own box. At first, they each simply physicalize a rasa pose and sound without one person paying attention to the other. But then they notice one another and begin to "dialogue" with the rasas. They can shift rapidly from one box to another. So, shringara confronts vira and then vira moves to adbhuta; after a moment shringara rushes along the line to bibhatsa and adbhuta jumps to bhayanaka. And so on, in no predetermined sequence.

9. At step 8, many new combinations appear. People begin to find things that are far from social clichés. Those on the outside are often amused, moved, sometimes frightened. Something is happening, though it is difficult if not impossible to put it in words. A few people are hesitant about going into the boxes at all. No one should ever be forced to enter. Rasaboxes, like all exercises in The Performance Workshop, must always be voluntary. My experience is that everyone, finally, participates; but the range of participation varies. Sometimes, the leader has to ask those who jump in again and again to hold back, giving the more timid an opportunity. The exercise is both bluntly expressive and a scalpel that cuts very deeply into people. Paradoxically, in performing different emotional masks, the participants discover aspects of their being that had remained hidden—not infrequently even from themselves.

    Texts are brought in—that is, speeches from known plays, letters, diaries, or something composed just for the exercise. Scenes from dramas enacted by two or even three people. The text remains fixed, but the rasas shift—with no preplanning. So, for example, Romeo is all shringara but Juliet is karuna;

then suddenly Juliet springs to raudra and Romeo to adbhuta. And so on—the possible combinations are endless. Occasionally, Romeo and Juliet are in the same box. At this stage, performers test out some of the many possibilities of any given text. Or rather, texts are revealed as not meaning one or two things but permeable, open, wildly interpretable.

10. Scenes are enacted with one underlying rasa, on top of which are bits played in different rasas. Rasas can be layered, one on top of the other, or combined. For example, Juliet's shringara—her love for Romeo—may be on top of her raudra—her anger against her parents; or she may mix shringara, raudra, and—at the end of the play—karuna. Or, perhaps, unexpectedly, the drama's end is infected with hasya, the absurdity of it all. There are so many possibilities. Here one begins to see how a whole production could be mapped as a progression of rasas. The progression could be scored or improvised for each performance (see Bowditch, pp. 280–293).

There are even more possibilities. The Rasaboxes exercise is designed to be unfinishable. It is not intended to be a true example of a *NS*-based performance. Indeed, what results from doing Rasaboxes is not at all like any traditional Indian performance. The exercises actually point to the creative possibilities suggested by the underlying theory of the *NS*. It *comes from* rather than *is an example of* that theory.

The Empty Box

What about shanta, the empty box at the center? What happens there? In the exercise, a person can enter that box only if the person is "clear." What that means, the person directing the exercise cannot say. Each person will have her own criteria for total, whole clarity. I think of shanta in one of two ways. Either, like white light, it is the combination of all the feelings so that individual colors (and each rasa has a color[16]) disappear; or, as in achieving nirvana, a person transcends all feelings and accomplishes "emptiness," which paradoxically equals totality. In the years that I've led Rasaboxes exercises, someone has entered shanta very rarely, one or two times. There can be no challenge to such a position. So, what if the person is not really "clear"? How can another person tell? And maybe it is so, maybe the participant has surpassed all *samsara*, all the clutter of feelings, the confusion of mixed emotions, the noise of change. I will not judge.[17]

Rasaesthetics in Performance

Let me turn from training to performance. Indian theatre, dance, and music are not banquets. In kutiyattam, odissi, bharatanatyam, kathakali, kathak, and so on, performers dance, gesture, impersonate, and sometimes speak and sing. Occasionally, there is burning incense thickening the air with odor. But for the most part, the data of the performance is transmitted from performer to partaker in the same way as in the west (and elsewhere), through the eyes and ears. How is this rasic?

Watching traditional Indian dance, one sees the performer looking at her own hands as they form different *hastas* or *mudras*—precise gestures, each with a very specific meaning. This self-regarding is not narcissism in the western sense. "Abhinaya" literally means to lead the performance to the spectators—and the first spectator is the performer herself. If the self-who-is-observing is moved by the self-who-is-performing, the performance will be a success. This splitting is not exactly a Brechtian *verfremdungseffekt*, but neither is it altogether different. Brecht wanted to open a space between performer and performance in order to insert a social commentary. The rasic performer opens a liminal space to allow further play—improvisation, variation, and self-enjoyment.

The performer becomes a partaker herself. When she is moved by her own performance, she is affected not as the character, but as a partaker. Like the other partakers, she can appreciate the dramatic situation, the crisis, the feelings of the character she is performing. She will both express the emotions of that character and be moved to apprehend her own feelings about those emotions. Where does she experience these feelings? In her body, including her brain; in her ENS, the gut inside the body that is dancing; in her ears, eyes, and brain that are hearing, seeing, and interpreting the performance; in her cognitive self that is enacting a dramatic situation. The other partakers—the audience—are doubly affected: by the performance and by the performer's reaction to her own performance. An empathetic feedback loop takes place. Experiencing this "theatre and its double" can be remarkable.

In orthodox western theatre, the spectators respond sympathetically to the "as if" of characters living out a narrative. In rasic theatre, the partakers empathize with the experience of the performers playing. This partaking can of course include delighting in the narrative and characters. But it also goes beyond—or, rather, to the side of such plot and character-driven empathy. This empathy with the performer rather encourages Indian theatre to wander, exploring detours and hidden pathways, unexpected turns, long descriptions, widely varying moods. Here rasa and *raga*[18] converge. The partaker's interest is released from the story and reengaged with the enacting of the story; the partaker does not want to see what happens next but to experience along with the performer what is happening. There is no narrational imperative insisting on development, climax, recognition, and resolution. Instead, as in kundalini sexual meditation, there is as much deferral as one can bear, a delicious, sometimes ecstatic, delay of climax and resolution.

I am here expounding a theory of reception—even to the extent that the performer's self-regarding is a reception of her own performance. This needs further elaboration. One treatise on abhinaya instructs the dancer to sing with her throat, express the meaning of that song with her hand gestures, show how she feels with her eyes, and keep time with her feet. And every Indian performer knows the traditional adage, "Where the hands go, the eyes follow; where the eyes go, the mind follows; where the mind goes, the emotions follow, and when the emotions are expressed, there will be rasa." Such a logically linked performance of emotions points to the "self" not as personal ego, but as the *atman*, or profound absolute self, the Self that is identical to the universal absolute, the *Brahman*.

Eating in a traditional manner in India means conveying the food directly to the mouth with the right hand. There is no intermediary instrument such as fork or spoon. Sometimes a flat bread is used to mop or hold the food; sometimes rice is used to sop up a curry. But in all cases, the food on the index and third finger is swept into the mouth by an inward motion of the thumb. Along with the food, the eater tastes his own fingers. The performer regarding her mudras is engaging in a kind of "theatre feeding." As with self-feeding, the emotions of a performance are first conveyed to the performer and the partakers by means of the hands.

Orthodox western performing arts remain invested in keeping performers separated from receivers. Stages are elevated; curtains mark a boundary; spectators are fixed in their seats. Many mainstream artists, scholars, and critics do not look on synchronicity and synesthesia with favor. Eating, digestion, and excretion are not thought of as proper sites of aesthetic pleasure. These sites—aside from rock concerts and sports matches—are more in the domain of performance art. In early performance art there were Carolee Schneemann, Allan Kaprow, Linda Montano, Chris Burden, Stellarc, Orlan, and others. Later came Mike Kelley, Paul McCarthy, Karen Finley, Annie Sprinkle, Ron Athey, Franko B., Cassils, Rocio Boliver, and more, all of whom insisted on making "the body" explicit.[19] Their work began to elide differences between the interior and the exterior; to emphasize permeability and porosity; to explore the sexual, the diseased, the excretory, the wet, and the smelly. Performances used blood, semen, spit, shit, urine—as well as food, paint, plastics, and other stuff drawn from the "literal" rather than the "make believe." This work is not very Asian on the surface, but at an underlying theoretical level, it is extremely rasic.

These kinds of performances need to be studied in terms of rasaesthetics. That means paying attention to the increasing appetite for arts that engage and interrogate visceral arousal and experience; performances that insist on sharing experiences with partakers and participants; works that try to evoke both terror and celebration. Such performances are often very personal even as they are no longer private but public.

Rasaesthetics opens questions regarding how the whole sensorium is, or can be, used in making performances. Smell, taste, and touch are demanding their place at the table.[20] Thus, I am making a much larger claim—and sending out a more general invitation. I am inviting an investigation into theatricality as orality, digestion, and excretion rather than, or in addition to, theatricality as something only or mostly for the eyes and ears. I am saying that performance practice has moved strongly into this place, and it is high time for theory to follow.

Notes

1 I've revised this essay several times since it first appeared in *TDR* (Schechner 2001): 45, 3: 27–50. The current version was revised in May–July 2018.
2 At the very start of the *NS*, Bharata claims for it the status of a Veda—the most sacred of ancient Indian texts. Such a claim to being the "fifth Veda" as a way of elevating a text is not unusual. Tradition finally, of course, assigned the rank of shastra to the *NS*, a position below the Vedas on the hierarchical ladder of Sanskrit sacred writings. As for the framing origin myth told in chapter 1—how Brahma composed this fifth Veda, its transmission to Bharata and his sons, and their performance of the "first natya" celebrating Indra's victory over *asuras* and *danavas* (two kinds of beings who revolted against the gods)—much can be made of it. The asuras and danavas are enraged by the performance of their defeat; they rush the stage and, as the *NS* tells the story, magically freeze "the speeches, movements, and even the memory of the performers." Indra, king of the gods, intervenes, thrashes the demons with a flagpole, which is then installed as a

protective totem. Brahma instructs the gods' architect Visvakarman to construct an impregnable theatre, well guarded by gods. This having been done, the gods say it is better to negotiate with the asuras and danavas than to forcibly exclude them. Brahma agrees, approaches them, and asks why they want to destroy natya. They reply, "You are as much the creator of us as of the gods" so why are we omitted from natya? "If that is all there is to it," Brahma says, "then there is no reason for you to feel angry or aggrieved. I have created the *Natyaveda* to show good and bad actions and feelings of both gods and yourselves. It is the representation of the entire three worlds and not only of the gods or of yourselves." Thus, natya is of divine origin, all-encompassing, and consisting of actions both good and bad. For an extended and highly sophisticated interpretation of the *NS'* framing myth, see Christopher Byrski (1974).

3 According to Kapila Vatsyayan (1996, 32–36) and Adya Rangacharya, whose English translation of the *NS* (1996) is the most readable, in 1865 the American Fitz Edward Hall unearthed and published several chapters of the *NS*. In 1874, the German Wilhelm Heymann (or Haymann, as Vatsyayan spells it) wrote an influential essay that stimulated further translations of several chapters by the French scholar, Paul Reynaud (or Regnaud, as Vatsyayan spells it). But it was only in 1926 that the first portions of the Baroda critical edition were published. The critical edition, edited by M. Ram Krishna Kavi, is based on 40 manuscripts coming from different parts of India. The whole Sanskrit text of the critical edition was not completed until 1954. Baroda is today's Vadodara in Gujarat, western India. *NS* fragments-manuscripts are kept in the Oriental Institute at the Maharaja Sayajirao University of Baroda. As Vatsyayan notes, "In spite of all these results, the final text is contradictory, repetitive and incongruent; there are lacunae too, but, what is worse, there are words and passages that are almost impossible to understand. . . . It is not only modern scholars who suffer this inability to understand; even almost a thousand years ago . . . Abhinavagupta . . . displayed this tendency" (Vatsyayan 1996, xviii). Vatsyayan (180ff) provides a "Database of the *Natyashastra*" locating and listing all 112 known extant texts and fragments. All the texts are Sanskrit but transcribed in a variety of scripts: Newari, Devanagari, Grantha, Telugu, Malayalam, Tamil, Kanarese. Thus, we know that from an early time the *NS* was widely distributed across the subcontinent.

4 Rasa as flavor is fundamental to not only natya but also ayurvedic medicine, the ancient Sanskrit system of health and healing. This chapter is not the occasion for a discussion of the relationship between rasa/*NS* and rasa/Ayurveda. I wish to note only the correspondence between the flavors of food and the flavors of emotion. The six flavors of ayurveda are: *madhura* (sweet), *amla* (sour), *lavana* (salty), *katu* (hot, spicy), *tikta* (bitter), and *kashaya* (astringent/dry). Some of these map onto emotions: "sweet love," "sour feelings," "salty tears," "hot rage," "bitter feelings," "dry response," etc. In relation to natyarasa, two correspondences are obvious: madhura to shringara and katu to raudra; other correspondences are more complex and cannot be reduced to one-on-one.

5 "In pre-Socratic thought the prerational notion of agon is used to describe the natural world as a ceaseless play of forces or Becoming" (Spariosu 1989, 13).

6 Lee Strasberg (1901–1982), an American actor and actor-trainer, headed the Actors Studio in New York from 1951 until his death. At the Studio, Strasberg taught his interpretation of Stanislavsky's system of actor training. Strasberg emphasized "emotional memory," wherein the actor recalls and relives specific personal, even intimate, events that parallel or are strongly metaphorically connected to the emotions of the character. The feelings aroused and expressed by means of emotional memory are used in performing the character.

7 I formed East Coast Artists (ECA) in New York in 1992. The first performances I directed with ECA were *Faust/gastronome* (1993), *Three Sisters* (1997), and *Hamlet*

(1999). Rasaboxes was developed during workshops I ran at NYU in the 1990s and with my colleagues in East Coast Artists. During the late 1990s and into the 2000s, I worked with Rebecca Wilenski Ortese, Ursula Neuerburg, Michele Minnick, Paula Murray Cole, Rachel Bowditch, Marcia Moraes, and Fernando Calzadilla further developing Rasaboxes, while they also developed it independently. These artists, as well as people trained by them, lead Rasaboxes workshops globally (see Chapter 1 for more on East Coast Artists, and Chapter 4 for further development of TPW and Rasaboxes).

8 According to the first chapter of the NS, Brahma created the *natyaveda* "to show good and bad actions and feelings of both gods and yourselves [humans]. It is the representation of the entire three worlds [divine, human, demonic] and not only of the gods or of yourselves. Now dharma [correct living], now artha [warring], now kama [loving], humor or fights, greed or killing. Natya teaches the right way to those who go against dharma, erotic enjoyment to those who seek pleasure, restraint to those who are unruly, moderation to those who are self-disciplined, courage to cowards, energy to the brave, knowledge to the uneducated, wisdom to the learned, enjoyment to the rich, solace to those in grief, money to business people, a calm mind to the disturbed. Natya is the representation of the ways of the world using various emotions and diverse circumstances. It gives you peace, entertainment, and happiness, as well as beneficial advice based on the actions of high, low, and middle people" (NS, 1:106ff; English adapted from the Ghosh [2009] and Rangacharya [1996] translations).

9 How similar is this to the Eucharist? The wafer and wine do not taste sweet as prasad does. But the god–human sacrifice at the core of the Eucharist is "celebrated." A Roman Catholic website states: "The celebration of the Eucharist is not a private devotion but rather a communal gathering much like a family meal" (Loyola Press 2018). The Eucharist represses its Orphic theophagy in favor of a Neo-Platonist/Augustinian abjection of the body. But what about an earlier epoch, when Greek, South Asian, Middle-Eastern, and Egyptian cultures were interacting with each other? Did Jesus and his disciples relish *as food* that first Eucharist? The first Eucharist happened, after all, at a Passover seder, a feast celebrating the liberation from slavery, the exodus from Egypt, and the defeat of the Egyptian army—all directly staged by God. And what of the Indian gods who receive prasad? The murtis are bathed in sweet milk, dressed in silks, and adorned with flowers. The Shiva lingam is drenched in ghee (clarified butter), sensual seminous stuff, as well as a key ingredient in fancy cooking. Not so long ago, after dressing the murtis and offering them sweets, *devadasis* danced for them. These performances by women dedicated to the temples were "private" in the sense that gods, dancers, and musicians were the only beings acknowledged as present. The priests, princes, and men of privilege who savored the performances, later gaining sexual access to the devadasis, were "invisible." They saw as if through the eyes of the gods. Indeed, who is looking at such performances? Who endows the murtis with life? And are the devadasis a species of prasad offered to the murtis but enjoyed by men? The power that gives life to the murtis is identical to that which transforms wine and wafer into Jesus' blood and flesh. He is eaten, devadasis are partners in love-making: both are offered. Depending on your religion or lack thereof: pretense or transformation, abracadabra or miracle, sexual exploitation or holy union. What holds Hindu temple practice and the Eucharist in the same fold of meaning is "theatricality."

10 Bhajans are celebratory, even ecstatic songs, in praise of gods such as Krishna and Rama. Sometimes, while singing bhajans, crowds will circumambulate sacred wells and trees. Bhajans are sung by ordinary people and by *sadhus* (holy people who have renounced daily life).

11 The peripheral nervous system (PNS) consists of the many nerve cells throughout the body connected to the brain via the spinal cord. The PNS receives sensory input, which is then transmitted to the brain where it is "interpreted" as various kinds of touch, heat–cold, pain, tickling, etc. Signals are sent back from the brain resulting in bodily movements and so on. The ENS is part of the PNS, but both structurally and operationally very different than the rest of the PNS. The ENS, for the most part, operates independently of the brain though it is connected to the brain via the vagus nerve.

12 Michele Minnick informed me that "In somatic and physical therapy practices, including yoga-based practices, there are ways of stimulating the vagus nerve through certain breathing and sounding exercises, etc." Indeed, the yoga that I always teach in my performance workshops and during rehearsals for productions does greatly increase performers' abilities to do rasic performing. A strong part of this training begins with yogic breathing or "pranayama." I add to this a wide range of other breathing exercises derived from the practice of Kristin Linklater and from my own work.

13 Note from the Editors: Here, as elsewhere in the book, Rasaboxes is capitalized when it refers to the entirety of the practice. It appears with a small "r" when referring to the rasaboxes grid, or an individual rasabox, such as the karuna rasabox.

14 I will not detail these exercises here (see Chapter 4). I describe some early, but still valid, exercises in *Environmental Theater* (1972, revised 1994). Since that time, I have added exercises, many of which are described in this book.

15 Artaud writes: "We must recognize that the actor has a kind of emotional musculature which corresponds to certain physical localizations of feelings. The actor is like a real physical athlete, but with this surprising qualification, that he has an emotional organism which is analogous to the athlete's, which is parallel to it, which is like its double, although it does not operate on the same level. The actor is an athlete of the heart ... and the sphere of the emotions is his peculiar domain. It belongs to him organically" ([1938] 1976, 259–60).

16 The *NS* associates each rasa with a color: shringara/green; karuna/gray; raudra/red; hasya/white; vira/orange; adbhuta/yellow; bhayanaka/black; bibhatsa/blue. Shanta—like hasya—is white, but I interpret this to mean clear, without color.

17 Note from the Editors: First and second wave teachers of the work have developed different approaches to the shanta rasabox (see Chapter 4, p. 150).

18 In Indian classical music, a raga is a specific progression of sounds, pauses, and rhythms that the musician uses as the basis for improvisation. Potentially, there are thousands of ragas. The musical artists often start with a specific raga and then play with it, vary it, both creating and following where it goes.

19 For a detailed discussion, see Rebecca Schneider, *The Explicit Body in Performance* (1997), and Amelia Jones, *Body Art/Performing the Subject* (1998).

20 David Howes, Constance Classen, and their colleagues at the Centre for Sensory Studies, Concordia University, Montreal, have developed an anthropology/aesthetics of the senses with significant publications and important conferences. Go to: www.centreforsensorystudies.org/.

Works Cited

Artaud, Antonin. "*The Theater and Its Double* (1931–36)." In *Antonin Artaud Selected Writings*, ed. Susan Sontag. New York: Farrar, Straus and Giroux, (1938) 1976, pp. 213–76.

Bharata-muni. *The Natyashastra*. Translated and edited Adya Rangacharya. New Delhi: Munshiram Manoharlal, 1996.

Bharata-muni. *Natyasastra: A Treatise on Ancient Indian Dramaturgy and Histrionics Ascribed to Bharata Muni.* Translated by Manomohan Ghosh. Varanasi: Chowkhamba Sanskrit Series Office, 2002–2003.
Blakeslee, Sandra. "Complex and Hidden Brain in the Gut Makes Cramps, Butterflies, and Valium." *New York Times*, 23 January: C1–3, 1996.
Byrski, Christopher. *Concept of Ancient Indian Theatre.* New Delhi: Munshiram Manoharlal, 1973.
Classen, Constance. *The Color of Angels.* London and New York: Routledge, 1998.
Dharwadker, Vinay. "Emotion in Motion: The *Nātyashāstra*, Darwin, and Affect Theory." *PMLA*, vol. 130, no. 5, 2015, pp. 1381–1404.
Diderot, Denis. *The Paradox of Acting (Paradoxe sur le Comedien).* Translated by Walter Herries Pollock. London: Chatto & Windus, (1773) 1883.
Geertz, Clifford. *The Interpretation of Cultures.* New York: Basic Books, 1973.
Gershon, Michael D. *The Second Brain.* New York: Harper Perennial, 1998.
Gershon, Michael D., Alcmene Chalazonitis, and Taube P. Rothman. "The Neural Crest to Bowel: Development of the Enteric Nervous System." *Journal of Neurobiology*, vol. 24, no. 2, 1993, pp. 199–214.
Gershon, Michael D., and S. M. Erde. *Gastroenterology*, vol. 80, 1981, pp. 1571–94.
Hadhazy, Adam. "Think Twice: How the Gut's 'Second Brain' Influences Mood and Well-Being." *Scientific American*, 12 February, 2010. www.scientificamerican.com/article/gut-second-brain/. Accessed 27 July 2018.
Howes, David, ed. *The Varieties of Sensory Experience.* Toronto: University of Toronto Press, 1991.
Jones, Amelia. *Body Art/Performing the Subject.* Minneapolis: University of Minnesota Press, 1998.
Lannoy, Richard. *The Speaking Tree.* London: Oxford University Press, 1971.
Loyola Press. "Celebrating the Eucharist in Community." www.loyolapress.com/our-catholic-faith/sacraments/eucharist/celebrating-the-eucharist-in-community. Accessed 27 July 2018.
Partridge, Eric. *Origins: A Short Etymological Dictionary of Modern English.* London: Routledge and Kagen Paul, 1966.
Sargeant, Winthrop, trans. *The Bhagavad Gita.* Albany: State University of New York Press, 1984.
Schechner, Richard. *Environmental Theater.* New York: Applause Books, (1973) 1994.
———. "Believed-in Theatre." *Performance Research*, vol. 2, no. 2, 1997, pp. 76–91.
———. *Rasaesthetics.* TDR, 45, no. 3 (T171), 2001, pp. 27–50.
Schneider, Rebecca. *The Explicit Body in Performance.* London and New York: Routledge, 1997.
Shipley, Joseph T. *Origins of English Words: A Discursive Dictionary of Indo-European Roots.* Baltimore: Johns Hopkins University Press, 1984.
Spariosu, Mihai. *Dionysus Reborn.* Ithaca: Cornell University Press, 1989.
Vatsyayan, Kapila. *Bharata: The Natyashastra.* New Delhi: Sahitya Akademi, 1996.
Winnicott, D. W. *Playing and Reality.* London: Tavistock Publications, 1971.
Zarrilli, Phillip. "What Does It Mean to 'Become the Character': Power, Presence, and Transcendence in Asian In-Body Disciplines of Practice." In *By Means of Performance*, edited by Richard Schechner and Willa Appel. Cambridge: Cambridge University Press, 1990, pp. 131–48.

PART II

Practice

FIGURE 4.1 Sketch of performers doing Rasaboxes by Joan Schirle. Dell'Arte International School of Physical Theatre, 2005.

Source: Courtesy of Paula Murray Cole.

CHAPTER 4

Inside The Performance Workshop

PAULA MURRAY COLE, MICHELE MINNICK, AND RACHEL BOWDITCH

Fundamental Principles and Practices

The Performance Workshop (TPW) is a flexible container for training performers, exploring self and identity, and creating performances, while simultaneously making a group out of a collection of individuals. It draws on the principles of environmental theatre developed by Richard Schechner (see Chapter 1, pp. 14–17). The physical and vocal training, as well as many of the improvisational exercises in the workshop, are part of an ongoing oral and experimental tradition going back to the 1960s. The suite of core exercises has evolved over time, and since 1999 has been adapted and expanded by Schechner's collaborators, who are now its primary teachers.

If performance studies is a field in which we can view and analyze anything *as* performance, in TPW everything *is* performance. TPW sessions are facilitated from this perspective—from the first to the last gathering of the group. The "liminality" (see Chapter 1, pp. 29–31) of TPW means inviting participants to consider that everything that happens within TPW—whether theatrical or quotidian—is content. All content can be shaped and incorporated into exercises, improvisations, and performance compositions.

This chapter is not a complete representation of what can or does happen in TPW. It best serves as a supplement to, rather than a replacement for, guided instruction led by an experienced facilitator. It is our hope that, by sharing core practices, we can offer readers a glimpse into the workshop and give support to those training as teachers of the work.

In Part I of this book, we outline some of the key concepts and fields of study that frame the practical work of TPW, including ritual and play and their relationship to the theory and practice of performance, as well as environmental theatre concepts and practices that forged this approach from the 1960s to today. They still inform our practice, along with Richard's configuration of rasaesthetics (see Chapter 3), and our own research on rasa in the contexts of performance and wellness. In this chapter we refer to Richard on a first name basis, rather than the more academic "Schechner" used elsewhere in the book. Because this chapter is an inside view of the work we have shared with him in TPW, during which he asks participants to call him "Richard," we thought it best that the writing reflect that relationship.

Here, before diving into the work itself, we would like to explain some spatial, temporal, and relational configurations that structure both group formation and individual participation in the workshop.

Four Phases of Performer Training

Richard outlines a trajectory of group training in the "Performer" chapter of *Environmental Theater* (1973, 125–71), which describes the bones of what we do in TPW. He explains the principle behind the progression of exercises we might do on a given day, over the course of a week, or a whole workshop. Here we offer a slight adaptation of the progression:

1. Getting in touch with yourself
2. Getting in touch with yourself face to face with others
3. Relating to others without narrative or other highly formalized structures
4. Relating to others within narrative or other highly formalized structures

(Schechner 1994, 130)

The early days of the workshop tend to focus on 1–3, and 4 begins to be elaborated as we work with more complex exercises and assignments. All of the more "highly formalized structures" are built upon the basics of movement, breath and sound, and the relationships we build with each other through the work, day after day. The process is cumulative, which is why presence and participation are so important. There is no way to "make up" an experience that has been missed, for the unique *experience* of "getting in touch" and "relating" is what emerges spontaneously in the moment of doing, showing, sharing, and watching in real time.

Presence and Absence

TPW offers an opportunity to explore participation in a variety of ways. The baseline agreement is to be present in the room. The Rules for Play (see p. 88) ordinarily do not permit more than one absence during a three to five-week workshop. There are no outside observers, but group exercises and performances do allow for degrees of doing, watching, or dropping out, as will be explained later. This creates a more ritual-like structure, in that there is no "audience" separate from the group that is training and performing. Being part of this temporary community means being present, even if a participant can do no more than observe on a particular day.

Consent and Boundary Checks

Since the 1960s when some of these exercises were first developed, Richard has introduced more opportunities for saying "no," or opting out. The right of refusal is not the same as consent, however, which is currently defined as a clear, affirmative, and enthusiastic "yes," both in the broader culture and in the context of intimacy direction for theatre.

TPW creates an environment in which participants may invite and play with desire of all kinds, and challenge themselves to take risks, sometimes at the edges of comfort. To continually interrupt exercises to ask for consent may make it impossible to drop into the kind of flow that is a creative force for the group and essential to developing trust. This play between setting boundaries and allowing them to shift, or even at times to dissolve, is a compelling paradox we continue to explore in TPW.

Prior to the introduction of exercises involving any form of physical contact (such as One Sound, Open Sound, Sculpting in Partners, etc.), establish consent procedures and practices for communicating physical boundaries. A boundaries check is one way that each participant can communicate areas of their body that can or cannot be intentionally touched or contacted by another. We encourage all participants to develop the habit of doing a boundaries check when working in partners or in small groups each time they encounter new opportunities for physical contact.[1]

Feedback and Discussion Circles

We pause exercises periodically to invite immediate feedback about the work at hand. As we become conscious of our own individual responses to the work—the collisions, confusions, resistances, desires, connections, and so forth—and if we are willing to share these experiences out loud, we often find that deeper, more personal connections develop among group members. These growing connections inform the quality and content of subsequent encounters we are having with others. Facilitators, guided by the feedback emerging from the group, can highlight principles that undergird the work, or segue into the next phase of an exercise, or change course.

We also hold sit-down Discussion Circles to hear feedback and process how each participant is responding to the work, or about a particular topic of interest. For both forms of feedback, we ask the group to phrase responses as "I statements." This ensures that you are speaking only for what you have experienced. I statements help you to:

- Avoid generalizations that may unconsciously imply that your experience of the work is shared by others, or even everyone in the group.
- Take responsibility for what you say without making assumptions about how others are receiving the work.
- Embrace your own experience as valid, whether or not others share the same perspective.
- Cultivate your own sense of agency and allow others to do the same.

In our experience, participants readily embrace this practice, easily understanding its purpose, even if periodic reminders and adjustments need to be made to uphold the practice throughout TPW. For those who are not fluent in the language used to teach the workshop, "I statement" rules are modified to accommodate their language use. All points of view are welcome as long as they do not cause interpersonal harm, injury, or insult, including of course denigrating someone's race, gender, culture, or sexual orientation.

To effectively facilitate feedback, it is important to develop comfort with silence. If we respond out of the anxiety of filling silence, rather than from a genuine need to speak, we may be short-circuiting other responses. Sometimes responses to the work are difficult to verbalize. Becoming comfortable with silence also means opening a space for those who do not often speak up to lean forward and participate in the conversation. People may dominate the conversation or hang back from participating for a variety of reasons. It's good to drop in a reminder now and then that we share responsibility for keeping this balance.

Another key element is that there does not have to be agreement. The facilitator can listen to diverse responses, without showing approval or disapproval. Simply witness what is being offered in the moment and hold space for whatever arises. Discussion Circles are moments for finding out what is coming up for individuals and/or for the group. These circles are in part a way for the temporary community of the workshop to navigate their relationships—between individuals, group, facilitator, and material—as much as anything else. Not everything needs to be solved or resolved (see Figure 4.5).

Time in TPW

Spatial and physical boundaries are configured and reconfigured throughout the duration of TPW. The ritual-based container of TPW also means approaching time in different ways. The way we organize time impacts our consciousness, social organization, and ability to respond creatively to our experience. Most of 21st-century western life is organized around "clock time," a relatively recent invention that shapes the operations of industry, learning, leisure, and almost every aspect of our everyday lives. We have both an objective and a subjective sense of time—something that takes an hour could feel like it took ten minutes, and vice versa. This subjective experience of time is related to "event time." Although the external boundary of the workshop is measured in clock time, we work as much as possible in event time within each session. Associated with ritual, play, and certain kinds of performance, event time is measured by the occurrence or completion of an event or activity. In event time, exercises have an organic relationship to their own intrinsic processes, and to individual and group needs, rather than chronologically imposed starting and ending times. The completion of a particular cycle of activities, rather than a set number of minutes or hours, determines when an exercise is over.

Richard has often shared this anecdote about becoming conscious of his expectations of clock time versus his experience of ritual event time when attending a temple ceremony in Bali, Indonesia:

I was invited to attend a ritual performance that I was told "begins at 9:00 p.m." I dutifully arrived at the temple at 8:45. The place was empty. Not even the ubiquitous monkeys were there. I sat, notebook open, and waited. 9:00, 9:30, 10:00, 10:30.... As the minutes and hours went by, people began drifting in, doing this and that, some more or less dozing, sitting, or slumped along the walls of the temple. Musicians arrived, tuned up, chatted, smoked. More and more people. Hubbub. The monkeys showed up, sensing there would be food. More people. Incense. And finally, I don't recall exactly when, probably after midnight—the Balinese love the small hours—the ritual began. Trance dancing, gamelan, sharing of *prasad*, smoke, and happy noise. When it was all over as dawn arrived, I had the temerity to ask someone who looked like he would know, "I thought it was to start at 9:00pm?" My informant fixed me in his gaze, eyes sympathetic to my strange foreigner's sense of time, "When it starts, that's 9:00pm," he said. Event time, not clock time, rules—or at least used to rule—in Bali.

(Schechner 2018)

Some sports games are played in event time, some in clock time. For example, a marathon or a tennis match ends when the winner crosses the finish line, or wins match point. Most soccer games are played in two 45-minute halves. Differences between clock time and other ways of marking time are not just cultural or aesthetic distinctions and are not politically neutral. The anti-racist ideas and practices that have been taken up in the academy, the arts, and other sectors of society in the US, with increased rigor and widespread engagement since 2020, include ideas about time. Of particular note is the sense of urgency that Tema Okun describes in "White Supremacy Culture," originally published in 1999, and circulating in an updated version in the 2020s. Urgency "makes it difficult to take time to be inclusive, encourage democratic or thoughtful decision-making, to think and act long-term, and/or to consider consequences of whatever action we take."[2]

There are strong cultural differences concerning the importance of being "on time," or the meaning of absence. By the same token, we have found that resistance to event time has increased in more recent years, particularly in places like New York City, where concerns about safety, making late-night trains, work, family, and other obligations, have superseded the possibility of allowing certain exercises to complete in event time. In short, facilitators must be sensitive to the ways time is approached in the specific cultural context of each workshop.

Navigation Guide

A Note About Language

We use the pronoun "you" to address the reader as an individual workshop participant and/or group. "We" are the facilitators of the workshop, and/or the collective group of participants and facilitators together. Among the many pronouns in use, we employ "they/them, he/him, and she/her" when referring to individual participants. The words "player, participant, individual, person, and performer" are used interchangeably. The words "game, exercise, and performance" are also used to describe practices that overlap and intersect. The connotation of each is somewhat different. When we talk about an exercise as a "game," your approach to doing it may be different than when we call it an "exercise" or a "performance."

A Note About Order

Rather than following the order of exercises as they would flow in a workshop, we have grouped related exercises together. All of the Crossings exercises, for example, which would normally unfold organically in relation to other exercises over the course of the entire workshop (see Sample Workshop, pp. 184–185), appear in this chapter together and sequentially, so that it is easier for the reader to follow the logic of their progression. We use section headings to facilitate the reader's encounter with the material, and at times, discussion and commentary may be included. We have provided theoretical information supporting the practical work, as well as additional exercises, within text boxes that are interspersed between exercises.

Instructions

Instructions appear in writing in much the same way we give them verbally to participants in a workshop. Characteristic of TPW, instructions intentionally involve as little detail as possible. If participants press for clarification, we offer what Richard often says, "Do what you think I mean," or "do what you think you heard." It is in these spaces of not knowing, of interpretation, and "mis"-interpretation that creativity and experimentation unfold. There is no correct way to interpret or do an exercise—each becomes what the participants make of it. Another aspect of TPW that cannot be represented here is the improvisational nature of its facilitation—instructors have a plan, but that plan is informed and re-formed at every moment, often reshaped in response to what happens. Keep in mind that any set of instructions for a given exercise is merely a single example.

Experience

To assist the reader's understanding, some exercises include first-person narratives from the perspective of a fictional Performance Workshop participant: an amalgamation of our experience of doing and teaching the work over many years. These descriptions are by no means meant to be prescriptive. Rather, our hope is that they exemplify and animate aspects of doing the work.

Discussion

Discussion sections are places for additional thoughts or advice for participants and facilitators. They may include things we would say during the course of an exercise, or afterwards, in a Feedback and Discussion Circle.

Rules for Play

- 100% attendance is required for the duration of the workshop.
- Be ready to begin on time.
- Everyone is responsible for keeping the space clean.
- Instructions are invitations; all participation is voluntary.
- No physical harm to anyone in the group is permitted, including to yourself.
- No outside observers are permitted.
- What happens in the workshop stays in the workshop.

Beginnings

FIGURE 4.2 Rolls of masking tape.
Source: Photo courtesy of Maurício Cuca, 2012.

Set Up

Prior to the first session of the workshop, participants are advised about what to wear and bring: movement clothes, water, food for the break, and a notebook, if desired. The workshop space has been prepared to achieve a sense of emptiness and a new beginning—furniture cleared, floors swept and mopped, lighting and sound equipment set up if available. A line of masking tape has been laid across the floor from wall to wall, with enough distance between this line and the entry door for participants to stow workshop materials and personal items.

Entering the Space

Once everyone has changed into their workshop clothing, we meet the group outside the workshop space.

Instructions

Welcome to The Performance Workshop. We encourage you to keep greetings and socializing to a minimum. There will be time for introductions and discussion once we are inside the workshop space. Bring your belongings with you—there will be a place to stow them inside the workshop space.

Over the course of the workshop, you will be given many sets of instructions. Think of them as invitations, or guidelines. Like the rules of a game, instructions set what we are doing as a group. You decide how to enact them. Most importantly, because this is a space of play, your participation is always voluntary. We'll be talking more about that as we proceed.

Here are your first set of instructions:
1. Enter the space together in silence.
2. Place your belongings as far as possible *behind* the line of masking tape.
3. Remove your shoes, socks, jewelry, and watches and stow them safely with your belongings.
4. When ready, stand with your toes just behind the line of masking tape without touching it.
5. Face the open space.
6. When everyone has arrived behind the line, the next instruction will be offered.

EXPERIENCE

I enter the space with the others in silence. There is an atmosphere of anticipation, mystery, confusion, and concentration—a kind of contained excitement. My sensations of doing are heightened as I try to remember and use the instructions we have been given. I pay attention to how I enter, where I place my belongings, then find my way to standing behind the tape line. There is a formal feeling within this preparatory activity.

Silence is an important element throughout the workshop. Sensing yourself, the environment, and communicating with others without words can generate new experiences of self and new modes of group interaction. Tasks are also usually accomplished more quickly and efficiently in silence.

Traditionally, the structuring of the space is accomplished with the most everyday of objects: masking tape. The *space between* the entrance door(s) and the line of tape is the space between the "outside world" and the "inside world" of the workshop. Water, notebooks, extra clothing, personal items, props, and so on are stowed in this area and accessed as needed during the workshop. This is also a place to rest, or to temporarily "drop out" without leaving the room entirely. The space outside the doors—the outside world—is where we socialize, take breaks, and deal with everyday life. We configure, deconstruct, and reconstruct the space many times throughout the workshop.

Crossing the Line

When everyone is standing behind the line, we give the next set of instructions:
1. Regard the space. What do you see? What do you imagine?
2. Sense the ground under your feet. How does it feel?
3. Sense your breath. Focus on your breath for a moment.
4. Become aware of the group and the individuals around you.
5. What other sensory information is available? What else is happening?

6. In your mind's eye, plan how to enter and what you will do in the space. Plan a starting moment, some physical actions, and an ending moment. This is your physical score—it can include improvisation.
7. When you cross the line, enact your physical score. Notice how you encounter the space and others. What thoughts and desires arise?
8. Stop when you have arrived at a sense of completion, or when you hear the next instruction.
9. If you forget any of the instructions, do what you remember.
10. When you are ready, begin.

EXPERIENCE

From behind the line I plan my physical score: two small steps to cross the line—lie face down—slide on my belly across the floor—roll into a ball shape—stand up—do full-body turns diagonally across the floor—stop. I notice I don't want to be the first to go. I sense tension, excitement, and resistance. I hear fans whirling and lights buzzing. Someone coughs. The space in front of me seems cold. I take my first two steps to cross the line—I lie down then slide on my belly. Someone crosses my path. Our eyes meet for a moment then break contact. Although this contact was not part of my physical score, it happened and I allowed it. I return to my physical score: I roll into a ball, then stand. I see the space, the others moving. I stop to watch. After a few moments, I resume my physical score by doing a few full-body turns diagonally across the space. Eventually, each person arrives in stillness. I notice the silence, my shape, and my position in space relative to others . . . I linger, breathing in the now, the beginning.

Entering the Space and Crossing the Line introduce a key element of the workshop: the *spatial boundary* that delineates the workshop space from the everyday space that lies beyond it. This primary boundary, which marks our entry into and departure from the play space of the workshop, is the only one that will remain in place throughout a group's time together. As different exercises and games are introduced and developed, many such boundaries will be created and removed. Boundaries may be created to define the nature of your participation in an exercise, or designate areas for specific activities and roles.

TPW exercises play with the use of *time*. Entering the Space in silence may heighten our awareness about how much time we use to stow our belongings, to take off our shoes, to arrive at the crossing line. Within a whole performance composition, or even within a very short phrase, the construction involves sculpting time in several ways. When does the composition start? When does it stop? What does it mean to arrive at completion? How long or short is each segment? Are there changes in rhythm or tempo? Is there repetition? Or, how does time parse or deconstruct form and meaning? How does the exercise or composition inform or even alter our perceptions of time while we are participating with it, as either a performer or observer?

Time also provides us with an important boundary to contain our work. As Richard says, we may be more willing to open ourselves fully and deeply within an exercise if we know it will end. Or if we know we have the choice to stop when we want. Instructions for performance composition work in TPW often include suggestions to structure time in simple ways, such as "make a performance lasting no longer than one minute." This can be either rigidly or loosely interpreted, or even ignored by the performer, but it does offer a parameter, a container within which the work can be made.

Names

Names exercises make personal introductions—often executed in conventional, perfunctory ways—into small performances. This is not about making introductions theatrical; rather, it means recognizing the performative nature of names. There are many name games in theatre and elsewhere, designed to learn the names of people in a group as a part of "getting to know you." This exercise shares that objective, but rather than rely on conventional social behavior, it explores introductory greetings as a first opportunity to *encounter* self and others. In TPW, an "encounter" is distinguished from everyday social interaction in that we attempt to set aside conventional social behavior in order to connect with one another in a more undecided, intimate, and unadorned way (see Nakedness, p. 113). This usually requires slowing things down and simplifying the content of each interaction so that we can focus on the *quality* of the exchange.

Instructions: Names, Round #1

Sit (or stand) in a circle:

1. Say your first name. It may be your given name, a preferred name, or a nickname. Leave out introductory words and phrases, such as "My name is _____."
2. Say your own name again.
3. Wait in silence until someone else says their name.
4. When no one else takes a turn, this phase of the exercise is over.

Allow silence in between each player giving their own name. Resist the temptation to discuss or ask questions. Simply receive each other and the names without comment. Notice the thoughts, feelings, and sensations that come up for you as you say your own name and receive the names of others.

Instructions: Names, Round #2

1. Say your own name.
2. Make eye contact with another in the circle. Say their name.
3. Make eye contact and say the name of each player in the circle (or as many as you like).
4. Avoid pointing or other gestures as you say their names.
5. When finished, say your own name again. There is silence until someone else initiates.
6. When no one else takes a turn, this phase of the exercise is over.

If you would like to say someone's name but do not remember it, without embarrassment say, "Tell me your name again." Simply receive it and say their name. Connection with the other person within each encounter is more important than memorization.

Take your time.

It's not a grocery list.

Performative Introductions

1. One at a time, improvise an introduction of yourself to members of the group.
2. Use any mode of performance you like: movement, text, singing, a game—anything you would like to offer as a performance of self at this moment.
3. Use your name in some way during your performance.
4. Begin when you feel the impulse. When you are finished, join the group again.
5. We will not applaud after performances, but instead leave space and silence for the next person to begin.
6. The game is over when no one else offers a performance.

Wait For It . . . Hold Your Applause

In TPW, except when the group agrees otherwise, we do not applaud when someone has completed their turn in an exercise, or after a performance, a feat, etc. Instead, we allow space for silence in order to sense the resonance of what has just happened and the potential for something new to emerge. Perhaps a Performative Response will be initiated by someone in the group following a Performance of Self. These moments emerge only when space is not taken up by applause, commenting, or side conversations.

Greetings

After names have been shared on the first day, and reviewed on the second, it is customary to add a greeting to the opening rituals of each workshop session. This can take place any time after everyone has crossed the line, and after any other initial workshop business is attended to. It could come before or after warm-ups. One greeting we often use is Arm Swings.

Instructions

1. Walk around the space, noticing who is there with you.
2. When you make eye contact with someone, offer your arm.
3. If accepted, link arms at the elbow and begin to spin around with one another, maintaining eye contact.
4. One of you will say the name of the other person. Allow that name to land.
5. If you don't remember someone's name, as in the Names exercise, simply ask.
6. The other person says your name.
7. When both people feel satisfied with the exchange, it ends. Walk around the space until you encounter another person with whom to arm swing.
8. This continues until there is no more swinging.

Variations

It can be fun to play with variations in speed of the swinging further along in the workshop when people know one another a little better. An effective way to do this is to demarcate slow, medium, and fast arm swing sections of the space, so you can make choices about how fast you want to swing. You may also experiment with different holds—taking one arm at the wrist, or two, for example, rather than linking elbows. Spinning, making oneself dizzy, and falling are activities young children often enjoy and are an important way to play (see Caillois 2001). Arm Swings can provide a quick burst of joyful, playful energy.

Discussion

The objective of Arm Swings is for participants to have a different kind of encounter, now using physical contact as well as names and eye contact. Not everyone finds these tasks accessible or easy. For neurodivergent folks, people on the autism spectrum, for example, sustained eye contact or certain kinds of touch can be very challenging. Different cultures also shape expectations around eye contact. Greetings offer opportunities for both facilitators and participants to challenge their habits and to find alternatives that enable an exchange to take place, if in unconventional ways.

Play Theory: Caillois

Play theorist Roger Caillois identifies four modes of play found in sports, games, festivals, gambling, and children's games, among other activities: Agon (competition, contests), Alea (games of chance), Mimicry (imitation and role-playing), and Ilinx (like vertigo, a child spinning in circles) (1961, 23). At least two modes can be found in TPW's exercises, games, and performances. Dressing up and costuming, a form of mimicry, is a central part of TPW as performers experiment with self and persona. Arm Swings and One Sound One Movement are exercises that may induce Ilinx.

Warm-Ups: Physical and Vocal Training
Yoga Asanas and Breath Work

In TPW, warm-ups serve multiple purposes:

- When practiced daily for a significant period of time, they *train* the body and voice.
- As *preparation* for a workshop session or rehearsal, they focus attention and awaken energies, helping to shift away from habitual, everyday ways of being toward more receptive and responsive modes that benefit the work at hand.
- They attune performers to sensation and feeling, integrating inner and outer life. They are a way of *connecting* and *relating to others* through breath, sound, and movement.
- They have the potential to transform a collection of individuals into a group.

Among the warm-ups used in TPW, yoga *asanas* (postures) and *pranayama* (yoga breathing exercises designed to increase the flow of *prana*, or vital energy) are fundamental components. The asanas constitute a set score of movements and breathing that function as a daily ritual of entering the space, attuning to the group, and centering the self. These exercises are vital to creating a mind–body–breath connection in the performer that helps cultivate the awareness and presence critical for the workshop. These are done in sequences taught to Richard in 1971 by Tirumalai Krishnamacharya (1888–1989), the "father of modern yoga," in Madras (now Chennai), India (see Chapter 1, pp. 24–26).

I've always found yoga to be like a sailing ship. You're looking at an island out there, and then you reach it and you realize there's more sea on the other side. It's always infinite. So, in my own mind, my infinite challenge is to inhale forever—or exhale forever. (Interview with Richard Schechner, Dale, 15)

The "Richard yoga," as we often call it, is rhythmically somewhere between the slow pace of Iyengar yoga and the fluidity of a vinyasa practice. Krishnamacharya taught his pupils individually, including Iyengar, addressing their personal physical, mental, emotional, and spiritual imbalances. The sequence taught to Richard attended to his particular needs, age, and physical condition at the time. It is moderate enough to be beneficial to many, and Krishnamacharya gave Richard permission to teach this sequence to others. Although somewhat challenging for the average person, this yoga sequence does not require extreme flexibility or strength to execute. If practiced well, the series can even enhance flexibility and balance, strengthen and tone muscles, improve musculoskeletal organization and breathing, and calm the mind.

Yoga Asanas

We offer here a glimpse of the yoga done in TPW through Fernando Calzadilla's drawings (see Figures 4.3 and 4.4) and a brief description of one of its first movements, Rising Up On the Toes. The yoga sequence involves standing, sitting, and lying down poses. Most of the asanas in the sequence are organized within a rhythm of slow, steady movements coordinated with the breath. Every movement takes place on an inhale or an exhale, with a slight suspension of breath and dynamic stillness between the inhale and exhale. The intention is to lengthen the duration of both the inhale and exhale and to do them as evenly as possible. Generally, we teach by modeling the yoga series three asanas at a time, then the group repeats them. We show and do them in sections over several days: first the standing sequence, then the sitting sequence, and finally the lying down sequence. In this way, we can minimize verbal instruction by demonstrating the movements and the slow tempo of this particular approach. There are also inverted poses, such as the shoulder stand and the headstand, which may or may not be included in workshops depending on time constraints and participants' abilities. The first movement in the standing sequence is a small but challenging one.

Instructions: Rising Up on the Toes

1. Begin standing, feet together, arms at sides, chin dropped slightly toward chest. Eyes gaze toward the floor at about a 45-degree angle.
2. Inhale. Pause.

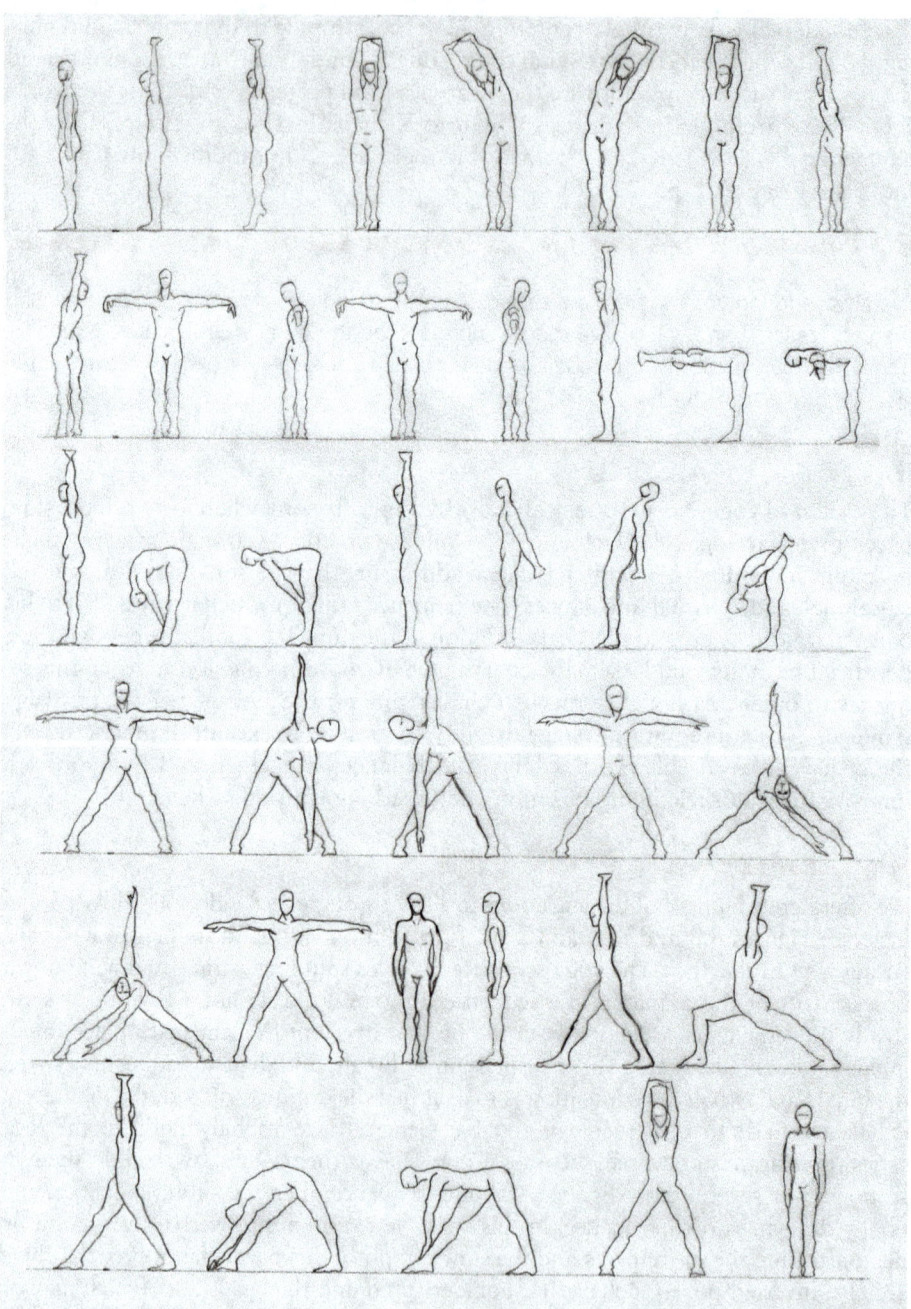

FIGURE 4.3 Yoga drawings by Fernando Calzadilla.

CHAPTER 4 ▸ Inside The Performance Workshop 97

FIGURE 4.4 Yoga drawings by Fernando Calzadilla.

3. Exhale while raising arms above head, then interlace the fingers, palms up. Pause.
4. Inhale. Pause.
5. Exhale while rising up onto the balls of feet. Pause.
6. Inhale while returning heels to floor. Pause.
7. Repeat (steps 4–6) two more times.

The integration of body, breath, and mind provided by the yoga serves as preparation for the creative process. The slowness and stillness integral to it are good preparation for Slow Motion Transformation exercises and other elements of the workshop that are physically rigorous yet contemplative. Richard often emphasized the idea of yoga as a "yoke" that links body to breath, breath to mind, and mind to the oneness of all things. Iyengar explains how this physical practice is aimed at developing in the practitioner "a poise of the soul which enables one to look at life in all its aspects evenly" (Iyengar 1979, 19).

Conveying performance knowledge and techniques orally is a core value of TPW. The yoga sequence is the single element of the workshop that Richard has done and taught in nearly the same way since he learned it over 50 years ago. When we teach the yoga, we always do so with an explanation of its origins and history, and with the caveat that TPW does not offer formal yoga instruction.[3]

Breath Work

Breath is the foundation of all TPW exercises, particularly Sound and Rasaboxes exercises. As part of the fundamental warm-up, we generally use four forms of breathing sequences, based on yoga pranayama. They are integrated before, during, and after the yoga asana sequence and vocal work:

- *Humming and Clearing* is a version of *bhastrika* pranayama modified and taught to us by Leeny Sack, who worked with Richard in The Performance Group in the 1970s (see Leeny Sack, pp. 34–35). It is good preparation for the yoga asanas, as it opens the nasal passages and deepens breathing. It also prepares for subsequent sounding exercises through gentle humming as well as resonator and pitch exploration. To practice it, maintain a continuous hum by buzzing the sound into the nose and mask of the face while massaging the nostrils, nose, and paranasal sinuses. When the mucus has been sufficiently warmed and liquefied by this process, exhale forcefully through the nose into a tissue held some distance from the nose, repeating this several times until the nasal passages are clear, and only then wiping the nose.
- *Ujjayi*, or Victorious Breath, is paired with the yoga asanas, each movement accompanied by a slow inhale or exhale. This breath is simultaneously energizing and calming. Ashtanga teacher John Scott describes it as a "soft sibilant sound made when breathing. Inhalations and exhalations are through the nose . . . the air is taken to the back of the throat where, by a subtle contraction of the muscles around the glottis, its flow is regulated. The quantity and length of inhalations and exhalations are equal, and it is this equality that sets the rhythm and meditative aspects" (Scott 2000, 18).
- *Nadi shodhana,* or Alternate Nostril Breathing, is a sequence in which breath is inhaled through one open nostril while the second is closed off with the

thumb, then exhaled through the second half-closed nostril, while the first is closed off with the fourth finger—alternating from one open nostril to the other half-closed nostril during each breath cycle. In between, each breath is suspended, at the top of each inhale, and the bottom of each exhale. The inhalations and exhalations can be done with counts as follows: inhale for 4; hold full for 8; exhale for 8 (through opposite half-closed nostril); hold empty for 4; then switch. When done for five minutes or more, it is calming and focusing. It can be used in preparation for work or in cooldowns from vigorous exercises.

- *Kapalabhati*, or Skull Shining Breath, is energizing and focusing and is used as a bridge between the yoga and resonator work. It is called Skull Shining Breath because forcing the air out through the nose creates the sensation of the breath brushing or "shining" the inside of the skull.

Instructions: Skull Shining Breath (*Kapalabhati*)

1. Sit or stand in a comfortable position that allows the feet or the sitz bones (ischial tuberosities) to feel equally balanced on the ground. If needed, these exercises can be done sitting in a chair.
2. Inhale and exhale slowly to release the breath.
3. Inhale again, then exhale sharply through the nose, mouth closed. This exhale is a quick and voluntary "pulse" from the belly. This is accomplished by having the intention of exhaling sharply through the nose. If you put a hand on the upper belly just between the ribs and navel area, you will feel a responsive muscle movement inward toward the spine with each exhale.
4. The inhale that follows is passive: like a sponge, the air will be replaced into the lungs naturally, as the belly releases.

Experiment with how little or how much effort it takes to accomplish the sharp exhale. Use enough pressure so that the air exits the nostrils audibly, but not so much that you are overly pumping the abdomen. With practice, you will find that it requires less and less effort to accomplish the strong exhale through the nose.

Instructions: Skull Shining Breath (*Kapalabhati*) in Sets

Once you have a feel for the active exhale and the restoration of the breath via passive inhalation, repeat several times, followed by a long, slow inhale and exhale. This can be done in several sets such as:

1. Inhale and exhale to slowly release the breath.
2. Inhale to prepare.
3. Ten short, quick exhales (the inhale happens passively after each).
4. Repeat steps 1–3 two to three times.
5. Inhale and exhale slowly to release the breath.

With practice, you can increase the number of exhalations in a set and/or increase the number of sets. This pattern becomes the breath "blueprint" used in Panting and Sounding with Resonators.

Clearing Breath

This breath and movement phrase is used in a few ways:

- To gather the group and "clear" in preparation for work at the start of a session.
- To clear and close the work at the end of a session.
- Groups or individuals can clear during or after psychophysical exercises.

Instructions

1. Stand with legs slightly apart, arms at sides.
2. Inhale through nose, exhale through mouth.
3. Inhale: raise arms laterally in a wide arc overhead.
4. Double exhale: drop the head and torso toward the floor, bending the knees as the arms swing closed (exhale), then swing open (exhale) across the front of lower legs.
5. Inhale: return to standing, moving both arms forward and up in parallel palms facing the ground. Let the hands float up, fingertips tracing the shape of a large ball in front of you. When the hands reach your chest:
6. Exhale: palms facing ground, gently press hands downward, passing an inch or two away from your torso, as knees soften.
7. Inhale: lengthening legs, gently and slowly release the arms back to your sides.
8. Exhale: come to stillness. This completes one cycle.
9. Repeat steps 3–8 for two more cycles.

Group Clearing Breath

Once everyone has learned the movement and breath phrases, we focus on the group/ensemble element of Clearing Breath.

1. Make a circle.
2. Anyone can initiate the first movement. Everyone joins.
3. When the group has completed three cycles, stand in stillness together for a moment or two without making any physical adjustments, then release.

The "together" of doing this exercise does not have to be perfect unison. Everyone should be able to respect both their own breath phrasing and their connection to the group.

Panting and Sounding with Resonators

"Panting," as we call it, provides a foundation for Sound exercises that build ensemble and explore individual and collective creativity. We begin by introducing Skull Shining Breath, then open-mouth panting with breath, followed by adding sound to the panting. Finally, we introduce resonator work. Richard adapted panting from world-renowned voice teacher Kristin Linklater (1936–2020), who taught voice work to members of The Performance Group in the 1970s. Her idea of "touch of sound," allows us to:

[S]hift the job of judging sound from the aural sense to the tactile and visual senses. As long as work on the voice includes listening to sounds to check their quality, there will be a conditioned split between the head and the heart, and emotion will be censored by intellect rather than shaped by it. By *touch* of sound I mean the feeling of vibrations in the body.... The impetus for sound is impulse, and the raw material is breath; in order to remove effort from the throat, it helps to imagine that sound, as well as breath, starts from the middle of the body.

(Linklater 2006, 65)

Panting with Sound

Initial panting exercises bridge breath work with sounding exercises. Panting with Sound happens in and out through the mouth like an animal panting, then adding vocal vibration (phonation) to the steady rhythm of the outgoing breath, as in Sounding with Resonators. Using the pulsation of breath in Skull Shining Breath, we begin to explore the "touch of sound" on each exhale, while allowing the throat to remain relaxed.

Instructions

1. Allow the mouth to open and, one exhale at a time, release a sound on each exhale. Start off with an "h" sound, so it most often comes out as a kind of unshaped "huh" (or schwa) sound. This is a short touch of sound, not a sigh.
2. Notice how the breath passively replaces itself on the inhale, like a sponge regaining its shape after being squeezed dry of liquid.
3. Increase the frequency of this sounding as you go, until you are doing a steady pant, "huh, huh, huh, huh" with passive inhales between.
4. Notice where the sound is resonating or vibrating in the body, particularly in the head, neck, and chest.
5. As you work, continue to reduce the physical effort you are using to pant, and alternate between breathing and sounding.

Sounding with Resonators

"Resonators" are specific areas of the body toward which we direct the breath, vibration, and sensation of sound, and/or from which the sound is felt or experienced. Richard's approach was greatly influenced by Grotowski's resonator work.

Grotowski: Resonators

The actor should be able to decipher all the problems of his body which are accessible to him. He should know how to direct the air to those parts of the body where sound can be created and amplified by a sort of resonator.... The actor who investigates closely the possibilities of his own organism discovers that the number of resonators is practically unlimited. He can exploit not only his chest, but also the back of his head (occiput), his nose, his teeth, his larynx, his belly, his spine, as well as a total resonator that encompasses the whole body and many others, some of which are still unknown to us (Grotowski 1968, 35–36).

In TPW, we start with four resonators in which we employ specific vowel sounds:

hah—chest/thoracic organs
hee—the mask of the face, nose, and paranasal sinuses particularly
huh—belly and pelvis
hoo—the head

After we have practiced accessing these four resonators individually, we do rounds of all four, alternating among them (this is done as part of each day's warm-up following the yoga). Next, we practice our focus and agility with a counting exercise: pant using each of the resonators in this order: hah, hee, huh, hoo, counting down from 16 of each, to 8 of each, to 4 of each, to 2 of each, and then back up—2, 4, 8, 16.

Although these sounds seem very simple, not everyone finds them easy to produce. We spend time discovering how and where to direct the sound, refining the vowel shapes, reducing tension, and focusing on sensing the vibration in the body. Detailed instructions may come with the introduction of each resonator, or after they have all been introduced and experienced by the group.

Group Sound Work

Open Sound

Setting Up for the Exercise

The whole group breaks up into smaller groups of at least three people, ideally four or five. There are a few different roles to play in the exercise, and each person in the group can play each role:

- The Base of Support
- The Sounder
- The Sounder's Assistants
  - 1 Player who shakes/vibrates sounder's diaphragm/abdomen/ribs
  - 1–2 Assistants who support the sounder's arms/legs (optional)

Instructions

Before you start, remember to do a boundaries check with your group (see Consent, pp. 83–84). Make accommodations and modifications accordingly.

1. The player who is the Base of Support (BoS) is on the ground on their hands and knees. Padding can be used if needed (such as a yoga mat or towel under the knees and/or hands).
2. The Sounder, helped by the others, lies face up along the spine of the BoS player, resting their head over, on, or near the BoS player's shoulder. The lower body drapes over the BoS player's pelvis. The feet may or may not touch the floor.
3. The Sounder, one breath at a time, sighs out one long sound, using a single open vowel sound such as "aaahhh," or "ooohhh," or "ooooo," etc. One breath, one sound. The Sounder allows for breath expansion on each inhale, then releases and sighs out another long open vowel sound. The Sounder repeats these open sounds for as long as they desire, or for as long as the BoS can sustain their position.

4. While the Sounder releases each open sound, the Player places their hands on the core of the Sounder's body to feel the breath and sound vibration, at least once or twice, before making anything happen.
5. The Player now gently but firmly presses/vibrates the diaphragm/upper abdomen area of the Sounder, sending waves of sound into the room. This is accomplished by fitting the palm/heel of a softly open hand just below where the ribs join together, soft fingers lengthening and draping toward the sounder's sternum or to one side of the ribs.
6. The player presses the palm/heel of their hand angling downwards and slightly toward the head, then releases quickly, repeating the action in varying rhythms so that it amplifies and further opens the sound the Sounder is making.
7. The Player releases the pressure and vibration, softening the hand and following the breath as the Sounder inhales.
8. Repeat steps 3–6.
9. The Player who is shaking/vibrating the sound may move to different areas of the Sounder's body, front of ribs, sides, navel area, just beneath the ribs, etc. Both hands can be used depending upon the area of contact.
10. (Optional) Once the Sounder and Player get going a bit, the other Assistants can take part supporting the weight of the Sounder's arms/legs. They can gently lengthen the arms and/or legs of the Sounder or add additional vibration through gentle shaking of the limbs.
11. Once everyone has played for a bit with Open Sound, they bring their exploration to a close.
12. They help the Sounder to stand while supporting the Sounder's head and neck area, and helping them to balance as they rise up from the back of the person who is the BoS.
13. The BoS recuperates by lengthening their back in child's pose, and/or by folding at the hips and hanging in a full spinal roll down over their bent legs while the other players offer gentle but quick surface massage and tapping of their legs and back to enhance circulation.
14. Offer feedback to one another about the experience using "I" statements.
15. Once finished, each player in the small group rotates into a new role and the next round of the exercise begins.

Discussion

Open Sound can be introduced into the workshop once the group has established a baseline of trust. The exercise also builds group trust through the contact and support needed to help each other do the exercise, and through the sometimes profound, or surprising, or fun discovery process of releasing big, unintentional sounds into the whole space.

Aiming and Passing Sound

In this exercise, we begin with using the four resonators previously learned to relate to the space and to each other in a creative, improvisatory way.

Instructions

1. Make a circle standing or seated on the floor.
2. Using one of the resonator/panting sounds, one player at a time, aim your sound toward an object or focal point in the space. Once you have made contact, use the sound to try to affect the thing you are aiming at.
3. Explore various resonators in various relationships to the space. How does the sound you are making affect you?
4. Find a few other focal points to send the sound, farther and/or nearer to your body, with or without changing the resonator.
5. As you explore, adjust the proximity, pitch, and intensity of the sound.
6. When you have completed your exploration, aim your sound toward another person in the group. They sound with you for a bit, joining you in both the sound and any physical expression you are making.
7. Drop out when they have begun to make the sound their own.
8. The person to whom you passed the sound now begins their own exploration from step 1.

Aiming and Passing Sound connects internal vibrations, the physical sensations of sound, with external relationships. The "touch of sound," rather than being focused inside your body, is now touching both you *and* something or someone else in the room.

Variation

This exercise can involve movement through space. If, for example, you see a spot on the wall on the other side of the room and wish to go closer, you can go there, and the group will follow. The group can support and reflect your sound by using audible breath in the vowel shape of the resonator you are using (but without vocal vibration). Wherever you stop, the group gathers around you, and again to the next place, and so on, until you pass your sound to the next person (see Step 5). In this version of the exercise, the shape of doing and partaking, sending and receiving, continually shifts, and the group becomes an active participant in the soloist's explorations.

One Sound

One Sound is a follow-no-leader exercise. The fundamental rule of these sound-based exercises is, "make the sound you hear." The objective is to discover collective creativity rather than the assertion of individual will. When participants truly surrender to making the sound they hear, the group's sound will transform on its own.

Instructions

Dim the lights in the room so that only silhouettes are visible.

1. Make a circle seated on the floor.
2. One person enters and sits cross-legged in the center of the circle and begins to pant, using one of the four resonator sounds (hah, hee, huh, or hoo). As long as that person is alone, they can change resonators or change the tempo, pitch, or volume.
3. Another enters the circle and sits back-to-back with the first person, making the sound they hear. As soon as there is more than one person, there is no leader.

FIGURE 4.5 Students in a Feedback and Discussion Circle. TPW at NYU.
Source: Photo courtesy of Ryan Jensen Photography, 2004.

4. Both now make the sound they hear, matching each other as identically as possible, in terms of rhythm, pitch, and quality.
5. Up to four people can enter, one at a time, to sit in the center back-to-back while sounding.
6. If you are left alone in the center, you may either come to silence ending the exercise, or continue or change the sound to keep the round going.
7. We play each round from silence to sound to silence.

Once participants become comfortable with One Sound, the four-person limit is released, and as many people as would like can join the center. Each person must find a way to make physical contact with at least one person in the center. It is possible for everyone to be in the center, or no one. All instructions are otherwise the same.

Rules of Follow-No-Leader in One Sound Exercises

- Make the sound you hear.
- There is no "original sound," or "right sound," only the sound you hear. Keep in mind that "the sound you hear" may also be a cough, a laugh, or any sound in the space.
- The only time you can "be creative" or change the sound at will is when alone in the center.
- You may exit at any time for any reason. You may reenter at any time.
- When you become distracted, or when you become aware you have deliberately changed the sound, you must take yourself out of the center and rejoin the outer circle.
- Each round of the game begins and ends in silence. It may cycle from silence to sound to silence multiple times.

Discussion

Ideally, One Sound exercises are done for an extended period and in event time (see Time, pp. 85–86). You are encouraged to push your limits, to stay in the center longer than you think you can, to allow fatigue to become a creative force in the process. When fatigue, combined with the repetition of the sound, has taken over, individual boundaries blur, enabling participants to surrender to the group. This blurring of self and other allows the group to enter a state of flow and an altered state of consciousness a state Richard often refers to as a "light trance state" (see Flow, p. 107).

Another effect of One Sound exercises is the dilation of time. The exercise can go on for an hour or more, though is often perceived as having lasted only minutes. Over the course of multiple cycles, if you surrender to making the sound you hear and allow it to happen, the sound begins to transform on its own. There is a balance to be struck; often it takes multiple cycles of the exercise to achieve the *doing without deciding*—which is the objective of One Sound. If achieved, a shift in consciousness and somatic experience happens through "groupness," facilitated by the exercises.

In the early days of a workshop, One Sound is a key exercise to juxtapose with solo Performances of Self and Crossings because it dissolves individuated energy into group energy. One Sound builds the group connection necessary to support the vulnerable revelations of self those exercises evoke. It is also an important preparation for sound and chorus work in Rasaboxes.

One Sound One Movement

Using the same principles as One Sound, One Sound One Movement (OSOM) begins standing, using movement together with the Sounding with Resonators sounds (see pp. 101–102). Sound vibrations felt and transmitted through the body are a means for finding connection in the seated exercise. In the moving version, the rhythm of footfalls, the movement of the body, and the panting sounds become sources of unity.

Instructions

The lights are dimmed to focus on movement and sound.

1. Stand in a large circle, at the outer edges of the space.
2. One person starts running counterclockwise in a large inner circle, close to the edge of the space. With each footfall, they sound one of the resonators (hah, hee, huh, or hoo) in a panting rhythm. One step, one breath, one sound. It must be a light run or jog, not a walk or any other movement.
3. Another joins the first person. Now, both do the movement they see, and make the sound they hear. Take in as much detail as you can about what another person is doing with a soft focus, perceiving movement with your whole body.
4. More people join—as with One Sound, as many as four or five at first, until everyone has a good sense of how the exercise works.
5. The group moves in a single direction in a large circle, unless this changes as a natural result of following-no-leader.
6. Join and leave the group as often as you wish, clearing to the outer edges of the space when not moving with the group. Everyone may be moving and sounding, or only one person may be in the center.

7. One round of the exercise goes from silence and stillness (no one in the center), to sound and movement (one or more moving and sounding in the center), to silence and stillness (no one in the center).

Remember that this is a follow-no-leader exercise. Because in each round of One Sound One Movement the group travels through space in a single direction, it is easy to develop a "follow *the* leader" dynamic. One solution is to run backward or alongside others, so there is more of a sense of moving and sounding *with* the whole group, rather than imitating another player's movement in overly rigid detail.

It takes longer to get into a groove while both sounding and moving together, so it is good to practice for 45 minutes to an hour the first time you do this exercise. Early in the exercise, people may tire quickly. Experiment with pushing through the fatigue rather than rejoining the outside circle. Often, people are surprised at how the energy of the group can propel them forward into a new state of consciousness, providing a burst of previously untapped energy and stamina.

Starting with a run in a big circle, one sound to each footfall, sets up an important limitation, from which all kinds of sound and movement will naturally arise. The variation and group creativity of One Sound One Movement will arise on its own. It can range in tempo from fast to very slow, but each new round should start at a moderate to rapid pace. Fatigue then plays even more of a role in transforming the sound and movement.

Flow

Flow, a core concept in both play and ritual, is a deeply pleasurable state defined by Hungarian-American psychologist and play theorist Mihaly Csikszentmihalyi as "the state in which people are so involved in an activity that nothing else seems to matter; the experience is so enjoyable that people will do it even at great cost, for the sheer sake of doing it" (Czikszentmihalyi 1975, 4–6). Flow occurs when our abilities are suited to the challenges of a particular activity. We can become so absorbed in such activities that "there is little distinction between self and environment, between stimulus and response, or between past, present and future" (36). Activities that induce such deep flow states, including extended group exercises in TPW, can produce a heightened sense of pleasure, presence, and awareness with a feeling of "total involvement" (43).

A shared sense of deep flow often occurs during rituals, festivals, or large group gatherings like music concerts. Victor Turner describes this phenomenon as *spontaneous communitas*, "an oceanic feeling of belonging, ecstasy, and total participation that many experience when ritualizing works by means of repetitive rhythms, sounds, and tones that effectively 'tune' to each other the left and right hemispheres of cerebral cortex" (1995, 20). In TPW, a feeling of communitas may occur when participants allow themselves to be completely absorbed in making "group sound" in One Sound exercises, for example. (See Victor Turner and Spontaneous Communitas, Chapter 1. pp. 30–31).

Crossings

Crossings I: Encounters

Crossings are a series of structured improvisations that invite encounters between players. Crossings I focuses on ordinary actions such as walking and looking, and simple nonverbal exchanges. Throughout these exercises, you are invited to examine gaps between private experience and public display, asking questions such as, "Which of my desires am I actually willing to perform?" and "What will be the consequences if I do?"

Instructions

Two parallel lines are taped down onto the floor, about 18 feet apart, and long enough to accommodate half the group on each side.

1. Choose a line of tape to stand behind, facing those on the opposite side.
2. Take a moment to regard those across from you. Sense the space between you—a space of potential in which anything could happen.
3. One person at a time, choose a destination behind the opposite line, walk to the other side, cross the line, then turn to face the line of players where you started.
4. You may cross alone or another person may initiate a cross from the opposite side.
5. If this happens, you will pass each other, stop, then turn to face each other.
6. Regard one another. Without speaking, receive one another by means of this looking and being looked at.
7. When you are ready to go, turn away from each other, complete your crossing, then turn to face the line of players across from you.
8. Another person begins to cross and the process repeats.
9. You may cross as often as you wish, but only two players can be crossing at the same time.

The exercise may end when it comes to stillness organically, or when stopped by facilitator.

EXPERIENCE

I am two steps into the space when someone from the opposite side begins to cross. We pass each other, then stop. I turn around and meet Y., a tall, sandy-haired man about half my age. We're standing about eight feet apart. I look into his eyes. I don't want him to feel as uncomfortable as I do, so I turn away quickly and finish my cross. My heart is pounding. I feel a bit embarrassed. I don't know why. A few more players cross and encounter one another. The atmosphere of the group seems a little stiff and nervous.

The facilitators pause the exercise for a moment and ask, "How's it going?" Someone volunteers "uncomfortable." Another "fun, but what's the point?" Another says, "I feel constricted." The facilitator replies, "So you have an extremely limited set of actions you can perform in this exercise. But here's the thing: The inner contents/experience are limitless. And what's more, no one except you will know what those inner experiences are. You don't have to tell or show anyone. Allow yourself to experience what is happening, that is enough. This can include your frustration with 'the rules.'" We resume the crossings. There's a shift in the quality of the encounters, an interesting tension that wasn't there before. It feels like those of us behind the lines are leaning in more to try to grasp what's happening between the two people in the center.

I cross the line, pass the other, then turn around. I am facing A. She regards me with a kind and open energy. I genuinely smile for a moment. A dozen thoughts float through my mind: What is she thinking? She reminds me of someone . . . who? I feel comfortable in her presence. I have no impulse to turn away. Time seems to have slowed down. I have a growing sense of "now-ness." I am more aware of my connection to A. and less aware of the eyes of the group. There is barely an expression on her face, but I notice an intensity in her eyes. It's hard to tell exactly why the exchange is over, but we both seem to sense that it is. We turn away from each other. I finish my cross without hanging onto my thoughts or feelings about the encounter.

Discussion

In the early stages of Crossings, we frequently pause for adjustments such as, "No acting or creating. Simply do the physical task." We challenge participants' notions of what "acting" should be, in order to get at the more fundamental task of being present with what arises. It is important that, in stripping down physical actions, the encounter is nevertheless fully, vitally alive inside the simple physical score.

We take time to discuss what "regarding" might mean. What does it mean to really *look* at another person? How does the phrase, "to hold someone in regard," affect how you look at and see someone?

It is tempting to look only into one another's eyes, and lock onto that gaze. As intense and intimate as it might be, eye contact is often a socially acceptable way of looking and being seen—varying from culture to culture and specific circumstances. In TPW, you are given permission to look, to really see and receive the whole person with your whole self. Once participants have had several rounds of practice, we invite them to really *look* at the other person's body, clothes. Notice every detail. Allow yourself to be observed and seen in this way. It doesn't have to be or appear to be comfortable. Whatever it brings up, either for you or the player being regarded, becomes the content for that instance of Crossings.

Variation: Names

After the group has thoroughly practiced crossing and encountering others without words, we introduce names as the first form of textual communication. During an encounter, you may:

- Offer your own name to the other.
- The other person may or may not offer their name in return.
- Allow a silence before and after the giving and receiving of each name.
- When you are ready to go, turn and finish the crossing.

After a few rounds of using your own name, continue the exercise using the other person's name. Each new element adds a new layer of complexity to the exchange. Who will say their name? Only one player? Both? How does saying either your own name or the other person's name inform the encounter in that particular moment? Notice how names can have a new significance within each encounter.

Variation: Renaming

- Try a new name for yourself. Instead of saying "Michele," for example, I could say, "Cleopatra."
- Another person may give you a new name. For example, instead of saying "Rachel," you say, "Sunshine." Rachel may accept or reject the name by repeating the name she wants to keep, for example: "Rachel" or "Sunshine."
- If you accept that new name, it remains your name for the duration of the exercise. You may rename yourself once. You may accept a new name from someone else once.
- At the end of a round of Crossings that involves renaming, a round of Names can be played, in which people say the name they will use for the remainder of the workshop.

Doing, Performing, Non-Matrixed, and Matrixed Acting

In the 1960s, Michael Kirby, a colleague of Richard's at NYU, and one of the first to theorize Happenings (see Chapter 1, p. 15), articulated distinctions between different kinds of performing that are still useful today. The differences between "matrixed" and "non-matrixed" performing he outlines in "Acting and Not-Acting," are particularly relevant for framing the continuum of performing we work with in TPW.

> To act means to feign, to simulate, to represent, to impersonate. As Happenings demonstrated, not all performing is acting. . . . The performers in Happenings generally tended to "be" nobody or nothing other than themselves [non-matrixed]. . . . There are numerous performances that do not use acting. Many, but by no means all, dance pieces would fall in this category. Several Far Eastern theatres make use of stage attendants such as the kurombo and koken of Kabuki. These attendants move props into position and remove them, help with onstage costume changes, and even serve tea to the actors. Their dress distinguishes them from the actors, and they are not included in the informational structures of the narrative. . . . Extras, who do nothing but walk and stand in costume, are seen as "actors." Anyone merely walking across a stage containing a realistic setting might come to represent a person in that place—and perhaps, time—without doing anything we could distinguish as acting. . . . If the performer does something to simulate, represent, impersonate, and so forth, he or she is acting. . . . Acting may be said to exist in the smallest and simplest action that involves pretense. . . . Acting becomes more complex [matrixed] as more and more elements are incorporated into the pretense. It must be emphasized that the acting/not-acting scale is not intended to establish or suggest values. Objectively, all points on the scale are equally "good." It is only personal taste that prefers complex acting to simple acting, or non-matrixed performing to acting. The various degrees of representation and personification are "colors," so to speak, in the spectrum of human performance, artists may use whichever colors they prefer.
>
> (Kirby 1987, *A Formalist Theatre*, 3–4, 6–7, 10, 20)

In the Workshop, we explore the full range of these possibilities, from framing everyday behavior as performance to performing "as oneself;" from taking on personas to inhabiting fully formed performance worlds that bring in the matrices of character, story, setting, and so on.

Leeny Sack's (see Chapter 1, pp. 34–35) mantra, "Everything is content," is useful because it allows us to relax artificial boundaries about what we think are "appropriate" thoughts, feelings, and impulses. Knowing we will not express or act on those impulses (in the first phases of the exercise), we are free to let ourselves play, to open our awareness to many possibilities. Another Crossing, a moment later, even involving the same people, may be completely different. As Richard often says, "create nothing, deny nothing." Full engagement in the present moment *is* the drama.

It is important that those regarding from behind the lines "hold the space," that is, activate the space for those crossing, giving the crossers their full attention. Avoid the temptation to put your hands in your pockets, cross your arms, or do anything else that communicates dropping out or losing energy and focus. Even while standing behind the line, you are performing.

Watching

Throughout the workshop, we explore multiple ways of watching and seeing, and being watched and seen. One Sound, Crossings, and Rasaboxes specify designated performing and watching roles. Other exercises blur the lines between the two. There are times when watchers are watching other watchers. It is a mutually provocative relationship, between performers deciding what to reveal, or not, and spectators deciding not only what to watch, but what we want others to see us watching (or avoiding watching). We explore relationships between performance and spectatorship, sensitizing ourselves to the inner experience of watching and being watched. This invites us to confront social conventions and taboos. Becoming aware of the many ways one can watch and be watched leads to being inventive when composing performances, too. Where is the audience situated? Do they have total or only partial visual access to the performance? Do they see one another? Are there other senses involved?

Crossings II: Display

In Crossings II, we move from basic encounters, which focus on simply being present with one another, to exploring what arises when we bring desire and doing into the encounter: the desire to see and to be seen, and the desire to show and be shown specific parts of the body.

Instructions

1. Make a few crossings as before: crossing, passing each other, turning to face one another, and regarding each other without words.
2. Make a few crossings as before using *your own name* as the text of the encounter.
3. Make a few crossings as before using the *other person's name* as the text of the encounter.
4. Next, cross, pass each other, then turn to face and regard one another, as before.
5. Then, *show a part of your body to the other*. Your display of the body part is the invitation to look; do not point to it. The part of the body you show must be visible, not covered by clothing. For example, if I wish to display my forearm, I may have to roll up a long sleeve to reveal it.
6. The other person moves as close as necessary to see what you are showing. No touching.
7. When that showing and looking have come to completion, regard one another once again. There may or may not be a reciprocal showing.
8. Once the final regarding of one another has taken place, both turn away and cross out.

EXPERIENCE

I start my cross and J. crosses from the other side. We turn, meet, and regard each other for a moment. We have been asked to resist the temptation to plan what we will show before we meet face to face. I wonder what J. will show? I have the impulse to show him my knee. I roll up my pants leg and uncover my left knee. I point my foot, toes on the floor for balance, and bend my knee toward him. I look into J.'s eyes. He smiles, taking a few steps closer to observe my knee. I allow him to do so. I watch him looking, wondering what he is noticing. Then I cover my knee again. J. stands up and we regard one another. I don't know if he will show me anything. When I am about to turn around, J. holds up his hair and turns around to reveal the nape of his neck. I take a few steps in so that I can see the details of what he is showing. I notice the topography of his skin, short fine hair sprouting out beneath his long mane of black hair. I observe the length and strength of his neck. I feel a kind of privilege in being allowed to look at something that seems so vulnerable, a hidden area except for those close with J. He lowers his hair and turns to face me again. We regard one another. We turn away and cross out.

Nakedness

Training and productions of The Performance Group sometimes involved full or partial nakedness, starting with *Dionysus in 69* in 1968. As TPW took shape as an independent entity, and the culture changed moving out of the 1970s into the 1980s, Richard gradually focused the exploration of partial dressing and total undressing within Crossings exercises. Sometimes Slow Motion Transformation includes the option for full exchanges of clothing between two people (see p. 130). As Richard wrote:

> I have explored nakedness in training and performance from the limited perspective of the middle phase of the cycle: undressing-naked-dressing. No TPG exercise or theater piece has ever presented all the performers naked throughout. So nakedness in the TPG context means undressing, doing something, and dressing. I admit a fascination for the exchange of clothes, for disrobing and re-robing again as another. When a person puts on someone else's clothes, a change occurs. I want to explore the way people display themselves.
>
> (1994, 90–91)

Literal, physical nakedness in TPW is never required. Facilitators must make appropriate decisions about whether or not to include the option of undressing as part of the vocabulary of performative actions available in specific exercises. In working with undergraduates, for example, it would be inappropriate to introduce nakedness. It is possible to explore "the exchange of clothes" and "the way people display themselves" without it. In any case, any performer's decision to undress, and the degree to which they do so, is their own. There is likewise no censorship of physical nakedness in the performances participants bring to the workshop.

In the "Nakedness" chapter in *Environmental Theater*, Richard notes:

> Nakedness reverberates in apparently contradictory directions. A naked baby, a naked corpse, a naked person asleep. A naked prisoner running a gauntlet of truncheon-wielding concentration-camp guards. Dreams of being naked alone among a crowd of the dressed. Naked and seductive; hundreds of naked people sunning on a Vancouver beach; films of naked lovers; pornography. Medical films. From innocence and helplessness to vulnerability and the inability to defend oneself to confusing images combining vulnerability and sadomasochism. From eroticism to clinical detachment. Also nakedness implies a public event: To be naked with no one watching is to adumbrate a process that needs another's acknowledgement. Nakedness is a social condition.
>
> (1994, 87–88)

Exercises such as Slow Motion Crossings are as much about the subjective experience of the performer as they are about performing. In that sense, the invitation to experiment with different states of dress and undress can be liberating. In exercises involving the display of parts of the body, or even the whole body naked, part of what we are exploring is the question, what is real nakedness? What is it to see and be seen by another? And what is at stake in wanting and expressing the desire to see others in their nakedness?

Crossings III: Desires

In the first phases of Crossings, the focus is on the other person as they are, on observing their physical and energetic presence. In Crossings III, we are deliberately opening the door to personal associations, projections, and fantasies—allowing them to arise in a way that is not planned or preconceived. They come into being during the encounter, in the present moment. We work with them as internal, unexpressed thoughts and impulses, then as outer expressions. We begin to explore what risks we are willing to take in relation to another person, and the consequences of taking them, or not taking them. What might be gained or lost through expression, action, and self-censorship?

Instructions
Part I: The Thought in Your Head

1. Cross as before and then, within an encounter, let a desire arise: something you want to *do to* or *do with* the other person, or something you want them to *do to* or *do with you*.
2. Allow this desire to take the form of words. Think the desire to yourself, for example, "I want you to do cartwheels across the floor"—or any other desire, however extreme—without speaking it aloud.
3. Make eye contact with the other person, energetically transmitting your desire without words or action.
4. When each has had a chance to connect and project their desire, turn and cross out.

Part II: Mouthing Desire
Invisible

Same as above, but now, for step 2, instead of forming the sentence only in your head, silently mouth the sentence of that desire while using a hand to cover your mouth, so that you can feel the shapes your mouth is making in your silent speech, but the other player cannot lipread it. Observe what happens—to you, to your partner—when you both expose yet conceal your desire.

Visible

Same as above, but now, for step 2, instead of concealing the silent mouthing of your desire, allow the other player to see your silent speaking. Observe what happens—to you, to your partner—when you expose your desire in this way.

Part III: Whispering

1. Cross and let a desire arise within the encounter.
2. One at a time, cup your hand around your mouth and *whisper* the desire in the other's ear. Do not let anyone else in the group hear you.
3. Your partner may fulfill your desire or not. To refuse, silently shake your head "no."
4. When the exchange is complete, cross out.

EXPERIENCE

The stakes feel a lot higher when we are invited to whisper our desires. I notice that I edit or censor my own desires, even when no one knows or will ever know what I am thinking or soundlessly saying. I want to challenge myself to really connect with someone in the encounter and allow myself to open to whatever occurs to me. Will the other person do what I ask of them or think it is crazy? If they ask me something that I refuse to do, will they think I don't want to play?

I begin my crossing and S. crosses from the other side. When I turn and face them, it takes a moment for a desire to form. I know they have a beautiful voice, particularly for traditional Irish folk tunes. In a whisper, I ask them to sing me one. They gently refuse, shaking their head "no." I am surprised because it is something they do well. I accept their refusal and continue to connect with S. They whisper in my ear, "make poses like a bodybuilder while singing 'Happy Birthday.'" I chuckle and fulfill their request, and have a lot of fun doing it. When I am finished, we reconnect for a moment, turn away, and cross out.

Discussion

Some of the things we say to participants:

- Observe what desire arises in the moment you turn to face the other person. Try not to anticipate what you might see or feel when the other person turns around, or what might arise in you as fantasy.
- Observe the gaps between what you think and what you express in language, and between what you express in language and what you actually do—no matter how boring, obscene, ridiculous, or inconsequential the desire may seem, observe any resistance that arises.
- Observe any self-judgment. Notice if and how you censor your desires or fantasies, if only within yourself.

Yes and No

The first time I participated in a workshop with Richard (1998) was the first time I was ever offered the "right of refusal," as it felt to me at the time, in a performance training workshop or rehearsal environment. In the early phases of Crossings, he said, "If you don't want to do something that I or another person asks you to do, silently shake your head 'no' and don't do it. A 'no' is as good as a 'yes.'"

In most of my previous actor training, and certainly in rehearsals for theatre productions, saying "no" was taboo. How did that come to be? For me, perhaps there is a connection to an oft-repeated principle when learning to improvise in groups: "always say yes." For example, in an improvisation when another actor offers you something like, "your pants are wet," instead of responding "no they aren't," and thereby denying the reality of the play world the other actor just created, I say instead, "yes, I was walking in the river. Lovely day for it . . ." Saying "yes" accepts the other actor's offer and builds upon it. Perhaps I am not the only actor who imported that principle into other contexts within the theatre until I arrived at the conclusion that I must always say "yes" in order to "play well with others" or to be a "good actor." In fact, the mainstream culture of theatre in the US sent me strong messages tantamount to "stay in your lane," and "don't voice resistance to those in the room with more power than you." I was taught never to refuse what was offered to me, either by another actor, fellow student, teacher, director, or costume designer.

So to play with the permission and possibility of refusal at any given moment—to observe and not play, or to drop out entirely—was a liberation. The invitation to rejoin the playing whenever desired was included in Richard's explicit guidelines. In addition to providing ways of saying "no" within exercises, space was given in TPW to express dissent, to challenge ideas, and to disagree. All these invitations were and still are built into the practices of TPW from the very first session.

By Paula Murray Cole

Performance of Self and Persona

Invitations to make performances are offered throughout TPW. Performances of Self invite participants to mine personal content for the creation of short solo performances. All of the work of TPW engages "self," but the following exercises focus on exploring the continuum of self–persona–character: Names, Performative Introductions, Crossings, Song of Self, Object Exercise, Animal Exercise, Slow Motion Transformation, and Rasaboxes.

Unlike traditional Stanislavsky-based actor training, rehearsal, and performance, performance compositions in TPW may never involve work on a role—that is, matrixed performance of a fictional character, a Juliet or Uncle Vanya (although these may be worked on, too) using the personal as a resource supporting a truthful performance of a character by means of "emotional memory" or similar techniques. Working with personal material draws on objects (articles of adornment, food, decorative or sacred things, everyday items), memories, past experiences, feelings—real or imagined—or skills (dancing, music making, drawing, roller skating—just about anything). A "persona," which in Latin means mask, is based on one or multiple identities of the performer. Personas may arise at any moment, from any element: a personal story, a vocal quality, an object, a rasa, an historical figure, or a character in a drama. Helpful in thinking about making performances sourced on our "selves" is Richard's theory of "restored behavior."

Restoration of Behavior

Restored behavior is living behavior treated as a film director treats a strip of film. These strips of behavior can be rearranged or reconstructed; they are independent of the causal systems (personal, social, political, technological, etc.) that brought them into existence. They have a life of their own. The original "truth" or "source" of the behavior may not be known, or may be lost, ignored, or contradicted—even while that truth or source is being honored. . . . Restored behavior can be of long duration as in some rituals or of short duration as in fleeting gestures such as waving goodbye. . . . Restored behaviors are "twice-behaved behaviors," behaviors behaved from the second to the nth time; never for the first time.

Restored behavior is the key process of every kind of performing: in everyday life, in healing, in ritual, in play and sports, and in the arts. Restored behavior is "out there," separate from "me." Restored behavior is "me behaving as if I were someone else," or "as I am told to do," or "as I have learned." But even if I feel myself wholly to be myself, acting independently and displaying originality, only a little investigating reveals that the units of behavior that comprise "me" were not invented by "me." . . . Most performances, in daily life and otherwise, do not have a single author. Rituals, games, and the performances of everyday life are authored by the collective "tradition," a grand "anonymous." Individuals credited with inventing rituals or games are actually synthesizers, recombiners, compilers, and/or editors of already practiced actions.

In fact, all behavior is restored behavior because all behavior consists of recombining bits of previously behaved behaviors. Mostly people aren't aware that they are doing any such thing. People just "live life." . . . Restored behavior can be actions marked off by the aesthetic conventions of theatre, dance, and music. Restored behavior can be actions reified into "etiquette," or diplomatic "protocol." Restored behavior can be a boy not shedding tears when jagged leaves slice the inside of his nostrils during a Papua New Guinea initiation; or the formality of a bride and groom during their wedding ceremony. The myriad known-beforehand actions of life vary enormously from culture to culture and circumstance to circumstance. Because it is marked, framed, and separate, restored behavior can be worked on, recalled, played with, rehearsed, made into something else, transmitted, and transformed (Schechner 2020, 10).

Song of Self

Song of Self (or Performance of Self) is often the first performance composition assignment. Instructions are given with little time to prepare, usually just one session before the performance is shared. The idea is to be as spontaneous as possible.

Instructions
1. Create a Song of Self—a brief performance that expresses some aspect of "you" that is no longer than three minutes.

2. Use any genre or framework to structure your performance score: ritual, game, story, drama, song, dance, to name several possibilities.
3. Use any medium: movement, music, text, or visual elements.
4. You may use objects and/or dress (articles of adornment).
5. You may use songs or music, but nothing prerecorded.
6. Make deliberate choices about your use of space.
7. Make deliberate choices about your relationship to the audience.

These performances may highlight aspects of identity, as well as the desires, fears, and quirks of each person in the group. They may reveal and/or conceal personal and cultural histories, artifacts, and specific performance skills. Once performed, they begin to create an inventory of shared experiences that the group can draw upon for future performance compositions. Elements of form and content combine, giving rise to an emergent performance culture unique to each workshop group.

What is a Performance Score?

A performance score is a skeleton, map, or frame that gives a performance its structure. It may vary from open instructions such as "go to a field, spend two hours there . . ." to something precise like a musical score in which every detail is predetermined. It can be as simple as a few gestures or as elaborate as a complex choreography. It can last less than one minute or extend across several years. It may be partly or entirely improvised. Its overall shape is determined by these and other choices that give it structure. Your score is not your performance; it is more like a set of instructions. The concept of "score" is useful for TPW because it does not depend on a script or text; it focuses on the structuring of performance itself.

Notes from Paula Murray Cole's TPW Journal 1998

Song of Self, Round #1

I struggled with this assignment. I wrote down ideas in my journal, a kind of poetic rumination on the topic. Then I spoke with another participant about our mutual anxiety of performing "the self." Ideas for what I considered a "performance" were not satisfying to me. Here's what I wrote in my journal after the performance:

> I gathered the group in a circle, dimmed the lights to a glow and asked them to turn their backs. I told them that making a "Song of Self" was difficult for me because I spend so much time speaking others' words, singing others' songs and "performing." I said what I wanted to do was to stand in silence. I did so. I was shaking nervously even at the prospect of this silent *unsong*. I closed my

eyes. I tried to ground my overly charged energy by putting my hands in prayer on my forehead with feet together. I tuned into the energy of the room. The others sat or stood in silence and stillness. I was still too, but I was not calm on the inside. After a while and before I was ready to do so, I stopped the performance. I admitted that it was an arbitrary ending—the scene could have gone on much longer.

Here are my observations about others' performances of Song of Self, Round #1:

- W. had two volunteers wrap her body in a long bolt of blue cloth, mummy-style, while singing a gorgeous sad song in Spanish. She asked us to "warn" her if we felt the urge to do so—no one did. She asked us to quietly say her name when the song finished. She asked only the women to do this, although Richard joined in too.
- J. made a corn-kernel homunculus as he sang, then shaman-like, "breathed life into it." Then he poured "blood" (ketchup) onto the kernels. Then he stopped.
- M. sang a song. Before she started, she asked us to think of our mothers, and to think about how we might feel if we had written a song like hers to our mother. It was a jazzy-bluesy love song to her mother. She had quite a powerful voice and the words seemed deeply felt.
- B. backlit himself and did three fragments of songs—the first songs he remembers learning, taught to him by his relatives.
- L. played the violin while we, as she requested, milled around the room and spoke about her.
- N. sang and taught us a song she sang to her son when he was young.
- G. recited a piece of doggerel she'd composed. It was sweet—she pleaded with us "not to hurt her" throughout.
- C. sang a child's song while doing gestures as if she were in agonizing pain.
- K. skipped around the room singing "I'm a very impressive person" to the tune of "I've Been Working on the Railroad." She escalated the drama by banging herself against the columns in the room while continuing to sing. She then stopped, sobbing behind one of the columns. She beckoned us to join her. We did so and she whispered twice, "I hate myself."
- A. behaved as a bird in a cage.
- D. told a story in Mandarin. He instructed us to act out all the parts: trees, a river, a bridge, birds. The song he sang seemed happy. He chased clouds while he sang but never caught one.

Song of Self, Round #2

Richard asked us to refine the Song of Self exercise for Wednesday night. We could change it in one of three ways:

1. Make it more personal.
2. Tell a story about a specific birthday.

> 3. Borrow someone else's [performance] and make it your own. If you choose to do this, ask permission and perhaps even get assistance from the person from whom you are borrowing.
>
> When the time came to perform our revised Songs of Self, Richard introduced a new element: the "preferred audience." He limited us to a choice of one to three people. Considering this option, I chose to limit my audience to only children because I am a twin. There were two in the group: M. and G. The rest of the group was told to hide but be voyeurs.
>
> I made an audio recording about my most recent birthday. I read cards from my mom, dad, two friends, and my twin sister. To develop this performance, I had to go out to the garbage to find the cards I had recently discarded. Luckily, I found them, and I brought the dress my sister had sent as a present. The cards led directly to a discussion of my twin and our co-mutual identity. I explained at the end the significance of using my voice on the recording: it is the way I felt we are most alike: the sound of our voices. Which I hate. Not hers, but my own. But her voice sounds like mine. Hmmm . . .
>
> In the feedback afterward, Richard suggested that my piece needed more formalization. His comments centered on his observation of "absence" in the contents of what I had presented. He recognized the cards and dress represented people who were absent. I need to work harder to find my subjective responses and *formalize* them.

Play and the Self: D.W. Winnicott

For British psychoanalyst and pediatrician D.W. Winnicott (1896–1971), play is at the center of both individual human development and the development of culture. His approach to therapy was based on the importance of play for a healthy self. Winnicott claimed that "[it] is in playing and only in playing that the individual child or adult is able to be creative and to use the whole personality, and it is only in being creative that the individual discovers the self" (Winnicott 1971, 54). Winnicott theorized the "transitional object," which from early infancy occupies the space between mother and child. The first transitional object is the mother's breast; and then things such as a baby blanket or favorite toy. The transitional object exists in a realm that is "not me, but not not me." This state of being is the basis for playing—and all art, including performance. For Schechner's take on Winnicott and the "not not," see pp. 128–129.

Performative Responses

In traditional western theatrical contexts, applause (or boos), laughter, or rapt silent attention are expected responses to a performance. Conventions determine whether some responses are welcomed only at the end of an act or a play, a movement, or a symphony. More often than not, in TPW we ask the group not to applaud—or visibly react in any way—as we move from one performance to the next. Instead, the performative response invites us to ask, "what if we responded to a performance with a performance?" Participants are invited to make space after and between performances for these kinds of acts to occur.

A performative response is an improvisation, a spontaneous eruption or creative addition, that is expressed by one or more participants, following any performance or exercise. It can be as small as a simple gesture, or as large as a song in which everyone participates. It might engage or repeat elements of the performance to which it is responding. There may be a single response, or, one response may ignite another, and then another. Here is an example based on a performative response that happened in a past TPW:

A Song of Self involved a large quantity of small stones the performer brought from their home country, arranged in a particular manner on the floor while they told a story from their childhood. Someone in the group responded to this performance by arranging the stones in a different pattern. Another did an elaborate dance around this arrangement of stones. Another discovered that the stones were on the bottom of the ocean, and became a deep-sea diver collecting them, using one hand as a breathing mask while vocalizing the sound of an oxygen tank accompanying her, and the other hand like a salvage grab to pick up each stone. Others caught on and joined in to collect rocks in the same way until the space was cleared, ready for the next Song of Self to begin.

There is no mandate to have performative responses. In fact, there may be no performative responses to anything for an entire workshop.

Object Exercise

Instructions

Participants are instructed to bring an object of personal significance to the workshop for the next session, and to have their objects available at the edges of the room until the exercise begins.

1. Display the objects in the space. How does the object want to be displayed? Consider all options. They can be placed on the floor, hung from the walls—the only requirement is that they be visible.
2. Once all the objects have been displayed, walk around in silence regarding the objects without touching them. Notice which objects you are drawn to.
3. Once everyone has seen all the objects, identify for the group any object that should be touched and handled only by you.
4. Sit or stand somewhere in the space to begin the exercise.
5. You may perform the "story" of up to two objects. This may be in the form of movement, song, words, or a game, for example. Be specific about how the group is arranged in the space and in relation to the object and to you. The objects you select may or may not be yours. Your stories of the objects may or may not be "true."
6. Performances will flow from one to the next, without applause, and without a predetermined order.
7. The exercise ends when no one moves or shifts in the direction of an object.

As the objects are taken up and their stories told, by both their real and fictional owners, unique personas, and sometimes hidden aspects of participants emerge in the moment of doing. This exercise is one way of introducing play with truth and lies, fact and fiction.

Songs

Singing and sharing songs has always been an integral part of TPW. Participants are invited to bring songs from their own personal lives, cultures, and performance traditions to share with the group. We have learned songs in Mandarin, Turkish, Hebrew, Spanish, Portuguese, English, and other languages. Facilitators often teach rounds, which enable the group to explore harmony and movement while singing together. We have used songs as part of the vocal warm-up, as ensemble-building exercises, and for transitions between exercises and cooldowns.

Animal Exercise

Unlike other animal exercises that have been developed in actor training pedagogies, in this exercise, the "animal" is not an imitation of animal movement—"moving like a monkey" or "moving like a cat," for example. The animal that emerges during this exercise is an expression of you, *the performer*. You discover your inner animal's nature—its likes, desires, drives, and how it gets what it wants. By moving on hands and feet, one's relationship to the floor and to others shifts—intensifying the senses of smell, taste, hearing, touch, and the kinesthetic sense. Engaging the senses as animal versions of ourselves, we experience bodily and social organization emerging in a visceral way.

Instructions

The day before, each person in the group is asked to bring one serving of their favorite fruit for the next workshop session. At the start of the session before warm-ups, fruit is prepared by cutting it into bite-sized morsels and laying it out on a large piece of paper, plastic, or tarp. The facilitator then puts it out of sight. Designated areas for interaction or behavior are taped onto the floor (see step 5). For the exercise, the lights are dimmed to almost total darkness so that the animals rely more on senses of smell, taste, touch, and sound.

1. Begin One Sound One Movement. Consciously increase the speed and intensity as you go.
2. At the highest point of intensity/fatigue, the group collapses on the floor.
3. Take a moment to catch your breath, then move into a fetal position (lying on your side with knees bent toward your middle) to start the next phase.

Lights black out. The lights slowly come up so that the space is still dark and only silhouettes are visible. Your animal awakens.

4. First, explore the space with your eyes closed. Use whole-body sensing—your snout, what you smell and taste, what you hear—to identify and relate to the space, objects, and other animals. Move onto your hands and feet (not knees) on the ground if able, or modify the movement that is available to you, activating as many parts of your "animal self" as you can. Little by little, begin opening your eyes.
5. Explore the five demarcated spaces taped onto the floor throughout the room. There are three dens (only one animal can be in a den at a time), and a larger fourth space for friendly interaction between animals through smelling, tasting, and making sound. The fifth is a drop-out space, located on the periphery of the entire room. Go there when you want to leave the exercise. Come back when you want to rejoin. The space between these five demarcated areas is "wild."

After some exploration, the facilitator slides the cut fruit into the center of the space.

6. There is food available now. Use smell rather than touch to select the food. Pick it up directly with your mouth and teeth, no hands. How does the food affect your animal? Your animal's relationship to the other animals? Explore the possibilities for action, interaction, and rest.
7. An optional phase of the exercise can include engaging the rasas, if Rasaboxes has been introduced. The eight basic rasas can be applied to eating, moving, and interacting with other animals (see below).

As the lights begin to brighten, the exercise comes to a close.

8. Go to the "drop-out space" *as your animal*, then gradually come back to yourself. When all are in the drop-out space, each player takes a moment to regard the animal world they have left behind (see Figure 4.6).

Lights dim to black.

Once basic group trust has been established by prerequisite exercises, the Animal Exercise can help you to discover new and deeper layers of relationship to self and other. It also organizes the body around the gut (enteric nervous system) and spine, the sense of smell and taste, and offers the opportunity to explore another layer of identity: the "animal me."

A fruitful way of exploring rasa in this exercise is to allow the rasic flavors to arise organically, moment-to-moment. How does your animal experience and express them and in what situation? The animals can be brought onto the rasaboxes grid, which can provide a deeper level of embodiment and connection, particularly for relating, chorus work, and other more complex Rasaboxes exercises. In shorter workshops, abbreviated versions of this exercise can help to connect body and senses in a more animal way.

FIGURE 4.6 After Animal Exercise. TPW at NYU.
Source: Photo courtesy of Michele Minnick, 2016.

Group Performances

Once the first solo performances, such as Song of Self, have been shared, that material along with other shared vocabulary in the workshop can be used as the basis for the creation of group compositions. Traditionally, we have stuck with Richard's motto of "building the house with the bricks you've got"—in this case, reusing and recycling the material produced, the doings and interactions of the workshop itself. This aligns with the principle that "everything is performance" (see p. 82). For example, two or more participants may combine elements of their Songs of Self to make new iterations. We do invite participants to introduce classic texts, myths, or other sources people may be familiar with, to be combined with other material. Once Rasaboxes has been introduced, rasas can be folded into working on text, character, and so on. We encourage exploration of different uses of space, different functions of performance (games, rituals, confessions, and so on), and different configurations and relationships with the audience. The progression of composition assignments often moves from solo to duet to group work, assigning longer times to each, ranging from 1–3 minutes to 5–10 minutes.

Creating Performance Worlds

FIGURE 4.7 Crossing the line in Slow Motion. Rasaboxes Summer Intensive, Dell'Arte International School of Physical Theatre.

Source: Photo courtesy of Rachel Bowditch, 2009.

Crossings IV: Slow Motion

Doing a Slow Motion Crossing is the first level of building a performance world, combining multiple elements of the workshop. Just as in Crossings I–III, conflict and drama arise out of the basic elements of desire, acceptance, consent, and refusal. Slow motion is movement so slow that it appears as if no one is moving—if one were to look away and look back a minute later, the performers may have advanced a millimeter or so. The physical and psychological challenges of moving continuously in super slow motion intensify everything that happens—encounters, discoveries, and disappointments. Moving very slowly widens the gap between our desires, impulses, and the actions they give rise to. This intensity may be perceived more by the doers than the watchers. In that sense, although it has an elaborate performance score, much of what "happens" in Slow Motion Crossings happens internally.

Preparation

Practice moving in super slow motion with the group at least a day before embarking on Slow Motion Crossings. Getting used to moving this slowly takes practice, as ordinary movements, such as level changes (from crawling to standing, for example), become very challenging. Invariably, we also find that when first asked to move in super slow motion, people have very different interpretations of what this means. Practice can attune your speed to the speed of others. Do at least 20 minutes of super slow motion in a Crossings context, or in open space before doing Crossing IV.

Setting Up the Crossing Space

Slow motion exercises require a bit more set-up than earlier versions of Crossings.

- Facilitators prepare the space by taping out a large, rectangular "crossing box."
- Two microphones are set up in two corners of this box, taping off each corner with just enough space for one person and the microphone stand inside it.

- Ample space is reserved around the periphery of the crossing box to allow players to periodically break out of the Slow Motion Crossing to run and pant, doing One Sound One Movement (see Figure 4.8).
- A watching box is taped out along one side of the crossing box, allowing facilitators as well as participants to watch the performance.

Instructions

Once the space is set up, the instructions are given to participants and repeated at least once before the exercise begins.

1. As in Crossings I–III, take your place behind one of the two shorter sides of the rectangle.
2. Notice who is across from you, who is next to you.
3. Look at the space. Plan your route across, from one side to the other without backtracking, by creating a map in your mind's eye—your performance score (see p. 118). Incorporate your desires to either encounter or avoid others—and imagine what might happen if you meet.
4. You will cross the space only once. Everyone must finish *at the same time*.
5. This crossing will take place in super slow motion. You have several opportunities to break out of super slow motion. When you do break out, you may (see Figure 4.8):
   a. Run around the outside of the Slow Motion Crossing Box, panting and repeating one of the four resonators each time your foot hits the floor. If anyone is already running and panting, join using the same resonator and in the same rhythm, doing One Sound One Movement.

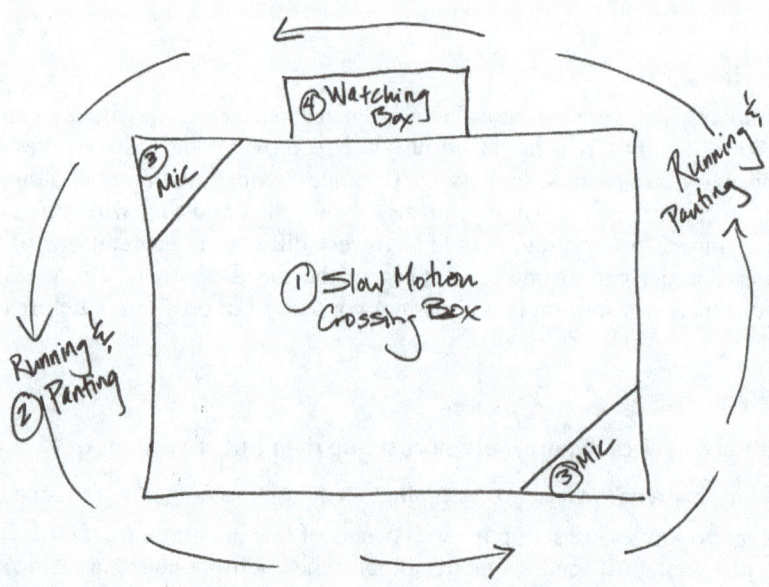

FIGURE 4.8 Slow Motion Crossing diagram by Michele Minnick.

b. Go to a microphone to:
   - Sing a song.
   - Tell a birthday story, either your first (which is likely a story that was told to you), or your most recent birthday. Or describe a dream—either one you had last night, or a recurring dream.
   - Narrate in great detail, in present tense, what a particular performer is doing. For example, "Rachel is reaching down toward Paula, who is crouched on the floor. Her fingers are opening very, very slowly. She is reaching toward the ribbon in Paula's hair." And so on.
c. Go to the watching box (see Figure 4.8) to observe the performance with the facilitators, but only through "binoculars" made with your hands, focusing on small areas of the interaction happening in the crossing space.

6. Once we begin, the exercise will run its course without interruption.

A Slow Motion Crossing exercise can end organically in event time—when everyone has crossed the opposite line from where they started, no matter the hour—or facilitators can freeze the players and ask them to move to a position one or two steps before crossing the line, then unfreeze, to complete the final crossing in slow motion.

Discussion

This introduction to Slow Motion Crossings offers the group the opportunity to get acquainted with its basic structure, the technical challenges of moving in slow

FIGURE 4.9 Shay Webster in a Slow Motion Crossing. Arizona State University.
Source: Photo courtesy of Rachel Bowditch, 2012.

motion, and the need to attune to one's own journey with that which is shared by the group. The extreme slowness allows participants to move between deep absorption in their own drama and the larger performance of which it is a part. The watching box allows people to get an overall view of the performance as it unfolds. From the vantage points at the microphones, one can both perform and observe what is happening in all locations within the exercise.

Crossings V: Slow Motion Transformation

Slow Motion Transformation exercises build upon Crossings IV, with the addition of personas and characters, and fleshing out more complex performance worlds. Instructions for dressing are given to participants, often in phrases like, "Dress to kill," or "Dress for your last day on earth," or, after working with Rasaboxes, "Dress as a rasa." The group is instructed to bring a complete change of clothing with them, including underwear, shoes, makeup, and whatever else. Participants are encouraged to create their attire from whatever they have at hand. For example, for a TPW at NYU, Rachel did not have many belongings with her, so for this exercise she created a fancy hoop skirt, corset, and headdress—all constructed with tape and pages from the *New York Times*. This was a far more creative and interesting process than if she had bought something at a costume shop—and it cost her less than five dollars. Outfits made of materials other than clothing may need considerable time for assembly. Dressing assignments should be given a few days in advance, to give performers time to assemble their materials.

Much of what occurs in TPW is non-matrixed performing (see Kirby, pp. 110–111). Slow Motion Crossings IV and V introduce more complexity, or more matrixed performances, as the encounters bring out elements of persona, even character. Individuals bring their own stories into the world, or perhaps stories emerge from the dressing, or during the exercise. Allegiances or conflicts may arise during a crossing, but they are not rooted in a shared narrative or pre-existing dramatic structure, as they would be in a play.

Dressing is one point of entry into persona. Just as yoga and Rasaboxes begin with the physical, external shape of the body, participants are creating both internal and external realities from the outside in. Crossings that involve partial or total exchanges of clothing involve shifts and transformations of persona (see Nakedness, p. 113).

Self, Persona, Character

The experience of performing a persona in Slow Motion Crossing makes visible, in the Brechtian sense, the separation between actor/self and character/persona. Richard explains:

> In theatre, actors onstage do more than pretend. The actors live a double negative. While performing, actors are not themselves, nor are they the characters. Theatrical role-playing takes place between "not me" and "not not me." The actress is not Ophelia, but she is not not Ophelia; the actress is not Paula Murray Cole, but she is not

not Paula Murray Cole. She performs in a highly charged in-between liminal space-time. Spectators help by not reminding Cole who she "really is" in her ordinary life. But during the curtain call, they applaud Cole, not Ophelia. Or rather they applaud Cole's ability to perform Ophelia.

Of course, it's not so simple. Many actors train hard in order to believe in the actuality of whom and what they are representing. And from the mid-50s, happeners and performance artists have explored many different ways of performing themselves. But even someone so insistent on performing his own life as Spalding Gray (see Chapter 1, pp. 34–35) played a character called "Spalding," a persona who was a framed and edited version of the "real" Spalding. Gray developed his life-narratives by keeping journals and by tape recording early in-process performances of his monologues. Gray listened to the recordings and carefully edited his texts. By the time Gray performed a "finished" monologue, his apparently casual self-presentation was honed in every detail, including slips and "mistakes." The audience enjoyed "Spalding" as presented by Gray.

(Schechner 2020, 151–52)

The slow motion space is a liminal or liminoid (see pp. 29–31) space where there is a playful distance between self, persona, and character. Participants' desires, actions, and reactions can express, expand, move toward or away from the "me," the "not-me," and the "not-not-me." There is no directorial framework for what happens in this space; rather, the action is negotiated by the performers.

Slow Motion Transformation begins with two simultaneous activities: *Setting Up Dressing Corners*, which participants do, and *Setting Up the Crossing Space*, which facilitators do, helped by participants once they finish setting up their dressing corners.

Setting Up the Crossing Space

Use instructions 1–4 in *Setting Up the Crossing Space*, Crossings IV: Slow Motion Crossing (see pp. 125–128).

Additional breakout spaces for this exercise may include:

- In the center of the slow motion crossing box, a smaller box, large enough for two people, may be taped down for exchanging clothing with another player.
- Another smaller box may be added inside the slow motion crossing box for performing a rehearsed piece of behavior, or some other designated activity.
- A music box for playing musical instruments and singing can be set up outside the slow motion area.
- A slow motion eating box can be added, inside or outside the Crossing Box.

Setting Up Dressing Corners

- Each corner of the room is supplied with chairs, lighting, and at least one full-length mirror. These corners are your starting places for the exercise.

- Gather your things and, in silence, determine where in the room and with whom you want to dress. This is your home base, and the people there will be your affiliated tribe, kin, or gang.

Instructions: Dressing

1. You and your group decorate your corner; make it "home." This place represents both each of your individual identities and your identity as a group (see Figure 4.11).
2. You will dress yourselves and one another. Ask (non-verbally) for help if you need it. Help one another to become the most fabulous versions possible of your personas.
3. If you require privacy, a small corner behind a curtain is set up for that purpose. Or, if necessary, participants may use a nearby restroom to change some of their clothing. Do as much as you can/are comfortable with in your dressing area.
4. At any point during the dressing, a member of your group may wish to take a walk to see the other groups. They announce this aloud by saying, "Going on a walk!" Then your whole tribe takes a tour of the other groups' dressing corners. Wherever they are in their dressing process, everyone else in the space must take a soft freeze until the touring group returns to their own corner. When they do, everyone resumes their activities where they left off.
5. As in all Crossings, the actions described previously are done in silence. There is no talking or mouthing during any Slow Motion Transformation, except for in the spaces that have designated speaking or singing.

Instructions: Slow Motion Transformation

When everyone is dressed and ready, each group proceeds to one of the crossing lines. They will begin as a group, but each individual performer will plot their own course for the Slow Motion Transformation. The instructions for Slow Motion Crossings 1–5 (see Slow Motion Crossing, pp. 125–128) are given once before Dressing, and again when everyone is standing behind the crossing line, ready to begin (see Figure 4.12).

Additionally, you may include these activities among the breakout choices (see Figure 4.10):

- Perform a rehearsed piece of behavior inside the behavior box.
- Play your musical instrument or sing in the music box.
- Eat a morsel of food in the slow motion eating box.
- Two kinds of undressing and dressing:
  - Inside the center box of the Slow Motion Crossing space, participants may completely change clothing (down to undergarments or totally).
  - Alternately, participants may exchange one item of clothing anytime during their slow motion cross. This is done as a part of the relating that takes place in slow motion and must involve consent of all parties (see refusal in Crossings III p. 114; in Yes and No, pp. 115–116). Consent will also happen in slow motion.

Keep in mind throughout that this is an exercise in deep listening; although there may be moments of cacophony, overall, you are aiming for a symphony. At all times,

CHAPTER 4 ▸ Inside The Performance Workshop

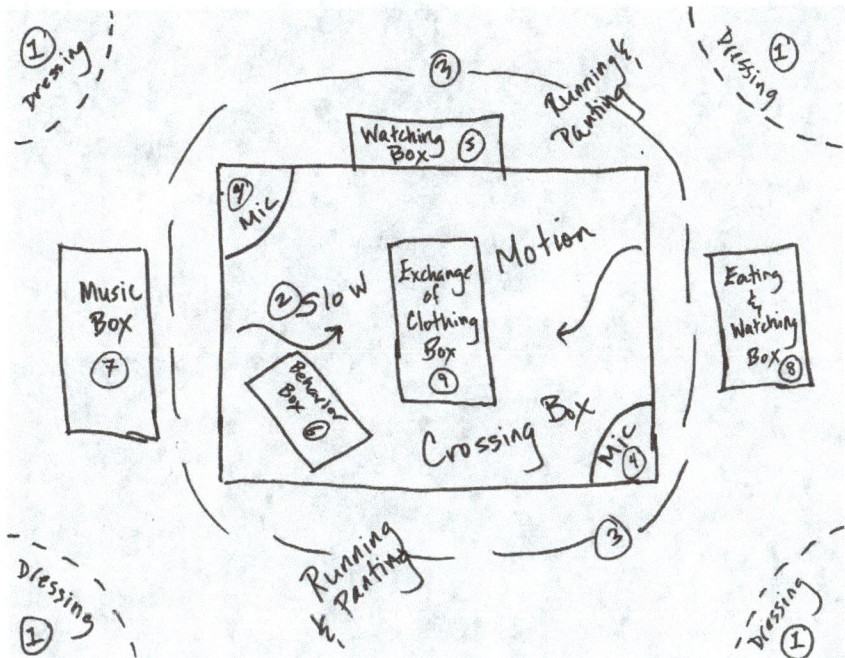

FIGURE 4.10 Slow Motion Transformation diagram by Michele Minnick.

you are tracking both your own journey, moment-to-moment desires, actions, and consequences, and how everyone's journey is creating the performance as a whole.

As in Slow Motion Crossings IV:

- When your breakout is over, return to the exact physical position you had when you left for your breakout. Resume your crossing in slow motion. You must return to slow motion before engaging in another break out.
- When you get to the other side, cross out of the box and stand or sit, striking a pose in stillness. The aim is for everyone to complete their crossing as simultaneously as possible.
- When everyone has exited the box and taken a soft freeze in a pose reflecting their current state of dress, inner state, and persona, regard one another and the space, as the lights fade to black.

EXPERIENCE

I stand at the edge of the crossing box ready to begin, "dressed to kill" from head to toe. I am wearing a red mesh dress, pink underwear and slip, my strappy black heels, eye makeup, and red lipstick. I carry a small, beaded purse that belonged to my grandmother. The instructions for crossing the space in super slow motion have been given, as well as the activities we can do for the breakouts. The workshop facilitator adds instructions periodically, so we don't have to remember everything at once:

132 **PART II** ▶ Practice

FIGURE 4.11 Dressing corners. TPW at NYU.
Source: Photo courtesy of Michele Minnick, 2016.

FIGURE 4.12 Slow Motion Transformation: at the Crossing Line. TPW at NYU.
Source: Photo courtesy of Michele Minnick, 2016.

"Notice others on the other side of the space . . ."

I see various interpretations of what "dressed to kill" means. Like me, some others are wearing fancy clothing. But others interpreted the invitation differently. D. is dressed as a pig, complete with a rubber pig snout mask. M. is dressed like a ninja warrior. Z. is outfitted in army green, a helmet, goggles, and carrying a plastic toy machine gun. B. wears a lab coat, gigantic black rubber gloves, and a surgeon's cap. E. is dressed like a Wall Street trader. I am impressed by the wit and breadth of these interpretations.

"Notice an object or item someone on the other side of space has that you want. If you encounter someone in the slow motion space, you may exchange an item of clothing or an object (see Figure 4.13).

I consider this and ask myself what I desire. The rubber gloves and goggles intrigue me. I like K.'s fedora hat. G. has a fly swatter that amues me.

"Whom do you desire to encounter and meet in the crossing space?"

E.'s Wall Street trader is looking at me. I think I could have some fun with her. It could be interesting to meet M's ninja warrior in this play space.

I follow the impulse to begin on my hands and knees, crawling into the crossing box. I regret this decision immediately, as working in super slow motion on all fours requires a lot more strength than I imagined. I sense my whole body. I can hear my own breathing. I crawl, noticing every shift of weight and balance moment-to-moment. I am at once completely absorbed in the doing and watching myself do it, as if from a distance...

Unexpectedly, B.'s foot appears in my view. I see the details of his brown wingtip shoe. Slowly I look up and notice the rubber glove on his right hand. I decide to reach for it—perhaps he will give it to me. As I am reaching, in extreme slow motion, we make eye contact. He notices my intention and slowly allows his right hand to come toward my reaching hand in a gesture of acquiescence. I am charged with a sense of excitement about getting the glove, yet it seems to take an eternity before I touch it, then another eternity before my grip is strong enough to gently tug on it. B. moves to free his hand from the oversized glove. Eventually it flops off. Now I have it in my grasp, between my left thumb and forefinger. A new problem: how will I put it on moving this slowly? I let the glove fall to the floor and slide my right hand along the floor searching for its opening. The big glove is roomy and stiff enough for me to slide all my fingers inside it, millimeter by millimeter. My body is aching from the effort. I need to break out.

I memorize my exact body position and shape so that I can come back to the same spot after my breakout. I run around the periphery of the space doing One Sound One Movement on the resonator sound "hah" with every footfall. It is a relief to be moving quickly after being in the slow motion for . . . how long . . . half an hour, 45 minutes?

I run to the corner designated for speaking and singing. Over the microphone, I sing a bit of "Someone to Watch Over Me." The notes float out into the space hauntingly, a kind of a soundtrack to the action I am observing as I sing. I notice E. She is in the process of giving her necktie to M., who is sliding on her back across the floor. K. has G.'s fly swatter now and G. has her fedora. When did that happen? Until now, I hadn't perceived many of the interactions happening around me, only those with which I was engaged. D. is in the music box occasionally ringing a Tibetan singing bowl. Its lingering resonance adds another dimension to the sound in the space. I finish my song and do One Sound One Movement back to the exact position I left in the Slow Motion Crossing box to continue my journey.

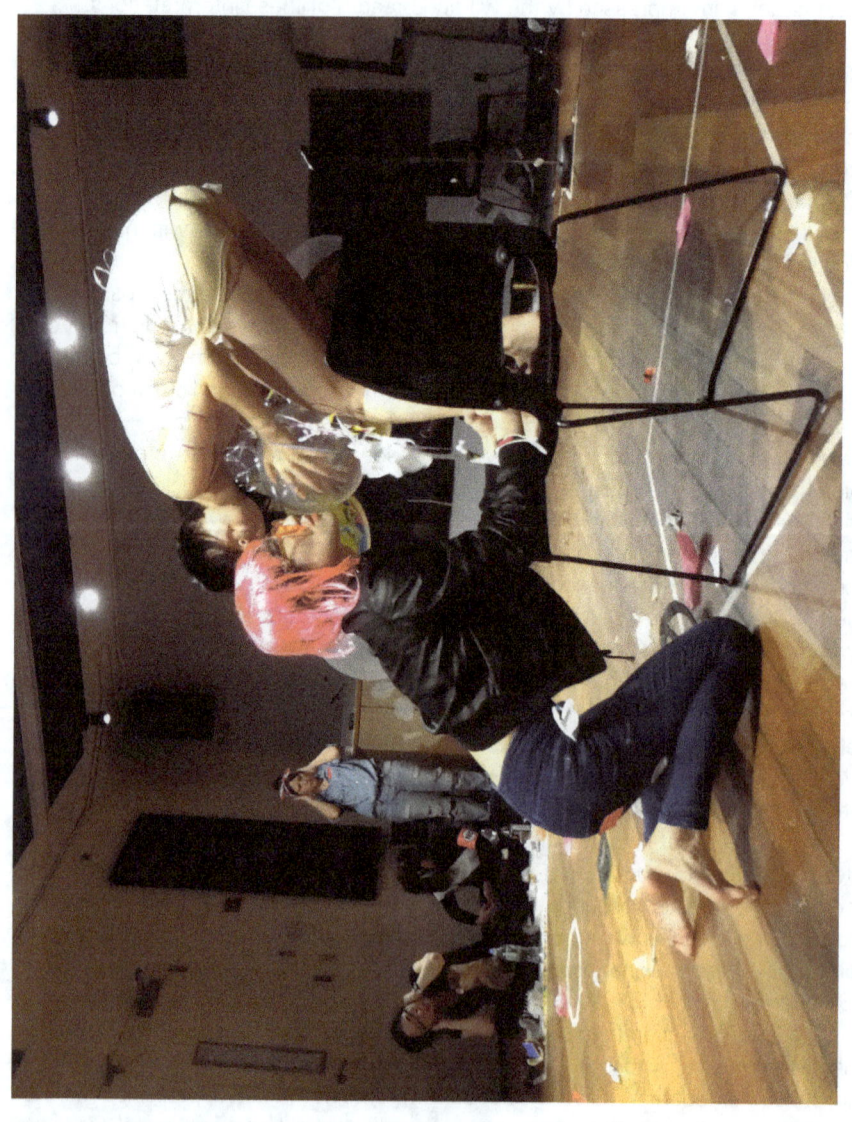

FIGURE 4.13 Encounter in the middle of Slow Motion Transformation. TPW at NYU.

Source: Photo courtesy of Michele Minnick, 2016.

Because so much of the Slow Motion Crossings experience is internal, it's important to do a Feedback Circle to share experiences. This may need to happen the next day, both because of time, and because it can be difficult to process the experience verbally immediately after completing it. Consider these questions as you observe one another and reflect on your journey:

Who did you meet out there?
What was exchanged?
What happened? What dramas unfolded?
Did you vary from your original score? How did this affect your journey?
Is your "tribe" still the same or did you forge new alliances?
How have you or your persona/character changed?

Slow Motion Transformation Variations

- Other activities within and outside the larger Crossings space may be incorporated—for example, expressions of character/persona, or the speaking of scenes or monologues could take place at microphones or in the behavior box. Other senses might be engaged in the slow motion eating box, and so on.
- The world of a play, poem, or other text and its characters, settings, and ideas can be used. Performers cast themselves in the role of their choosing. Sometimes these instructions involve a layering of elements, such as "Dress as a character from the play and choose a base rasa for that character." In this way, you could wind up with three different versions of Blanche Dubois, for example, with raudra, karuna, and bibhatsa as a base (see Layering Rasas, pp. 173–174; Bowditch p. 172; Cole pp. 174–176; and Calzadilla, pp. 269–274).
- Source material that creates textures, landscapes, moods, or worlds can be used in these exercises. For example, one summer at NYU, the group explored themes of climate change, and our relationship to the more-than-human world of animate and inanimate things. Theoretical texts such as Timothy Morton's *Hyperobjects* and Jane Bennett's *Vibrant Matter* met with the rasas, and with personas who gathered for an "End of the World" Slow Motion Transformation exercise.

Rasaboxes

FIGURE 4.14 Aerial view of rasaboxes grid. TPW at NYU.
Source: Photo courtesy of Ryan Jensen Photography, 2004.

Overview

Of all TPW exercises, Rasaboxes is perhaps the most well known. Building on previous exercises in the workshop, Rasaboxes introduces an important concept: *rasa*. Rasa—flavor or juice in Sanskrit—is a theory of emotion in performance. Rasaboxes, Richard's unique interpretation and application of rasa theory, gets its name from the rectangular grid on the floor housing the eight basic rasas of the *Natyashastra*, plus shanta, added in later interpretations (see Pillai, p. 49, and Schechner, p. 61). In this chapter, our focus is on the practice of Rasaboxes as we have developed it in classrooms, workshops, and productions since 1998. The Rasaboxes exercises offered in this book are a representative selection drawn from a vast and ever-expanding array of possibilities. Our objective is not only to communicate an approach to working with Rasaboxes but also to make clear the key ways it relies upon and is integrated with the other exercises in TPW. The number of exercises described is far more than can fit into the standard three-week format of TPW. A three-week workshop focused mostly on Rasaboxes could incorporate many more.

Rasaboxes reintroduces emotion in new ways: 1) as a fully embodied, expression-based gateway for discovering and shaping performance actions; 2) as a shared, social domain of play, rather than a private domain of memory and experience, and 3) as a form of tasting, savoring, and enjoying performing. Everything introduced up to now—warm-ups, Crossings, One Sound exercises, Performances of Self—provides a foundation for the level of communication and connection necessary for the group to explore the complex psychophysical world of Rasaboxes. The rasas, and the boundaries between them marked by the grid structure, are learned by performers over the course of several sessions. Once the basics are mastered on the rasaboxes grid, this structure is internalized, allowing performers to explore other exercises and performative explorations rasically, on or off the grid.

"Rasaboxes," with a capital "R," refers to title of the practice as a whole; "rasaboxes" with a lower case "r" refers to all of the rasaboxes on the grid. The singular "rasabox" refers to an individual box on the grid within which is placed the transliterated name of a rasa: shringara, raudra, bibhatsa, karuna, vira, adbhuta, hasya, bhayanaka, and shanta. Therefore, we refer to players entering the "karuna rasabox," the "vira rasabox," and so on.

Why Rasa?

Schechner's and Pillai's chapters have answered the question "what is rasa?" by introducing the concept of rasa as taste, flavor, or essence, as well as specific ways that Richard has interpreted this concept in order to theorize about contemporary performance. But *why* is the concept of rasa useful on the ground, in studio practice? *How* is it valuable to people who have no direct connection to Indian culture or performance? Without direct contact with the *Natyashastra* and the Sanskrit terms for the rasas, without experience or knowledge of the historical or contemporary uses of rasa in an Indian context, do we risk misunderstanding, or worse? As Nisha Sajnani warns in a recent article addressing the use of Rasaboxes in drama therapy, there is a danger that we may exoticize rasa, or the "ancient Indian" context from which it comes (Sajnani and Gopalakrishna 2017). As the invention of an American theatre director, Rasaboxes is certainly not a direct interpretation of its Indian inspirations. The exercises offer an idea of rasa as it has been understood and envisioned by Richard, and as it has evolved through the teaching and development of subsequent generations of performers and teachers. We are not borrowing techniques or methodologies from classical Indian performance forms. So why not just use familiar emotion words from our own languages? Here are a few key ideas to keep in mind as you read on, and as you practice:

> **Rasa as flavor, juice, or essence:** The concept of rasa grounds the work in the senses and sensations of the performer, and that which is shared with the audience, or the "partakers." The idea that what we are exploring are emotional *flavors* can free performers from personal, biographical, and psychological associations and allow them to explore the psychophysical aspects of emotions as they are tasted and shared with others. In Rasaboxes, we can find pleasure and enjoyment in playing with emotional expressions that, in life, might be experienced as difficult or unpleasant. Although the Sanskrit term *bhava* (emotion) and its corresponding voluntary and involuntary manifestations more accurately names what we are doing—performing particular emotions—we

use the rasa words instead because we prioritize the sharing of emotional flavors. The rasa words point to the *result* of the doing: the relational, sensorial involvement, and enjoyment exchanged between performers and partakers. By using rasa in the name of the exercise, and the Sanskrit names for each rasa, we are putting not only embodiment, but *enjoyment* at the center of performer training.

The use of the Sanskrit terms: The Sanskrit terms *as we use them in Rasaboxes* contain far more possibilities than single words for emotions in English or other languages. Rather than exoticizing Sanskrit, the intention is a kind of "making strange" in the Brechtian sense. For most people who practice Rasaboxes, Sanskrit provides some distance from our usual habits, associations, and memories. We preserve what we understand to be the "original" meanings of the Sanskrit terms, while also allowing a great deal of exploration and experimentation. We seek to embody the essential qualities that can be tasted in raudra and shringara, as well as the myriad possibilities offered by individuals playing within these categories. The resulting expressions may differ from what was intended by Bharata-muni or what is understood by contemporary performers of classical Indian dance.

Rasaboxes as research: Rather than a codified system of expression as described in the *Natyashastra*, or as deployed in classical Indian dance forms, in Rasaboxes we improvise expressions by using each rasa as an essence. Each performer works intimately with themselves and with others to discover, deepen, and widen their own range of expression of that essence. As we explore both familiar and new modes of experiencing and expressing emotions, we discover stimuli and actions associated with each rasa and individual ways of accessing their flavors psychophysically.

The way we introduce Rasaboxes varies, but the objectives of the first two or three sessions remain the same: to understand the overall concept of rasa and its usefulness in training the affective, energetic connection *between* performer and spectator; to learn general meanings of the rasas and discover interpretations for each; and to practice the embodiment of each rasa alone and in relating with others, using still poses, facial expressions, breathing, and simple movement phrases.

Paul Ekman and Facial Expression of Emotion

To understand how Rasaboxes works on a neuro-muscular level, we rely on both Michael D. Gershon's "brain in the belly" (see Chapter 3, Rasaesthetics) and the work of Paul Ekman (1934–). Ekman is an American psychologist and a colleague and friend of Richard's.[4] He is a leading authority on the expression of emotions in the human face, and one of the founders of the field of emotion science. Ekman builds upon ideas pioneered by Charles Darwin (1809–1882) in his *The Expression of the Emotions in Man and Animals* (1872) and by William James (1842–1910) and Carl Lange (1834–1900), who linked human emotions to survival reflexes. His research suggests that humans across cultures produce and recognize the same facial expressions for six "basic emotions"—anger, fear, enjoyment, sadness, disgust/contempt, and surprise.

Ekman explains in *Emotions Revealed* (2003) that emotions evolved to allow humans to respond to and cope with their environment. Humans developed auto-appraisers, adaptive instinctual mechanisms, to scan the world around both to warn of danger and to develop emotional bonds. Ekman describes nine pathways to emotion, from automatic unconscious processes to deliberate shaping:

1. Auto-appraisal—automatic response of the nervous system to the environment: sensing danger, for example.
2. Reflexive emotion that follows auto-appraisal, tensing up in fear, for example.
3. Memory—remembering a past emotion.
4. Imagination—images, visualization, sounds, smells, and sensory triggers evoking emotions.
5. Talking about an emotional experience.
6. Empathically experiencing emotion when witnessing someone else's emotional expression.
7. Others instructing us how to feel about something.
8. Violating social norms.
9. Producing emotions through physical instruction, muscle by muscle, which arouses the nervous system—psychological/body/emotions feedback loop (Ekman 2003, 21–27).

Ekman's work is relevant to Rasaboxes training in several ways. These nine pathways are important to articulate, to younger actors in particular, who may have a limited perspective on how to access emotional states without triggering traumatic responses. His research revealed that instructing people to shape a facial expression of an emotion muscle by muscle—to "make the face" of an emotion—results in feeling that emotion. Furthermore, Ekman's "six universal basic emotions" overlap the *Natyashastra*'s eight basic emotions.[5] This points to the fact that emotions are both cultural and personal. Finally, Ekman's attention to the detail of facial expression helps performers develop an awareness of its importance in building rasic expressiveness.

Orange Exercise: Rasa, Literally

Orange Exercise[6] is an exercise in experiencing rasa literally, by seeing, touching, smelling, and tasting. Like any work with food/flavor in Rasaboxes, it is a bridge between taste-rasa, and the enjoyment of emotion-rasa in performance. The *experience* of rasa unfolds throughout the encounter *with and between* the fruit and the person seeing, touching, smelling, and tasting the fruit. Perceptions about its properties might be shared, but the experience is unique to each participant. Working with oranges, or with any food, requires a clean surface and then cleanup—put paper or paper towels on the floor and make sure a mop and water are available.

Instructions

Gather in a circle and pass out one orange per person. Then ask:

1. What do we "know" about oranges? (shape, place of origin, taste, etc.)
2. What personal associations do you have with oranges (cultural, familial, geographical, any)?

3. Look at your orange. What can you experience of this particular orange using your senses? As you investigate the orange, its color, texture, weight, sound, and smell, name and share your experiences with the group.
4. Next, peel your orange. Pause to notice the different ways people peel their oranges.
5. How do you receive the smell of the orange? What sensations, associations, and/or memories arise?
6. Next, taste it—very, very slowly—savoring each moment and each texture, sensation, smell, and flavor. Is it sweet? Sour? Describe the flavors you experience to the group.
7. Consider where the flavor, smell, and substance of the orange are now. Inside the fruit? Inside you?

Consider how the orange's juicy essences are released throughout the space and experienced by others. This points to the relational aspect of rasa, its relationship to and between the performer and their partakers. How is rasa released in performance, making the emotional flavors available to others? We also ask you to notice *how* you are doing what you are doing. For example, while one person peels their orange in a continuous spiral, someone else might pick off little pieces, one at a time. Similarly, not everyone has the same way of savoring the flavors in the orange. Although they may all be exploring the same thing together, each player must discover their own secrets to opening themselves and their audience to the experience of each rasa. It is important to go step by step, sensing without rushing the process. Experiencing rasa is savoring.

Variation

The Orange Exercise may introduce rasa at the beginning of Rasaboxes, or, it may come in once the meanings of the rasas are learned, at which point participants can take the fruit on a journey through the rasaboxes. How does the essence of the orange change in each rasabox? Does it taste, smell, or feel different? What are the various ways participants interact with the orange and with each other as they move around the grid? Later in the process, it can be interesting to explore all kinds of flavors and foods in the Rasaboxes. They offer an immediate way of discovering the mouth-to-belly-to-bowel connection in performance and provide a powerful sense of the different flavors within each rasa. For example, how is a spicy vira different from a salty vira? What is a chocolatey shringara versus a meaty shringara? The orange is also often the first object we introduce in Rasaboxes, so although it is a food, as an object it can be explored in a multitude of unexpected ways.

Ayurveda and Rasa

Ayurveda is a philosophy of balance, well-being, and medicinal and culinary practice originating in India at least 2000 years ago. The theatrical theory of rasa is historically and culturally linked to Ayurveda's six basic flavors: sweet, salty, bitter, sour, pungent (spicy), and astringent (dry, like the taste of black tea or plain cooked lentils). In this system, the flavor, color, and properties of foods are themselves medicinal. They are understood to have a direct effect on our mental and emotional states, as well as on our physical health. Ayurveda is founded on the idea that the same elements that compose all matter also compose the human body. The flavors in foods are produced by combinations of elements—ether (*akasha* or emptiness), air, earth, water, and fire. Ayurveda takes literally the idea that you, or at least the physical–emotional aspects of you, "are what you eat." The elements in nature combine to make doshas, which are constitutional qualities affecting body type, emotional tendencies, and so on. When the doshas are out of balance, combining appropriate foods and spices is a primary remedy (see Lad 2002).

Setting Up the Rasaboxes Grid

We begin Rasaboxes by making a grid on the floor using masking tape, approximately 18' × 15', creating nine equal-sized rectangles of at least 6' × 5', and leaving space around the outside for participants to enter and exit the exercise. The size can be adjusted so that the tallest person in the group can lie down inside each rasabox with room to spare. Larger spaces can accommodate a larger grid.

Next, we assign each of the eight rasas, randomly to each of the eight outer boxes. Participants label the boxes with the transliterated Sanskrit word for each rasa. (see Table 4.1. Note: the translations are there for your reference. Do not write them in the rasaboxes.) We always leave the center rasabox unlabeled to

TABLE 4.1 Sample layout of a rasaboxes grid.

RAUDRA	HASYA	BHAYANAKA
(anger)	(humor)	(fear)
BIBHATSA	[SHANTA]	ADBHUTA
(disgust)	(peace) Leave box empty	(surprise/wonder)
SHRINGARA	VIRA	KARUNA
(love/the erotic)	(courage)	(sadness)

represent the "emptiness" of shanta. We will explain some ways of using the shanta rasabox later.

If available, it is ideal to work in a space in which sidewalk chalk can be used directly on the floor. Chalk is messy, in a good way—it rubs off on skin and clothing, literally imprinting "rasa dust" of the boxes onto participants. Otherwise, paper can be taped to the floor and crayons or markers used instead of chalk.

Introducing Each Rasa

When all the rasas are in place, basic descriptions or experiences may be verbally offered about each rasa, both in its traditional context as described in the *Natyashastra* and in our own experiences of working with these eight flavors of emotion. For example, we might talk about shringara as erotic or romantic love, but also as physical pleasure, such as smelling sweet odors, tasting savory food, and so on. Alternatively, we non-verbally demonstrate a rasa through sound, breath, facial expression, physicalization, etc., while the participants name what they see, hear, feel, and associate with the demonstration. Sometimes, participants are invited to "taste" the rasas by entering a rasabox and physicalizing the rasa. This method is experiential and experimental, facilitating the participants' understanding that there are many ways to express each rasa, rather than one "right" way.

Writing and Drawing in Rasaboxes

After the rasas have been introduced, each person, working simultaneously with the whole group, writes and/or draws the personal associations they have with each rasa (see Figure 4.15). We do this exercise at the beginning of each Rasaboxes session, until the rasas are thoroughly learned by the group.

Instructions

1. Enter the rasabox of your choice. In silence, draw or write your personal associations for the rasa. These may include abstract designs, your own words, quotations from literature, evocative images, gestural markings, or anything that comes to mind. Writing can be in any language you speak. These are *your* associations, and they are for *right now*. Tomorrow they may be different.
2. Enter all eight rasaboxes (except shanta rasabox in the center of the grid) to write and/or draw your associations. When finished, exit the grid.
3. This phase of the exercise is over when there is no one left writing or drawing inside the rasaboxes, and all are standing or sitting outside the grid.
4. Next, the group walks around the outside of the grid to regard all the contributions made inside each rasabox. Notice how they affect you. What are the commonalities and differences? (see Figure 4.16).

CHAPTER 4 ▸ Inside The Performance Workshop   143

FIGURE 4.15 Michele Minnick drawing inside the rasaboxes grid. TPW at NYU.
Source: Photo courtesy of Ryan Jensen Photography, 2004.

EXPERIENCE

I noticed that people had very different associations and ways of naming and representing each rasa. For bibhatsa, for example, someone drew a cartoon-like face vomiting. Another wrote the words, "I have lost all respect for you," and someone else drew a picture of a cockroach. While we were writing and drawing in silence, the atmosphere was meditative, each person taking time to connect with each rasa.

Embodying Rasas

After the group has finished Writing and Drawing in Rasaboxes, we begin the physical work of embodying the rasas at a high level of intensity—extreme physical shapes, audible breath, and exaggerated facial expressions. This approach makes the basic essence of each rasa palpable to the players in a fun, theatrical way, making clear that this is *play*—not often how emotion is approached in actor

FIGURE 4.16 Drawing in raudra rasabox from workshop led by Richard Schechner, Norway.

Source: Photo courtesy of Richard Schechner, 2013.

training. We focus first on the "outside," *showing* the rasas to one another, by first making big and still shapes with the entire body in each rasabox, adding the breath, movement, and the voice in subsequent exercises.

Around the World I

A warm-up focusing on body shapes in the rasaboxes:

1. Evenly distribute yourselves around the four sides of the grid.
2. When you hear the signal (e.g., a hand clap, or "Go!" from the facilitator), jump into the rasabox in front of you and make a still shape with your entire body—including hands, feet, and face—that expresses the rasa in that box.
3. When you hear the signal, jump out of the rasabox.
4. Move one rasabox to your right (or counterclockwise).
5. Repeat steps 2–4 until you have worked in all rasaboxes, or as many as you like.

Around the World is done at a fast pace with no time for thinking or planning. Participants are invited to complete one circuit of the whole grid. By the end, each

FIGURE 4.17 TPW participant in hasya rasabox. TPW at NYU.
Source: Photo courtesy of Ryan Jensen Photography, 2004.

person has entered each rasabox at least once. The facilitator may draw focus to different elements of physical sensation and expression, such as skin, eyes, spine, extremities, open or closed shapes, the degree and location of muscle tension. The objective is to experience and express each rasa by engaging a specific pose, a body shape including the face (see Figures 4.17 and 4.18). Of course, if you do not want to work in a particular rasabox, no matter the reason, that is your choice.

Sculpting in Partners

Sculpting focuses on body shape and facial expression by having people work in pairs. Participants are invited to create still poses or "sculptures" for two or three rasas. This exercise is done in silence. All communication is nonverbal.

Instructions

1. Find a partner to work with for this exercise. Do a boundaries check-in (see pp. 83–84).
2. Enter a rasabox of your choice and make a full body pose that expresses the rasa as fully as possible.
3. Your partner regards the still pose you have created. Without seeking to *change* what you are doing, your partner silently asks themselves, "How can

FIGURE 4.18 Performer in bhayanaka rasabox in workshop with Michele Minnick. Casa da Ribeira, Natal, Brazil.

Source: Photo courtesy of Maurício Cuca, 2012.

I help you clarify or intensify the expression of this rasa? Does it need to be bigger, more intense? Does it need adjustments to the shape, the facial expression? Is the whole body engaged in this expression?"

4. If you are the helping partner, be creative in finding nonverbal ways to coach your partner. Physical contact is one option (taking your partner's consent boundaries into consideration). You can also communicate with sounds, or with mirroring, for example.
5. When you, the helping partner, are satisfied with the sculpture, give your partner a positive signal, a "thumbs up" or something else.
6. The partner being sculpted memorizes the enhanced still shape and then jumps out of the box and back in again, as many times as it takes, to seal the body's memory of the pose.
7. Change roles. Repeat steps 1–5.

Each person should end up with two or three practiced and memorized still poses in different rasaboxes after completing Sculpting in Partners. Next, we learn how to move from one rasabox to another on the grid.

Rasaboxes: Rules for Play

Except for shanta, which always occupies the center rasabox, the rest of the rasas can be placed in any box anywhere on the grid. The spatial relationships between and among rasas should shift each time the grid is set up.

- The space outside the grid and the inner tape lines of the grid are neutral—without rasa.
- There is no neutral inside a rasabox. If you're in a rasabox, you're in that rasa, tasting and expressing it.
- Instantly transform your entire body, breath, face, etcetera, when you cross a line into a new rasabox.
- When you cross to the outside of the grid, drop the rasa instantly.
- Outside the grid, your role is to be an engaged spectator, tasting the rasas that are shared between performers and the other partakers.

Instructions for Moving Between Rasaboxes

Now that we have mapped out what happens inside the rasaboxes and around the outside of the grid, focus on how to move between them. This can be accomplished in three ways:

- Jump immediately from one rasabox to another (no neutral).
- Use the inner lines of the grid as a temporary neutral space for traveling or briefly pausing between rasaboxes.
- Use the neutral space outside of the grid to travel from one rasabox to another.

Showing and Regarding

After exploring Sculpting in Partners, the next step is to allow time to both show and regard the still poses, or sculptures. Showing allows you to practice your memorized still poses, while also growing your tolerance for being looked at by others in the group. Looking at or regarding others in Rasaboxes takes practice, too, as we learn to give ourselves permission to taste, savor, and enjoy what we are observing. Or to be repulsed. Or frightened. Or surprised, saddened, and so on.

Instructions

1. Surround the grid, this time about two feet away from the outer edge of the tape to allow players enough room to enter and exit the rasaboxes.
2. Up to four players at a time can enter/jump/cross into their memorized still poses on the rasaboxes grid, built during the Sculpting in Partners exercise.
3. Stay for as long or as short a time as you like showing your pose.
4. Do not allow for any neutrality while inside the box. If you are inside the rasabox, express that rasa with all your being.

5. When fewer than four players are showing on the grid, another may jump onto the grid to show a pose.
6. The rest of the group will regard the players' still poses from outside the grid by looking closely at specific details of a pose, and/or watching one or more players from various locations in the space.
7. For both sets of players, consider: What are you receiving? How are the rasas being communicated?
8. When players on the grid are finished showing a pose, they may exit the grid or cross into another rasabox to show another pose they built during Sculpting in Partners.
9. This exercise continues round-robin—players either showing poses on the grid or regarding those who are showing from outside the grid—until no more players are on the grid.

Share feedback with the group about what you are experiencing using "I" statements. The introduction of "no neutral" inside the rasaboxes is extremely important. Once it is introduced, participants will need to be reminded that each rasabox is a three-dimensional rasic space with its own qualities, rhythms, and possibilities.

Making a Breath Phrase

Next, we bring still poses more fully to life by engaging the breath and sensing how it can fill and animate the body. The still pose then becomes a short breathing and moving phrase, a loop with a beginning, middle, and end, that can be repeated. Breath is the beginning of movement, and an essential element of relating to others in Rasaboxes.

Instructions

The group works round-robin with some players making breath phrases inside the rasaboxes and others regarding them from outside the grid, then switching roles as desired. During each step, allow breath to lead body and body to lead breath.

1. Begin by re-entering one of the rasaboxes you have already worked on, embodying one of your memorized still poses.
2. Improvise animating your still pose with breath. As you inhale, how does the breath fill the shape you made? As you exhale, how does it flow out? Pay attention to whether you are breathing through the nose, or the mouth, whether the emphasis is on the inhale or the exhale, and so on. Are there pauses in between inhale and exhale?
3. Notice your body's sensations as the breath draws in, then discover how the body wants to release/move as you exhale.
4. Keep improvising with the incoming and outflowing breaths, allowing the physical life to enliven and shift until a repeatable movement/breath phrase begins to emerge, grow, and evolve.
5. Once you have developed a phrase, repeat it a few times and exit the rasabox. As before, reenter and exit the rasabox a few times, until the phrase is fully memorized.

CHAPTER 4 ▸ Inside The Performance Workshop

6. Do the same for as many of your remaining still poses as you like.
7. This part of the exercise ends when no one enters the rasaboxes to make a movement/breath phrase.

Next, as with the still poses, do Showing and Regarding with the movement/breath phrases, then share feedback with the group about what you experienced. What changes about your experience, either as doer or watcher, when breath and movement are added?

Discussion

During early phases of the work, concerns may arise about "authenticity." When working at high levels of intensity, with extreme physical expressions and exaggerated breath, sometimes you don't "feel" the emotion you are embodying. It is helpful to know that exaggeration serves to clearly and strongly imprint the rasas into the body's psychophysical system.

Subsequent exercises will focus on scaling the intensity levels of the rasas, from extreme to subtly nuanced expressions, and on building connections between inner sensation and outer expression that can be tailored to any genre, style, or scale of performance. Also, the training places the emphasis on rasa—what is received by the partakers. A particular expression may feel "false" to the performer, while still conveying the rasa to the partaker. We are not endorsing "fake" or disconnected acting, but at the same time, do not insist on a "real" emotional experience. We have learned through practice that, over time, this work connects inner sensing and experiencing with outer expression and communication as familiarity with Rasaboxes grows.

Candace B. Pert: Molecules of Emotion

Pioneering neuroscientist Candace B. Pert (1946–2013), author of *Molecules of Emotion: The Science Behind Mind-Body Medicine* (1997), discovered the opiate receptor. Pert's major scientific breakthrough paved the way for a significant paradigm shift toward greater understanding of the inextricable link between mind and body, as well as the important role emotions play in health and wellness. Pert's study of the molecular basis of the emotions showed "how the molecules of our emotions [neuropeptides] share intimate connections with, and are indeed inseparable from, our physiology" (18). Pert argued that the emotions are in fact the link between mind and body. She wondered, "Do they [emotions] originate in the body and then get perceived in the head, where we invent a story to explain them, as William James said? Or do they originate in the head and trickle down to the body, as Walter Cannon posited?" (135). According to Pert,

> The new work suggests there are almost infinite pathways for the conscious mind to access—and modify—the unconscious mind and the body. . . . [W]e have found that in virtually all locations where information from any of the five senses—sight, sound, taste, smell, and touch—enters the nervous system, we will find a high concentration of neuropeptide receptors.
>
> (141–142)

Pert's work aligns with what many people have discovered doing Rasaboxes—that the entire body, not merely the brain, or the facial muscles, participates in the generation, reception, and interpretation of emotion. The idea of a multinodal/biochemical system suggests that emotions do not trickle down from the central nervous system (CNS), but rather can be launched from any kinesthetically connected area, any stimulus or sensation, inner or outer.

Shanta Rasabox: First Taste

Shanta always occupies the center box of the grid but is not represented in writing or drawing. Common conceptions of shanta include peace, balance, and equanimity. Whatever its quality, it is a unique space on the playing field. Shanta is usually introduced sometime between the first and third day of a workshop, usually within the context of a game or exercise. We note that for Richard, shanta was not possible to experience—except to those who had achieved Buddhahood, which in his experience was no one (see Schechner, p. 73). He limited entry to shanta to rare occasions, and often required vigorous work through the other eight rasas as a requirement for entry, calling upon the performer to recognize when she reaches something approaching a balancing of all the rasas in the body, and only then to enter the center box. We feel that shanta is an important element of the training and find the shanta rasabox useful for creating a variety of dynamics on the grid and training specific skills. Next is an example of an initial exploration of the shanta rasabox. We recommend introducing shanta before the exercise that follows, Shopping for Rasas, as it invites players to use the shanta rasabox.

Instructions

1. Complete Drawing and Writing in the eight rasas surrounding shanta.
2. In silence, everyone uses the grid lines (the masking tape between the boxes) to walk to the center box.
3. As you enter the center box, breathe shanta into your body; let it affect every cell. Notice how sensations are different here than in other rasaboxes.
4. When ready, look around at each of the eight rasas, regarding and receiving them through the lens of shanta, one at a time. Notice how you perceive the images and words in the raudra rasabox, for example, from a shanta perspective.
5. When you have made contact with all eight of the outer rasas, turn your attention to those inside the shanta rasabox with you. How do you perceive others through the lens of shanta? What helps you to stay connected to shanta, as you regard others and allow others to regard you?
6. When this process is complete, use the grid lines to exit the shanta rasabox and return to the neutral space outside the grid. How is shanta different from neutral?

Shopping for Rasas

Shopping for Rasas is a game that combines all of the first steps of learning Rasaboxes. It can serve as a beginning for relating exercises, as this game is usually played in the second or third Rasaboxes session.

CHAPTER 4 ▶ Inside The Performance Workshop

Instructions

Use the one or two short and repeatable movement/breath phrases you built during the first Rasaboxes session. Alternatively, build only one or two new short and repeatable movement/breath phrases in the rasaboxes. Exit the grid.

Shopping for Rasas involves rotating among four possible roles/activities. Everyone who is outside the grid must balance the grid—making sure there are people on every side, or as many sides as possible at all times, to hold the space for those working inside.

Role 1:

Do one of your own movement/breath phrases in a rasabox. Perhaps someone will join you to learn your phrase, perhaps not.

Role 2:

Enter a rasabox where someone is working and learn their movement/breath phrase, as precisely as possible, mirroring every detail (as in One Sound One Movement, but with breath). Once you have learned another's movement/breath phrase, you may use it as your own. You may initiate doing the phrase as if you had created it, and others may learn it from you.

Role 3:

Witness/regard the work from outside the grid.

Role 4:

Witness/regard from the shanta rasabox. Play in the shanta rasabox as a place to be present and receive what is happening around you. First, connect with shanta breath and sensation in the body. Then, regard/witness others working on the grid without allowing yourself to be moved by the energy of the other eight rasaboxes. Play with the difference between blocking sensation and allowing it to pass through you without a ripple.

Everyone in the group works at the same time. You are in charge of which role/activity you play and when, but balance your activities with those of the whole group.

Additionally:

- You may play with or repeat the same movement/breath phrase as often as you like.
- As many as can fit in a rasabox can simultaneously play in it.
- More than one movement/breath phrase at a time can happen in the same rasabox.

EXPERIENCE

When the game begins, I enter adbhuta rasabox to copy a movement/breath phrase that E. is doing. I am standing in front of E. and mirror her breathing and movements as precisely as possible while E. repeats her phrase. After a few rounds, E.'s adbhuta movement/breath phrase is now fully in my body and breath, too. After a few more rounds, E. exits the rasabox while I continue to do the adbhuta phrase I learned from her. Next, G. enters adbhuta and learns the phrase with me. After a few rounds with G., I exit the rasabox. I regard others working in various boxes. I notice B. is alone in raudra, a tornado of breath, fists, and stomps. J. weeps with his breath and body shape in karuna. E. has now joined J. in the karuna rasabox but initiates a different movement/breath phrase. They are both sharing the karuna flavor, though different expressions of it.

From the outside of the grid, I notice my body/breath responding to what I am seeing/hearing from the others in the rasaboxes. The flavors I experience shift depending on what I am regarding. Next, I dip back into adbhuta and do the phrase I learned from E.—which is now mine too—for a few moments. From there I go into the shanta rasabox. I sit cross-legged on the floor, inhaling and exhaling in long slow breaths. I watch R. working in bibhatsa. Their nose wrinkles and lips recoil, their eyes nearly shut against smelly fumes. I become aware that I am slightly mimicking their expression in the muscles of my own face. I want to stay in shanta without tasting R.'s bibhatsa, so I refocus on my breath and relax my muscles—tuning into porous sensations in my skin and bones, the space between my cells—allowing the other rasas to pass through me while I remain with shanta.

Relating in Rasaboxes for Two Players

All Rasaboxes exercises involve relating. The very concept of rasa is relational, occurring between the taster and the partaker. "Relating exercises" in Rasaboxes refer to games in which players encounter other players or objects on the grid. In Rasaboxes, the kinds of encounters participants had in Crossings are now shaped and flavored by the rasas the players are embodying. Relating in Rasaboxes explores moment-to-moment give and take. You respond and make choices connected to the rasabox you are in, while staying attuned to the other, who is in a different rasabox. We do this exercise with breath and movement before sound is added, then repeat it with sound, then again when text is added, and so on. This game is played as a round-robin, which encourages you to move briskly around, on, and off the grid (see Figure 4.19).

Instructions

Two players at a time relate to each other on the grid. The rest of the group witnesses/receives from outside the grid, making sure to balance all sides of the grid to support the players. Be ready to enter at any moment.

1. Enter the rasabox of your choice.
2. Immediately establish your connection with the rasa through movement and breathing (and sound if the group has integrated sound).
3. Then, notice the other player. Take each other in through breath and eye contact.
4. Regard and respond to the other through the lens or flavor of the rasabox in which you are working.
5. Either player may change rasaboxes or leave the grid at any time.
6. The moment you or your partner exits, another player from outside the grid enters immediately, keeping the scene in play. If you both exit at the same time, two others enter.
7. The game is over when no player steps onto the grid to relate.

FIGURE 4.19 Participants relating in the rasaboxes grid. TPW at NYU.
Source: Photo courtesy of Ryan Jensen Photography, 2004.

Variation

A player from outside the grid can also tag out one of the players. "Freeze" the player you want to replace by tapping them on the shoulder. Take on their frozen pose, and as they leave, resume the game with the other player.

Discussion

It is easy to get "stuck" in one particular relationship or rasabox long after the dynamic of the relationship has stagnated, and this round-robin format keeps players moving—there is no limit to the number of times you can go in or out. The more dynamically you play, the more fun you will have, and the more the unfolding "scene" takes on a life of its own. Sometimes the tempo will slow and the work will become very nuanced. Allow for and attend to these qualitative shifts, engaging with the other players and allowing yourself to be witnessed by the partakers outside the grid.

Noticing when sensations shift is a key element of the training. If they shift away from the rasabox you are currently working in, and/or if you cannot resist the rasic "contamination" of another, you have choices: change to the rasabox you are drawn to, reconnect with the rasabox you are in, or to leave the rasaboxes grid entirely.

Transitions in Rasaboxes

Rasaboxes proposes a complete physical transformation *from the moment you cross the line* into any rasabox from the space outside the grid or from one rasabox to another.

Both beginning and more advanced players often "cheat" the first moments of crossing the line into or out of a rasabox. When this happens, entering a new rasabox appears undefined, neutralized, or carries over qualities of the previous rasa. Attending to the very first moments of transition into and between rasaboxes is a productive exercise that strengthens our work in all the other exercises. Separating elements of physicalization of the rasas into distinct components—posture, breathing, facial expression, muscle tension, and sensations of the skin, for example—can help us make transitions with greater nuance and precision and develop more conscious awareness of what and how we are both sensing and communicating each rasa.

This exercise can be done once participants have achieved a familiarity with the basic elements of the game and are familiar with all the elements to be addressed in the Transitions exercise. All of the following work should be done very close to the tape lines of the grid so that in a single breath, or a single step, performers can move from one box to another.

Instructions

Working Individually

1. Surround the grid, no more than two players at the edge of each rasabox.
2. Choose one element of physicalization to focus on: posture/shape, breath, facial expression, muscle tension. This is your *Focus element*.
3. Pay particular attention to the moment of crossing the line, rather than jumping into the rasabox with the whole body at once.

4. As you cross from outside the grid into a rasabox and back again, pay particular attention to how your focus element transforms as you transition in and out several times. How detailed can you be? For example, if working with facial expression, what happens with the mouth? The eyebrows? The eyes? The tongue? The ears? The nose? What changes first?
5. Repeat with other focus elements. Work slowly at first. Then, see how quickly you can cross back and forth, and how quickly you can change.
6. Change the rasabox or focus element whenever you like.

Putting the Pieces Together

1. Cross the line between two rasaboxes, making a total body–breath–face transformation from one rasa to the other.
2. Repeat the same transition, focusing on different elements. What happens if you begin the transformation with breath? With posture? How is it different if you change direction? For example, instead of moving from karuna to raudra, start in raudra and move to karuna.
3. Notice how focusing on the details of physicalization affects your inner state. Slowing down and focusing on details helps connect the external to the internal, encouraging inner/outer feedback and psychophysical transformation.
4. Repeat the same process with one or two more pairs of neighboring rasaboxes, staying with a pair long enough so that you can move back and forth between them quickly, making the transformation as instantaneous as possible.

For now, don't worry about repeating yourself, using the same shape, breath phrase, or facial expression. The specific expression is not as important as becoming conscious of the process. It can even be helpful when starting out to use the idea of set poses or breath phrases as departure and arrival points for each rasa.

While Working Individually is primarily focused on doing, and the *experience* of transitioning, Transitions in Pairs is focused primarily on the *communication* of the rasas and the experience of a partaker in the moment of transition. For this you will need a partner. One player will be working on the grid, the other *observing* and "coaching" from outside the grid. This exercise is a verbal elaboration of the nonverbal feedback offered in Sculpting in Partners. Care must be taken about how verbal feedback is offered. This is not a directing exercise but rather an exchange of doing, observing, and experiencing. Use language such as "I noticed," "What if you . . ." rather than correcting your partner.

Transitions in Pairs

1. With a partner, go to the border between two rasaboxes, staying outside the grid. One player begins in the role of the Performer, the other as the Observer. The Observer will always be outside the grid. The Performer may begin each transition either from outside the grid or in a pose inside a rasabox, close to the line they are about to cross.

2. The Performer repeats the same process as in Working Individually, of entering and exiting the grid, and between two rasaboxes, focusing on one physical element at a time and attempting to transform as fully as possible.

3. The Observer watches their partner in an embodied way, paying attention to what they see/hear/sense, as well as to their own bodily responses. Notice what elements are changing and which ones are communicating the shift to the new rasa.

4. After watching for a bit, the Observer offers feedback (off the grid), helping the Performer to become conscious of what they are doing in terms of breath, shape, and facial expression. What happens first? Does anything lag behind? What is communicating the rasa most strongly? Is anything left out?

5. The Observer may suggest things for the Performer to try. For example, "What if you focused only on the transformation of the shape of your body as you cross?"

6. Work in a few different spots around the grid, exploring possibilities for total transformation.

7. Performers and Observers may switch roles either between one set of working on Transitions, or after each person has gone through the entire process.

Depending on time and energy levels, an optional final moment for this exercise can involve free movement and play around the grid. It is important to integrate the work on transitions back into more open improvisation. As each new exploration of Rasaboxes is added, it is useful to return to this exercise, as transitions may fall away again when the complexity of relating to a partner or working with the text is introduced.

Sound Sensation in Rasaboxes

In Rasaboxes training, as in TPW overall, vocally produced sound is treated as an extension and expression of the body. To that end, we spend time freely playing with a wide range of vocal sounds before working with words, and before moving into texts that involve interpretation.

After working on exercises that shape the body and breath in Rasaboxes, sound can be added. When introducing exercises to connect with vocalized sound, we speak of "sound sensation," as distinct from the linguistic components of speech. The focus is first on the *feeling* of sound that is not yet words—the sound that gets *ex-pressed* from the body, perhaps like freshly squeezed juice, infuses the breath with flavors of vibrations. It is fueled by the inhalation, literally *in-spired*. We talk about breath as a means of drinking in (or sipping, sniffing, or gulping) the rasa. One cycle of rasa inhalation and rasa out-sounding fuels another. Changes in the rhythm or tempo of the breath emerge, bodily sensations change in response.

There is a tremendous variety of rhythms, tempos, and intensity levels for the incoming and outgoing breaths in each rasa. In hasya, perhaps a quick inhale is followed by many pulses of outgoing breath before the next inhale. A short chuckle can engender giggles that grow into peals of laughter, then guffaws. Or not. It depends on what happens, and on what you choose to follow.

Exercises such as One Sound One Movement that integrate movement and vocalization are introduced before beginning sound work in Rasaboxes. You can also do sound and movement explorations off the grid as a warm-up for sounding on the grid.

Phonemes

The smallest unit of vocal sound is called a "phoneme," made up of vowel sounds, and voiced or unvoiced consonants. It is fun and illuminating to take these small units of sound into the rasaboxes to discover how each rasa informs them. The [f] or "fff" sound when explored in bibhatsa is different than the same sound explored in shringara, and so on. In fact, the same phoneme can fuel wholly different experiences even in the same Rasabox.

Phonemes can be combined into sequences of sound. Work with combinations that are not yet consciously derived from specific words: "Dra, myt, shla," and with non-human sounds such as motorboats, barking, gurgles, swooshes, and so on. Each rasabox will inform these explorations differently. Allow your exploration to inform breath, body, and imagination, deepening these connections as you play.

Syllables in Names of Rasas

Use the name of the rasa with which you are working to play with phonemes and syllables. Any sound or part of the rasa name can be explored in isolation, in any combination, and in any order: *adbhuta* can be "ah-ah-ah" or "ooo-ooo-ooo," or "ah-d-bh ooo t ah" or "bhu" or "dah-ad-tah."

Ground all sounding in body sensation/shaping/moving and, of course, always with the breath connecting it all.

FIGURE 4.20 Performer in bibhatsa rasabox in a workshop with Michele Minnick. Casa da Ribeira, Natal, Brazil.

Source: Photo courtesy of Maurício Cuca, 2012.

As the exercise progresses, the full rasa names can be sounded. Building from phonemes, syllables, and rasa names creates a foundation for playing with any text you are bringing into the rasaboxes.

Resonators in Rasaboxes

After exploring sound freely in the rasaboxes, re-introduce the four resonators (hah, hee, huh, hoo). These simple syllables can expand your sense of the range of pitch, tone, and quality available in each rasabox. In addition to the rhythmic possibilities explored in "panting" exercises, here we use the resonators to find new tonal possibilities. What is raudra with a high and sustained "hoo" sound? What about adbhuta with a low "huh" sound from the belly? What about a shringara on the "hee" sound in the nose and facial mask? These sounds suggest specific ways of connecting with the body by dipping into unexpected rasa-resonator combinations, offering additional flavors to experience within each rasabox.

Around the World II

An exercise in soloing with breath, sound, and movement in the rasaboxes grid.

1. Surround the grid on all four sides.
2. One player at a time, enter the rasabox in front of you and improvise moving, breathing, and sounding.
3. When ready, move into the next rasabox on the grid. Remember there is no neutral in the rasaboxes, so you must move, breathe, and sound the rasa you are in until you enter the next one.
4. Do as many or as few rasaboxes as you like, leaving the grid when you like.
5. Do three Clearing Breaths after you exit, to neutralize or rebalance your breath/body/mind/sensation (see Clearing Breath, p. 100).

EXPERIENCE

I tiptoe across the line into the bhayanaka rasabox on the grid sensing into the energy of bhayanaka. I crouch down but remain on tiptoe, fingers splayed on the ground for balance, spine alert. I am low to the ground, ready to move quickly as I listen for danger. My open mouth draws in a quick breath. My breath stops. I cannot hear it or see it but sense a menacing presence. Perhaps the danger is behind me? I spin around to see what's there and I let out a loud yelp. My own breath/sound and movement startle me. I sit on the ground. My forearms/hands fly up to cover the area around my head. Quick breaths come in then sharply spurt out. My legs and feet propel me backward, then kick away from what I fear. I curl myself into a tight little ball to cower and hide. I quickly roll out of the bhayanaka rasabox into the adjacent rasabox. My whole body spirals luxuriously across the floor of the shringara rasabox, releasing the sensations of bhayanaka. My muscles soften and yield as a pleasurable, sweet-tasting breath fills me. I tune into a warm sensation on my face. My fingers gently explore the smoothness of the floor. I exhale a contented sigh enjoying the sound of buzzing lights. I join the sound with my own "zzzzzz" sound for a bit. I inhale and stretch myself long then slither into the next rasabox . . .

Shanta as Witness

In Richard's workshops in the 1990s, shanta was often described as "white light" that might result from perfectly balancing all the other rasic colors, or as a kind of emptiness, but also possibly as "bliss" or "enlightenment"—in any case, it was clear that it was a higher state, different from the rest. We weren't allowed to enter it often, because "who among us is enlightened?" This is a valid observation. But the more I have worked with Rasaboxes as a training ground, and the more I have learned about and practiced Buddhist-oriented forms of meditation, the more the shanta rasabox has become an essential invitation, a key place to *practice*. In many ways, shanta has become the center of my teaching of Rasaboxes and TPW.

The role of shanta in my approach to the work became clear when, as part of my recovery from a devastating health crisis in 2005, I began to meditate. I tried various methods before eventually coming to vipassana, one of the earliest forms of Buddhist meditation, which I have practiced mostly in a form developed in the U.S., known as Insight Meditation. Its initial focus is the breath, to ground the mind in sensations of the body. This practice encourages one to develop a sense of equanimity, so that we can meet any person, circumstance, thought, or emotion with a sense of spaciousness, rather than attachment or aversion. When teaching Rasaboxes, I usually present the shanta rasabox as a place to train this ability—commonly known as "mindfulness"—and to practice the role of witness.

Performances since the 1980s—particularly those of women, LGBTQIA artists, and artists of color—have borne witness to difficult and traumatic histories. Through this work, witnessing became a key function in the genres of performance art and solo performance. My experiences working with Leeny Sack,[7] who has explored her history as a child of Holocaust survivors, as well as a survivor of chronic illness, and who first introduced me to vipassana meditation, has deepened my relationship to shanta as a place of witnessing, and the sense of responsibility and ethical engagement inherent in that role.

I invite TPW and Rasaboxes workshop participants to enter the shanta rasabox in a variety of ways. Responding, reflecting, and reacting is natural and easy, for most of us, when encountering others in Rasaboxes. For me, shanta is a space that demands more: it asks us to *be with and for the other*, no matter what they might be expressing or experiencing. This makes it very clearly distinct from the non-rasa, "neutral," or more relaxed place of enjoyment outside the grid. The shanta rasabox requires a willingness to experience things as they are, without judgment, with full presence.

As performers and creators, the shanta rasabox also offers us the opportunity to develop our *inner* witness, the observer within, the eye of our own personal storm. It can be both a calming and energizing space to manage the flux and flow of rasa, a place of spaciousness *inside* the rasaboxes where we can pause before stepping into another rasabox with its desires, aversions, attachments, and exertions—which we love in theatre but when out of balance in life can exhaust and deplete us. In practical everyday terms, shanta can serve as a training ground for widening the gap between our initial feelings and impulses in response to what the world throws at us—giving us a *choice* in how we respond. For those working in educational and healing fields, it is an essential place to practice the role of listener and witness.

By Michele Minnick

Relating with Shanta

This is an exercise for partners, part of the trajectory of Relating exercises that explores shanta in a more sustained way, and in equal measure to the other rasas. It is a great way for the player in the non-shanta rasaboxes to explore rasa as tactic.

Instructions

1. One partner enters the shanta rasabox; the other player enters another rasabox, anywhere on the grid.
2. The player in shanta remains there, while the other player moves into and out of various rasaboxes, relating to the player in the shanta rasabox with sound and movement, with or without text.
3. The player on the grid uses everything at her disposal within various rasaboxes to try to communicate with, affect, and influence the player in the shanta rasabox.
4. The player in shanta is researching what is necessary to maintain a state of equanimity in the face of the intensity and turbulence of the other rasas.
5. Switch roles.

FIGURE 4.21 Alyssa Duerksen exploring karuna rasa with body, paint, and canvas. Ithaca College.

Source: Photo courtesy of Marla Montgomery, 2007.

Scaling Intensity

Each rasa can be expressed and felt along a vast continuum of intensity. Raudra, for example, can range from mild annoyance to wrath of mythic proportions. These explorations allow performers to modulate levels of intensity within each rasa and to learn about the expressive scope and scale of each rasa using movement, breath, and sound. They serve as a prerequisite to working on text, character, and composition, and prepare the performer for Mixing and Layering Rasas (see pp. 171–176).

Preparation: Scaling Speed—Off the Grid

The first time the group plays with Scaling Intensity, participants practice scaling the speed of physical movement without rasa. The facilitator leads the group by verbally calling out the various speeds throughout the phases of this exercise.

Instructions

Step 1: Scaling Speed

1. Begin anywhere in the playing space. Choose a simple action: walking, jumping jacks, chopping wood, etc.
2. As you perform this action, scale the speed at which you do it, from 1 to 100% of your total capacity for speed, in small increments. What is moving at 1%? A thought? Stillness and breathing? Is 3% a subtle weight shift? Is 5% super slow motion? Perhaps 25% is a comfortable walking speed?
3. As you play up and down the full range of speeds on the scale, adjust percentages as you learn.

Step 2: Scaling Inner/Outer Speed

After exploring up and down the scale using faster and slower speeds, you can begin playing with "inner" and "outer" speeds in two ways:

Fast Inner Speed/No Outer Movement

1. Move at your speed of 60% or so. Suddenly stop moving. If you were doing jumping jacks, for example, stop the physical movement but imagine that you are still doing jumping jacks at the speed of 60%, but do not enact them. What do you notice?
2. Resume both the inner and outer speeds at 60%.
3. Repeat several times at various speeds, stopping the outer movement while really sensing you high inner speed.

Fast Inner Speed/Slower Outer Speed

1. Resume both the inner and outer movement at your speed of 60%.
2. Keep your inner speed at 60%, but move with a *Slower* outer speed of 20%, for example.

3. Resume moving, matching inner/outer speeds, to clean the slate for subsequent combinations.
4. Explore several different inner/outer speeds: 60/40%, 70/30%, 80/20%, etc.

What associations do you have moving with a higher inner speed with no outer movement? A slower outer speed? Some typical responses are it feels like "having high stakes in a scene," or "having to keep a secret," or "being emotional but not wanting to show it." What if the inner speed is slower and the outer speed is higher? Experiment freely.

Scaling Intensity of Rasas—Off the Grid

Step 1: Moving Up and Down the Scale of Intensity

1. Repeat Steps 1 (1–3), only now with rasa instead of speed. The group selects a rasa: hasya, for example. Everyone begins in a comfortable position, lying down, sitting, or standing, and improvises movement as dictated by the rasa. Allow movement to arise as the rasa awakens and increases in intensity level.
2. As you move up and down the scale, 1 to 5% at a time, explore the rasa at each increment. What is hasya at 1%? Is 20% a smile? 25% a slight giggle? 50% playfulness? 70% mocking your classmates? 80% uncontrollable howls of laughter? Play around until you have a firm sense of the relative differences among intensity levels of hasya.
3. Come to neutral, then repeat the previous steps with another rasa. After two or three rasas, begin to explore differing inner and outer intensity levels.

Step 2: Scaling Inner/Outer Intensity—"Cooking" the Rasa

This exercise teaches you to scale inner/outer intensity levels of rasa with a single cue: "Cook it!" Intensifying and compressing a high-intensity inner rasa, while containing its outer expression, is called "cooking" the rasa.

1. Start working in a rasa until you are at about a 70% high-intensity range. When the facilitator says "cook it," quickly contain your outer expression of the rasa. For example, keep the inner rasa at 70%, but only let it show "on the outside" at, say, 10 to 20%. You decide how intensely you contain, limit, or dial down the physical expression of the rasa. For example, what happens if you are in hasya at 70%, laughing until your sides hurt, when suddenly you need to suppress or even stop laughing altogether?
2. Allow the higher inner intensity to build and burst through the outer containment so that both inner and outer intensities are the same again: 70/70%, for example. Then "cook it" and release it again. Notice what happens.
3. Freely explore containing and releasing the rasa at various inner/outer levels. In between, clean the slate for subsequent combinations by returning to the same inner/outer intensity levels.
4. Explore simple activities while cooking the rasa, such as sitting, drawing/writing on a chalkboard, exchanging greetings with others—whatever is available.
5. Choose a different rasa and repeat the exercise.

As you explore, discover and log your own sensations at various levels of intensity within each rasa. Notice your associations as you work. Do any images, stories or circumstances, environments, or relationships emerge? What effect does containing the rasa have on your experience of it? Like so much of TPW, this is a kind of self-training where you must take the initiative to find your own answers. Taking intensity level explorations back onto the grid, where you have to make sudden shifts from one rasa to another, will lead to further discoveries.

Intensity Arc—On the Grid

Emotions are episodic. They have an onset, perhaps an increase of intensity, followed by a decrease of intensity and eventually, a resolution of some sort. The Intensity Arc exercise is an improvised episode using Rasaboxes that can be done once participants have worked with Scaling Intensity. Up to eight participants can work on the grid simultaneously, but only one person per rasabox (shanta is excluded from this exercise). The rest of the group surrounds the grid.

Instructions

1. Enter any rasabox and make a high intensity, animated breath/movement/sound pose/phrase. Once you have learned it, exit the rasabox.
2. Using the same rasabox, make a low(er) intensity still pose or breath/movement/sound phrase. Once you have learned it, exit the rasabox.
3. When you have a beginning and end point, enter the rasabox again and improvise a journey from your high intensity pose/phrase to your low intensity pose/phrase. When completed, exit the rasabox.

An intensity arc can be made going from low to high as well.

EXPERIENCE

To make my high intensity phrase, I enter the adbhuta rasabox spinning slowly around, widely embracing, sensing, seeing, and hearing all the space around me. I pause and drink in the air through my nose and mouth sensing the inflow of breath, curious to find how my chest rises and expands in all directions. "Hoo" is the sound that bounces out in response to the discovery. Now on tiptoe, arms overhead, I am both floating upward and dangling downward somehow, suspended and expanding in time and space—"Hooooooo!"—a marvelous epiphany. My eyes open to take in the jaw-dropping view of all that is— "Hooooooo!"—all that has ever been— "Hooooooo!"—all that will ever be. I repeat this phrase several times, then exit the rasaboxes grid.

To make my low intensity phrase, I roll from the outside of the grid into the adbhuta rasabox. I sprawl on my back like a big letter "X" floating on water. I lower the inner and outer intensity of adbhuta by crossing one elongated leg over another, one hand to belly, the other to heart. I breathe easily with a "Hmmm" sound, sensing the afterglow of my connection with all beings that now reside within me. "Hmmm." After some breaths, I roll out of the rasabox.

To begin the Intensity Arc, I reenter the adbhuta rasabox spinning slowly around, widely embracing and seeing all the space around me as before. "Hooooo!" When I arrive

FIGURE 4.22 Michele Minnick in adbhuta rasabox. TPW at NYU.
Source: Photo courtesy of Ryan Jensen Photography, 2004.

at the end of my high-intensity phrase on my tip toes, I improvise a middle for the Intensity Arc, connecting the high-intensity phrase with the low: my sounding and moving becomes more sustained, arms drift downward as I regard my left arm, then right arm. "Ooo"—the colors and textures of my skin, the lines in my hands, fascinate me. The ground beckons me as my fingers touch its surface, "Ooo." I plunge in and down into its waters. I sprawl on my back, a big letter "X" floating on water, then snow! I make snow angels with my arms and legs. I sense both joy and discovery as my body moves, especially when I notice the cool temperature with my skin contact on the floor "Hoo!" I am curious if it feels cool on other parts of the floor. I search for spots of cool and find both warm and cool spots as I slow down the rate of my arcing snow angel limbs. I see a shining bright light in the sky! I think it has a message for me "Hoo" . . . I listen in stillness. I cross one elongated leg over another, one hand to belly, the other to heart. I breathe easily with a "Hmmm" sound, sensing the afterglow of my connection with all beings that now reside within me. "Hmmm." After some breaths, I arrive at the end of my low intensity phrase, then roll out of the rasabox.

Text in the Rasaboxes: Monologues

Text work in Rasaboxes will benefit any style or genre of performance that involves language, including sung language in musical theatre, opera, and other performance forms. Text work shapes Sound Sensation into a felt embodiment of language. It is essential to keep exploring your gut-based feelings and your connection to sensation throughout the body, particularly in the face, mouth, chest, belly—parts associated with sound production. When first using a text, select a single phrase

FIGURE 4.23 Drawing in shringara rasabox in workshop with Richard Schechner, Norway.

Source: Photo courtesy of Richard Schechner, 2013.

to explore the possibilities of language—from the phonemes to the full phrase. Ground the work in physical choices. Text is an extension of sound, which is an extension of breath, which is a movement of the body. As always, participants may work with texts in any language in which they are fluent.

Intelligibility is not important at this point. The key is to release all notions about meaning, context, or the character who speaks the text. A facilitator might say something like, "You don't know. I don't know. Only the rasa knows, and will tell you, in the moment, what this text might be saying. Let's find out." Let go of your preconceived ideas and give in to rasic sensation, allowing discoveries to arise.

As we begin to work with text, which engages the intellectual part of our brains, often we abandon all the work we've done to stay grounded and connected to the body. Implicit in all instructions that follow is the necessity to integrate body, breath, sound, and text. If people are struggling, it can be helpful to have participants start their work with text low to the ground, rather than standing (see Animal Exercise, pp. 122–123).

Instructions

Depending on the size of the group, this exercise may be done with everyone working on the grid at once, or with half the group observing from outside, and the other half working.

On the Grid:
1. Take the first sentence, or a key sentence in the monologue, and begin to explore it in each rasabox, beginning with the smallest elements—individual phonemes, syllables. Take your time to arrive at a full word.
2. Build up to a whole sentence gradually, working through each phoneme, syllable, word, then phrase, looping back, using repetition to explore nuances of rhythm, tone, etc.
3. Once you have explored the entire monologue in this way, moving freely between the rasaboxes, begin to challenge yourself by changing rasaboxes in unexpected places, mid-sentence, even mid-word.
4. Use varying levels of intensity, work with different "inner" and "outer" intensity levels—containing versus freely and fully expressing raudra, for example.

There are a number of ways to work with text off the grid. Here is one approach to working with monologues whose aim is to separate rasic choices from intellectual analysis of the text. Work with a well-memorized monologue. Choose three to five rasas to work with.

Off the Grid:
1. Create a short, simple physical score based on the five rasas, choosing in advance when you are going to change.
2. Work the transitions between rasas. Transitions can be tricky, and one has to find an organic logic to them—which is often a logic of the breath or body that literally "makes sense" of the changes.
3. Add the monologue to the score, deciding what parts of the text will be performed in each of the rasas.
4. Perform the monologue with the physical score (this may be followed by some feedback from other participants and facilitator).
5. Then, release the physical score, and try speaking the monologue—simply allowing the rasas to arise moment-to-moment. The rasas you had scored may float up organically, or others may arise. Allow yourself to flow with whatever comes, as you integrate your intentions with the rasic shifts.

For monologues, scenes, and devised works that use text, Rasaboxes is a great way to explore layers and complexity of meanings and relationships. Rasas can flavor the psychology of a moment, or they can *generate* the psychology of moments. They give rise to actions, just as they can provide the quality of an action. Once language comes into the process, playing with rasas can change perspectives and provide useful new information about a character's backstory or relationship with other characters. In preparing a role, you may never use a particular rasa in your performance but, having explored all of them, the character work that emerges will be more nuanced.

Chorus Work in Rasaboxes

The foundations of chorus work have been laid in preceding Rasaboxes exercises—particularly Shopping for Rasas, Sounding, and Scaling Intensity levels. Chorus Work also employs skills learned in follow-no-leader exercises, such as One Sound One Movement.

Instructions: Open Chorus

1. Divide into groups of at least three but no more than seven people. All but the group who starts surround the grid on all sides. The starting groups stands together in front of a single rasabox.
2. Enter together into that rasabox and immediately start connecting with, tasting, experiencing, and expressing the rasa through breath, sound, and movement.
3. Once you've connected with the rasa, allow it to become contagious, responding to and interacting with the others in the rasabox with you. Your improvisations fuel, and are fueled by, the rasa, by others, and by shifts in intensity levels as you play.
4. When one player initiates a cross into another rasabox, the rest of the chorus follows immediately, without thinking or judging, shifting into the new rasa the moment each crosses the line between the boxes. Remember to sense and express the rasa of the box you are in until you cross over.
5. When one of you crosses out of the grid, the others follow, and the round is over.

The chorus is both a single organism and a collection of individuals within that organism (see Figure 4.24). Its rhythms, intensities, shapes, and sounds are sometimes shared, sometimes divergent. It is important to pay attention to the flow, intensity, and rhythm of each rasa; to the arc of the phrasing of each episode. Neither rush nor stay too long in any rasabox. Sometimes the group waits until the intensity level drops and the energy begins to dissipate before moving to the next box. Instead, make the shift while the rasa is still fully alive so that an energized transition fuels the experience/expression in the next rasabox.

Chorus with One Sound One Movement

This exercise builds on the principles of One Sound One Movement adding rasa to the mix. Instead of the chorus entering a rasabox together with individual expressions, one person leads the entry into each rasabox with a sound and movement that is immediately taken up by others as they enter.

FIGURE 4.24 Participants doing chorus work in vira rasabox. TPW at NYU.
Source: Photo courtesy of Ryan Jensen Photography, 2004.

EXPERIENCE

Seven of us are standing outside the raudra rasabox. Z. enters first, landing in the box in a wide stance; the muscles of her thighs tighten. Her arms make a wide-reaching gesture that subsequently closes in toward her body as her fingers and hands clench into fists. Her jaw is thrust forward, her eyes are open wide. Each time she repeats the gesture she makes a kind of growling sound as her arms pull in toward her body. Once her phrase is established, we jump in to mirror what she is doing. With each repetition of the gesture and the growl, the intensity of our sound and movement increases. As we work, variations of Z.'s phrase begin to emerge among us, like variations on a theme in music. We are not always in total unison or making the same face, breath, sound, or gesture, but share the same energetic intensity, focus, and basic phrasing.

Chorus with Text

Chorus exercises with speakers/chorus leaders are highly dynamic exercises that challenge your ability to manage your own expression in relation to the ensemble. The energy of the chorus can free the chorus leader to explore their text, using a range of intensity levels, in relation to a small group who move through the rasaboxes with them. This version of chorus work can use any text—poetry or prose, song lyrics, the text on the back of a cereal box—from sentences to monologues, shared by the group or not.

Instructions

1. Enter a rasabox with your group and immediately begin connecting, tasting, experiencing, and expressing the rasa through breath, sound, and movement.
2. Once you feel connected to the whole group and the rasa, one of you becomes the chorus leader by speaking your text.
3. Those of you in the chorus turn your attention to the leader, adjusting intensity level and volume. You now respond together—chorus to the chorus leader—using breath, sound, and movement. You may also echo the physical expressions of the chorus leader, as well as words and phrases from their text (this can be particularly fun when the speaker is using a language the chorus does not understand).
4. The chorus leader can move anywhere on the grid and the chorus follows, immediately taking on the new rasa when they change boxes.
5. The chorus leader may decide to give up their role and dissolve back into the group, or a new chorus leader may emerge, signaling to the first leader to relinquish their position.
6. This round will continue until everyone in the chorus has had at least one chance to speak their text as chorus leader.
7. Everyone exits the grid together.

Chorus with Speaker and Listener

The exercise proceeds the same as Chorus with Speaker, except now there can be a listener in a separate box from the chorus and chorus leader. The listener can emerge from the chorus or can enter from outside the grid. This is an excellent way to practice the *listening* side of relating, giving players the chance to explore what it is to *receive* in different rasaboxes. Listening exercises can be introduced earlier in Relating in Rasaboxes for Two Players, for example, with one partner more focused on receiving and the other on doing/pursuing a response, with or without text. When you are free to listen without having to respond or communicate verbally, you can investigate the active and flavorful listening that happens on the grid. This kind of relating does not allow for any neutrality: the listener is always hearing and seeing from a particular rasic point of view. It brings home the classic adage that "acting is reacting"—that being present for one's partner by taking in and responding to what she is doing is not only the springboard for one's next action or speech—but also a communication in itself. Playing with intensity levels and degrees of inner/outer containment are also very valuable here.

Relating with Text: Scene Work

Scene work in Rasaboxes is a complex balancing act. As in all relating exercises, you must maintain the rasa of the box you are working in while responding to your partner, who is in another rasabox. Text must stay grounded in the body to avoid relying on predetermined meaning, given circumstances, or on a preconceived or "natural" response to your scene partner. Instead, respond according to what the rasas require in the moment.

Before doing the round-robin one-on-one relating game, it can be helpful to warm up to relating by having everyone work on the grid simultaneously. In pairs, participants can explore relating using preverbal sound and movement with a focus on relating from *different* rasaboxes. Each player can change boxes when they wish.

Instructions

When introducing text, begin with a very simple exchange, like:

"I am Michele, who are you?"
"I am Paula, who are you?"

Remember, just because text is available to you, you do not need to be speaking all the time.

1. Enter a rasabox, connecting first with your own rasa before connecting with your partner.
2. Notice your partner and begin using/exchanging the text of the scene, infused by the rasas, to relate to each other.
3. Enter or leave the grid at any time.
4. The moment you or your partner exits, another player from outside the grid enters, keeping the scene in play. If you both exit at the same time, two others enter.
5. The game is over when no one enters the grid.

Variations

Tapping Players In and Out

You can enter the game while two others are relating by entering the rasabox of one of the players and tapping them on the shoulder, which signals both players to freeze. You take on the exact shape (body, breath, facial expression, etcetera), intensity level of the rasa, and relationship to the other as the "tapped out" player, who then exits. The new pair resumes the action.

Third Player in Shanta

When you are ready to stop playing, you may exit the grid or enter the shanta rasabox to observe/witness. You may enter the shanta rasabox only from within the grid, not from the neutral space outside the grid.

Once in shanta, you may stay there for the duration of the next pair's scene, or longer. You may exit at any time.

Working with Scene Texts

The text can be an open scene (dialogue without a fixed set of given circumstances) or a short scene sourced from a play that can be used as an open scene. We lean toward scripts with simple vocabulary so those with English as a second language or participants less familiar with classical texts can easily understand and use the material. As always, participants may work monologues and even experiment with scene work in their native languages. In the context of a production or scene study class, a more individualized approach can be used with everyone working with the actual text of their scenes. Rasaboxes has been used during rehearsals to explore text, character, and scene work (see Bowditch, pp. 280–293, Calzadilla, pp. 269–274, and Cole, pp. 174–176).

Mixing Rasas

Two or more rasas can be mixed to create complex combinations. For example, what rasas would you combine to make jealousy? Indignation? Morbid fascination? Think of Rasaboxes as a painter's color palette, from which a variety of hues or color combinations can be made. The possibilities are infinite. In early phases of training, it is natural for mixing to happen unconsciously. In Mixing and Layering, we make conscious choices to combine two or more rasas. Players must be experienced in Scaling Intensity of individual rasas before effective mixing can occur.

Instructions

1. Improvise with movement, breath, and sound in a rasabox, vira for example, until you have a short, repeatable phrase to use as your "base."
2. Enter a different rasabox, hasya for example, with your base phrase, and allow the new rasa to infuse your base phrase, mixing the two flavors in various proportions. The "flavor" of both rasas is expressed and modulated through breath, contraction and relaxation of muscle, facial expression, and any other element that has been explored.
3. Return to your base rasa to unmix, before going to another rasabox.

EXPERIENCE

To establish my base rasa, I cross the line into the vira rasabox. I feel my legs/feet strongly connecting through the floor. Both arms/fists thrust above my head, as if celebrating a victory, as I exhale strongly and quickly on a "Ha!" sound. My fists pound my chest twice as I inhale strongly through my nose. I repeat the first gesture again, arms/fists above my head, adding a stomp with my left foot as I sound "Ha!" then I stomp my right foot with another "Ha!" A rhythm grows as I repeat this phrase. After a few repetitions to memorize the phrase, I cross out of the rasaboxes grid.

To mix my base rasa with a different rasa, I enter the hasya rasabox and repeat my vira phrase, which is now the movement motif with which hasya starts to have fun. Immediately the breath changes, my fists fly upward with the inhales and when I pound my chest, I exhale with more of a "Heh, Heh!" My pelvis starts to swivel. I play around with rhythms and sounds, all in a kind of mockery of the vira phrase with which I started. Now I am punching my fists and stomping my feet all over the place, as if provoking rivals to fight with me. I am having a great time playing freely by mixing hasya with my vira motif and it makes me laugh too. I exit the rasaboxes grid.

When the group is mixing, we often hear the comment, "This is the first time I have really connected with (or felt) the emotion . . ." It is true that emotions in everyday life are experienced as mixed more commonly than as "pure" or unmixed emotions. For performers in theatre, mixing gives "authenticity" and complexity to characters responding within the given circumstances of a dramatic situation.

Creating a Rasic Persona

The following example from Rachel Bowditch illustrates an extended exploration of the development of a persona from the 2006 New York University TPW, prompted by an invitation to "dress as a rasa" for a Slow Motion Transformation (see pp. 128–135). This is also an example of Mixing and Layering Rasas:

One of my first times experiencing Slow Motion Transformation, we were asked to come dressed as a rasa—I chose *bibhatsa*—my favorite rasa. I began to visualize and imagine a persona that would have bibhatsa as their base rasa. In preparation, as I walked through the streets of New York City, I tried on bibhatsa to see what kind of person saw the world this way—how did they walk, what was their point of view. For me, an image of the costume came first—a black slip, fishnet stockings with rips, platform boots, a messy bun, smudged black eyeliner, and black lipstick—somewhat goth and definitely a smoker. As a non-smoker, I bought a pack of cigarettes and envisioned this persona as someone always having a cigarette dangling out of their mouth—whether lit or unlit. This person looked at the world through the lens of disgust—it was a world that had been unfair, hostile, and cruel. There was both an external and an internal bibhatsa working in tandem—she was immersed in a world of disgust. Externally, as the world viewed and judged her, I imagined that she preferred night time and walked the streets experiencing the world through the lens of bibhatsa. Internally, she hated herself and was disgusted by the things she had done and had been forced to do. She was deeply disgusted with herself—feeling violated and broken—damaged goods.

During the Slow Motion Transformation exercise, I slowly dressed in the dressing corner, layer by layer, transforming into the physical persona I was embodying. I spent the next three hours moving in slow motion with a bibhatsa base, mixing and layering other rasas as I moved through them. As a performer, it was a powerful experience to sustain that level of engagement to go deeper into this bibhatsa persona. Who and how did she love (bibhatsa/shringara)? What was she proud of, if anything (bibhatsa/vira)? What was she afraid of (bibhatsa/bhayanaka)? What made her laugh (bibhatsa/hasya)? What angered her (bibhatsa/raudra)? Over the course of the crossing, I lost one of my boots and had to limp with only one boot on—in my imagination, as the night wore on, her self-disgust accumulated as her costume unraveled and her situation worsened (bibhatsa/karuna). As I prepared, dressed, and performed as this persona, her backstory unfolded with each encounter. She developed from a persona into a character, with layers of psychological complexity. She left an indelible mark on me.

Layering Rasas

Two or more rasas can be layered to create combinations that may seem like mixing but are in fact very different. There are several possibilities. As in Rachel's example of her bibhatsa persona, in Layering, we work with a base rasa, *over which other rasas are layered*—from the deepest, sometimes secret core layer, up to the interactive social or surface layers. A Blanche DuBois of Tennessee Williams' *A Streetcar Named Desire* played with raudra as her base rasa would create a very different character than one played with a base rasa of karuna. Or Nora from Henrik Ibsen's *A Doll's House*, could be played with a base rasa of bhayanaka, while masking it with hasya and shringara—concealing her fear as she plays at being Torvald's happy housewife. As with Mixing, players must be experienced in Scaling Intensity before effective Layering can occur.

Instructions

1. Improvise with movement, breath, and sound in a rasabox, karuna for example, until you have a short, repeatable phrase to establish your base rasa.
2. Enter a different rasabox, adbhuta for example, with your karuna base and allow the new rasa to *contain* or conceal your base rasa, layering the two flavors, one nested inside the other.
3. Return to your base rasa to unlayer, before going to another rasabox.

EXPERIENCE

To establish my base rasa, I cross the line into the karuna rasabox. I sense my legs/feet weakly melting as I surrender to gravity and sink toward the floor. My head and spine follow the downward path; my left hand helps support my weight on the floor. My right hand cups the top of my head. I can feel my face breaking into a grimace of agony. Meanwhile, a long exhale slowly keens "Oooooooohhhh!" until it becomes little repeated sobs of "oh, oh, oh, hoh." My belly tightens, my spine undulates lightly upward as my heavy heart opens and pours out the sound. After a few repetitions of this phrase to memorize it I exit the grid.

To layer a different rasa over the base rasa I enter the adbhuta rasabox. I start my base karuna phrase, then adbhuta wraps around the karuna to contain it. I can sense the pulses of the karuna phrase happening deep inside of me, but my external body remains upright, resisting the temptation to give into gravity. My head tilts back and I regard the stars. A surprised but slightly whimpering "oh!" is released. My right hand cups my forehead as before, but this time my left hand alights on my solar plexus. I inhale, my jaw drops open and I wonder in thought "Am I dreaming?" Everything seems new and beautiful and sad.

The base rasa may live within your body's center, or in a posture, gesture, facial expression, breathing pattern, or any combination of these. The important thing is to keep the base rasa alive from within, while layering other rasas onto it. The base rasa can be a resting or default position of the character or persona. Or, it may be hidden most of the time, then revealed in a crucial moment, a literal "dis-covery."

The idea of layering rasas can be extended to scene work. One might set an entire scene in a tonal key of a particular rasa (or combination of rasas), while individual characters or moments are played in other rasas. In the third act of Anton Chekhov's *Three Sisters*, for example, while everyone else is traumatized and operating in a state of emergency because of the fire (perhaps bhayanaka or karuna, or both), Masha reveals her love (shringara) for Vershinin. Sometimes, rasas emerge logically out of the text, as if the playwright is working with a rasic palette, but it is also possible to apply rasas (or their combinations) experimentally to a text to discover unexpected interpretations.

Building a Character with Rasaboxes[8]

by Paula Murray Cole

In 1999, I played Ofelia[9] in Richard's adaptation of Shakespeare's *Hamlet*. I used Rasaboxes in a few ways in this production: 1) as a tool to discover the emotional content of the play through both text analysis and physicalized exploration in scene rehearsals; 2) as a way of creating the psychophysical structure of the character; and 3) as a mode of offstage emotional preparation.

Whenever I begin work on a play, like most actors I comb the text for clues about my character by looking at the given circumstances and how all of her relationships take shape.[10] I begin to get a sense of my character's objectives (what she desires from others), the obstacles she faces in pursuit of those objectives, and the specific actions she takes to achieve them. Based on information culled from and inferred by the text, I develop a biography for the character, which helps me to get a handle on her psychology: what and who has shaped her sense of self, her emotional needs, her connection with others and the environment, her behavior in response to all these factors. This preparatory work helps me to consider the rasas I may want to use. I begin to get a feel for which rasic emotions are most accessible to my character, which will best support the text, my own interpretation of the role, and the director's vision for the production. Although I make notes about all this work on paper, more importantly, I do it in-body, out loud. It is my private rehearsal and preparation time for group rehearsals. I then begin to freely play and experiment with the rasas in scene rehearsals. One of the ways I began to incorporate this work during *Hamlet* was to play whole scenes in a single rasa, full tilt. For example, the scene in which Ofelia tells her father, Polonius, that Hamlet has frightened her by behaving in a strange manner, I first played in bhayanaka (fear), then karuna (grief or compassion), then shringara (love), then raudra (rage), and so on. I noted how each rasa affected the actor playing Polonius and how it informed the actions I chose. This kind of exploration helps me to discover the range of emotional and active choices I want to keep and to limit other choices that seem less useful.

Next, I experiment with layering rasas to create the internal and external conflicts that drive the character's choices throughout the play. For Ofelia, I chose to work with four primary rasas: two "surface" rasas, those to which I felt she habitually gravitated: bhayanaka (fear) and karuna (grief); one "mask" rasa: shringara (love), a rasa with which she identified but also strategically used to gain familial and social approval, making it a consciously held mask; and one core or base rasa: raudra (rage), deeply repressed until her final scene. I used these rasas in varying weights or levels of intensity, depending on the challenges Ofelia faced in a given scene. The key element in my interpretation of the character was the way in which I used the core rasa, raudra: it was her unconscious psychological base from which I built my through-line of action. I decided that Ofelia's survival at home with Polonius and her brother, Laertes (and later, by extension, her lover Hamlet), hinged upon her ability to suppress any degree of objection she felt in the face of what they wanted from her. From an early age, I imagined, any jot of resistance was completely quashed by her father's disapproval and threats of rejection. Conversely, she was pleasurably rewarded for being lovely, kind, affectionate, and compliant. She understands, however subconsciously, that she must hide her core feelings of rage (raudra) behind the mask of loving affection (shringara) in order to survive or thrive in her relationships. So, I denied Ofelia full access to rage until her final scene (though it peeked out in quickly squelched flares at the end of the nunnery scene and in the player's scene, as her situation and relationships became strained). Raudra was, however, the rasa always creating the tension from beneath, shaping the others—the irritating grain of sand creating the pearl of her personality.

Given this psychological character structure, what happens to Ofelia when her father is murdered by her lover while her brother is absent and the whole thing is covered up by

FIGURE 4.25 Paula Murray Cole in shringara rasabox.
Source: Photo courtesy of Ryan Jensen Photography, 2004.

the king? What happens when she feels the "forbidden feeling" of outrage because her murdered father is buried without ceremony? What does she do when the relationships that necessitated the repression of her core rasa and adherence to her mask rasas are gone, violently stripped away? Luckily, Shakespeare lets us find out in Ofelia's famous and final scene: the mad scene.

In brief, my physical score and psychological action in the mad scene focused on: 1) performing a funeral for my father; 2) punishing and humiliating the king and queen for my father's death; and 3) secretly warning my brother of their treachery. For Ofelia, the scene is quite logically motivated, but her psycho-emotional conflicts overwhelm her, displacing and fragmenting her interactions. My four primary rasas were energized to the absolute extreme as I abruptly switched gears between them. In this scene, I allowed Ofelia to fully experience and express raudra. The force of that rasa, finally unleashed, was exhilarating, giving rise to new rasas: hasya (ridicule when mixed with raudra) and bibhatsa (disgust/contempt), all the better with which to blast and humiliate the king and queen.

Indispensable to the process of building this production was composer–choreographer Elizabeth (Liz) Claire. She (and the other musicians) created music that wove throughout the fabric of both the rehearsals and performances of this production. Liz is trained in Rasaboxes work, and I had the luxury of working with her on Ofelia's scenes, mostly scored to the sound of her solo violin. Between the two of us, we composed movement and music that supported, amplified, and greatly enhanced the rasic choices that were made.

Lastly, I used this work as offstage preparation before and during performances in order to gear up for scenes. While training in Rasaboxes, I learned to locate places in my body that, when moved (or held) in certain gestures or rhythms, initiated the sensations and physiology of a particular rasa. For example, my first experience with a complete psychophysical connection to karuna happened when I slowly and gently turned my forearms skyward in a gesture of helplessness. Karuna rasa arrived in a matter of seconds. I learned to quickly engage karuna using other physicalizations after this initial breakthrough. So, to prepare for my entrance into the mad scene, I engaged this rasa offstage in order to seem and feel as if I'd been crying inconsolably for weeks. My face would actually become red and puffy, tears streaked my cheeks, long strands of rheum ran from my nose! This was easy and fun to do; not painful, not personal. As I hit the boards to play the scene, I sensed the audience felt the rasa and experienced it with me. Their response fueled me even further, fueled the rasa shared between us. The effect, it seems, was both persuasive and harrowing.

Rasaboxes training helped me to plot Ofelia's journey throughout the play, to access her emotional and psychological behaviors, and to shape the moment-to-moment action. In rasic terms, perhaps I will say the work helped me to discover my own performance recipe: which ingredients to mix together, how long to stir and cook it, to "taste" and make adjustments, and finally, to offer up my creation to be shared and enjoyed.

Rasawalk: Site-Specific Explorations

Since the early 2000s, we have explored taking *rasawalks*, working outside the workshop space in various environments—constructed and natural, indoor and outdoor. The primary goal of a rasawalk is to explore an everyday environment through the lens of the rasas. The environments also open up previously undiscovered aspects of each rasa. In New York City, we have explored Penn Station, Washington Square Park, and Central Park. We have rasawalked on beaches, glens, and forests in California and Brazil, in downtown and rural environments in Ithaca, NY, the bucolic campus of Rose Bruford College in the UK, and elsewhere.

A rasawalk can happen anywhere—on Zoom, we might do them in our living room—and can be structured in a variety of ways. In natural environments, a person can connect the rasas to the elements—water, wind, earth, fire, and so on; to plants and animals; and to other people. In urban environments, participants have the chance to interact with concrete and metal architecture, escalators, benches, and signs, the myriad flavors found in shops and kiosks, as well as tourists, residents, and other group members. Similar to the ways flavors of food activate each rasa internally, the external environment stimulates us through our outwardly oriented senses (see Mee, Chapter 12).

Instructions

The following is one example of a rasawalk. The only requirement is that participants have developed an embodied relationship to the rasas on the grid before

FIGURE 4.26 Matt Watkins rasawalking on Moonstone Beach, CA. Rasaboxes Summer Intensive, Dell'Arte International School of Physical Theatre.

Source: Photo courtesy of Rachel Bowditch, 2009.

working outside or in public space. The group meets inside the workshop space and receives instructions for getting to the designated place for our rasawalk. Belongings are safely secured in the workshop space so that participants are as free as possible to explore.

Step 1: Moving to the Rasawalking Site

1. Choose a partner. Keep this partner in your view for the entire exercise, though you needn't do all or even any activities together. Partners may be quite far away from one another sometimes, or work closely together at other times.
2. In silence, the group makes its way to the perimeter of the designated rasawalking place, where further instructions may be given. Participants are encouraged to use all their senses to begin to attune to and notice elements of their environment.

Step 2: Rasawalking

1. Move slowly at first, perhaps even in slow motion (see Slow Motion Crossing, pp. 125–135), as you explore the environment. What rasas do you receive as you encounter different sights, smells, tastes, sounds, textures? Allow the rasa(s) to infuse you at a conscious level, breathe and pay attention to what you are taking in, in/gesting, in/haling, and so forth.
2. Play within a particular rasa, using it as a lens to experience the environment, to explore how it informs the quality of every encounter.
3. Deliberately change rasas at any time. Or change your focus to encounter something new in the same rasa.
4. Let the rasawalking happen without words. Instead, use breathing or Panting with Resonators if you want to get someone's attention. Or express the rasa you are experiencing through nonverbal sound.
5. The exercise ends when you hear a signal sound from the facilitator (a bell, whistle, etc.).
6. Find a starting place in the rasawalking area. After all instructions are given, begin with three Clearing Breaths.

Within the exercise you may do any of the following:

- You may include other participants in your exploration. Or not. Up to you.
- Break out by moving quickly with One Sound One Movement to get to another area. Once in the new area, slow your tempo again to engage with what you find there.
- Use Clearing Breaths at any time. Feel free to "cross out" or step out of the exercise as needed. You can cross back into rasawalking again at any time.

Step 3: Closing the Exercise

1. When you hear the signal, gather in a circle. Do three Clearing Breaths to end the rasawalk.
2. Share experiences in a Feedback Circle, either in the rasawalking location or back in the workshop space.

FIGURE 4.27 Performers in shavasana in workshop with Michele Minnick. Casa da Ribeira, Natal, Brazil.
Source: Photo courtesy of Mauricio Cuca, 2012.

Variations

Participants may dress up as a rasa persona or choose a dominant rasa as a base for the rasawalking experience. If so, time is given for the group to dress before leaving the workshop space for the rasawalking place.

Cool Downs

In TPW, cooling down is essential, both at the end of each session, and sometimes after individual exercises. A cool down can consist of a wide variety of activities with an intention of regulating the nervous system using either calming or energizing practices, depending on which activities have preceded it. Examples include Feedback and Discussion Circles, Clearing Breaths, songs, group sound or music circles, or lying-down in *shavasana* or "corpse-pose," or other resting and transitioning practices from a range of somatic traditions (see Figure 4.27). Cooldowns can provide an opportunity for not only recuperation but also digestion and integration of what has been learned or experienced.

Many of the exercises in TPW are vigorous. Some lead people into an altered state from which it can be difficult to move immediately into another exercise, or into conversation. Giving people ten minutes to journal, draw, rest, and reflect alone and in silence can help process those experiences, restore energy, and bring people into a state of readiness for the next activity. A Feedback Circle after an exercise can both cool down the group and allow the chance to metabolize what just happened.

Facilitators report that cooldowns are often neglected or absent, especially if ending workshop sessions "on time" is a priority. Sometimes we must find other ways to cool down, and there are many. Participants can be encouraged to be responsible for their own cool downs after the workshop, either in groups or individually. This can take the form of informal gatherings, such as socializing in hallways or other areas outside the workshop space, in restaurants or bars sharing food and drink, or in participants' homes. Whatever your cool down consists of, use it as a way of integrating what has been done, of letting the work go until the next session, and returning to life outside the workshop.

Waterfall: Recuperating from Rasaboxes

Consent and boundary check-ins need to be established before this exercise. This entire exercise happens in silence as a meditation.

1. The group stands in a circle with one person in the middle with their eyes closed.
2. One by one, beginning at the top of the head of the person in the middle, apply gentle yet firm touch, both hands pressing the sides of the body toward the center, in a descending sequence.
3. As soon as the first person's hands move, another person's hands start at the top of their head, and so on, so that as the hands move down the body, there is a feeling of a cascade or waterfall of touch that continues until everyone in the group has moved their hands down the person's body from head to feet.
4. A new person in the group stands in the center and steps 1–3 are repeated until the entire group has gone.

The effect of human touch can help to ground, rebalance, and reset the nervous system, especially after exercises like Rasaboxes.

Shanta Waterfall[11]

The lights in the room are dimmed to almost darkness.

1. Enter the shanta rasabox in silence.
2. Imagine you are standing under a waterfall that is washing away all the emotions and energy. Allow yourself to come to a peaceful place. This may take a few minutes.
3. When you feel ready, one at a time, exit the shanta rasabox and gather around the outside of the grid.

Closings

The Banquet

The culminating event of TPW is The Banquet. This is an extension of Crossings V: Slow Motion Transformation, and a ritual of closing for the workshop. The space is emptied at the end of the previous workshop session. If props and costumes or personal items have accumulated in the space during the workshop, participants remove unneeded things before the final session. The group must be able to leave the room with all their belongings in hand at the end of the final session. What is left behind is an empty space.

The space is set up with a long table(s) and chairs, so that the whole group can sit around a single banquet table, and a ladder for photo taking. Mirrors can be placed throughout the room for dressing. TPW facilitators participate in The Banquet as members of the group, bringing the same items as everyone else.

Each person brings:

- Clothes to wear at The Banquet: the most elegant and beautiful attire you can imagine. Dress for the occasion: a final Banquet to celebrate TPW. Come as your best self. Or, come as the superhero/goddess/rockstar/fantasy version of yourself.
- Food and drink: a single serving of your favorite food and drink. Bring just enough for yourself and maybe a little extra (rather than enough for the whole group). Facilitators may check in with the group about food allergies.
- Decorations and table settings: lighting, candles if allowed, flowers, tablecloths and/or place mats, bowls, plates, glasses and/or cups, utensils, napkins, etc.). Everything to make the table as beautiful as possible.
- Decorations for the space: lighting, party paraphernalia, etc. Any item used during the workshop can be used as decoration.
- Cameras: participants may take still photographs at designated times. This is one of the few times when cell phones are allowed in the workspace.

After the warm up, instructions for The Banquet are given one segment at a time:
In silence:

1. Place all your clothes neatly in a designated space (against the north wall, for example).
2. Place all food, table settings, room decor in a different designated space (against the south wall, for example).

Once the items are placed, then:
In silence:

1. Together, set up the banquet table and place chairs around it.
2. Decorate the space and table. Put your food and table settings on the table. Place your camera (if you brought one) on the table.
3. As people make choices about placement and decor, anyone is free to adjust or change anyone's choice. The decorating and placement phase is over once no more adjustments are made. The group moves to the edges of the room, then takes the time to regard what's been accomplished.

A ladder is placed near the table for posed photo taking, then:
   In silence:

   1. You may leave one or more pieces of your clothing or accessories on the chair in front of your place setting at the table, if desired.
   2. Display the rest of your clothing in a place at the edges of the room, where you feel comfortable changing.

When all have settled on places for displaying their clothing, the whole group dresses:
   In silence:

   1. Get dressed in as much of your Banquet attire as you have placed in this spot. Take your time.
   2. When you have completed dressing, take a standing still pose at the periphery of the space.

Once everyone is dressed and ready:
   In silence:

   1. In your mind's eye, design a slow motion physical score to get to your place at the table. You may plan to meet other people in the space as part of your score, or spontaneously interact with others in the moment.
   2. You may take breakouts from the slow motion by doing One Sound One Movement around the periphery of the space, then returning to the spot you left to resume your slow motion score.
   3. If you left one or more items of clothing at your chair, put it on in slow motion when you arrive at your place.
   4. When everyone has arrived and seated themselves at the table, strike a still pose—the first Banquet tableau.

After this has been accomplished:
   In silence:

   1. One person at a time rises from the table and takes up to three photos of the group. You may use the ladder or some other angle.
   2. While one person is preparing to take their photo, the group shifts from one still pose to a new still pose—creating a new tableau for each photographer.
   3. The photographer returns to the table, allowing the next person to prepare to take a photo while the group shifts into a new still pose, and so on.

When no one else takes a turn:
   In silence:

   1. The feasting begins, *but only in slow motion*.
   2. Do not feed yourself, *only others*. Offer a morsel of food or a sip of drink to someone.
   3. A person may accept, or refuse by slowly shaking their head "no," as in Crossings exercises.
   4. Move around the table feeding as many others as you wish from any dish you like, but only in slow motion.

After some time, the facilitators say "Pause." Then they say:

> *Now, move normally. Eat any way you like. Play music, talk, dance, have fun.* (People can play recorded or live music over the sound system, as at a party).

After people have danced, eaten, and drunk their fill, a facilitator says:

> *Now anyone can make a statement, reflection, performance offering, etc. to the group, or to particular participants or facilitators about their experience of the workshop. The statement can be in words, a song, a dance, or any kind of performance.*

When everyone who wants to has shared, a facilitator instructs:

> *It's time to clean the space. In silence, please throw away or recycle any unwanted food, trash, etc. in the containers provided and sweep and mop the space. Stow all personal belongings in your bags. Change into your street clothes (or not).*

This phase of the exercise is over when the space is totally clean, when everything is packed, and placed at the end of the space furthest from the entrance.

Uncrossing the Line

To begin the closing ritual of the workshop a facilitator says:

> *In silence, gather your personal belongings. You must carry them with you as we leave the space. Line up side-by-side facing the far wall opposite the crossing line, just a few inches away from the wall.*

Once everyone has gathered, the final actions are performed, in silence. The group "Uncrosses the Line" by moving slowly backward through the workshop space. As people move, a facilitator says something like:

> *Remember all that happened in this space during the workshop. When we arrive on the far side of the crossing line, we will pause, and take one last look.*

When everyone has stepped backward over the crossing line that defines the workshop space, a facilitator removes the masking tape. The group takes one last look at the space, and the facilitator turns off the lights. Moving backward, the group exits the studio. Once everyone is out, a facilitator closes the doors.

Out beyond The Performance Workshop world, ordinary life goes on.

Structure and Practice of TPW

Sample Outline for Three-Week Workshop

The following Sample TPW outline gives a basic sense of the progression of exercises, rather than a full account of everything that might happen day to day. It is not possible to do all the exercises included in this book in a 75-hour workshop, and exercises may be moved around to accommodate the unfolding of the work from one session to the next. We have not listed all daily rituals such as Greetings, Clearing Breaths, cooldowns, song sharing, etc., but focused on mapping out sequences of yoga, breath and sound work, Performances of Self, Group Sound, Crossings, Rasaboxes, and Group Performances. Due to the necessity of feeling out in real time the best moments for taking long and short breaks during the workshop, we have also not placed breaks in this sequence. Midway through each session, we take one long break that involves leaving the workshop space, for socializing and a bio (bathroom, food, water) break.

Week One

Week One, Day 1

Entering the Space
Crossing the Line
Names and Performative Introductions
Workshop Overview and Housekeeping
Yoga: Standing Poses
Breath Work: Humming and Clearing, Skull Shining Breath
Crossings I
Feedback and Discussion Circle
Assign: Song of Self

Week One, Day 2

Greetings: Arm Swings and Names
Yoga: Add Seated Poses
Breath Work: Add Alternate Nostril Breathing
Sound Work: Panting with Resonators
Crossings II
Songs

Week One, Day 3

Yoga: Add Lying Down Poses
Breath and Sound Work
Group Sound: One Sound
Perform: Song of Self
Performative Responses
Feedback and Discussion Circle

Week One, Day 4

Yoga, Breath, and Sound Work
Perform: Song of Self (continued)
Group Sound: One Sound One Movement
Crossings III
Assign: Song of Self II, Crossings IV
Introduce and Practice Slow Motion
Songs

Week One, Day 5

Yoga, Breath, and Sound Work
Aiming and Passing Sound
Crossings IV: Slow Motion
Feedback and Discussion Circle

Week Two

Week Two, Day 1

Yoga, Breath, and Sound Work
Open Sound
Perform: Song of Self II
Feedback and Discussion Circle

CHAPTER 4 ▸ Inside The Performance Workshop

Rasaboxes: Introduction, Orange Exercise, Writing and Drawing, Sculpting in Partners, Showing and Regarding
Assign: Group Performances

Week Two, Day 2

Yoga, Breath, and Sound Work
Rasaboxes: Making a Breath Phrase, Shanta Rasabox: First Taste, Shopping for Rasas, Shanta Waterfall
Feedback and Discussion Circle
Songs

Week Two, Day 3

Yoga, Breath, and Sound Work
Rasaboxes: Sound Sensation, Chorus Work, Relating in Partners, Relating with Shanta
Feedback and Discussion Circle
Assign: Crossings V: Slow Motion Transformation

Week Two, Day 4

Yoga, Breath, and Sound Work
Animal Exercise
Rasaboxes: Scaling Intensity, Intensity Arcs, Transitions, Chorus, and Relating with Text
Songs

Week Two, Day 5

Yoga, Breath, and Sound Work
Perform: Crossings V/Slow Motion Transformation
Feedback and Discussion Circle

Week Three

Week Three, Day 1

Yoga, Breath, and Sound Work
Perform: Group Performances
Feedback and Discussion Circle
Rasaboxes: Monologues, Chorus with Text

Week Three, Day 2

Yoga, Breath, and Sound Work
Perform: Group Performances (continued)
Feedback and Discussion Circle
Rasaboxes: Mixing and Layering Rasas, Scene Work
Assign: Banquet

Week Three, Day 3

Yoga, Breath, and Sound Work
Rasawalk
Feedback and Discussion Circle

Week Three, Day 4

(Catch Up Day/TBD)
Yoga, Breath, and Sound Work
Group Performances (continued)
Feedback and Discussion Circle

Week Three, Day 5

Yoga, Breath, and Sound Work
Banquet
Cleanup
Uncrossing the Line

Notes

1. We encourage anyone leading TPW exercises to adopt consent practices that work for them. Resources for establishing boundaries around physical touch and consent can be found in Adam Noble's "No-Fly Zones" and "Permission and Touch" (2011, 4–5) in "Sex and Violence: Practical Approaches for Dealing with Extreme Stage Physicality" and *Staging Sex: Best Practices, Tools, and Techniques for Theatrical Intimacy* by Chelsea Pace and Laura Rikard, Routledge (2020, 17–32).
2. www.whitesupremacyculture.info
3. TPW facilitators are not required to be certified yoga instructors; however, of the seven core teachers, more than half have significant yoga experience in more than one form of yoga. Most have extensive somatic movement education training.
4. The editors met Ekman in 2003 when Schechner invited him to observe Rasaboxes. Subsequently, Rasaboxes trained actors were invited to present at the 2004 International Society for Research on Emotion (ISRE) conference in New York and modeled facial expression of emotion for a *National Geographic* article, "On Assignment: Playing with Emotions," The Mind Issue, March 2005. Photographed by Cary Wolinsky.
5. See comparison of facial expressions of emotion of kathakali actor and Ekman models in "Magnitudes of Performance" in *Performance Theory* (Schechner 2003), pp. 306–309.
6. Other fruits may be substituted for health or taste reasons, but they should be juicy!
7. See Minnick (2016).
8. First published in "The Actor as Athlete of the Emotions: The Rasaboxes Exercise," by Michele Minnick and Paula Murray Cole in *Movement for Actors* (2017, 285–97).
9. This was the spelling used in Schechner's adaptation, which was a mixture of several versions of the play text.
10. The following compact description relies on the reader's foreknowledge of *Hamlet*. My intention is to be concise about how I used the Rasaboxes work together with Stanislavsky-based acting techniques in building a character.
11. The exercise was inspired by Anna Halprin's story of a healing ritual that included standing under an imagined waterfall (1995, 67).

Works Cited

Caillois, Roger. *Man, Plan, and Games*. Champaign, IL: University of Illinois Press, 2001 (1961).
Cole, Paula Murray. Personal TPW journal, 1998.
Czikszentmihalyi, Mihaly. *Finding Flow*. New York: Basic Books, 1997.
———. *Beyond Boredom and Anxiety: Experiencing Flow in Work and Play*. San Francisco: Jossey-Bass, 2000 (1975).
———. *Flow: The Psychology of Optimal Experience*. New York: Harper Pere Classics, 2008.
Dale, Daniel. "Richard Schechner's Notebook." *Namarupa*, vol. 05, 42, no. 13, May 2011, p. 15.
Ekman, Paul. *Emotions Revealed: Recognizing Faces and Feelings to Improve Communications and Emotional Life*, 1st ed. New York: Holt Paperbacks, 2003.
———. "On Assignment: Playing with Emotions." *National Geographic*, March 2005. The Mind Issue. National Geographic.com/Magazine
Grotowski, Jerzy. "The Theatre's New Testament." In *Towards a Poor Theatre*. London and New York: Routledge, 2012 (1968), pp. 35–36.
Halprin, Anna. *Moving Toward Life: Five Decades of Transformational Dance*. New Hampshire: Wesleyan University Press, 1995.

Huizinga, Johan. *Homo Ludens: A Study of the Play Element in Culture*. London: Routledge, 1949.
Iyengar, B. K. S. *Light On Yoga*. New York: Schocken Books, 1979.
Kirby, Michael. *A Formalist Theatre*. Philadelphia: University of Pennsylvania Press, (1987) 2011.
Lad, Vasant. *Textbook of Ayurveda: Fundamental Principles of Ayurveda. Volume One*. Albuquerque, NM: The Ayurvedic Press, 2002.
Linklater, Kristin. *Freeing the Natural Voice: Imagery and Art in the practice of Voice and Language*. Hollywood: Drama Publishers, 2006.
Minnick, Michele. *Breathing Worlds: Somatic Practice, Performance and the Self in the Life/Art Work of Leeny Sack*. Dissertation, 2016.
Minnick, Michele, and Paula Murray Cole. "The Actor as Athlete of the Emotions: The Rasaboxes Exercise." In *Movement for Actors*, edited by Nicole Potter, Mary Fleischer, and Barbara Adrian, 2nd Rev. ed. New York: Allworth Press, 2017 [2002], pp. 285–97.
Noble, Adam. "Sex and Violence: Practical Approaches for Dealing with Extreme Stage Physicality." *The Fight Master*, Spring 2011, pp. 2–6.
Pace, Chelsea, and Laura Rikard. *Staging Sex: Best Practices, Tools, and Techniques for Theatrical Intimacy*. London and New York: Routledge, 2020.
Pert, Candace B. *Molecules of Emotion: The Science Behind Mind–Body Medicine*. New York: Simon and Schuster, 1997.
Pollock, Sheldon. *A Rasa Reader*. New York: Columbia University Press, 2016 (paperback 2018).
Sajnani, Nisha, and Maitri Gopalakrishna. "Rasa: Exploring the Influence of Indian Performance Theory in Drama Therapy." *Drama Therapy Review*, vol. 3, no. 2, 2017.
Schechner, Richard. *Between Theatre and Anthropology*. Philadelphia: University of Pennsylvania Press, 1985.
———. *Environmental Theater*. New York: Applause Books, 1994. 1st ed. Hawthorn, 1973.
———. *Introduction to Performance Studies*, 4th ed. London and New York: Routledge, 2020.
———. Interview with Rachel Bowditch, Paula Murray Cole, and Michele Minnick, 2016.
———. Personal email correspondence with Michele Minnick, 2018.
———. *Perfomance Theory*. London and New York: Routledge, 2003.
Scott, John. *Ashtanga Yoga: The Definitive Step-by-Step Guide*. Hachette, UK: Gaia Books, 2000.
Turner, Victor. *The Ritual Process: Structure and Anti-Structure*. London and New York: Routledge, 1995.
Winnicott, D. W. *Playing and Reality*. London and New York: Routledge, 2005.

PART III

Facilitating The Performance Workshop

FIGURE 5.1 Sketch of performers doing Rasaboxes by Joan Schirle. Dell'Arte International School of Physical Theatre, 2005.

Courtesy of Paula Murray Cole.

CHAPTER 5

Principles of The Performance Workshop

An Interview with Richard Schechner

WITH PAULA MURRAY COLE, MICHELE MINNICK, AND RACHEL BOWDITCH
June 19, 2016; edited January 12, 2022

What are some of the key principles of TPW?

RS: The first principle is presence. As in *Waiting for Godot*, you have to be at an appointed place at an appointed time. Be there ready to work in an alert state of bodymind. And once you are there, be present. Attend all workshop sessions for the full time. The workshop is a temporary world, a whole unit, and if you're absent from it even once, you are amputated from the collective body. It's better to be in a sling, broken limb and all, watching and listening when you can't be fully participating than to be amputated from this world. So, either come to the workshop, even if it is just to watch, or take another workshop later, when you are better. You cannot be in the workshop, unless you're in the workshop.

Second, you have to have dual respect: internal respect for your own feelings, associations, and impulses; and respect for others, your workshop colleagues, and leaders. This respect commands physical safety first and psychological safety next. But this respect does not mean pussyfooting. The work is demanding.

Third, you should join a workshop willing to go beyond your ordinariness. This kind of workshop is designed to be experimental, literally: "ex-peri," outside the perimeter of your daily life. Be hungry for the extraordinary, generated by the simplest means.

And lastly, a willingness to not be too strictly bound by the clock, the time of each workshop session, and maybe even more importantly, the time of any exercise. It may take a whole session to do a single exercise; or maybe you don't finish it. What you learn from a workshop flows as night follows day and day follows night: you learn about your own processes of feeling, thinking, and relating, each in relationship to the other two.

A workshop, as I run it, should not be about the "I" but about the "we." The smallest social unit is two. Three or more is even more interesting, but not one. In the workshop, as you stand on the crossing line waiting to begin, or as you

FIGURE 5.2 Richard Schechner with an early sketch of Rasaboxes in his 1993 journal.

Source: Photo courtesy of Michael Kushner Photography, 2016.

cross a line into this or that rasabox, you're always aware of somebody next to you, somebody across from you, somebody else in the room. Each and every person in the room. Once, in The Performance Group, Stephen Borst said, "There's a little bit of you in each of me." That's what it comes to.

I would not do a one-on-one workshop. I need a critical mass, eight or nine, with 15 to 20 the most before the group becomes a crowd. You need enough people because part of the process is the chance to drop in and drop out, the possibility to hide, to experience the workshop as ocean waves: sometimes you're up, you're cresting; sometimes you're coming down, riding; sometimes you swim back against the current. And sometimes it's "selective inattention."[1] Once in a while, I'll doze. Or be in a hypnagogic state. Sometimes the work takes me into a twilight zone, into fantasies and dreams. That happens to participants, too. If people are doing slow motion, or singing repetitively, or carefully preparing "worlds" to inhabit—as preparation for the Slow Motion Transformation exercise, for example—I go off into my own whatever. Then, suddenly, I snap back. Maybe 20 years ago I would've said, "Oh my God! What am I doing sleeping here?" But I now feel that that's part of the process, a psychophysical/emotional state of half sleeping, half being awake. Its own kind of wakefulness—to that which can't be paid attention to, but just happens. So, it's a paradox. You want to be alert to your sleepiness. And you want to be in the kind of open sleep brain wave function. A lot of very creative things happen in that realm.

You have always made it a cardinal rule not to talk about the work outside of the workshop group.

RS: Yes, no gossiping. If you want to talk about someone, make sure that person is present. The interaction becomes a confrontation rather than gossip. It is essential to keep the work focused in and on itself, to let it recalibrate as it goes along. And if someone has a question about the work—why this exercise and not another; how to do something, and so on—this kind of discussion when done in a circle with all workshop participants present can advance the work collectively as well as individually. There may be some instances when an intimate just-you-and-me conversation is necessary. But that should be done when possible in the workshop space during the workshop time.

No observers—can you speak about that rule?

RS: People, when they're in something together, are more likely to disclose themselves, to go forward, if there's no one with a free ticket just watching. The workshop is not a show. However, once you get to open rehearsals and previews of a performance you obviously have observers as part of the process, but before that, don't compromise. No observers.

If I'm a performer, what can I expect to learn from TPW?

RS: Drop your expectations. In the workshop, you learn a little yoga, you learn basic breathing. You learn to slow down. You learn, in the paradoxical way I spoke of before, to pay and not pay attention at the same time. You learn to play with your fantasies and dreams, daydreams and night-dreams. You learn to make performance worlds. And you learn about others by learning about yourself; and the other way around, too. Maybe most of all, you learn that the boundary between yourself and another is porous, and in some circumstances, doesn't exist. How, if you're a sphere and somebody else is a sphere, how do those spheres overlap and interact with each other? It is hard to put this into words. At a very basic level, feelings can be sense perceptions. The metaphors are very powerful if you take them literally. So "How do you feel?" means "*How* do you feel?" What's the technique, the "how"? I can learn to feel an emotion with my fingers or taste it with my tongue or smell it with my nose. The rasas work that way, as immediate sense perceptions, in your gut, your mouth, nose, and so on. Yes, eyes and ears of course. But a core part of the Rasaboxes exercise is learning to engage the other senses. At their root, all the senses are to some degree tactile. They require contact. The most intimate sense is taste; it happens inside the body, inside the mouth and nose. You have to bring things not only close, but inside yourself to taste. Then touch with the hands, feet, or other body parts. Next is smell. Smell goes further than touch; it can fill a room or even an outdoor space. Sound goes further than smell. And sight, the farthest of all. In the workshop, we explore the senses we ordinarily do not examine closely. Of course, we do in eating and lovemaking. But there we are immersed, maybe overwhelmed; we are too excited or stimulated to examine these senses. In the workshop, you get the chance to slow down, examine, analyze even as you experience. You learn to play with these senses and get a feeling for each of them in their own domain, how they are in themselves and how they interact with each other.

In workshops, if I have enough time, I move from the visual, say Crossings, to sound such as Open Sound, and other ways of making sounds, to touch, and then to tasting. We do a lot of eating, sharing food, especially in Rasaboxes and in The Banquet. For a workshop that lasts a few weeks, we end with The Banquet.[2]

What happens over the time of the workshop is the processual evolution of individuals becoming a group. People join the workshop as individuals; they learn to become a collection of individuals, and if the workshop works, they end as a group. When it's over, everyone's a little sad. Over a few weeks, we've formed a community, a world.

Presumably, you invented or originated a lot of this work because something like it didn't already exist?

RS: I invented or adapted the work of others because I was directing plays and I wanted to work with a trained company but I wasn't satisfied with the training that was out there. Some of it was good, but performers needed more, needed something different.

My three-and-a-half-week workshop with Grotowski in the fall of 1967—from November 6 through November 30—a workshop he was running along with his company member and actor Ryszard Cieslak for NYU's Graduate Acting program—was very important. I took some of what Grotowski and Cieslak taught and used it immediately with people who would become The Performance Group. Then in 1971 I went to India. I saw a lot of different kinds of performances. And for several weeks I studied yoga with Tirumalai Krishnamacharya,[3] a great teacher-master, who said I could pass on what I learned, and I did, to The Performance Group. I also invited teachers to work with us on voice, Kristin Linklater, and on body-awareness, Elaine Summers, and other teachers, too. This work then became integrated into what I did in the performance workshops I led. Like with all practices, some was from what I learned, some was adapted and changed, and some was invented.

You weren't satisfied with the way people were being trained?

RS: Right. No matter how good they were as individuals, they hadn't worked together. So, the first thing I did was to have the people work together, not on a production but on what comes before a production, on the basics. Body-awareness, yoga, breathing, vocal production, and movement. And then later, emotional training such as Rasaboxes. At the same time, moving forward with complex exercises and improvisations. Enacted storytelling, devising, bringing in or writing texts, and so on.

How far back does that go, Richard? Did that start with The Performance Group or earlier?

RS: Wanting to have a company of trained performers started earlier. Ever since I was a grad student at the University of Iowa in 1957–58 and then after I came out of the army and went for my PhD at Tulane in 1960. It was at these places that I learned about the Moscow Art Theatre and the Berliner Ensemble. I formed theatre groups—the East End Players in Provincetown in the summers of 1957, 1958, and 1961, the New Orleans Group, which I co-directed in 1966–67 with musician Paul Epstein and painter Franklin Adams. Theatre is done best by trained teams. It's true in sports, it's true in business, it's true even in family life. In the modern era in western theatre, the great productions have been made by trained companies: Stanislavsky, Meyerhold, Brecht, Brook, Grotowski. And in our own day, The Performance Group and Wooster Group, the SITI Company, Mabou Mines, the Builders Association, TEAM, and others. Theatre companies are families, actual or invented. There are conflicts, like in all families, but the given is that the group will stay together, that there is basic trust. If trust is lacking, the group will disintegrate, and most often the project at hand will fail. But if there is trust, people can argue, bicker, and love the way a successful family does. In Asia, Africa, wherever there are traditional performing arts and rituals, the people who make the performances are families. The skills pass from parents to children. And the stories are about families, often enlarged into aristocrats and gods. In modern and postmodern Europe and America, the people who make the performances usually are not literally a family, but they become one through the group. And again, the stories they enact are all family dramas. Whether it's Ibsen or Beckett, Chekhov, the Greeks, or Shakespeare. Family dramas through and through.

What happens when there is a crisis within the group? How do you handle this when it does emerge?

RS: Yes, it often happens. Victor Turner said that social dramas go through four phases: breach, crisis, redressive action, reintegration or schism. So, whenever you have a crisis, there's the chance for the whole thing to break up. Or you work through the crisis so that when it's resolved the union is stronger.

The classic definition of drama is conflict. I've directed lots of plays. I don't want the person playing Claudius to hate the person playing Hamlet for real. I know that in sports you're playing for real. But then the whistle blows and you stop. The game ends, and you should embrace your opponent. It's the same in a workshop. And in Rasaboxes. Inside each box, you're all in. But once you step out, everything stops. You are an "athlete of the heart," Artaud's phrase. The idea is to fully engage and just as fully disengage. Like that, in the twinkling of an eye. That's a big thing to learn in the workshop: how to engage and disengage, to commit and stop, to be all in and all out. That's a very good lesson for all kinds of performances in life and in art—to deeply engage in your life and your work and then after work disengage with it. Don't bring everything home with you. I think the workshop helps with that.

Let's talk about how the workshop facilitator establishes the rules.

RS: The sports analogy works here, too. The workshop leaders are like umpires and referees, the keepers of the rules and the enforcers of the rules. They are also like coaches, guiding, teaching, and calling the plays. Playing in a rule-bound world allows the players to play intently, as hard as they can. The rules guide them, protect them, enable them. In the work process itself I'm able to sense when I need to intervene and when not. If people disagree with each other, how do you, as leader, moderate? What gets played out and what gets stopped? Finally, in a workshop as in everyday life, sometimes people don't like each other all the time, there's no way around it. Get over it, work through it, but in a performative way.

I wonder if you have any thoughts for today's theatre practitioner about the relevance of this work today, and looking toward the future?

RS: It's very hard for me to answer that, because I have no idea what people need. I'm not doing this work in order to meet somebody else's needs. I'm doing this work because people want to do it. And because I profoundly enjoy doing the work. Why they want to do it is their business. As long as they want to do it and I want to do it, there's a convergence. Truthfully, as I get older, I personally don't want to do it that often; that's why I've helped and authorized and done everything I can to encourage you and others to do it.

What advice would you give to teachers of this work?

RS: Keep practicing until the work becomes second nature. Don't teach what you don't know, but know that you can always learn more. Reaching from what you know to what you don't know. On and on. Work from and with the basics of awareness, body and vocal work, exercises like Crossings and Rasaboxes. There will come a time, when you know how to start an exercise but don't know where it will go. That's better than OK, that's good. You may not know the answers—for sure, you won't know all or even many of the answers—but you need to know the means of asking the questions.

There is ignorance and *ignorance*. Not knowing the basics is not acceptable. But not knowing the results can be very creative. Cultivate a young green mind. A young green mind can grow, be wounded, and re-grow. It is supple, it seeks what's going on. It doesn't feel it owns the only truth. It knows there are multiple truths depending on circumstances. I would also say the teacher should be as physically adept as she or he can be. As you grow older, this becomes more difficult. Because I am older, I do more physical work in the gym than I did 30 years ago. That doesn't mean I'm better, it means my body is worse, and therefore needs more maintenance. So, and maybe this seems ironic, the older you get, the more you have to learn, the more intently you have to study. Knowledge is a tiny ship sailing the ocean of ignorance.

Notes

1 See Schechner, "Selective Inattention," *Performing Arts Journal*, 1, 1 1976 (reprinted in all editions of Schechner's *Performance Theory*).
2 See Chapter 4, pp. 181–183.
3 See Chapter 1, pp. 24–26 and Chapter 4, pp. 94–98.

CHAPTER 6

The Unavoidable Guru
Roles of The Performance Workshop Leader

SCOTT WALLIN

An effective leader of The Performance Workshop (TPW) must play a variety of roles, beyond simply organizing the workshop and explaining the exercises. Here, I argue that one such role is the "guru." In *The Dionysus Group*, actor and theatre scholar William Shephard recounts how his desire to learn from theatre guru Jerzy Grotowski led to his participation in Richard Schechner's 1967 performance workshop in New York:

> My initial reading of Grotowski's essay, "Towards a Poor Theatre," was an astounding experience for me. I found that the work of the Polish Theatre Laboratory confirmed my conviction that the work of the actor was at the core of the theatrical experience, and, in addition, Grotowski was able to articulate my innermost presentiments. . . . I returned to Schechner with my enthusiasm for Grotowski's work, and that very same evening after class he informed me that Grotowski was coming to NYU to conduct a five-week seminar for selected students and guests at the School of the Arts in the near future (Oct.–Nov., 1967). I was overjoyed at the prospect—what luck! Unfortunately, however, I was not one of the students selected to participate in the seminar, and no amount of pleading with the school administration changed my circumstances.
>
> Schechner had been invited to participate, and I could do nothing but literally wring my sweaty hands with envy and frustration as Schechner talked, in class, about his forthcoming work with Grotowski. Schechner, however, assuaged some measure of my pain over the blind injustice of school administrators by telling me that he intended to start a workshop, himself, after Grotowski's departure. In addition to his own ideas for environmental theatre, Schechner said that he would be using elements taken from his work with Grotowski.
>
> (1991, 3–4)

For Shephard, the fact that he could not participate in Grotowski's workshop was almost too much to bear. But happily, Schechner offered himself to the young artist as a surrogate guru.[1] Schechner's historic workshop in the Tompkins Square Community Center in Manhattan's East Village, in which Shephard participated,

198 PART III ▸ Facilitating The Performance Workshop

FIGURE 6.1 Discussion circle with participants in workshop with Richard Schechner, Norway.

Source: Photo courtesy of Richard Schechner, 2013.

evolved into The Performance Group (TPG), which starting in March 1968 had its home at The Performing Garage, where the company created *Dionysus in 69* (see pp. 20–23).

Shephard's story expresses the same yearning that led me in 2005 to New York University's graduate program in performance studies. As an undergraduate I had studied acting and directing and, like Shephard, quickly became disenchanted with the mainstream theatre Peter Brook condemned in *The Empty Space* (1968). I passionately embraced the ideas of various experimental theatre artists such as Grotowski, Brook, Antonin Artaud, and Joseph Chaikin. When I discovered Schechner's writings, I had found my guru and embraced performance studies as my interdisciplinary home. I eventually quit my day job as a clinical social worker and moved to New York to study with the scholar and artist I felt I had come to know so well—at least on paper.

When I arrived for the first semester of my program in the summer of 2005, I learned with sharp disappointment that Schechner was away on sabbatical until the following spring. However, The Performance Workshop he had developed was now being taught by two members of East Coast Artists, Michele Minnick and Paula Murray Cole. I enthusiastically applied for the course. Walking home in the late evening after the first session, I knew that I had come home to like-minded artists, even though my expected "guru" was absent. In the weeks to come, I discovered that TPW creates a liminoid space structured by ritual, play, and spectatorship (see Turner 1982, 20–60) in support of its psychophysical and environmental theatre practices. The exercises (see Chapter 4) combined discipline and silliness, tradition and transgression. We deconstructed everyday social norms, personas of self, and ways of engaging with our bodies, emotions, objects, texts, and others in the ensemble in order to explore new temporal, spatial, physical, psychological, and interpersonal experiences, perceptions, and meanings.

After the workshop concluded, many of us wished to continue the work. We met on our own on a weekly basis in the performance studies studio, repeating and experimenting with the exercises we had found so enriching earlier that summer. But the atmosphere in the studio felt different than what we had experienced in NYU's Abe Burrows Theatre. Even though the studio space was smaller, it felt empty, sterile, and less inviting than the much larger theatre. Our yoga sessions were cursory, and we felt like individuals practicing in the same room instead of an intimate ensemble. The Rasaboxes work seemed somehow less "authentic." Although the One Sound One Movement exercises remained productive, they were isolated events that did not hold the sessions together. Attendance became spotty. Ten weeks after we began, we stopped meeting altogether. I was frustrated with our seeming inability to carry the work forward and asked myself why we had failed. Was this not the same group of individuals who had carried out such strong work only a couple of months ago? Was our inefficacy attributable to our busy schedules as graduate students? Was it because we were no longer enrolled in a costly class that demanded strict attendance for university credit?

True as these reasons were, I suspected there was something else that went beyond schedules and institutional sanctioning: we lacked a leader. Although another student and I facilitated each meeting by suggesting and leading individual exercises, we modeled our group as a collective. No one was in charge. Because of this, something integral was missing from the process, even though collectively we knew everything needed to conduct the exercises. As people drifted away, I cynically suspected that the others lacked self-discipline and required an authority figure to keep them on task. Or perhaps someone needed to literally stand in as the "guru" in order for the others to collectively render the studio space ripe for exploration, play, and risk. I wondered if, without such a leader, some necessary link to tradition had been broken. Even though I enthusiastically attended each meeting, I felt that the magic was lacking. It was as if we had become artistic orphans, lacking our bridge to the past, the spark necessary to animate the work and infuse it with life. Ten years later, after having participated in, assisted with, and co-led additional workshops with Cole and Minnick, as well as incorporating many TPW exercises into my acting courses and rehearsals, I now see that the demise of our collective does not have a mystical explanation. Our group's failure provides evidence that the leader is the keystone of TPW. During the summer, Minnick and Cole were indispensable. This leadership role needs to be understood in order to ensure that the rich work that began with Schechner continues to develop.

In order to examine this topic, I interviewed Schechner, Minnick, and Cole to see how they articulate what it takes to make the workshop the kind of positive experience I had. The complete workshop and some of its component exercises have been taught by second-generation and even third-generation leaders. With each new leader, the work evolves. What does it take for a leader to be both a facilitator and a guru—one who not only teaches the exercises but also inspires future leaders? In my attempt to pinpoint the essence of the successful workshop guru, I have followed my personal lineage of workshop leadership. By focusing on Schechner's thoughts and writings, Minnick and Cole's reports of their work with Schechner, how they have maintained and adjusted his ideas and exercises to fit their own personalities and interests, and my own experience with all three leaders, I seek to clarify the leader's role and symbolic function in creating the sort of workshop experience that I have come to know and value. The tensions, dualities, and paradoxes of the role that these three have revealed provide insight into how a leader might perform most effectively.

Haunting my exploration of the leader's role is the term "guru," which can be cryptic and misleading without clarification. This guru is not a single person but rather the personification of the workshop's traditions, the best practices of any particular lineage of leadership, and the seemingly mystical qualities of a leader that some participants, such as myself and Shephard, have sought. Grotowski and Artaud have remained two of my mythic, historical gurus, haunting the workshop space with the promise of passion and commitment. Schechner's writings and his explication and implementation of others' ideas, including Grotowski and Artaud's, led me to seek him out as my guru in 2005. He did serve as my professor and advisor while I was a graduate student at NYU, but our practice together has been limited to stand-alone, single-day workshops—never the long-term, in-depth experience I had sought. He therefore remains at arm's length, an iconic but distant figure to me in terms of The Performance Workshop. In the actual workshop I participated in, Minnick and Cole successfully performed as practical—but, importantly, also proxy—gurus for me.

The Many Hats of the Workshop Leader

During our conversation about TPW, Schechner was eager to demystify the term "guru" and quickly pointed out to me that the Sanskrit word basically means teacher.[2] But I am considering the term as it has been appropriated by many western theater practitioners over the past century. When these artists refer to a "guru," we must understand such usage in its new context rather than how the term was and is used in India. Much of TPW, such as its yoga[3] and application of rasa theory, borrows and builds upon South Asian performance theories and practices. Regardless of whether we laud such adoption as creative borrowing or condemn it as orientalist misappropriation, such adapted concepts and practices need to be defined and assessed as separate and unique from what they are derived from. Yes, in Sanskrit, "guru" means teacher. However, a teacher may perform many roles and functions, and The Performance Workshop leader does much more than transfer knowledge to participants. Theatrically speaking, a TPW leader serves as stage manager, director, and primary audience. In ritual terms, they are the shaman, a transporter or bridge to the workshop's liminoid space. In terms of play, the leader is a coach, referee, and trickster. In terms of therapy, they are the analyst: both the disinterested target of transference and the projector of countertransference. In familial terms, they are the parent, the authority figure who both supports their charges and pushes them out on their own, simultaneously taking responsibility for them and letting go of that role.

The Bridge and the Holder of the Space

TPW centers on the Crossings exercises (see Chapter 4) through which participants are transported from everyday reality into a liminoid space-time where daily roles and identities are held in abeyance. Crossings is a complex set of exercises that share one action: the movement of performers across a line into a liminal space, having specific experiences in that space, and then crossing back into ordinary space. Within the liminal arena of ritual, play, and theatre, participants experience different rules, expectations, and possibilities than in the spaces of daily life. Time may slow down, the spoken word may be silenced or transformed, songs may be sung, rhythmic physical and sonic actions of endurance may be explored, personas may be tried on and performed, fantasies and free association may be pursued, and affects may be engaged, explored, and shared. None of this can occur without some sort of "crossing," which naturally needs a bridge. Although the visible bridge may be nothing more than a piece of tape on the floor, the workshop leader officiates the crossings of that threshold. They function as both a stage manager and kind of lay shaman to organize, sanction, and support these transportations.

In the fall of 2005, our workshop collective lacked someone who officially initiated and ended each session by framing the temporal and physical space and inviting the others to cross into it (see Chapter 4, pp. 90–91). By traversing the line that facilitators of The Performance Workshop set in place, participants viscerally experience the change from the outside everyday space to the space of the workshop and ritually affirm for themselves and others their commitment to the work at hand. Crossing the line can be understood as the embodied equivalent of an Austinian speech act, a performative, because it physically engenders the liminoid space (see Austin 1975). I do not recall anyone in our collective carrying out the seemingly mundane task of taping down the line at the door of the studio to demarcate where we would cross the line to begin our work each night; certainly no one oversaw our crossing into the workshop space. This omission might seem trivial for a group who had already "crossed" together many times. Perhaps the act of taping the line was so associated with the functions and responsibilities of the workshop leader that no one in our group was audacious enough to do it, thereby symbolically asserting themselves as the leader. We unconsciously chose to ignore the taped line's significance, treating it as inconsequential, acting as if we had already crossed. The ramification of this omission is profound. Not only did we lack a group director to decide what exercises to practice in the space, we had no one to mark the space itself. Because no one had delineated the space and then invited the rest of us to cross into it, our unspoken performatives of entry were never initiated. We never ritually entered the space.

After the initial crossing, the leader acts as the shaman figure to assist the participants in transporting themselves during various exercises. There is nothing magical about this task, but transportation itself can feel somewhat mystical.[4] In conversation with me, Schechner explained that:

> The shaman is not such an extraordinary person. The shaman is kind of self-selected, and selected by his or her group, to be a link between one set of powers—which are strong, useful, and dangerous—and society. There needs to be a bridge between them. That's also true in religion. *Pontiff* is related to the French word *pons*; it's Latin for bridge. And the pope is the bridge between the world of the Catholic community and the world of the clergy and the institution of the church. Also, the institution of the church is the bridge to heaven, to the Divine. So, the shaman is a bridge but not necessarily so powerful. Temporarily powerful, in-the-midst-of-the-rites powerful.

Along with bridging their group to the extraordinary, the shaman also provides an anchor to tradition. In my first workshop, Minnick and Cole similarly served as links to Schechner's previous workshops, and therefore to him. Because they had participated in those workshops with Schechner and had been sanctioned by him to lead us, I believed in their guidance and assurance that our group's efforts followed the original TPW's structure and practices. I entrusted them with the power to oversee and sanction our transportations.

At the same time, a link to tradition alone is not enough. Minnick and Cole's role as bridge to tradition was legitimized by their own abilities and proclivities as leaders. They recreated the liminoid space with their own unique style of leadership, using as well the interests and abilities that the other participants brought to the work. In other words, my first performance workshop—like all such workshops before and after—cited the authority of tradition and past leaders while generating new traditions born from the evolving work and the culture of each new group of participants.

As supervisor of the workshop's many crossings, the leader does more than give guidance, permission, and encouragement. They serve as the default audience member. Our collective lacked this person. Because no one functioned primarily as the watcher, the group could not experience being truly watched, a vital component of most performances (see Chapter 4, p. 111). We proceeded to perform in a rather unheeded and arguably incomplete way, much like speaking into an anechoic chamber or releasing air into a vacuum. No wonder the space felt vacuous despite its small size. It follows that one of the primary functions of the workshop leader, after delineating the space and sanctioning the crossing is to "hold" the space, to contain and define it. There must always be someone on the perimeter watching the others work. The leader need not always be the one to perform this function, but their presence in the room assures the group that someone will always be appointed to take this role. Once the leader has demonstrated their ultimate responsibility for this duty, the participants trust them never to allow the work to proceed untended.

The primary material of The Performance Workshop is the participants' own bodies, thoughts, feelings, and performed identities. Thus, an important aspect of holding the space is helping participants embrace their own sense of self while encouraging them to explore and expand their boundaries of self-expression, representation, and interactions. When most effective, the workshop playfully teeters between the known and unknown, conformity and transgression, safety and risk. It does so by offering an enticing and unnerving tension between performing, in Schechner's well-known formulation, the liminal tension between "not me" and "not not me."[5]

> People who have signed up for a workshop probably know a little bit about me or whoever the leader might be, and so they have preselected themselves for a certain kind of experience. Amusement parks give it to us in a physical way. You know, you want the roller coaster to be scary. You don't want to come off the roller coaster and say, that was nothing. At the same time, you don't want to die on the roller coaster. So when you get into the car and it starts moving, you know, what's your limit? A good one is right at that limit. Carnival gives that with identity. You can put on a mask and be who you are not. In a workshop, I'm providing an arena for these kinds of experiences within a framework where you are going to hopefully learn certain techniques or skills that will help you: a) if you want to make performances; and b) in your ordinary life. And it drives a wedge between what or who you are pretending to be and what or who you are.

Part of trying on and exploring new identities includes crafting performances of self, which we craft, in part, with tools of personal expression that Goffman terms "personal fronts" (1959, 24). These may include clothing, posture, speech patterns, facial expressions, bodily gestures, various props, language, markers of sex, gender, race, ethnicity, age, ability, and more. But what they all require by definition is an audience of at least one other person to whom the performance is played. The leader thus not only demarcates a liminoid sandbox in which the group can experiment with such fronts, but also offers themselves up to each participant as the recipient for those performances. Minnick describes the role of the leader-as-holder:

> I, as the leader, am the stand-in for the audience who is not there. And I think of myself as an anchor. There are moments when it's really important to get others to hold the space with me, but I'm always the primary holder of the work. As the primary witness, I give people freedom because they know that there is someone out there watching. The practice is always moving between doing, watching others, and being watched watching, just like the lines on the floor, which both contain things and give you a clear boundary within which you can be free.[6]

Holding the space not only affirms the participants' performances, it also allows them the freedom from concern about certain details of the work or the underlying structure that holds the entire world of the workshop together. Additionally, they know that someone is actively striving to maintain the participants' physical safety and basic human rights during the work. Minnick notes that participants, free from such responsibility, experience a "total immersion in a world that is emerging as the group moves through it." Because the world is unfolding in real time, no one knows what will happen next. This uncertainty or first-time-ness brings anticipation and immediacy to the work for the participants. In order for this to occur, however, the process needs a director who maintains an outsider's perspective, manages the workshop's substructure, and attends to the physical safety of the group.

In order for the work to have a sense of immediacy and organicity, the workshop leader cannot set or know what exactly will happen on any given day or even within any exercise, although they have an outline of the progression of various steps that the group may aim for. How much a group will do in an evening or what that work will look like is contingent upon the makeup of each individual, the relationships between individual members of the group, the chemistry of the group as a whole, and all other factors related to the time and place of the work. The leader is always anticipating and responding to the group's energy, inclinations, and choices. In doing so, they strategically parse out information in doses, giving participants only enough information to engage with the immediate task at hand. This leads to productive anticipation and a sense of mystique for the participants. However, the leader unavoidably becomes in many ways the decision maker and authority figure of and for the group.

Schechner notes that when participants enter the workshop, they agree to "surrender their little bundles of freedom to the leader for the time of the workshop." This surrender, he explains, is empowering for everyone:

> It gives power to the leader, of course. But it also liberates those who are giving up that freedom and don't have to think about, "What am I doing here?" She or he has to only say, "I'll do what I'm told to do" [meaning, "I'll surrender to the process."] We know this from Zen. We know from meditative practices that if you give up desire, as it were, if you give up your individual originality, you'll come upon a profound originality. And you'll come to understand your desires better. So that's what the meditative practice, and person coming to the workshop is saying: "I don't want anything." I mean, insofar as they're able. "You tell me what I want, what to do."

Although this surrender is integral to the workshop, the question of potential risk arises. The line between withholding information and manipulating participants is not always clear, even though some manipulation might be welcomed. In *Environmental Theater*, Schechner describes an early workshop experience at Goddard College where he misled, ostensibly for her own good, a participant who felt that she couldn't trust three of her group members and was therefore afraid to let them touch her ([1973] 1994, 155). Instructing her to keep her eyes closed during a physical "rolling" exercise, Schechner silently substituted her original partners with the three people she had refused to work with. Once disabused, the participant reportedly expressed positive feelings and growth. Today, most would consider such use of deceit around the issue of consent disrespectful, unethical, and potentially harmful. But it is easier now after the #MeToo movement has increased awareness and public discussion of consent, sexual assault, and the abuse of authority in the workplace, to clearly recognize such an error. It is reasonable to assume that today we remain ignorant of other issues around consent and abuse of authority that we will develop a better understanding and appreciation of in the future. Schechner's candid examples of past mistakes made at Goddard College therefore serve as warnings for current and future leaders that participants, by relying upon the workshop leader, assign them a great responsibility because the work necessarily embraces uncertainty, a sense of danger, and flirts with rule-breaking.

What participants get out of the workshop correlates with how far they push against their comfort levels and take risks. How far is too far? Schechner offers a speech at the beginning of each workshop:

> I'm going to ask you to do whatever I ask you to do. I will never ask you to do something that is physically harmful. I have no idea what might be psychologically dangerous for you. . . . For me to be free and you to be free, we have to have this rule: I will ask whatever comes to my mind, because some of the things I've prepared and some I haven't. And you're free not to do it. You do it or not do it. But if you do it, you're responsible for it. I'm not. You're deciding to do it. And you can stop any time. It's not about braving it out. At the same time, I can be very seductive about wanting you to go forward. And I will try to urge you to go forward.

Reflecting on this, Schechner observes that

> there's a paradox that I'm saying that they don't have to do these things if they don't want to do them, but if they don't do them, they're not going to get what the workshop's about. So, they are both responsible, and maintain their authority, identity, whatever it is, and surrender it at the same time.

Any person in a position of authority, be it a teacher, parent, therapist, or theatre director, must adhere to a code of ethics to safeguard those in their care. But unlike the traditional psychoanalyst who figuratively or even literally places themselves in a position safe from scrutiny, the workshop leader is far from a neutral component of the group work—although how much a leader will use their own self, desires, and aesthetic proclivities in the work varies. Among the currently discussed leaders, Schechner has brought perhaps the greatest amount of his own imagination and desire into the workshop.

> [What's rewarding about being a workshop leader is that] you see and reverberate with these fabulous performances. And you get a chance to help structure those performances. When I watch, there's a lot of selective inattention. I'm watching, and in watching sometimes I go off into a hypnagogic fantasyland, and that gives me something to say. I'm also not working from a prepared script. I'm working from a kind of emotional contact improvisation. What I'm getting from what I'm seeing is also what I'm giving back as instructions. Yes, I do know the opening stuff with the crossing exercises. Yes, I do know with Rasaboxes the sequence of first writing the words and then speaking them, and so on and so forth. There is a sequence to how it all unfolds. But at a certain point, like at a sports match, within the rules there's an awful lot of room for variation and improvisation. So that is extremely creative.

In inserting their own fantasies, desires, and aesthetic proclivities into the group's work, the leader, to at least a certain degree, asserts their cultural values, morals, and perspectives, which are invariably influenced by their own subject position, including sex, gender, race, ethnicity, age, socioeconomic status, and abilities. By using themselves in the work, the leader is not offering the group anything less than what the other participants might contribute, except that the leader has greater influence over the proceedings. This is not necessarily a problem, but it should be recognized because the workshop process is not evident to the participants from the outset, when they are still at a point when they can decide whether or not to embark on the journey in the first place.

The leader's subject position not only influences the work, it also appears to inform just how much they infuse their personal self and desires into the group's work. Although Cole says that Schechner would ultimately "manage to decentralize himself and put the participants in relationship to each other as the primary focus [of the work]," he has arguably taken the most liberties in shaping workshop proceedings as they unfold, both by spontaneously handing out modifications whenever he feels moved to do so and by sometimes suggesting how someone might redo an exercise or performance.[7] Relevant to his personal imprint on the group work are Schechner's other roles outside of the workshops: notable director; prodigious scholar; and the primary progenitor of the workshop. Cole, in contrast, has primarily worked professionally as an actor, acting trainer, and licensed massage therapist, roles that prioritize serving others' ideas, growth, and needs.

> The way that I facilitate a workshop, I put myself in connection with the material, but my desire is not a central component of it. I'm trying to say, "What happens *between* you guys is the important thing, not my particular desire as a director or what I'd like to see." I'm not trying to move you towards a particular goal. If there is any goal, it is . . . more of a trainer's goal than an artist's. I try to make myself as invisible as possible. I want people to feel themselves in the work. I'm not interested in them feeling me in the work.

This tension between pedagogically driven facilitation and that which is at least partially driven by the leader's own creative desires and fantasies can also be described in psychodynamic terms. In traditional Freudian psychoanalysis, the analyst serves as a blank screen for the analysand's emotions to be transferred and illuminated. Then, as the analysand projects their thoughts and feelings, the analyst may note their own emotional reactions, i.e., countertransference, in order to better reveal and understand the analysand's conflicts and other issues. In TPW, the leader's "blank screen" extends beyond the leader herself to the workshop space she delineates and holds for the others. For Schechner, the leader will then insert his "countertransference" into the work as desired not only to facilitate the workshop process but also for his own pleasure and creative needs. For Cole, however, as a leader she expresses little countertransference because she sees her own desire and creative urges in response to the participants' contributions as unnecessary and, perhaps, distracting or intrusive. As the decider, she sets the agenda in terms of structure and the skills and creative processes to be practiced, and while she dictates little of the content that her students explore, her choices (to be "invisible," for example) unavoidably configure the work according to her particular desires.

The Trickster

The workshop leader is integral to the workshop's ritual nature, but they also serve as a jokester or trickster in order to facilitate the play, transgression, and anti-structure[8] necessary to ignite the group's creativity. According to Minnick, Schechner is a good role model for this aspect of the leader.

> [Schechner] has this presence as an instigator, but then he could also sit back and hold whatever was happening and not be particularly invested in what happens. One thing that was clear right away was the importance of his playfulness. When people started asking a lot of questions about his directions, he would say, "Do what you think I mean." The fun part for him is discovering how people understand what he's asking for or discovering that people don't want to do what he's asking and want to do something else. It was so exciting and different because in his other capacities as director and scholar he has such an authoritative presence. In the workshop he lets go of that to a great degree. He's also very spontaneous. And he's always inventing.

One way Schechner functions as an instigator is by introducing, expressing, or making room for that which is often repressed. For example, even though mass media in the United States prominently displays sexuality and the erotic in the public and private spheres, the public exploration of the personally erotic via our own bodies is much less common. Actors who have no difficulty taking off their clothes as long as it is their "character" doing so may hesitate doing so in a workshop setting (see Chapter 4, p. 113). A disrobed actor on stage or a film set is following a socially and publicly sanctioned code of behavior and is therefore still somewhat "clothed" by their professional status and dramatic role. This sense of protection or shielding is reinforced by the use of industry intimacy consultants and closed sets that help demarcate clear lines between the performer and their character. In contrast, TPW encourages participants to use and perform, i.e., reveal, their own sense of selves. Cole relates how, many years ago as a participant in Schechner's workshop, she faced the choice of whether or not to disrobe:

> All of these invitations were a self-challenge. [Schechner] didn't ask us to do that, but he gave instructions that would give rise to that possibility in different exercises; and I, who had confidently taken off my clothes in theatre [productions], felt very challenged in this space, you know, because it was me. There was no mediation of character in between.

Although such work can be challenging, its risk is tempered by the playfulness of the workshop space. Play theorist Johan Huizinga (1971) defines playful behavior as not entirely real, serious, or within the domain of ordinary life. Within the framework of play, behavior is not taken at face value. Gregory Bateson notes that when a dog plays by pretending to fight, its playful nip denotes a bite while also communicating "this is not a bite" ([1972] 2000, 180). The ludic condition of the workshop can also be framed in terms of the aesthetic element of the work. For example, for Cole, what prevents the engagement of the participants' intimate and personal feelings from becoming pure therapy is the fact that such work is "always channeled through the aesthetic." The primary purpose is creative exploration, not personal problem solving. However, neither are workshop performances and exercises completely separate from "real life." The participants use their own bodies, feelings, and subjectivities, which means that the workshop soon fills with intimate connections to the group's sense of self outside the ludic arena. This is what makes the play both risky and performative. Ultimately, the temporary and provisional nature of the workshop allows for a great expansion of and experimentation with self that is both manageable and an effective testing ground for behavior, ideas, and even values that later might be performed "for real" and "for keeps."

The workshop leader models and sanctions the group's playful anti-structure, which in turn partially—yet productively—undermines the leader's direction and control over the proceedings. When workshop participants asked Schechner to clarify his instructions, he responded that participants should simply follow their own interpretations of his words. This invites creativity and demonstrates an openness to all that may occur. It embraces risk and playful revolution because such open-ended instructions will upend Schechner's vision of how the exercise would otherwise proceed. Playfulness can thus be seen as the counterbalance to concern about the leader's power as the decider—the authority figure the participants trust to give up their "little bundles of freedom." Furthermore, if there is a danger that the leader, as the primary screen for the group's transference, might also produce excessive countertransference that imposes unwanted perspectives, values, and desires onto the group and thereby hinders the participants' own views and authorship, this risk is tempered by the leader's sense of play, which, by promoting anti-structure, undermines some of their authority and direction of the workshop proceedings. Although such play continues to insert the leader's personality and desires into the work, it does so from the position of leader-as-participant instead of leader-as-director.

Informed by theories of play and ritual, Schechner performed the trickster holy man in his own workshops, facilitating with a passionate commitment to both structured ritual and ludic transgression. This mix of qualities may seem a tall order for future workshop leaders, but not every leader must play the role of instigator. As participant, assistant, and co-leader, I have experienced Cole as playful but not impish, more of a trainer who enjoys and guides the work than a jokester who mischievously stirs the pot. As a theatre director and workshop participant, I love to follow my own desires and realize my visions. But as a nascent workshop leader, perhaps because of my background as a therapist, I also tend to take a more conservative role in the group by stepping back, holding the space, and focusing on others' exploration.

Conclusion

Each performance workshop leader will come to the work with their own unique background, skill set, and personality. As essential as being able to teach rasa theory or demonstrate Krishnamacharya's yoga sequence is the leader's appreciation of their basic role in constructing and facilitating the workshop's dual process of ritual and play, which is vital to the group's ability to be transported into the workshop space and each individual's capacity for experimentation. Although not all participants will come to the work seeking a "guru" per se, the leader who serves as a bridge will allow individuals and the group to tap into the traditions and passion that bring productive respect for the work and enrich the liminoid space with a spark of mystique. These are the qualities that empower the participants to work and grow. By faithfully understanding the roles of TPW leader as embodied and modeled by predecessors such as Schechner, Minnick, and Cole, current and future leaders will maintain the integral components of conservative ritual and transgressive play necessary to facilitating the construction of liminoid space, and innovate in ways that keep the work relevant to the contemporary moment.

Notes

1 I use the word "surrogate" advisedly. By 1967, Schechner was already well known as editor of *TDR*, a producing director of the Free Southern Theater, and a founding director of the New Orleans Group. *TDR* in hand, he arrived in New York in the summer of 1967 to become a professor at NYU. In reference to the years that followed, Schechner reports, "Group-wise I became a guru, loved and hated by the people I worked with. The nature of some of the exercises—... the hours-long improvisations evoking both mythic and intimate material, encounter and confrontation work—corroborated my position" (1994, 257).
2 Unless otherwise noted, all quotes attributed to Richard Schechner are from our conversation in June 2016.
3 Schechner learned yoga in Chennai in 1971 from the great master, Krishnamacharya (see Chapter 1, pp. 24–26).
4 In *Between Theater & Anthropology*, Schechner distinguishes temporary change from permanent within liminal space (1985, 117–50). After a "transportive" performance, performers return to ordinary life and their previous social identities, whereas "transformative" performances, such as initiation rites, intend to permanently change the participants' social identity or status (see "transport and transform," p. 30).
5 Merging psychoanalyst D.W. Winnicott's idea of "transitional objects and phenomena" (see Winnicott, p. 120) anthropologists Arnold Van Gennep's and Victor Turner's concepts of rites of passage and the liminal/liminoid (see Chapter 1, pp. 30–31), and Gregory Bateson's concept of the "play frame," Schechner argues that adults, during artistic and religious activity, can enter a temporary social and personal field of "double negativity" where ordinary hierarchies are dissolved and the ordinary actualities of identity are deconstructed through playful choice and experimentation (1985, 110).
6 Unless otherwise noted, all quotes attributed to Michele Minnick are from our conversation in July 2016.
7 Unless otherwise noted, all quotes attributed to Paula Murray Cole are from our conversation in July 2016.
8 Victor Turner argues that liminoid spaces can offer social arenas where typical social roles, relationships, and codes of behavior are set aside for a temporary time and place. Freeing participants from such strictures, this "anti-structure" allows them to experience "undifferentiated, equalitarian, direct, extant, nonrational, existential, I–Thou relationships" that in turn may facilitate exploration and experimentation of self (1974, 274).

Works Cited

Artaud, Antonin. *The Theater and Its Double.* New York: Grove Press, 1958.

Austin, J. L. *How To Do Things With Words.* Cambridge, MA: Harvard University Press, 1975.

Bateson, Gregory. *Steps to an Ecology of Mind.* Chicago: University of Chicago Press, (1972) 2000.

Brook, Peter. *The Empty Space.* New York: Grove Press, 1968.

Chaikin, Joseph. *The Presence of the Actor.* New York: Atheneum, 1977.

Goffman, Erving. *The Presentation of Self in Everyday Life.* New York: Anchor Books/Doubleday, (1954) 1990.

Grotowski, Jerzy. *Towards a Poor Theatre.* New York: Simon and Schuster, 1968.

Huizinga, Johan. *Homo Ludens.* Boston: Beacon Press, 1971.

Schechner, Richard. *Environmental Theater.* New York: Applause, (1973) 1994.

———. *Between Theater and Anthropology.* Philadelphia: University of Pennsylvania Press, 1985.

Shephard, William Hunter. *The Dionysus Group.* New York: Peter Lang, 1991.

Turner, Victor. *Drama, Fields, and Metaphors.* New York: Cornell University Press, 1974.

———. *From Ritual to Theatre: The Human Seriousness of Play.* New York: PAJ Publications/John Hopkins Press, 1982.

PART IV

Notes From the Field

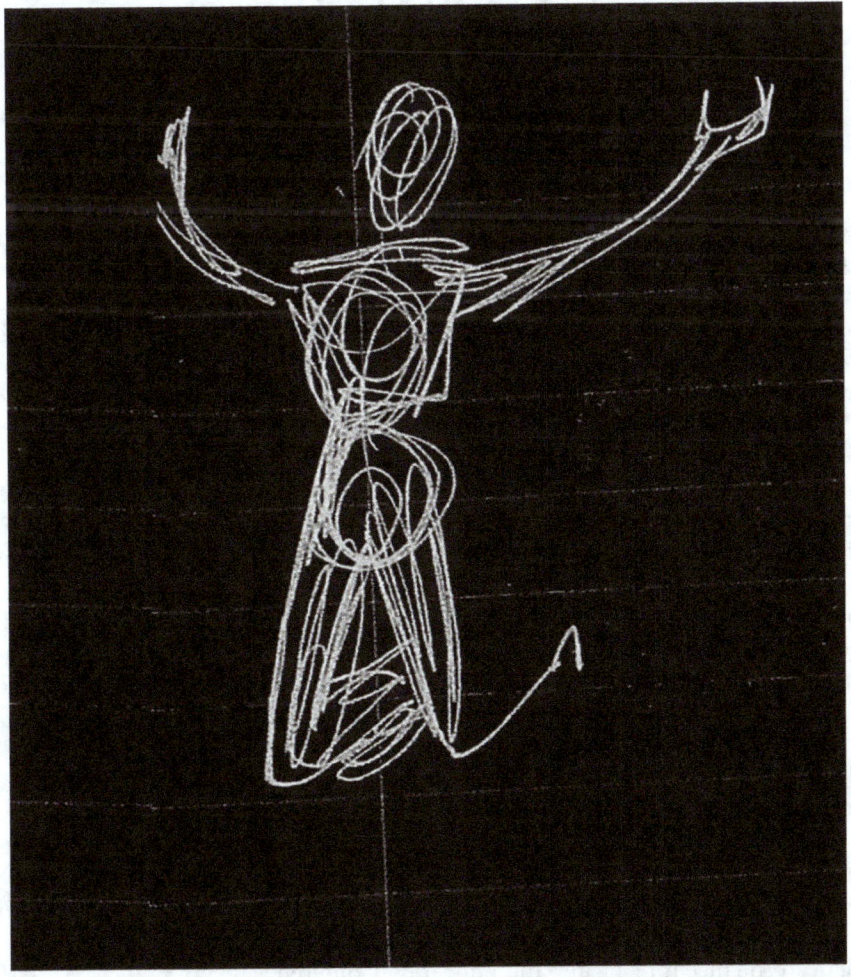

FIGURE 7.1 Sketch of performer doing Rasaboxes by Joan Schirle. Dell'Arte International School of Physical Theatre, 2005.

Source: Courtesy of Paula Murray Cole.

CHAPTER 7

Freeing Emotional Expression in Young Performers
Rasaboxes in K–12 Context

ELISE FORIER EDIE

A variety of primary and secondary school teachers throughout the United States and Canada have used Rasaboxes, or adaptations of Rasaboxes, in their school's performing arts programs for over a decade. The Rasaboxes activities and exercises offered in this chapter are for school age populations kindergarten through 12th grade (K–12) and were compiled from interviews with some of these educators and with participants in Rasaboxes workshops. Many of the teachers I interviewed for this chapter were part of the Central Washington University (CWU) Summer Institute for Theater Arts. This three-year summer master's degree program is designed for working elementary and secondary school teachers, enabling them to take classes and pursue a degree in theatre production while actively teaching and directing high school, middle school, and elementary school programs during the school year. Paula Murray Cole initially offered week-long Rasaboxes workshops as part of the Institute. The teachers who studied the techniques were able to integrate them into their programs and report back on the results. Summer Institute teachers have continued to use Rasaboxes in their public and private secondary schools in Washington, California, Idaho, South Carolina, Utah, Texas, and Tennessee in the US, and in British Columbia, among other locations. The in-field observations, exercise modifications, and experiences of these teachers are recorded here. I also interviewed educators and high school age students from the 45-minute to 3-hour Rasaboxes workshops I taught for the College of the Canyons in Santa Clarita, California (2014–15); the Utah Theatre Association in Provo, Utah (2012); the Dance Educators Association and the British Columbia Arts Educators Association Conferences in Vancouver, Canada (2011–12); and the American Alliance for Theater and Education Conference in San Francisco (2010). In addition, as a full-time Associate Professor of Theatre Education and Acting at CWU from 2005 to 2013, I trained a number of students in educational theatre in Rasaboxes. Some currently head up high school drama programs and/or work as drama educators in Washington State and elsewhere in the country. They were also consulted for this chapter.

Because the needs of high school students are so different from elementary school students, I have divided this chapter into two sections: Rasaboxes for middle school and high school–aged youth (ages 12–18) as part of a drama curriculum and in rehearsal; and modified Rasaboxes for use in elementary classrooms, and in productions for ages 7–10. I realize also the degree of support and time available for such activities varies greatly from school to school.[1] Not every drama teacher has a theater, for instance. Some must cram their performances and classes into libraries and found spaces, moving tables and chairs daily while sharing quarters with cafeteria workers, coaches, or choreographers. A few teachers can chalk their floors and mop them every day with the blessings and cooperation of the school custodial staff, but others risk the wrath of the maintenance department, or have to tussle with the assistant principal to obtain a box of chalk, let alone for permission for students to use it on the floor. The Rasaboxes exercises described below can be adapted to any space, and with a variety of materials. The suggestions and exercises in this chapter are meant as a jumping off point, to inspire educators and drama directors, and to give them a sense of how Rasaboxes may be explored with grades K–12 students, regardless of their individual schools' resources and facilities. Rasaboxes lends itself to creativity, innovation, and free play, whatever the program. Classes can be flavored with a little sprinkle or a whole carton of Rasaboxes.

Rasaboxes with Middle and High School Students

Because opportunities for middle and high school students to engage in whole-body physical and vocal expression seem few and far between these days, Rasaboxes seems especially appropriate for them right now. Many 13–18-year-olds spend the majority of their free time absorbed in the internet. A 2016 Common Sense Media Poll for instance reported one in two teens "feels addicted" to their phones. It also reports typical teens can spend as much as nine hours a day on the internet. I know that I often have to pry my students away from their devices before beginning college classes. And even if my students stay off their phones while in rehearsal, they are almost always plugged into them again immediately afterwards, picking up their devices and headphones with obvious relief, happy to be back in the virtual world. The toll that this constant electronic stimulation takes on young people is still being studied, but preliminary findings indicate teens who are addicted to cell phone use have less brain connectivity in the parts of the brain that regulate emotion (Hong et al. 2013). One thing is certain: as long as teens are hooked on their screens, they certainly are not engaged in much physical activity, nor do they have opportunities to see other people face to face or interact with them physically, especially while exploring and expressing emotion.

At the same time, most students today have been subjected to frequent standardized testing, which sends a message to them that, when it comes to school at least, there is always a "right" way and a "right" answer. Often when my students show up for their first drama class, where the emphasis is on free imaginative play, deep emotional expression, and vigorous physical activity, many are unsure what to do. They freeze up. They ask, "But what do you want?" "How do I do this right?" Eventually, this initial resistance relaxes, and my students become bolder. Later on, they start to crave the exercises. As a result, I like to think Rasaboxes gives them a welcome opportunity to practice being human, as opposed to being plugged into the internet, or demonstrating benchmarks in academic achievement. It also opens their minds and bodies to a wider palette of emotional expression. As British Columbia-based secondary school drama teacher Moroz writes, "[My students] used to have three emotions: happy, sad, and mad. But with Rasaboxes, they have a new range of expression, and we all use a new language to talk about it" (Moroz 2010).

Using the Whole Body

For the reasons mentioned earlier, many teenagers today need to practice using their full physical being as a mode of expression. Unsure and unused to using their bodies as an expressive vehicle, they can be very hesitant about any kind of movement. For this reason, the warm-up yoga sequence from The Performance Workshop can be crucial to building body-awareness, as are frequent reminders to "explore sitting in the rasa," "explore lying down in the rasa," and "explore moving through the rasa" when using Rasaboxes. Many middle and high school students will be tempted to lie passively inside a rasabox and "think about the rasa." The teacher must be vigilant about providing instruction and opportunities for movement. Eventually, the students catch on, enjoy, and even welcome opportunities for physical expression. But in the early stages, they might need to be reminded frequently to "dive in," "fill your feet and toes and belly with the rasa," and "put that rasa in your elbows, your throat, your knees!" I have also found that reminding students to "breathe with the rasa" is a useful way for them to begin relating fully to the work. Teenagers can be physically and mentally frozen in a limbo of excruciating self-consciousness. However, I have found this self-consciousness often can be quickly overcome by simply reminding the students to breathe. "Breathe with the rasa," "play with the sounds of the rasa," "activate the rasa with your breathing" are all side-coaching suggestions that can help move a teenage student from stiff self-consciousness to full rasa immersion.

Rasa with Music

Once they are familiar with them, this age group loves to dance in the rasaboxes. A good, fun warm-up—one my students ask for repeatedly—involves chalking up a gigantic grid, choosing a piece of music, and letting the students improvise and respond to the sounds and to one another in the boxes. They will inevitably use most of their body to express and commit more fully to the rasas—and love doing it. This can be a great exercise for adults and college students, too.

Leaving Taboos Alone

Sexuality, sensuality, rage, fear, grief, and hate are all experiences with which young people grapple. But expression of them can sometimes be taboo in a school or workshop setting. I urge teachers using Rasaboxes in their classes to be sensitive to the taboos of the students they serve. Frequent reminders such as, "no one has to go into a box, if they don't want to" and "if you want to get out of the box, get out of the box" are necessary and encouraged. At the same time, creating a safe space where students can express themselves fully and explore their emotions freely will produce wonderful work. As with very young groups, a "no touching others" rule is adhered to when it comes to exploring shringara and raudra. And while some youth populations are quite comfortable with sexual feelings and sexuality, others benefit more by focusing on other physical pleasures when exploring shringara, such as "tasting delicious desserts," "the feeling of sunshine on bare shoulders," "the smell of your favorite scent," and so on. With these images, the focus is still on pleasure and joy, but many student populations (and presumably parents and administrators) don't immediately object to them, letting the students explore Rasaboxes more fully.

Interestingly, the Sanskrit terminology used in Rasaboxes can help diffuse students' concerns about what they perceive to be emotional taboos. For instance, Moroz describes how much easier it can be to engage his young male students in discussions about their emotions since introducing Rasaboxes study to his drama classes. Moroz notes, "Ask a high school boy to describe his deepest, darkest sadness, and he's likely to freeze up. But my male students will talk about karuna, and they will very willingly explore karuna" (Moroz 2010).

Feedback and Discussion

Many students in this age group enjoy talking and intellectualizing about everything. I allow "download discussions" after a session of Rasaboxes, but I use a timer. With this age group it also seems especially crucial to remind them to use "I statements" when describing their experiences, instead of the inclusive "you." Eventually, the discipline becomes second nature. Rasaboxes explorations have touched off some great discussions in class. In one acting class I taught, for instance, an analysis of Macbeth's character journey became a philosophical investigation in which students talked about how even the most "vira-like" intentions can devolve into "total bibhatsa and karuna" if evil tactics are employed to achieve an end.

Rehearsal: Working With Text

Many high school students are uncomfortable with reading and using text. This discomfort can translate into stilted performances and sometimes agonizing rehearsals. All sense of play, freedom, and creative experimentation disappears, while the young actor plods through the lengthy and time-consuming process of rehearsal and memorization with script in hand. Instead of subjecting my high school students (and myself) to this painful process, in early rehearsals I employ a version of Viola Spolin's "shadowing"[2] while working inside the rasaboxes. In this exercise actors do not carry scripts. Instead, a partner stands near with a script and "feeds" lines to the actor by speaking in their ear or just behind their shoulder. This frees up my actors to listen and respond to one another, without having to refer to a script in their hands.

In the early stages of rehearsal, I might simply tape out a grid and experiment with a scene, letting actors jump from one rasabox to another as the impulse moves them and as the scene progresses. Partners feeding the lines must enter the rasabox and embody the rasa with the actor they are shadowing. This has made for some very potent improvisation and discovery, as the shadowing partner naturally intensifies the rasa while feeding lines to the working actor. I have found lines are learned much more quickly this way, and there is an emotional freedom and willingness to experiment throughout the rehearsal process. Refining the play becomes about experimentation, going in more deeply, and polishing, as opposed to memorizing lines and "getting off book."

Once lines are memorized, it can be both fun and useful to create an impromptu rasa "grid" on the set, too. Nick Hutchinson, who taught drama at Skyline High School in Utah, describes a rehearsal exercise to keep his students from being limited by obvious emotional choices. He might say, "For tonight's rehearsal only, the couch is karuna, the table downstage left is where bibhatsa lives, the stairs are raudra, and the bed is hasya. If you are blocked in those spaces, you must inhabit and express those rasas. Go." He found that with such direction, new discoveries were made, the work was kept alive and interesting, and the students made emotional connections they might not have otherwise made with a traditional run-through.

Rehearsal: Scaling Intensity

Crowd scenes in large musicals and plays can be a trial for a high school drama director. Simply coaching "More energy!" and "Stay in the play!" can help. But I have also found that Rasaboxes opens a whole new way to create variety and engagement in such scenes. Here, teachers can give very specific instruction using the rasas and also specific levels of intensity (see Scaling Intensity, Chapter 4, pp. 161–164). For example:

> Okay, Tiffany and Moisha—on a scale of 1 to 10, 1 being a very low intensity level and 10 being a very high intensity level of the rasa—for tonight, in scene two, everything that happens should be filtered through bibhatsa, with intensity level 3. Let all your actions and reactions come from that perspective. George and Chandresh, you two are all adbhuta—and take it up to an intensity level of 8 or 10—everything you do, everything you hear, filter it through that. Keisha and Brad, you two are hasya at intensity level 5. Don't forget to listen, give focus, and stay involved with the scene. Okay, let's have fun and see how this goes.

Needless to say, "See how this goes," is a good catchphrase for rehearsal. It reminds the students that they don't have to "get it right," they just have to commit to something. Hutchinson describes the greater ease students have rehearsing,

> particularly during scenes that demand a lot of emotion. They used to freeze up and get self-conscious. I would be standing in the back of the auditorium yelling, "More! More!" But now, I just tell my students, "give me a full blown raudra at [intensity level] 10" and they will jump right into it.
>
> (Hutchinson 2010)

Tennessee-based drama teacher David Crutcher remarks on the usefulness of working with intensity to engage specificity in young performers: "[The direction] 'this is an [intensity level of] 8' in the raudra box produces an immediate, visceral, whole body response in the actor(s) in rehearsal, and later in the audience, in performance" (Crutcher 2017).

Rehearsal: Character Analysis

Rasa-based character analysis opens a whole new way of discussing and analyzing text for teenagers. While long, abstract discussions about psychological motivations are often intellectually interesting to this age group, my experience has been that this kind of work rarely yields any applicable techniques they can use or results in any real difference in their performances. For example, two students might talk for a long time about how Amanda bullies Laura at the beginning of Scene Two of *The Glass Menagerie*, but their actual performances will not change much after the talking. But Rasaboxes offers an immediate physical format for exploring emotional nuance and can create solid, tangible, impactful images and moments that lead to immediate understanding, often in a way that discussion cannot. Give young actors a direction like,

> In scene two, Amanda is filtering through vira and bibhatsa, because she's disappointed in Laura but trying to encourage her to strive. Laura is embodying bhayanaka and karuna, because she's frightened of her mother and ashamed of her infirmity. Let's do the scene with full physical expression and try to make the other person switch to your rasa. Go!

An exercise like that can make for a potent improvisation that no intellectual discussion can spark. Or as Kate Wold, drama director for Eastlake High School in Sammamish, Washington, put it, "Seeing someone in the fetal position in karuna, while you're standing tall with clenched fists in vira, naturally illustrates dynamic character differences my students may not have thought of with just a talk and a read through" (Wold 2017).

Rasa Maps

Rasa maps, both a spatial and temporal visualization of the rasic journey of a character, can also be effective when rehearsing. I sometimes tape out the rasa map directly on the set, allowing young actors to "walk through" the rasas while in rehearsal. When rehearsing *Jesus Christ Superstar* in the acting studio at CWU, for example, I had the student playing Jesus devise a map to help score the dramatic "Gethsemane" ballad, which Jesus sings just before his arrest. In the ballad, Jesus confronts God, begging first to be released from his fate, moving from raudra and karuna to a kind of mournful acceptance, incorporating vira into the mix. In rehearsal, we first taped a path that outlined the actor's blocking for the scene. We then filled in the path by chalking the various rasas and rasa mixes (see Mixing and Layering Rasas, Chapter 4, pp. 171–176) that corresponded to each moment of the song. As we rehearsed the song, Jesus moved through bhayanaka, karuna, raudra, bibhatsa, vira, karuna, and even hasya. If we needed to change the rasas or move them around, we rubbed out the chalk marks and made new ones.

Or, referring to the previous example, a student's scene-by-scene rasa map for the character of Laura in *The Glass Menagerie* might include a base mix of raudra/bhayanaka. But in Laura's first scene, at a family dinner, in addition to these base rasas, she might also experience and express hasya (joking with her brother, secretly laughing at Amanda's antics) and bibhatsa ("chew, chew your food!"). In the next scene, when Amanda confronts Laura about leaving typing school, Laura might veer from shringara (immersion in her glass animal collection) to bhayanaka/raudra (the shame at Amanda's rage) and deep karuna (the agony of being in typing class and of disappointing her mother). In this way, a student can outline the rasas Laura moves through in the play, engaging karuna, raudra, bibhatsa, shringara, and vira—all at various times in the action, while keeping the performance and character alive and responsive in the moment. Instead of using only intellect to analyze texts, students learn to use their bodies and emotions as well. Text analysis thus becomes a deeply integrative experience.

Mapping a character's journey through a scene or an entire play does not mean indulging in emotions and sacrificing intentions, objectives, and actions. In fact, being clear about the rasic point of view moment-to-moment can help clarify the action of a character and prevent young actors from getting stuck in a particular emotion. With rasa-based text analysis, "one note" performances give way to more nuanced, interesting explorations of character. In *The Glass Menagerie*, Tom and Amanda's contentious relationship automatically develops more depth if the actors mix their raudra-filled scenes with karuna or hasya. As Kate Wold says about her high school students,

> [m]any young actors get stuck in anger, and scenes with tension can turn into screaming matches without anywhere for the scene to continue. I've had students explore a scene that was stuck in raudra by putting them in hasya and bibhatsa instead, and then discussing afterwards how the other emotions change up the intention of their characters.
>
> (Wold 2017)

Used as a tool for analysis, the rasas can provide a variation in tactics, ultimately creating more interesting, nuanced, and realistic performances.

Rasa, Intimacy, and Emotional Intelligence

As of this writing, there has not been any formal study of how Rasaboxes can contribute to a curriculum that includes studies in "anger management" or "emotional intelligence." However, Twin Falls Idaho drama and English teacher Jennifer Blackburn, who worked almost exclusively with at-risk youth in Magic Valley High School, reports that Rasaboxes has proved to be an effective emotional exploration tool for her students, many of whom are victims of emotional and physical abuse or have been incarcerated for violent behavior. She writes, "Every [rehearsal] day starts with my students asking, 'Can we play in the boxes?' They can't get enough of it. And it's so safe! Especially on those days when everyone's emotions are a bit close to the surface" (Blackburn 2009). She posits that confining emotional exploration and expression to a box, which her students can jump into or out of at will, makes exploring raudra, bhayanaka, and karuna—emotional states that might be dangerous for them in "real life"—suddenly seem accessible, safe, and even fun. Blackburn suggests putting soft toys or pillows in the rasaboxes and encouraging students to interact with them (instead of one another) while immersed in a rasa. She also mentions that her students responded positively to bringing their own tokens—personal objects they associated with the rasas—into the boxes and then interacting with them.

Mike Moroz also reports increased intimacy and emotional bonding when working in Rasaboxes. His students reported feeling "more attuned" and "more in touch" with one another after a session of Rasaboxes. "A class that does Rasaboxes winds up sharing energy in a very unique way," he explains. He related a story of touring a production of A.R. Gurney's *What I Did Last Summer* to a neighboring high school in British Columbia. Before performing, his student actors requested to tape out a grid and do a session of Rasaboxes in their new performing space. "It was how they claimed the space and found each other. [Rasaboxes is] what gave them the courage to perform" (2010).

Using Rasaboxes with Kindergarten Through 5th Grade Students

Because K–5th grade drama programs are so rare in the US, there is not as much "from the field" material about using Rasaboxes in K–5 theatre classes as there is for middle and high school drama programs. Most of the elementary educators I interviewed were music or dance teachers who adapted the exercises to enhance and inform their annual recitals. That said, I do think there is a great deal to be gained by bringing rasa study into the elementary classroom. Rasaboxes provides a context to explore emotional experience and empathy and lends itself well to identifying, experimenting with, and learning to manage the full range of human emotions. At the same time, since Rasaboxes is a movement-based approach, it is particularly well suited to very young people. Children are physical beings, and Rasaboxes provides them with opportunities for physical learning and imaginative play (see Davis 1997; Sylwester 1995).

Getting Started

With Rasaboxes, as with all learning activities for the K–5th grade age group, it is more effective to work in short bursts of time, switching up modes and activities frequently. Fifteen minutes of Rasaboxes twice a week, over a period of weeks, is more effective than trying to cram everything into a 90-minute block class. When Kelly McFadden, a Richland, Washington, music teacher, was teaching Rasaboxes to first and second graders, she commandeered the school's multipurpose room and used 10- and 20-minute blocks of time to teach Rasaboxes as a supplement to her regular music lessons (McFadden 2010).

Warm-Ups

With students in grades K–3, it is best to work with the whole class in a circle, instead of on the grid. This allows the teacher to keep an eye on all the participants and provide immediate intervention if behavior problems develop. I suggest incorporating a gentle physical warm-up, one that encourages students to gradually focus on their full physical and vocal selves. A typical day's narration, as everyone stretches in the circle, might include something like this: "Wiggle your fingers . . . now add your wrists . . . now your whole arm . . . where's your elbow? . . . Can you wiggle your elbow? . . . What about your shoulders? . . . Can you find your shoulders?" I include facial muscles in the warm-up, too—eyebrows, mouth, nose, and even scalp and ears—so students begin integrating their facial expressions into the work.

After warm-ups, students can take turns creating shapes and gestures for other students to imitate. Typically, individual students take turns moving to the middle of the circle, where they show the whole group a frozen, full-body gesture. Once it has been observed, everyone else in the class mirrors the statue all at once. This gives the students practice in performing in front of a group, using their whole body for expression, while allowing maximum participation for everyone. It also allows for quick, positive side coaching. For example, if a demonstrating student brings facial muscles into the gesture, one can immediately call attention to it and praise the demonstrator ("See how Carrie's using her face? Are you using your face, too?"). In this way, students gradually learn to include their face as a mode of physical expression, along with the rest of their body.

Introducing the Rasas

It is helpful to introduce a single rasa at a time, while still working in a circle. It is advisable to spend several sessions exploring each rasa in brief, energetic bursts, rather than attempting marathon sessions of activity. With this age group, five to fifteen minutes and one or two rasas at a time is enough. Like adults and teenagers, young children can have all sorts of taboos, habitual expressions, and anxieties about certain rasas. It is good to anticipate these and be prepared for them. Most children will engage in hasya, for example, but might become tense or nervous about karuna, because it's "babyish" to cry or be sad. Raudra, if not controlled, can easily devolve into wrestling and fighting. Bibhatsa is rarely a good idea right after lunch. Shringara can be uncomfortable for young people who have been brought up to feel shame and guilt about physical pleasure. Understanding and anticipating cultural norms within each group, and integrating rasas in a gentle, fun, and voluntary way will meet with the most success.

The most effective way to connect with a rasa for very young students (ages 5–9) and even some less emotionally mature older students is for the teacher to attach contextual, imaginative scenarios that invite vocal and physical play. When introducing karuna, for instance, I might bring this story to the circle:

> Karuna is the sensation I feel when I see a little puppy that is all alone and scared or hurt. Imagine a little puppy right in front of you. Don't touch him yet. Just look at him. He is tiny and furry. He has a little tail and long ears. He's scared, I think. His tail is between his legs and his ears are drooping. Shhh! I think we probably should be quiet, so we don't scare him. Poor little puppy. Let's make ourselves small so he knows he's safe. Aw! Can everyone make that sound? Aw! What are we going to say to him, so he feels better? What can we do? Jamal has an idea. Jamal, show us what you can do or say to gently show the puppy you care about him.

CHAPTER 7 ▸ Freeing Emotional Expression in Young Performers   221

This introduction to karuna accomplishes several things:

1. Physical engagement is introduced: "Let's make ourselves small."
2. Vocal exhalation and sound are introduced: "Aw!"
3. Playing with and in the rasa is introduced: "Show us what we can say or do."

Even beginning this study of karuna with its "compassion" aspect is strategic—it allows an "accepted" expression of the rasa to be shared right away. Children who might initially criticize or shy away from sadness, or tears, will readily get down on all fours and try to help an imaginary puppy feel better. This easy engagement paves the way for the next step in the introduction of karuna:

> Karuna is also what I feel when I'm "sad." Do you know what sad is? What do people do with their bodies when they're sad? What sounds do they make? What sensations do you feel inside your body when you're sad? My lip feels heavy. What does my lip do when it's heavy? My heart hurts. What do I do when my heart hurts?

It can be helpful to invite personal stories from the students at this point and allow them to express their own experiences. "Did something happen to you recently that made you feel karuna? I think Lucila has a story she would like to share. Lucila, what made you feel karuna?" By inviting students to tell stories and explain their emotional experiences, they will begin to make personal associations with each rasa, which will reinforce learning and recognition.

Rasa Collage and Rasa Bureau Exercise

After physical and vocal exploration of a rasa, I find it helpful if everyone switches it up and draws a picture and/or writes a short story about a "karuna moment" that happened to them. These can then be shared with the class as a whole. Once a collection of stories and pictures is assembled, they can be arranged into a "karuna collage" on a nearby wall or bulletin board. Eventually, there can be a set of bulletin boards, one for each rasa. Or, as one teacher with limited wall space did, a special "Rasa Bureau," can be established, with a drawer for each rasa. Or, nine sturdy boxes—the ten-ream paper boxes are perfect—can be decorated, one for each rasa. Whatever method is used, these boards, boxes, and drawers can store a treasure trove of objects, images, poems, and so forth, all collected by students, each of which demonstrates aspects of a rasa. These collections can be drawn upon later for artwork or inspiration. In this way, students will begin to associate emotional expression and engagement as something always present in their work, art, and play. Use of the rasa vocabulary becomes part of the classroom language. Recognizing emotions and emotional expression becomes commonplace. In this way, studying and playing with rasas contributes to social and emotional learning.

Applying the Rasas to Other Subjects in the School Curriculum

Once the rasas are established and the students understand and recognize the physical and vocal expressions of them, rasa work can be used in art projects and lessons. Educators who include classroom projects like reader's theatre, storytelling, choral poetry, recitation, music, dance, and oral interpretation will have a whole new, extremely effective vocabulary, using rasas to coach their students for performances.

For example, when McFadden was preparing her elementary age students to read text aloud as part of a music and drama recital, she had them take turns expressing the same line of poetry, each through a different rasa. Even the most basic line, "I've never seen a purple cow," took on different meanings as it was interpreted through karuna, adbhuta, raudra, and bhayanaka. Her students caught on very quickly to using rasas in their text and started to have fun with them right away. A lot of the usual self-consciousness that can come with public speaking with this age group disappeared, as the students made a game of interpreting words with rasas. "There was a dramatic difference," McFadden writes, "Between students who 'read the part' and the students who 'expressed the part [using rasas]'" (McFadden 2010).

Students can also learn simple choreography, circle dances, or line dances and have fun interpreting them through different rasas. A couple of verses of the "Hokey Pokey," where students dip their right hand, or left hand, or right foot in a different rasa, can help review the sensations and get the whole body involved in emotional expression. Dance instructors at the British Columbia Dance Conference in 2012 reported to me that rasa work can be of great benefit when preparing students for recitals and complex ballets. The annual *Nutcracker*, for instance, can be enhanced with the incorporation of raudra/vira mice, adbhuta/shringara flowers, and a Clara gradually growing in her movement from adbhuta to bhayanaka to vira and shringara.

As with any authentic emotional exploration, for both elementary school age groups and high school students, there will be giggling and shyness; there will be stumbles and false starts. There will be rasas that some kids just won't engage in, and others (like raudra) that will have to be strictly supervised and, if necessary, curtailed. But perfect rasa expression shouldn't be the goal with young people. Neither should the full, deep expression of every rasa. It's enough for most students to recognize the rasas and express them, discuss them, and begin to create with them. Just like youngsters don't really need to eat a lot of spicy food, or caffeine, or sugar—just like they might not like to watch scary horror movies, or a lot of violence—they also don't need to spend a lot of time in Rasaboxes trying to reach the deepest expressions of their feelings. My rule of thumb is: Keep it light, keep it fun, keep it short.

Conclusion

It should be noted that without exception, all educators who reported back to me about Rasaboxes in their classrooms and rehearsals were uniformly enthusiastic about its effectiveness. They reported over and over again that their students felt empowered by the exercises and loved exploring emotional expression with rasas. I have found this to be true, too. Recently, for instance, I taught a brief workshop to high school students in South Carolina, at the state theater conference. The facilities couldn't have been worse. We were crammed in a carpeted art room with tables stacked against the wall, butcher paper tearing on the floor, students practically piled on one another in the rasaboxes, gamely striking poses. But even in these circumstances, performers and witnesses were wide-eyed with wonder, marveling at the effectiveness of the work. At the end of the workshop, I asked if there were any questions. The first one was, "Will you be our drama teacher forever?" The second question was, "How can we learn more about this?"

No matter what the reason, young people really like to explore Rasaboxes. Its seemingly immediate effectiveness helps them trust the techniques. The endless possibilities for play keep them exploring. The meaningful connections they make with themselves and each other provoke discussion and thought. Best of all, young people have fun with Rasaboxes. The grid becomes a playground for them, with emotional exploration providing a framework for storytelling, growth, analysis, and stimulation. I hope Rasaboxes becomes an integral part of every school arts program, so that all students can benefit from it. Whether they are 5 or 15, Rasaboxes has something to offer young people, by increasing emotional intelligence, deepening emotional connection and expression, and finding authentic moments for performances, whether it's a full blown high school production of *A Raisin in the Sun* or an elementary chorus singing "Jingle Bells" for a holiday concert. Working with rasas can enhance, entrance, illuminate, strengthen, and empower student populations everywhere.

Notes

1 I have been lucky to regularly work in an acting studio with black painted floors that could be easily marked up with chalk and then washed with a mop. For teachers without these amenities—and they include many high school drama teachers—the use of butcher paper, taped to a floor and drawn on with crayons and marking pens, has sufficed. For students with a working knowledge and familiarity with Rasaboxes exercises, especially in rehearsals on set, I have also used laminated 12 × 18-inch cardboard signs with the rasa names printed on them. These I taped to the walls, furniture, and scenery, thus creating an easily changed and dismantled "grid."
2 Viola Spolin is the internationally recognized originator of Theatre Games and an early proponent of improvisational theatre. She is the author of the seminal theatre text *Improvisation for the Theater* ([1963] 1999), in which her "shadowing" exercise is described on page 177.

Works Cited

Blackburn, Jennifer. *A Production of Bang Bang You're Dead at Magic Valley High School*. MA thesis. Central Washington University, 2009. Print.
The Commonsense Census: Media Use By Tween and Teens. Web. www.commonsensemedia.org/sites/default/files/uploads/research/census_researchreport.pdf. Accessed June 15, 2019.

Crutcher, David. Email Interview. 13 February 2017.

Davis, Kim. "The Value of Movement Activities for Young Children." *The Reporter*, vol. 2, no. 3, 1997, pp. 1–3.

Hong, S-B., A. Zalesky, L. Cocchi, A. Fornito, E. J. Choi, H. H. Kim et al. "Decreased Functional Brain Connectivity in Adolescents with Internet Addiction." *PLoS One*, vol. 8, no. 2, 2013, p. e57831.

Hutchinson, Nick. Personal Interview. 20 July 2010.

McFadden, Kelly. *A Production of Circus Circus for Kennewick School District*. MA thesis. Central Washington University, 2010. Print.

Moroz, Mike. Personal interview. 17 July 2010.

Spolin, Viola. *Improvisation for the Theater*. Evanston, IL: Northwestern University Press, (1963) 1999. Print.

Sylwester, Robert. *A Celebration of Neurons: An Educator's Guide to the Human Brain*. Alexandria, VA: ASCD, 1995.

Wold, Kate. Email interview. 8 February 2017.

CHAPTER 8

Psychophysical Preparation for Rasaboxes with Strasberg and Stanislavsky

URSULA NEUERBURG

As a researcher and practitioner, I am drawn to identifying tools that give performers access to the emotional states that render and sustain provocative, vibrant work. As a founding member of Schechner's East Coast Artists, I was directly involved in the early explorations that led to the creation of Rasaboxes exercises. In this chapter, I focus on my sustained examination of the subconscious (in Stanislavsky's and Vaghtangov's terms)[1] in Rasaboxes, when prepared and combined with principles from the Stanislavsky system and elements of the Method as developed by Lee Strasberg. I offer a quick snapshot of one of the exercises I teach in a semester-long class called Rasaboxes. The class first introduces Rasaboxes exercises and later investigates how to integrate a number of other acting techniques, focusing particularly on how Rasaboxes exercises can tap into the subconscious, while simultaneously functioning as a safety net for the performer and a way to situate the subconscious within a given circumstance.

According to Russian actor and director Yevgeni Vaghtangov (1883–1922),[2] the subconscious retains creative material that is not necessarily accessible through the conscious mind or cognitive processes.[3] He suggests,

> Consciousness does not create anything—ever. . . . Only the subconscious does. It has an independent ability to choose material for the creative process, bypassing the conscious mind. Apart from this, one can consciously send material for the creative process into the realm of [one's] subconscious.
>
> (Evans 2015, 109)

In this chapter, I focus on just a few elements of Stanislavsky's and Strasberg's approaches to acting, designed to access what they called "the subconscious," but what today is perhaps more often thought of as a state of pre-cognition and/or part of the self that is activated by psychophysical or somatic practices. I am purposefully sidestepping discussions around the term "subconscious" or the debate over the validity of the Method or the true meaning of the System: the former is treated here by me as a historical term that has still recognizable meaning in practice; the latter has been discussed in depth by many (Carnicke 2009; Benedetti 2007, 2016; McConachie 2006; Kemp 2012). My focus here is practical: first I show how different approaches employ and access the subconscious by describing exercises from these approaches as I learned them,[4] then by demonstrating how they can be mixed and layered in various ways with Rasaboxes exercises as preparation for the actor working with any aesthetic or style of theatre.

The Emo Lab: Rasaboxes

As part of the curriculum in the undergraduate BFA program at Concordia University in Montreal, Canada, the Emo Lab, now called Rasaboxes, is a semester-long course where the performance of emotion is investigated by the participants and the facilitator within a laboratory setting. The work was first developed as part of a three-year research grant workshopping Rasaboxes exercises with paid student participants. It then became integrated into my teaching load as a full-term class, meeting twice a week (2.75 hours each).[5] I chose the original course name, "Emo Lab" (2010 to 2015), because it allowed for more flexibility for both the instructor and the participating students when adjusting course content according to interest and progress rather than to raise the expectation of learning (and "mastering") a specific method. I believe that all acting methods need to be in flux so as to better adapt to changing trends and demands on the performer. In addition, while the Sanskrit term "rasa" is unknown to most students or else evokes the idea of cultural appropriation, the name "Emo Lab" clarifies that the class is about the performance of emotion (Neuerburg 2011). With regard to heightening the visibility of Rasaboxes (course name since 2017) as a valuable approach to actor training, it is good that the name itself is now on Concordia's university calendar.

The core principles and basic exercises of Rasaboxes are taught during the first four weeks of the semester. In that introductory phase, students learn about some of the sources for the exercises, such as excerpts from the *Natyashastra*, "Rasaesthetics" (Schechner 2001), and "High Emotion: Training in the Emo Lab" (Neuerburg-Denzer 2014). At first the students use "the self" in the "here and now" as their source. In week three or four, they begin to use text (a monologue of their choosing) or, on occasion, a song (folk or traditional) as a basis for their explorations. In the following seven weeks, and while continuing to practice on the grid, small groups of students present on other acting techniques such as Stanislavsky's system, Brecht, the Method, Meisner's repetition exercises, Viewpoints (Overlie, Bogart), mask work (commedia, Lecoq, Mnouchekine), somatics (Body–Mind Centering®), Laban's Effort Actions, and more. They guide the class in appropriate warm-ups and exercises as they are attempting to demonstrate how these techniques can be merged with Rasaboxes. We dedicate a few follow-up sessions to deepening each of these explorations. Working material turns from individual monologues to scene work (scenes are taken from one play, chosen by instructor, so that all performers move in the same "world"). During the final weeks of the term, more focus is put on applying the discoveries made to the scenes of a play. The class ends with a studio showing, sharing some of the scene work with invited guests.⁶

During the course, students are introduced to methods and exercises that explore accessing specific, repeatable emotional states through a psychophysical route. Despite previous exposure to a variety of acting techniques, it seems that students have more commonly approached working with emotions through mental processes alone—through imagination, memory, and the play's given circumstances. These components of acting technique build actors' skills in connecting text analysis with themselves, and the character, and are necessary avenues of investigation particularly well suited for work with plays from the canon of American realism. I agree with Phillip Zarrilli (2009) and others, however, that actors in the 21st century need to be able to perform in a wide variety of forms—from psychological realism to the postmodern or posthuman, from the performance of character to the performance of self or objects, with or without plot structure or scores—and in a multitude of settings. With these challenges in mind, I base the participant-centered Emo Lab/Rasaboxes on the students' experience and skill level, adjusting the course layout according to their progress.

The Psychophysical

Constantin Stanislavsky is often credited with bringing psychophysical acting to the West (Zarrilli 2009), but the concept had already taken hold in other disciplines half a century earlier (and of course many centuries earlier in other parts of the world, particularly Asia, from where Stanislavsky took much inspiration). In the mid-19th century, in reaction to Cartesian dualism, Austria's newly founded discipline of *Seelenkunde*, literally "study of the soul" (what we now refer to as psychology), pointed to the indivisible connection between body and mind. A study of early somatic practices cites the etymology of the term "psychophysical" as first appearing in print in 1845 in Viennese psychologist Ernst von Feuchtersleben's text book *Lehrbuch der ärztlichen Seelenkunde* (Huxley 2011, 25–42). Feuchtersleben points out that "psychologists are not only to concern themselves with the treatment of mental illness. . . . their mission includes the reciprocal relationship between the psycho-physical and the physio-psychological in general" (1845, 348; my translation). While not as explicit as later authors, Feuchtersleben highlights the indivisible body–mind relationship. The term soon found resonance with those concerned with activities of the body–mind, such as performers and movement specialists. In 1892, Delsarte authority Genevieve Stebbins "used the word in relation to performance, writing about 'psychophysical culture' in *Dynamic Breathing and Harmonic Gymnastics*" (Whyman 2016, 157). Rose Whyman suggests in her discussion of the psychophysical that Stanislavsky might have borrowed the term from Stebbins as he was familiar with her work even though he was not a proponent of Delsarte. The principles of the psychophysical were of course familiar to him through his studies of yoga and other Asian philosophies and practices. In 1923, Frederick Matthias Alexander writes: "The term psycho-physical is used both here and throughout my works to indicate the impossibility of separating 'physical' and 'mental' operations in our conception of the working of the human organism" (1923, 5).

Stanislavsky writes in detail about the necessity of relaxation for actors. He emphasized relaxation as a pathway to relieve blockages of both body and mind in order to heighten one's ability to concentrate and access the subconscious, activating deep imagination. His description of the sleeping cat draped on sand, every muscle relaxed, is evocative and immediately recognizable (2008, 124–25). But rather than doing a full floor relaxation, inviting students' body parts to grow heavy and melt into their surroundings, I introduce them to Strasberg's chair relaxation. This exercise keeps the performer upright and trains them to relax against and with an obstacle—the chair, which at the same time also functions as a support system and pressure point release tool.

Chair Relaxation Exercise[7]

As an introduction to Strasberg's Method, I lead the group through a guided chair relaxation, an exercise using progressive relaxation. This technique reminds us of Stanislavsky's insistence on knowing how to tense and relax each muscle separately (Stanislavsky 2008, 130) for better overall physical control, as well as for its relaxing effect. The depth of the relaxation that can be achieved in this exercise is due in part to the duration of the process: between 30 and 45 minutes. Through the mere passage of time, people transition into different frames of mind, enabling them to tap into layers of conscious and subconscious body knowledge. By staying upright on a chair, the performer stays anchored in space, thus making the process quite accessible, even to less experienced practitioners who feel "more in control" staying seated.

Instructions

Each person in the group sits on a chair facing straight forward toward the same wall. The instructor sits facing them.

1. Keep your eyes open in a soft focus to create a small circle of attention (Stanislavsky) around yourself in the chair, letting your neighbors and the instructor slip from your field of vision and concentration.
2. Allow the facilitator's voice to guide you through the exercise, which begins by tensing and then releasing each muscle in your body, one by one.
3. Begin by tensing your hands—make a fist and squeeze it tight for one, two, three, four, five seconds—let go and release. Now stretch the fingers as long and far apart as you can, hold five seconds, release. Be as detailed as you wish and make sure that after tensing, the muscles fully release.

The exercise continues in a very slow, step-by-step process as the facilitator leads the participants through the tensing and relaxing experience—from the outer appendages to the internal organs, including reproductive organs, head, and face. Going stringently through all the parts of the body allows the mind to map the body, and provides a framework for the process for participants to return to when distractions arise.

4. When distractions and tensions arise—from yourself, the people around you, or the environment—you can acknowledge them by vocalizing in some way. The vocalizations can be done in any language, gibberish or without words. This serves as a way to diminish the fear that someone will overhear personal thoughts. The point of the vocalization is to acknowledge the thoughts that arise and, by doing so, to let go of them. You may also yawn loudly, sigh, shout, or make other sounds as tension is released. Often, it takes some practice, or a certain level of familiarity among the participants, to fully vocalize.

Distraction and mental tension are usually a much greater hindrance to the success of the exercise than physical tightness. While being "more in control," the participant is also more exposed when sitting up, distractions are more likely to enter participants' awareness than relaxation exercises conducted on the floor in which the eyes are closed. Thus, the exercise also serves to train the mind to concentrate, follow instruction, and focus on mapping the body. It is an active form of relaxation, as tensing the muscles involves effort in order to lead to the release. It challenges and changes participants' focus, leading to greater seriousness and dedication to the work. As participants become familiar with the exercise, I do less whole group guidance and turn to individualized coaching by walking from person to person.

Transitioning from Chair Relaxation to Sense-Memory Work

A classic Strasbergian approach would be to lead from the chair relaxation into a sense-memory exercise. Sense memory is triggered and/or enhanced through the relaxation work. Because participants have opened up their subjective sensory awareness, they are able to access sense memories, which lead to imagining situations. When done successfully, this yields very different results from those reached through intellectual approaches to acting, such as reading a script, defining given circumstances, and arriving at the resulting tasks. Rather, this process leads to mining the bodymind, which is a repository for a whole range of nuanced sensory and affective experiences, memories, and knowledge, for "as ifs" that later can be applied to the theatrical situation. Some classic sense-memory exercise prompts, such as "bathing in sunshine," "taking a shower," "drinking from a cup," and "exploring your childhood room," can be explored while remaining in the chair, standing, or moving freely in space.

Sense Memory

Sense memory is meant to be enacted or physicalized rather than simply imagined; however, the focus is much different than in conventional miming. The imagined object within the world of memory—for example, a chest of drawers from your childhood room—is explored sensorially through the fingertips or other body parts, scent, and sound. Slowly, the dimensions and material details of the object are investigated. The process is not concerned with the accuracy of the movement or outward performance but instead with the imaginatively and sensually reconstructed qualities of the remembered objects. Through the sensitization of tactile or other senses, specific memories become enhanced, helping the whole self invest more strongly in the remembered environment.

Putting sense-memory work inside the rasaboxes grid tests the emotional value of the memory. By shifting between rasaboxes, the performer might find some rasas more "fitting" than others. They might also discover rasas they would not have considered relevant to a particular memory, suddenly becoming enhanced or meaningful. This process raises the performer's awareness of detail in everyday observation and theatrical work. Performers discover the strength and significance of their own experiential knowledge. They come to recognize sense memory as a pathway into more profound performance work.

Mixing Rasaboxes with Sense-Memory Work

When the students have established a sense-memory based on one of the earlier prompts, such as "bathing in sunshine" (one prompt per session for the whole group), they can take that onto the grid, to experience it with different rasas. This often results in a deepening of both rasa and sense-memory work, allowing greater access to the subconscious, which expresses itself through the emergence of unexpected memories and breadth of emotional states. The memory of forgotten details about a place or time emerges when prompted, for example, to explore "what is the consistency of the surface you are standing on?", or other elements that come to mind when focusing on touch, smell, hearing, sometimes taste, and, to a lesser degree, seeing. Ultimately, the goal of a sustained Strasbergian sense-memory practice would be to repeatedly access certain memories, creating a library of memory triggers for emotional states. In class, I use it as an exploratory tool to show ways into mining the subconscious for future use.

But not all participants are able or willing to do it. Some people have blockages, others resist the work, and from the feedback I receive, this is a resistance to exploring a layer of the self through memories and states of vulnerability that are hidden in everyday life, or the fear of what might happen when doors to the subconscious are opened. These fears are often based on the idea that the Method can harm performers by using personal memories in an exploitative way. It is important to point out that the students are advised not to explore memories more recent than five years ago. Also, the focus of the exercise remains on the physical/sensual aspects of the memory, as it is such details (a remembered smell of oranges for example) that turn into useful triggers. But most importantly, by moving into the rasaboxes, the performers learn to switch the emotions associated with a memory rather than getting "stuck" and overwhelmed in one emotion. In this way, the rasaboxes grid becomes the performers' safety net.

CHAPTER 8 ▸ Psychophysical Preparation for Rasaboxes with Strasberg

Toward the end of the chair relaxation exercise, I lead participants into a standing sense-memory exploration, and then remove the chairs. At times I place nine rasa cards[8] on the floor in the rasaboxes, while inviting the group to stay in their sense-memory work. I then verbally "activate" the rasaboxes, allowing the participants, in their own time, to connect their sense-memory exploration with specific rasaboxes. Another possibility is to not use the physical boxes, but to verbally guide the group through some or all of the nine rasas.

Transitioning from Chair Relaxation and Sense-Memory to Rasaboxes

Following the chair relaxation and sense-memory exercises, there are different ways to transition into the rasaboxes, for example:

- Get up and immediately enter the rasaboxes in a state of deep relaxation and simply explore the different rasas.
- Take the sense memory into the rasaboxes and explore different emotional values with the same memory.
- Do the same but in response to an improvisation prompt, i.e., a situational or narrative frame.
- Individually transition into character, enter the rasaboxes in character, and do character biographical research overlapping with your sense memory.

Tactics for Cooling Down

Sometimes, the student is not ready to do this type of work, or the student is emotionally raw for personal reasons, so accessing memories might open the performer to seemingly uncontrollable emotions. In cases where students feel overwhelmed, I employ different tactics:

- Encourage the student to change boxes in order to counter the effects of the rasa that led to overwhelm with an opposing rasa.
- Coach the student to step out of the rasaboxes and "shake it out," like dogs do after encountering a stressor. The action of shaking neurologically rebalances them. (This same technique is used in Trauma Release Exercise (TRE) for PTSD therapy).
- Invite them to verbally check in with the instructor.
- Encourage the student to journal.
- Invite them to drink some water.
- Invite them to quietly sit and direct their attention away from themselves and onto watching other members of the group who are still working.

Rasaboxes as a "Catching" Device

In part, the mistrust associated with the Method is due to the lack of a built-in mechanism to "catch" the participant, who has become potentially vulnerable when fully participating in a sense-memory exercise. Transferring the work from the chair directly into a physical and spatial framework allows the student to safely manipulate these states or memories. They can switch or counteract the connected emotions, or cross out of the rasaboxes altogether. It does require a firm grounding in Rasaboxes exercises to use it as a safety net. The beauty of Rasaboxes is that it provides a framework that immediately situates the deeply engaged bodymind of the performer. In that way, working with Rasaboxes confirms what Rebecca Loukes suggests, that "new scientific paradigms of 'enaction' and 'situatedness' understand that the bodymind cannot be separated from the space around it, the environment it inhabits" (2013, 225).

Conclusion

My goal in the Emo Lab/Rasaboxes course is to guide the performer to an understanding of how the emotional and sensory life of a character or role can be made multifaceted and layered but still analyzable, controllable, and repeatable in performance. While it is fair to say that the majority of my students will perform in relatively realistic types of theatre works, I encourage them to use these tools and to take the work to more exploratory forms of performance. When folded into Rasaboxes exercises, sense-memory work loses its exclusive connection to the Method, and to psychological realism, and becomes more pliable and applicable to a variety of styles of performance. Additionally, including the use of elements from the Stanislavsky system such as "circle of attention," and "progressive relaxation," this progression renders a potent mix that allows performers to achieve intense, gutsy performances.

With respect to psychophysical work, Rasaboxes can function as a springboard for improvisational explorations, while also contributing to precise character analyses. One could posit that, through the physical separation of emotional states into boxes, the rasaboxes grid functions as a cognitive playground, where the performer's mind differentiates between emotional states by navigating through physically distinct spaces. At the same time, this process of cognition is accessed via deep psychophysical immersion within each rasabox, a state in which the subconscious stays activated or, as Vaghtangov suggested, "one can consciously send material for the creative process into the realm of [one's] subconscious" (Evans 2015, 109). In this way, Rasaboxes exercises can make direct use of, and may even be considered a further development of, the Stanislavsky system and Strasberg's Method.

Notes

1 I am not, however, directly referring to Stanislavsky's work on emotions. A refreshing reread on his chapter on "emotion memory" has been done by Bella Merlin (2003, 60–64).
2 A student of Stanislavsky's, colleague of Meyerhold's, and mentor of Michael Chekhov's.
3 I am not personally trained in Vaghtangov's method; thus, I do not refer to his practical work in class or in this essay.
4 I was taught the exercises in the 1980s in the Arne Baur-Worch Acting School in Berlin; the process might be different from how it is taught by other third-generation teachers.

5 The majority of students who take the course are specializing in acting, with a few performance creation students, and occasional students from the humanities. They are in their second or third year, and we are occasionally joined by some fourth years and grad students (Quebec students take only three years for their BFA as they all do two years of junior college following high school graduation after grade 11). The course fulfills requirements for the BFA in Acting, while students in other areas take it as an elective.

6 The order in which the students encounter the work during the course of the semester is similar to the one used in The Performance Workshop, moving from "getting in touch with yourself" to "relating to others within narrative or other highly formalized structures" (see Chapter 4, p. 83). I took Schechner's Performance Workshop in 1991 while getting my MA in Performance Studies at NYU.

7 I studied chair relaxation as part of the Method at the Arne Baur-Worch Acting School in Berlin from 1984 to 1986. Strasberg had taught in Germany in the early 1980s, and his Method had become famous. Baur-Worch had trained with Walter Lott, an important Method teacher in Berlin at the time and one of the first teachers at the Actors Studio in LA and NY. Baur-Worch had also trained with Decroux, Grotowski, and Barba and taught a combination of these styles in his school. This did not seem to be unusual at the time and, in fact was considered to be a potent mix in order to achieve deep, gutsy performances.

8 I use laminated sheets for each of the nine rasas in class that can be easily placed and taped to the floor.

Works Cited

Alexander, Frederick Matthias. *Constructive Conscious Control of the Individual*. New York: E.P. Dutton, 1923.
Benedetti, Jean. *The Art of the Actor*. London and New York Routledge, 2007.
——. *Stanislavsky: An Introduction*. London, UK: Bloomsbury Methuen Drama, 2016.
Bharata, Muni. *The Natyashastra*. Translated by Manomohan Gosh. Calcutta: The Royal Asiatic Society of Bengal, 1951.
Carnicke, Sharon. *Stanislavsky in Focus. An Acting Master for the Twenty First Century*, 2nd ed. Abingdon, London and New York: Routledge, 2009.
Daboo, Jerri. "Stanislavsky and the Psychophysical in Western Acting." In *Acting: Psychophysical Phenomenon and Process*, edited by Phillip Zarrilli, Jerri Daboo, and Rebecca Loukes. Basingstoke, UK: Palgrave Macmillan, 2013, pp. 158–63.
Evans, Mark. *The Actor Training Reader*. London and New York: Routledge, 2015.
Feuchtersleben, Ernst von. *Lehrbuch der ärztlichen Seelenkunde*. Wien, 1845. https://archive.org/details/b29309700. Accessed 22 February 2017.
Huxley, Michael. "F. Matthias Alexander and Mabel Elsworth Todd: Proximities, Practices and the Psycho-Physical." *Journal of Dance and Somatic Practices*, vol. 3, no. 1–2, 2011, pp. 25–42.
Kemp, Rick. *Embodied Acting: What Neuroscience Tells Us about Performance*. London and New York: Routledge, 2012.
Loukes, Rebecca. "Beyond the Psychophysical? The 'Situated', 'Enactive' Bodymind in Performance." In *Acting: Psychophysical Phenomenon and Process*, edited by Phillip Zarrilli, Jerri Daboo, and Rebecca Loukes. Basingstoke, UK: Palgrave Macmillan, 2013, pp. 224–55.
McConachie, Bruce. *Performance and Cognition*. London, UK: Routledge, 2006.
Merlin, Bella. *Konstantin Stanislavsky*. London and New York: Routledge, 2003.
Neuerburg-Denzer, Ursula. *From Rape to Rapture: The Art of Performing Emotion*. PhD thesis. Freie Universität, 2011. https://refubium.fu-berlin.de/handle/fub188/5239?show=full, online deposit 2015.

———. "High Emotion: Training in the Emo Lab." In *New Essays in Canadian Theatre, Vol. 5: Theatre of Affect*, edited by Erin Hurley. Toronto: Playwright Canada Press, 2014.

Schechner, Richard. "Rasaesthetics." *The Drama Review*, vol. 45, no. 3 (T171), Fall 2001.

Stanislavsky, Konstantin. *An Actor's Work: A Student's Diary*. London and New York: Routledge, 2008.

Whyman, Rose. "Explanations and Implications of 'Psychophysical' Acting." *New Theatre Quarterly*, vol. 32, no. 2, May 2016, pp. 157–68. Accessed 26 January 2017.

Zarrilli, Phillip. *Psychophysical Acting: An Intercultural Approach after Stanislavsky*. London and New York: Routledge, 2009.

CHAPTER 9

Adapting Rasaboxes to Rasa≈Therapy

Clinical Applications in Drama Therapy

ANDREW M. GAINES

Drama Therapy and Distance

While many Rasaboxes performers have described their training as "therapeutic" (Minnick 2001, 41), drama therapists have intentionally adapted Rasaboxes exercises to provide psychologically healing experiences for over two decades. Interestingly, the *Natyashastra* portended an alliance with drama therapy, noting that drama "brings composure to persons agitated in mind [and] give[s] relief to unlucky persons who are afflicted with sorrow and grief or [over]-work" (Bharata-muni 1967, 15). The synergy between Rasaboxes and drama therapy is palpable, yet the union is imperfect. By hyphenating rasa≈therapy with the algebraic symbol for a close approximation, I coined this term to acknowledge the substantial modifications drama therapists have made to typical Rasaboxes practices in service of specific populations and settings. The ≈ symbol also honors the therapeutic-but-not-necessarily-therapy nature of Rasaboxes, a power which can be harnessed when done so with care.

Rasa≈Therapy Practices in Context

Drama therapists utilize the same principles of traditional verbal psychotherapy but extend beyond the domain of spoken words by engaging clients' imaginations and bodies, through both improvisational role-play and rehearsed productions. Clinical issues are addressed symbolically and metaphorically, typically through fiction and often with charged projective objects such as puppets, masks, or costumes.[1] This psychological distance allows clients to address difficult issues in a way that would otherwise be overwhelming. However, drama therapy can also release blunted or suppressed emotions with more authenticity. Irrespective of a drama therapist's particular theoretical orientation,[2] their ultimate goals for patients are widely shared among practitioners: gaining insight, expanding their default range of expression (*role repertoire*), and self-regulating independently. From the perspective of drama therapist Robert Landy, drama therapy helps clients discover a healthy expression that is neither devoid of emotion (*over-distanced*) nor flooded with feeling (*under-distanced*). Landy (1983) describes *aesthetic distance* as the healing state created by balancing these two emotional extremes.[3]

Through the lens of aesthetic distance, Rasaboxes offers a framework that deftly balances freeform psychophysical embodiment of emotion with rigorous structure. The grid design acts as a life-sized aesthetic distancing device; the lines on the floor provide a clinical *holding environment*—a container for dramatic reality in which clients can safely project and externalize their inner worlds. For people who have difficulty managing their affect, the rasaboxes grid can be especially beneficial by concretely delineating emotional arenas and developing stronger internal boundaries.

Gaye Doner-Tudanger[4] was one of the first drama therapists to experiment with Rasaboxes clinically. She started working with outpatient psychiatric clients at the Post-Graduate Center for Mental Health in New York City to develop original theatre pieces. Doner-Tudanger reported to me how one selectively mute patient eventually relearned to speak fully by incrementally expressing himself in Rasaboxes, buoyed by the nonverbal physicality. In 2013, Doner-Tudanger also used Rasaboxes in the devising process for her self-revelatory theatre performance at New York University (NYU), *Cancer as Change Maker*, five years before she died.

Alexandra Devin, a member of Doner-Tudanger's ensemble, integrated what she learned from studying with her to treat a private practice client with dissociative identity order, a condition in which a person develops alternate identities, or *alters*, that are often summoned unconsciously when triggered by traumatic memories. As an empowering alternative, Devin's client was able to consciously create fictional "alters," i.e., personas, with her body in Rasaboxes. These sessions segued into art therapy as the client processed her healing independently.

Robert Landy's version of Rasaboxes directed clients to take a mini hero's journey (Campbell 1968) through the boxes. Clients preselected boxes to represent "Obstacles," and potential "Guides" to encounter along their way to their expected "Destination" (Landy 2013). In 2011, Landy led a plenary session for a European Arts Therapy conference with over 300 delegates representing 30 languages. Each participant selected different emotions to represent their points of departure before the symposium, imagined Obstacles, Guides they hoped to meet, and anticipated Destinations (Landy 2013).[5]

Nisha Sajnani and Maitri Gopalakrishna have explored both codified and improvised forms of expression in their collaborative work (Sajnani and Gopalakrishna 2017). Gopalakrishna learned a performance system developed by the Adishakti Theatre Company in Pondicherry, India, inspired in part by *kudiyattam*,[6] the ancient Sanskrit performance form. She has been using her adaptations of Rasaboxes with young women in Bangalore for empowerment, personal development, and devising performances. Sajnani studied Bharatanatyam, another classical dance form,[7] and used Rasaboxes to train drama therapists at Lesley University and NYU, where she has been Director of the Program in Drama Therapy since 2017.

David Socha, a drama therapist who trained as my clinical intern, subsequently taught emotional intelligence to early elementary school children in New York City after-school programs, including some operated by the Morningside

Center. Socha labeled six boxes with superpowers (invisibility, super smart, flying, super strength, super speed, and my superhero/neutral). Costume pieces aided the children's dramatic play. Socha also worked with toddlers to help normalize difficult feelings by locating emotions and roles in their bodies, which assisted the children to access and de-escalate their affective responses without overtaking their tolerance levels.

Rasa≈Therapy and Addiction Rehabilitation

In my clinical practice from 2007 to 2009, I structured monthly rasa≈therapy sessions to treat adults recovering from drug and alcohol addiction on a 28-day inpatient unit at Interfaith Medical Center, located in the Bedford-Stuyvesant neighborhood of Brooklyn, New York. Since the population changed every day, clients sometimes experienced only one rasa≈therapy session during their stay. These sessions augmented verbal psycho-educational counseling, which taught patients about their condition and how treatment strategies worked. For instance, clients learned that emotions triggered their cravings, and that greater self-control could be achieved by avoiding people, places, and emotions associated with their preferred substances.

While avoidance can be a very useful coping strategy for some clients, my rasa≈therapy sessions offered an alternative view: managing difficult feelings requires practice in order to mitigate situational influence. I affirmed clients' concerns that self-regulating affect is not easy, especially under the pressure of habit. However, I offered that if actors can become "athletes of emotion"[8] by training in Rasaboxes, they too could develop similar emotional control through the regular practice of rasa≈therapy.[9] I framed my sessions as an opportunity to safely explore and expand patients' range of tolerance for emotional turbulence, as well as a chance to build supportive connections with other participants by sharing stories, thoughts, and feelings—both fictional and real—inspired by the enactments.

Rasa Hoops Exercise

Space was extremely tight on the inpatient unit; it doubled as the dining room and barely fit five small square tables for meals. When tables were flipped onto each other and pushed to the periphery, we were left with roughly 6 × 8 feet of playing space. Working with up to 12 patients in nine rasaboxes was just not feasible. As an alternative, I laid four hula-hoops on the floor.[10]

As a warmup, the group brainstormed and selected four emotions (using English words) they deemed useful to explore. Using a sheet of paper, I labeled each hoop with one of the four emotions selected. While I did not use the Sanskrit words in these shorter sessions, I still used bhava and rasa concepts (see Chapter 2, p. 49 and Chapter 3, p. 61 and Bharata-muni 1967, 105) to prompt clients to think in terms of emotional categories that contain a range of intensities and nuances. For instance, "anger" could include annoyance, irritation, frustration, and rage.[11]

In the middle of the hula-hoop cluster, I replaced the center rasa of *shanta* with a fifth sheet of paper labeled "peace."

For additional containment, I invited participants to use the central peace-zone from the outset of a session as a sanctuary space for introspection, rest, and temporary psychic safety. Before participants entered the hoops, I spent substantial time guiding them to physically and mentally locate their sense of neutrality as a point of reference. I compared neutrality to a palate cleanser between tasting emotions, aiding us to receive the next flavor. Returning to neutral reinforced emotional containment skills as well. Tranquil poses and calming breaths helped my clients locate a neutral state to begin from, then restore to, after exiting the rasa hoops.

Using a drumbeat or a handclap, I invited four volunteers to enter the rasa hoops. Simultaneously, I side-coached them to play with body shapes, breath phrases, and vocalizing. As I called out various levels or percentages of intensity, the players modulated their emotional explorations accordingly. To prevent under-distancing, I typically avoided guiding patients into the most intense levels of expression, especially if someone was new to me or rasa≈therapy.

After a few moments, I cued the players to exit the hoops, relax in neutral, and then go through the same series for three more rounds switching hoops each time. After four rotations, the group had a chance to savor all four emotions within the limited time available. To keep the rasic exchange activated (the notion of spectators/partakers "tasting" the performed emotions they observe), I encouraged those outside the hoops to track how the performances affected them and actively experiment with altering their physical proximity to the action.

Once fully warmed up, individuals could psychodramatically (Moreno 1934) tell their stories of addiction and recovery as they traveled through the hoops. Some clients could independently pace themselves, whereas others benefited from my cues to switch hoops, based on when I sensed they were stuck in a particular feeling, or if I felt a change would support their unfolding story with more dramatic turns.

I also had success introducing symbolic objects related to recovery into the rasa≈therapy storytelling. For instance, if the substance of choice was beer, they would interact with a disposable cup on which I had pasted the image of a popular beer brand. The cup's lack of verisimilitude did not deter most clients from delivering emotional and meaningful performances, perhaps as a testament to the power of aesthetic distancing.

Some clients become stuck recounting their stories of addiction and relapse cycles with helplessness and frustration. Just as Minnick (2001) notes that new insights about familiar fictional characters can be discovered by taking a monologue through Rasaboxes, rasa≈therapy allows patients to rewrite their ossified autobiographies with greater dimensionality, renewed perspective, and clarified perceptions.

Jumping Into New Roles

In some sessions, I did not refer to "emotions" at all. Rather, I used a more distanced approach by substituting rasas with role types such as Victim, Child,

Lover, Villain, Wise Elder, Critic, Coward, Trickster, or Hero (Table 9.1) inspired by Landy's (1993) taxonomy of roles in drama therapy. Whereas Rasaboxes performer training "values immediacy over-distance, savoring over judgment" (Schechner 2001, 31), my role-based form privileged more emotional detachment and cognitive engagement. For example, enacting the role of the Victim predictably encourages sad feelings. Yet at the same time, playing a generalized role type obscures potentially overwhelming affect. Enacting stereotypical personas based on social, cultural, or archetypal associations can serve as a protective scaffold for clients as they risk entering into unknown and threatening emotional territory. By jumping in and out of roles, players traverse states of emotional over-distance and under-distance as they approach aesthetic distance. The drama therapist can also help clients modulate distance based on the portrayal of the role's style, ranging from stark realism (under-distance) to caricature (over-distance). Eventually, stereotypes can be fleshed out with more emotional specificity and personal authenticity. In this regard, both Rasaboxes and rasa≈therapy move between the fictional and the real, the artificial and the personal, to arrive at a dynamic point that transcends these dualities. One key distinction here is the therapeutic intention: drama therapists using adaptations of Rasaboxes tailor their interventions to facilitate emotional and psychological transformation in service of individual and group treatment goals.

Another distinguishing feature of rasa≈therapy is leveraging physical engagement to enhance a parallel verbal group psychotherapy process. This work leads to rich reflections about how emotions are rooted in our bodies: "gut feelings," "butterflies in the stomach," "shaking with fear," "laughing until we cried," and having our "breath taken away." Jumping into roles also becomes a primer to internalize the impact of how being cast in a certain role (e.g., the Addict), influences the way we see and feel about ourselves. These insights naturally lead clients to draw connections to their recovery process and to declare powerful affirmations about making healthier choices in the future.

The next step in exploring role types was to place them in the rasa hoops. The types were either generated by the group or from a given list including Child, Healer, Survivor, Martyr, Son, Judge, Witness, Outcast, Bully, Demon, Dreamer, and several others.[12] Clients embodied the role types just as they would rasas or

TABLE 9.1 Converting rasas into role types.

Karuna	Adbhuta	Shringara
Victim, Mourner	Child, Seeker	Lover, Parent
Raudra	**Shanta**	**Bibhatsa**
Hothead, Villain	Wise Elder, Spiritual Leader	Critic, Misanthrope
Bhayanaka	**Hasya**	**Vira**
Coward, Martyr	Clown, Trickster	Hero, Warrior

English emotion words. Over time, many clients were able to expand and enrich their role repertoire by inhabiting a wider variety of roles. Freezing the action, I asked those watching to imagine a specific scenario suggested by the tableau. The narratives clients offered were often related to issues that triggered addictive behaviors, but also included generic scenes about work and family, or more fantastical fiction. I guided the group to experiment with alternate versions of these scenarios in the roles/hoops, allowing the archetypes to shift the narrative. These shifts often revealed brilliant solutions to dramatic conflicts or lampooned the ways emotions and attitudes get the better of us. For example, frequently a drug dealer would be conjured from the role of the Demon, manipulating a desperate, vulnerable Addict—spawned from the role of the Child—to buy more product. Jumping into adjacent hoops, the Dealer could become a Survivor and the Addict could become a Healer. The Healer-Addict might now empathize with the Survivor-Dealer's past trauma as the Survivor-Dealer confronts their own reflection in the death spiral of the Healer-Addict. This type of encounter often leads the characters to help each other choose sobriety in fellowship. Regardless of how unrealistic the scene might be, disrupting and rewriting seemingly infinite cycles of addiction and relapse offers a healing corrective experience, for players and witnesses alike. Even without the layer of storytelling, this rasa and role-based approach helps clients transcend the confining identity of the Addict and reclaim a more holistic, healthier self-concept.

Feedback and Cool Downs

Debriefing is an essential component of the rasa≈therapy process; clients frequently shared powerful takeaways. One patient said he finally understood that when he feels an emotion driving his need to drink, he only needs to wait because the emotion will eventually pass, followed by the next inevitable feeling, one emotion at a time, until he feels safe. Another patient declared with astonishment that rasa≈therapy made recovery *fun*. Others described how vicariously tasting emotions or roles from outside the hoops increased their empathy for others, which subsequently helped them feel less alone. By and large patients jumped in with enthusiasm and lamented when group time was over. However, groups usually included at least one person too intimidated to enter the hoops. Inspired by the bravery of others, clients who were initially more reserved became emboldened to take a taste-test the next time I brought out the hoops.

The containment qualities of rasa≈therapy also helped me encourage clients to disclose their self-assessments. Drawing on Jacob Moreno's (1934) sociometric technique *locograms*, I asked patients to place a foot (neutrally) in the hoop they found easiest to express, and talk to the people near them (or the whole group) about their experience and what they had learned. As we repeated this activity for the most difficult rasa/role/emotion, we observed how the group's patterns converged and diverged. For clients who had a chance to repeat the rasa≈therapy session, we could track progress when it occurred. Lastly, each member of the group stepped one foot between all the hoops to complete the phrase, "I'm in shanta/at peace when . . ."

Rasa≈therapy sessions always ended with participants helping to dismantle the floor design. This activity served as a way for clients to further *de-role*, a common practice drama therapists use to help clients intentionally reclaim a sense of self and reality. I encouraged patients to bear witness to the emptiness and honor the power of our collective imaginations and bodies to transform spaces—and ourselves. The moment would become imbued with both adbhuta (awe) and bhayanaka (fear), reminiscent of when scenery is cleared off a stage for the next production, but here signifying a renewed preparation for encountering a triggering person, place, or emotion. Invariably, someone would pick up a hoop and spin it around their waist, bringing in the playfulness of hasya (humor) to break a solemn moment. The hula-hooping always struck me as an apt way of de-roling themselves and the space, but it also epitomized aesthetic distance as individuals danced symbolically with the rasa/role/emotion and playfully internalized it on their own terms.

The final stage of my rasa≈therapy sequence was an open discussion format. Patients shared how substances can and cannot help them cope emotionally, the sources of these emotions, and healthier responses to prevent relapse. Some patients realized that emotions are not inherently good or evil; supposedly "negative" emotions can be valuable to keep us safe, and "positive," celebratory emotions can also lead to overindulgence.

Conclusions and Caveats

The clinical hour is so precious; therefore, drama therapists need to be highly strategic about which aspects of Rasaboxes they adopt, modify, and embellish. Moreover, elements should be carefully scaffolded within one session and over time, based on the needs of particular populations and settings. Participants who have extreme difficulty managing their emotions consider it to be a great achievement to work intensely for one hour and pushing too far beyond their limits might be more harmful than helpful. That said, just as performers require a substantial amount of training to embody all the rasas improvisationally, most clients need repeated exposure to rasa≈therapy with attuned guidance and modulation to approach a bonafide healing experience, albeit in shorter exposure intervals than those afforded to actors practicing Rasaboxes.

Finally, I caution Rasaboxes practitioners who are not qualified mental health professionals against experimenting with rasa≈therapy with vulnerable populations. Schechner (2001) similarly warned that Rasaboxes "is both expressive and a scalpel that cuts very deeply into people" (43). The goals of rasa≈therapy are different than Rasaboxes for actors, and the format needs to be carefully modified by trained drama therapists with clinical supervision. Lastly, readers should note that the rasa≈therapy approaches I have outlined do not constitute a comprehensive approach to psychotherapy, but rather serve as an additional set of tools in the drama therapy repository.

Notes

1 Drama therapy is similar to but distinct from *psychodrama* (Moreno 1934), a practice in which clients enact stories drawn explicitly from their real lives.
2 For a comprehensive overview of the field of drama therapy, see *Current Approaches in Drama Therapy* (Johnson and Emunah 2009).

3 These concepts might be tacitly familiar to performance theorists because both Landy and Schechner based their praxis on a similar broad body of knowledge integrating theatre, psychology, sociology, and anthropology—one major shared influence being the work of Erving Goffman (1959). Indeed, Schechner's (1985) "not not me," an extension of Winnicott's (1953) transitional space between the "me and not me," overlaps considerably with Landy's aesthetic distancing theory in drama therapy. Also, in one of his earliest writings on the topic, Landy cites Schechner and Schuman (1976) to acknowledge their scholarship on the psychological benefits of more under-distanced elements found in "the extreme states of ecstasy, trance, and meditation, as they relate to both theatre aesthetics and healing" (1983, 184).
4 Doner-Tudanger was introduced to Rasaboxes in the context of The Performance Workshop at NYU in the late 1990s (the editors).
5 Landy was exposed to Rasaboxes in 2004 at a demonstration given by Cole, Minnick, Bowditch, and others. He then invited Minnick to teach an introductory workshop for graduate students in the NYU Drama Therapy program.
6 Kudiyattam is performed (mostly) in Kerala by a family lineage called "chakyars."
7 See Pillai, Chapter 2, p. 52.
8 The phrase "athlete of the heart" was coined by Antonin Artaud (1966), and then adopted by Schechner (2001, 43) and Minnick (2001, 40) to describe the ideal Rasaboxes performer.
9 Drama therapists commonly reference the concept of enactment as a rehearsal for real life. For an extended treatment on this idea, see Daniel Weiner (1994).
10 The use of hula hoops was recommended to me by Gaye Doner-Tudanger based on her previous Rasaboxes experiments at an outpatient adult psychiatric clinic. However, Gaye had enough room to use nine hoops.
11 When I have more time with motivated and high functioning clients, I add Devanagari script to my pre-made labels. I speculate that adding a foreign language with transliterated Sanskrit might magnify the aesthetic distancing effect.
12 See Gaines (2005) for a comprehensive analysis of Landy's (1993) taxonomy of roles.

Works Cited

Artaud, Antonin. *The Theatre and Its Double*. Translated by Mary Caroline Richards. New York, NY: Grove Press, 1966.

Bharata-muni. *The Natyasastra*. Translated and edited by Manomohan Ghosh. Calcutta: Manisha Granthalaya, 1967.

Campbell, Joseph. *The Hero with a Thousand Faces*, 2nd ed. Princeton, NJ: Princeton University Press, 1968.

Gaines, Andrew M. *The Role Taxonomy Checklist: An Exploration of Drama Therapy Assessment*. Unpublished master's thesis, New York University, 2005.

Goffman, Erving. *The Presentation of Self in Everyday Life*. Garden City, NY: Doubleday, 1959.

Johnson, David Read, and Emunah Renee, eds. *Current Approaches in Drama Therapy*. Springfield, IL: C.C. Thomas, 2009.

Landy, Robert J. "The Use of Distancing in Drama Therapy." *The Arts in Psychotherapy*, vol. 10 1983, pp. 175–85.

———. *Persona and Performance: The Meaning of Role in Drama, Therapy, and Everyday Life*. New York, NY: Gilford Press, 1993.

———. "The Distancing of Emotion through a Confluence of Rasa Aesthetics and Drama Therapy." In *Arts Therapies and the Intelligence of Feeling*, edited by Salvo Pitruzella, Malcolm Ross, and Sarah Scoble, 47–52. Plymouth, England: University of Plymouth Press, 2013.

Minnick, Michele. "Rasaboxes Performer Training." *TDR: The Drama Review*, vol. 45, no. 3, 2001, pp. 40–42.

Moreno, Jacob L. *Who Shall Survive? A New Approach to the Problem of Human Interrelations*. Washington, DC: Nervous and Mental Disease Publishing Co, 1934.

Sajnani, Nisha, and Maitri Gopalakrishna. "Rasa: Exploring the Influence of Indian Performance Theory and Technique in Drama Therapy." *Drama Therapy Review*, vol. 3 no. 2, 2017, pp. 225–39.

Schechner, Richard. *Between Theater and Anthropology*. Philadelphia: University of Pennsylvania Press, 1985.

———. "Rasaesthetics." *TDR: The Drama Review*, 45, no. 3, 2001, pp. 27–50.

Schechner, Richard, and Mady Schuman, eds. *Ritual, Play, and Performance: Readings in the Social Sciences/Theatre*. New York: Seabury Press, 1976.

Wiener, Daniel J. *Rehearsals for Growth: Theater Improvisation for Psychotherapists*. New York: W.W. Norton, 1994.

Winnicott, Donald W. "Transitional Objects and Transitional Phenomena: A Study of the First Not-Me Possession." *The International Journal of Psychoanalysis*, vol. 34, 1953, pp. 89–97.

CHAPTER 10

Rasaboxes, Drama Therapy, and Stability Through Dynamic Change
A Case Study

DANA ARIE

Being an Emotions Junkie

I used to be an "emotions junkie." I didn't realize that at the time. It stood in contradiction to the way I perceived myself—rational, analytical. Thought and reason were my origin, my destination, and my defense. My background was deeply rooted in hard science, and pursuing an interest in theatre was perceived by others around me, as well as by me, as a detour, an adventure, before returning to my vocation in science. Little did I know that theatre would open a window to explore a new territory: the vast land of human emotions, in all their intensity.

My training as an actor enabled me to experience emotions in a way I had never permitted myself in real life. At its extreme, I felt skinless; every nerve in my body felt awake and stimulated. It was painful and exhilarating at the same time. I kept searching for that experience, that flood of emotions, in the theatrical process. Unfortunately, it also felt like an addiction.

Searching for Balance

I was introduced to Rasaboxes at an early stage of my training as a therapist at the Drama Therapy program at New York University. That work marked the beginning of a personal and professional journey. In my previous actor training, intense emotional experience had felt like chaotic energy that overflowed my body. Rasaboxes offered me a sense of shape, integration, a container—the external container of the grid, but more importantly, the container shaped by the body itself. The experience of containment the boxes gave me provided a new sense of balance, an ability to use the larger spectrum of experiences—thoughts, sensations, and narratives that come up in the journey through the grid—to process the content that arose in each specific box, rather than merely to indulge in or be overwhelmed by it.

Working with Rasaboxes, somatic sensations and emotional experiences allow for roles and narratives to emerge. For Dr. Robert Landy, founding Emeritus Professor of the NYU Program in Drama Therapy, "role" is one of the basic concepts in drama therapy, and his theory is central to the field. In short, a role serves as a projected part of the self; thus, personality can be perceived as the sum of all roles and the dynamic play between them (Landy 1993). The flexibility to appropriately transition between roles we play in life and between emotional states helps us to better adapt to changes and demands in the physical, personal, and social environment. The work with Rasaboxes holds the potential to train the participant to be not only an "athlete of the emotions" (Artaud 1958; Schechner 2001) but also an athlete of roles.

Why Emotions?

Emotions contain and convey information necessary for our survival. They set off chains of responses to both external and internal events and deliver social information of high biological relevance. The neuroscientist Antonio Damasio (1994) suggests not only that the body is important to constitute the feeling of an emotion, as suggested previously by American philosopher, historian, and psychologist William James, but also that emotions are necessary to the process of making advantageous decisions, particularly under conditions of uncertainty. This becomes even more significant when addressing decisions of personal or social value (Bechara et al. 2003; Bechara and Damasio 2005; Damasio 1994; Naqvi et al. 2006). Neural connections are established in the brain in response to our interactions with the world, and these connections integrate information regarding the circumstances under which they were created: pleasant or unpleasant physical sensations, somato-visceral and autonomic changes, or emotional memories, as well as projected negative or positive outcomes; future decision making processes will activate these neural markers, which contribute to the prediction of possible outcomes (Bechara and Damasio 2005; Damasio 1994). Somatic changes are therefore intimately connected to both emotional and cognitive processes.

Our ability to use the knowledge we gain from our own bodies, and our ability to experience and utilize our emotions, is mediated by interoception—the ability to sense subtle bodily changes such as changes in heart rate. (Pollatos et al. 2007; Wiens 2005). Not surprisingly, similar brain structures associated with emotional processing are also involved in the detection and processing of bodily changes (Cameron 2001; Critchley et al. 2004; Phan et al. 2002). This capacity is enhanced in people with specialized training in body awareness, such as dancers or meditation practitioners (Sze et al. 2010).

Regulatory Processes: From Homeostasis to Allostasis

In order to adaptively function in the real world, emotions need to be regulated. Emotional regulation refers to the process of selecting (either consciously or not) the appropriate emotion—the magnitude of its expression, duration, and associated behavior, as well as other components (Gross 2002). The use of Rasaboxes in drama therapy can help people improve their ability to regulate emotions and to be flexible in their responses, while at the same time gaining a sense of stability and control in their ever-changing life circumstances. Two concepts from biology—*homeostasis* and *allostasis*—are particularly useful in demonstrating how to achieve the balance between flexibility and stability.

In the past few decades, neuroscience and psychology have seen a transition in the perception of stability. The traditional concept of homeostasis—maintaining equilibrium when the environment changes—has been expanded into the more dynamic concept of allostasis, maintaining stability through constant adaptation to change. Homeostasis is about being reactive. It is a biological process that continuously senses internal and external environments in order to detect threatening changes and make required accommodations for self-preservation (McEwen and Wingfield 2010; Sterling 2012). It is an automatic, lower-level mechanism that incorporates primitive brain structures and does not require conscious awareness (Sterling 2012).

Allostasis maintains stability primarily by predictive efforts, which depend upon our awareness. It is a process of continual learning that makes predictions based on prior knowledge and current changes. It anticipates needs before they become critical and flexibly allocates available resources for the most efficient adaptation (McEwen and Wingfield 2003; McEwan and Wingfield 2010; Sterling 2012). A key characteristic of allostasis is the ability to integrate multiple visceral and somato-sensory signals with pre-existing cognitive and emotional information, and coordinate multiple regulatory mechanisms in concert. Hence, allostasis engages the living system in its entirety. It is therefore the key to regulation of complex (even social) behaviors (McEwen and Wingfield 2010; Romero et al. 2009; Sterling 2012). While deviations from the homeostatic state are often treated pharmacologically, allostasis requires a different approach. Allostatic load is the result of a prolonged activation of stress mechanisms in the body, usually due to maladaptive regulatory processes, and takes a significant physiological and psychological toll. Addressing it requires changes in perception, thought, and behavior. The therapeutic goal when addressing allostatic processes would therefore be to restore flexibility of responses, leading to an increased sense of control (Sterling 2012). As a therapeutic technique, Rasaboxes is an ideal mechanism for conscious learning and regulation through the allostatic process.

Rasaboxes as Training for Emotion Regulation: From One Box to Entire System

The Rasaboxes grid is an interactive environment that provides a unique opportunity to intently and actively explore emotional experiences as they unfold in time and space. It serves as a container with a clear frame, permitting safe exploration of emotional content. For the actor, Rasaboxes training enriches and expands emotional expression and representation. In therapy, the goal is to be able to flexibly regulate the emotional experience represented in that box (in order to alleviate allostatic load). Using the Sanskrit words enhances the freedom to experiment with new expressions and behaviors that are often not immediately available to clients in their behavior repertoire, particularly under conditions of stress.

The co-presence of other rasas/emotions in the same environment facilitates a dialogue between them—how they influence each other, how they mix and layer to create more complex emotions, how the sequence of boxes a participant chooses to follow affects the development of the story they tell. This means emotion regulation processes do not occur merely within one box. Rather, at any given time, emotional resources are dynamically shifting between and within the boxes, to ensure the most effective adaptation to the environment. The rasaboxes grid provides an environment for the client's own narratives (either real or imagined) to be enacted. The journey through the grid brings forth the exploration of different perspectives, experiments with new behaviors, and eventually incorporates them into the person's existing knowledge and repertoire of behavior.

Incorporating Body and Narrative in Drama Therapy: Developing Adaptive Mechanisms

The many approaches to drama therapy can be described collectively as *embodied narrative*. Drama therapy provides clients with the opportunity to bring their narratives to life, to try on new behaviors, and to have new experiences—feelings that may not yet be practiced in daily life. People often seek therapy because aspects of their lives are out of balance. The goal of the therapeutic process is to regain autonomy and control, relieve allostatic load, and restore flexibility of responses that we sometimes lose in the social and cultural adaptation process. In therapeutic work, it is the dynamic journey through Rasaboxes that the client learns to activate their emotional system in its entirety. By becoming aware of and comfortable with the sensations and reflections that arise in process, the client gradually incorporates these new discoveries into existing knowledge, so that in the future they become available and can hence support more adaptive behaviors. To demonstrate this, I will use excerpts from my Rasaboxes drama therapy work with a patient.

Case Study: Working with Michael in Rasaboxes

Michael[1] is 14 years old, an adolescent who seeks therapy for social anxiety. He is bright and very artistic. He has strong physical features that stand in contrast with his childish manners. He often shrugs his shoulders and raises his eyebrows in expressions of bewilderment. His affect rarely changes even when describing his own painful experiences. His demeanor and body language suggest he is trying to minimize the space he occupies in the world. At first, Michael appears to be self-aware as he openly shares his difficulties. However, any attempt to reach deeper into his feelings, or his here-and-now experience and reactions, always faces the same response—a shrug, raised eyebrows—partly apologizing, partly expressing embarrassment, and muttering "I don't know." For the first few sessions we talk. It is hard to bypass his highly rationalized approach, and any attempt at projective techniques[2] constantly triggers the defense mechanism of "I don't know."

While at home Michael is loud, vocal, and mostly angry. At school he barely speaks. Although not a social outcast, he has no intimate connections and therefore no sense of belonging. His experience in the world is that of detachment from himself and others. This detachment numbs his emotional life. And it sets a cycle in motion—Michael's inability to be authentic and to relate to others around him results in others finding it difficult to relate to him. His presence in the world has been narrowed down to repetitive patterns of behavior that intend to keep him "safe" but compromise his sense of well-being.

Michael is a very gifted artist. In most of his drawings he uses colored pencils and crayons—materials that suggest a very reserved emotional investment in the process. His drawings are realistic, featuring mostly human figures with no distinct emotional facial expressions. In his difficulty relating to his emotions, Michael demonstrates restricted expressiveness and rigid behavioral patterns that limit his ability to adaptively manage constantly changing and demanding social situations. For these reasons, I decide to introduce him to Rasaboxes. The invitation to draw on the paper-covered floor appeals to him. He works slowly, beginning with karuna, shringara, and hasya. The other rasas, as he describes it, are too difficult to grasp at the moment. Choosing to work with his preferred material of colored pencils, his sketches in the rasaboxes resemble his artistic work—humans devoid of emotional expressions, or expressions disconnected from humans. While he is drawing in the boxes, I take the role of witness to the emotions that fill the room—his and mine, conscious and unconscious.

We use the same paper sheets every session and add to them, which generates continuity. The content becomes layered and expanded upon each time we work. Through the drawing, he gradually externalizes his inner self, his perceptions, his "emotional vocabulary." On occasion, he expands into short verbal narratives. Over the course of a few sessions, he manages to draw in all the boxes. The embodiment of emotions, however, even in the form of a still pose, is too demanding for him at this point. Asking him to take on a pose at this stage feels as if I'm inviting his habitual rigid patterns into the room. Instead, I invite him to simply breathe in each of the rasas: to step into a box, close his eyes, and allow the content he drew on the paper to fill him. I ask him to pay attention to the sensations in his body, to observe the pattern of his breath, and eventually, to observe whether he notices any differences between the boxes.

To help facilitate active embodiment, I step into the boxes with Michael and we start with playing the mirror game—beginning with facial expressions and gradually incorporating the entire body. We each mirror each other; there is no fixed originator. The transition from passively taking in the content filling the grid to being active provides a new perspective: from merely maintaining the role of an observer, Michael now becomes involved.

During the following few sessions, Michael continues to experiment with the embodiment of the rasas. Each session begins with drawing, enriching the content that fills his boxes. Minor changes in mood or perspective are reflected in the drawings, but instead of dissolving and disappearing unnoticed, they are now present, addressed, and can be incorporated into his previously rigid approach to himself and the world around him. His body becomes more malleable, lending itself to the embodiment of the rasa. As a therapist, I am an observer, a spectator taking in the rasas conveyed by the performer. However, in the therapeutic context, something is also returned to the performer/patient—the material that has been taken in by the therapist is processed, digested, and returned to the client in the form of a look, an expression, a gesture, or even a comment or suggestion. I invite Michael to pay attention to his somatic sensations in different boxes, and to begin to distinguish those boxes in which embodiment felt more comfortable from those that were difficult. To this he easily responds—hasya and bibhatsa were the easiest. The most difficult boxes for him? Michael points at vira and raudra.

To one session, Michael brings a story regarding an incident at school. Another kid had made fun of him during a school trip. I invite Michael to pick the box that matches the essence of the story. He selects bhayanaka. Surprisingly, he chooses to work with oil pastels, a material that fosters more emotional release than Michael usually gives himself permission for. When he steps into the rasaboxes, Michael's body molds into the pose more easily than before. His breath becomes active and engaged. For the first time since we started the work, Michael is able to integrate a personal experience with physical sensations, actions, and sounds.

I then suggest one more thing. I ask him to find a box to which his body is drawn "right now." Without hesitation he steps into raudra. In this rage box, for the first time, he adds words—an internal monologue that has been shut inside for so long that even he could not access it until now. Michael can retell the being-made-fun-of incident with appropriate affect, as well as recall similar feelings from the past. At the end of the session, Michael begins to reflect on how fear and anger play a role in his life—how they inform his presence in the world and guide his decisions and actions. Being able to physically tap into them, explore and become familiar with them from within and without, Michael begins to understand and regulate them, rather than be dominated by them. During our last session I ask Michael where he wants to go from here. He points at vira and says: "I know I am not there yet, but I am not afraid of it anymore."

Closing Notes

My own personal journey with Rasaboxes, as well as my experience as a drama therapist, led me to appreciate the potential of this work as a method for developing adaptive reactions to unstable environments through a dynamic process of change. The movement that begins from the act of drawing in the boxes gradually expands to physical embodiment of emotions and from there to sounding and speaking. Narrative emerges. Rasaboxes allows clients who are emotionally over-distanced, like Michael, to become familiar and comfortable with their physical–emotional expressiveness. For clients who are under-distanced and overly emotional, they can learn to attenuate their emotions. The practice of transitioning through embodied emotions triggers the emergence of personal narratives that have been associated with these somatic emotional states. The playfulness of the work provides an opportunity to experiment with new perspectives in the safety of the therapeutic space. This enables the client to form new connections between somatic states and emotional and cognitive content, which expands adaptive capacities that can help them to achieve confidence and control.

Notes

1 The name of this client has been changed for confidentiality purposes.
2 Projective techniques are methods used in psychotherapy and psychological assessments to bypass conscious resistance, and provide access to hidden psychodynamic content.

Works Cited

Artaud, Antonin. *The Theater and Its Double*. Translated by M. C. Richards. New York: Grove Press, 1958.

Bechara, A., and A. R. Damasio. "The Somatic Marker Hypothesis: A Neural Theory of Economic Decision." *Games and Economic Behavior*, vol. 52, 2005, pp. 336–72.

Bechara, A., H. Damasio, and A. R. Damasio. "The Role of the Amygdala in Decision Making." *Annals of the New York Academy of Sciences*, vol. 985, 2003, pp. 356–69.

Cameron, O. G. "Interoception: The Inside Story: A Model for Psychosomatic Processes." *Psychosomatic Medicine*, vol. 63, no. 5, 2001, pp. 697–710.

Critchley, H. D., S. Wiens, P. Rotshtein, A. Ohman, and R. Dolan. "Neural Systems Supporting Interoceptive Awareness." *Nature Neuroscience*, vol. 7, no. 2, 2004, pp. 189–95.

Damasio, Antonio. *Descartes' Error: Emotion, Reason and the Human Brain*. New York: G.P. Putnam, 1994.

Gross, J. J. "Emotion Regulation: Affective, Cognitive and Social Consequences." *Psychophysiology*, vol. 39, 2002, pp. 281–91.

James, William. "What Is An Emotion?" *Mind*, vol. 9, 1884, pp. 188–205.

Landy, Robert J. *Persona and Performance*. New York: The Guilford Press, 1993.

McEwen, B. S., and J. C. Wingfield. "The Concept of Allostasis in Biology and Biomedicine." *Hormones and Behavior*, vol. 43, no. 1, 2003, pp. 2–15.

———. "What's in a Name? Integrating Homeostasis, Allostasis and Stress." *Hormones and Behavior*, vol. 57, no. 2, 2010, p. 105.

Naqvi, N., B. Shiv, and A. Bechara. "The Role of Emotion in Decision Making: A Cognitive Neuroscience Perspective." *Current Directions in Psychological Science*, vol. 15, no. 5, 2006, pp. 260–64.

Phan, K. L., T. Wager, S. F. Taylor, and I. Liberzon. "Functional Neuroanatomy of Emotion: A Meta-Analysis of Emotion Activation Studies in PET and fMRI." *NeuroImage*, vol. 16, 2002, pp. 331–48.

Pollatos, O., B. M. Herbert, E. Matthias, and R. Schandry. "Heart Rate Response After Emotional Picture Presentation is Modulated by Interoceptive Awareness." *International Journal of Psychophysiology*, vol. 63, 2007, pp. 117–24.

Romero, L. M., M. J. Dickens, and N. E. Cyr. "The Reactive Scope Model—a New Model Integrating Homeostasis, Allostasis, and Stress." *Hormones and Behavior*, vol. 55, no. 3, 2009, pp. 375–89.

Schechner, Richard. "Rasaesthetics." *The Drama Review*, vol. 45, no. 3, 2001, pp. 27–50.

Sterling, Peter. "Allostasis: A Model of Predictive Regulation." *Physiology & Behavior*, vol. 106, no. 1, 2012, pp. 5–15.

Sze, J. A., A. Y. Gyurak, W. Joyce, and R. W. Levenson. "Coherence Between Emotional Experience and Physiology: Does Body Awareness Training Have an Impact?" *Emotion*, vol. 10, no. 6, 2010, pp. 803–14.

Wiens, S. "Interoception in Emotional Experience." *Current Opinions in Neurology*, vol. 18, 2005, pp. 442–47.

CHAPTER 11

Rasaboxes in the Training of Drama Therapists

NISHA SAJNANI

Mental health providers, like actors, are called to be "athletes of the heart" (Artaud 1938). Learning to navigate emotional experience is central to the training and practice of mental health practitioners, whose job it is to be present with another while remaining aware of their own internal experience. Rasaboxes has been a useful way to support drama therapists and therapists-in-training in traversing the emotional geography of human experience, enabling a greater capacity for understanding and care for themselves and others. What follows are anecdotes of how I have used Rasaboxes to explore interrelated dimensions of being and becoming a therapist. These examples are drawn from my experience training drama therapists and other mental health practitioners in the context of professional development at New York University (NYU).

Emotional Aesthetics: Giving Form to Feeling

In the graduate-level Drama Therapy program that I lead at the Steinhardt School at NYU, students begin with experiential courses aimed at deepening their own self-knowledge. This self-knowledge includes *emotional intelligence* (Salovey and Mayer 1990; Goleman 1995)—the skills necessary to recognize, understand, and manage one's own emotions and influence the emotions of those who seek care. Self-awareness, in the context of the creative arts therapies, also involves giving symbolic form to feeling. Cultivating one's imagination and range of expression is necessary to our practice. Rasaboxes enables the development of *emotional aesthetics*, the sensory perception and expression of emotional experience, which offers a visceral, embodied understanding of one's own dynamic, internal, affective map.

At a conference hosted by the Institut für Theatertherapie (Institute for Theatre Therapy) in Nürtingen, Germany, I began by asking participants to practice the recursive cycle of *noticing, feeling, animating*, and *expressing* their responses to internal and then external stimuli, which I drew from Developmental Transformations (DvT).[1] I integrate this practice in my use of Rasaboxes because I find that it aids participants in attuning and giving form to their experiences while also developing flexibility, responsiveness to change, and a playful attitude. After a series of physical, breath, and vocal warm-ups,[2] coupled with exercises designed to support a sense of ensemble, I asked them to imagine the taste, shape, sound, and substance associated with each rasa.[3] This sequenced orientation to each rasabox elicited rich layers of sensations and associations. In an adaptation of this exercise at an interdisciplinary arts and health conference in Liverpool, UK, I asked participants to physicalize and vary the intensity of their expression along a continuum from 1 to 10 in each rasabox in order to practice modulating expression (see Chapter 4, pp. 161–164). I also asked participants to attend to the transition between rasaboxes in order to explore the relationships that, for example, disgust (bibhatsa) may have with wonder (adbhuta), or compassion (karuna) with anger (raudra). This sensory encounter was followed by an invitation to write and draw in each rasabox. This gave participants the opportunity to shift between physical and cognitive associations, thereby offering an experience of *aesthetic distance*, the capacity to be both emotionally engaged yet reflective at the same time (Scheff 1981; Landy 1997).

In these training workshops, I noticed that imagining each rasabox as a flavor made it easier for participants to discover culturally specific references to talk about the residue of what lingers in the body when a particular emotional state has been activated in the clinical milieu or therapeutic encounter. For some participants in Bangalore, India, for example, sadness was associated with the taste of raw, bitter gourd and wonder was associated with the taste of ladoo, a sweet besan-flour dessert. Articulating each emotion in the body with images, sensations, and words gives therapists a complex, aesthetic language with which to identify, explore, reflect, and communicate their own inner life. Participants indicated that practice with Rasaboxes heightened their awareness of their own associations to various emotional states and the variable effort taken to shift between them.

Being with Another Over Time

I have adopted Richard Mollica's perspective that the work of psychotherapy involves "a shared empathic partnership between two [or more] people working together in a community to create a new worldview" (Mollica 2014). Empathic attunement, the process by which an individual is affected by, can share in, identify with, and express the emotional state of another, is a critical factor in developing a positive therapeutic alliance (Wampold 2015).[4] However, the research on empathy in psychotherapy is often critiqued because, as Bruce E. Wampold writes,

> It is clearly easier for a therapist to be warm and caring toward a motivated, disclosing and cooperative patient than to one who is interpersonally aggressive, and the former types of patients will most likely have better outcomes than the latter, making the empathy/outcome correlation an artifact of patient characteristics rather than therapist action.
>
> (2015, 272)

The challenge then becomes how to be with another human being during their most difficult moments, especially when their approaches to coping are off-putting. Rasaboxes has been helpful in this regard because it offers therapists and therapists-in-training an opportunity to practice *affective resonance*, the dynamic of moving and being moved in relationship (Mühlhoff 2014), and *relational aesthetics*, a term that I have repurposed in the context of drama therapy to describe the interlacing of empathic and aesthetic attunement in the context of the therapeutic relationship (Sajnani 2017).

In a Rasaboxes workshop in December 2016 at NYU, Michele Minnick used an exercise called Shopping for Rasas (see Chapter 4, pp. 150–152) whereby participants were invited to mirror the movements made by other participants in a rasabox, thereby expanding their own range of emotional expression. I adapted this exercise with drama therapists-in-training at NYU and at Tel Hai College, Israel. I asked participants to divide into two groups and invited the first group to step into the center box, shanta, a space configured as a place of peace or bliss in Schechner's original vision (2001), which has also been theorized and practiced as a space to cultivate mindfulness.[5] I suggested the second group move to a rasabox that they had found challenging to enter or to leave, and to practice giving physical and sonic expression to being in that box. The result was a spectrum of dissociated, withdrawn, ambivalent, and exaggerated movements that gave aesthetic form to the challenge of emotional regulation when faced with reminders of distress. I asked the group in the middle to observe their internal experience and to practice joining any one participant from the other group by matching and mirroring their movements. They were given the option to do so from within the shanta rasabox or to join the other's rasabox. I asked participants from both groups to notice when they felt like they were connected to or in relationship with the other and, at that point, to allow their sounds and movements to organically transform together. Feedback from participants emphasized the relief that comes with being noticed and met by another, especially when it is hard to feel connected to oneself. Feedback from those who began in the center indicated a renewed awareness of their own associations and preferences as they considered who to join and how. Both groups made associations to the challenges associated with being with another when their movements gave rise to feelings of shame, fear, and, for some, deep sadness—reinforcing the potential of this exercise to call attention to how the process of therapy may affect both the therapist and client and the need to practice being and transforming in relationship with another even when it is difficult.

Performing Care

Mental health providers engage in *emotional labor* (Hochschild 1983) in that they are frequently exposed to emotional suffering, suicidal ideation, and the traumatic life events of those in their care while simultaneously regulating their own feelings and expressions. Further, they often do so within the paradox of "being ordered to care in a society that refuses to value caring," as expressed in under-resourced and neglected work environments (Reverby 1987, 5; see also Dreison et al. 2018). Sociologist Arlie R. Hochschild (1983) employed dramaturgical analogies used by Erving Goffman (1959) to describe twin processes involved in emotional labor: *surface acting* and *deep acting*. Surface acting refers to the suppression of negative feelings in order to display positive ones (i.e., faking it or putting on a mask) and *deep acting* refers to the attempt to align oneself with organizational goals in order to feel more authentically engaged while risking alienation from one's actual feelings. The ongoing suppression of genuine feelings associated with work-related stress coupled with the performance of positive feelings has been demonstrated to lead to burnout, a "degree of emotional exhaustion and fatigue, depersonalization (cynicism), and reduced personal accomplishment" (Kristensen et al. 2005, 197), which seriously affects between 21% and 67% of mental health providers (see Morse et al. 2012; see also Pandey and Singh 2016). It also leads to tiredness, non-involvement, loss of effectiveness, and negative consequences for patients and institutions, especially given the expense of recruiting and training staff (Morse et al. 2012). In addition to strategies that emphasize supervision, education, and social support, emerging approaches point to the benefits of meditation, mindfulness, art and music making, and physical engagement (Alexander et al. 2015; Brooks et al. 2010; Hilliard 2006; Huet and Holttum 2016; Mosek and Gilboa 2016).

Rasaboxes offers a model of performing care in that it can be used to facilitate a visceral awareness of the experience of moving between *surface acting*, when participants engage in expressions of emotional states they may not authentically feel, and *deep acting*, when they join and adopt the movements of others in order to accommodate what is required even if it does not fully reflect one's experience. Both are required skills in mental health practice (and most places of work). However, Rasaboxes also provides a means of noticing suppressed affect. The center shanta rasabox that I referred to earlier invites a contemplative stance and strengthens one's capacities to bear witness to oneself. The practice of oscillating between the shanta space and other spaces on the grid deepens the skills required to move flexibly between affect appropriate to hearing about a painful loss, for example, to restraint in staff meetings, followed by entirely different emotional demands at home.

Plotting Your Daily Life Exercise

In a training workshop in Beijing, I invited practitioners to plot a day in their life through the rasaboxes and to have their transitions between rasaboxes witnessed by a partner who observed from the shanta box. Adapting an exercise with text used by Minnick, I invited practitioners to write down a three-line poem about a challenge faced in their workplace or about a challenging colleague or client. They read the poem to a partner and then to the group before and after they experienced the full Rasaboxes exercise. The outcome revealed the degree to which practitioners are accustomed to suppressing the full range of their affect in daily life and the relief associated with discovering new possibilities for expression in situations where they previously felt blocked.

Summary

How do we remain present to our own suffering and that of others? How do we prevent ourselves from becoming so overwhelmed or desensitized that we fail to offer comfort and empathic understanding? Rasaboxes responds with generative possibilities for mental health providers to practice the skills needed for sustainable care. Drama therapists, with their familiarity with embodiment, improvisation, projection, and with their understanding of health as involving a flexible and expanded emotional and role repertoire, are uniquely positioned to benefit from this approach. In my experience, the structure of the training offers opportunities for a wide variety of care providers. In closing, I draw on the words of Audre Lorde who encouraged us to see "pain [as] an event, an experience that must be recognized, named, and then used in some way . . . in order for the experience to be transformed . . . into strength or knowledge or action" (1984, 171). Rasaboxes offers a map to uncover and encounter our own pain and that of others, to cultivate flexibility and presence, to sustain care, and to explore possibilities for action.

Notes

1 My approach to Rasaboxes is influenced by the improvisational practice of Developmental Transformations, an improvisation-based approach to drama therapy. See www.developmentaltransformations.com for more information.
2 Exercises included progressively slowing down one's inhalation and exhalation to a count of five, mimicking stretches offered by members of the group, a flocking exercise that involved grouping together and following the movements of one participant and then another, a facial stretch exercise where one tightened and then expanded their facial expression, and a vocal resonance exercise.
3 The language of taste, shape, substance, and sound came from instructions offered by Michele Minnick in a Rasaboxes workshop that I attended in December 2016 at New York University in New York City.
4 Therapeutic alliance consists of the quality of the intersubjective relationship and agreement about the goals and tasks of therapy. See Bruce E. Wampold (2015) for research on common factors that contribute to successful therapy.
5 Personal communication with Michele Minnick, December 2016 (see also Shanta as Witness, and Relating with Shanta in Chapter 4, pp. 159–160).

Works Cited

Alexander, Gina, Kari Rollins, Danielle Walker, Lily Wong, and Jacquelyn Pennings. "Yoga for Self-care and Burnout Prevention Among Nurses." *Workplace Health and Safety*, vol. 63, no. 10, 2015, pp. 462–70.
Artaud, Antonin. *Le Théâtre et son Double*. Paris: Gallimard, 1938.
Brooks, Darlene, M., Joke Bradt, Lillian Eyre, Andrea Hunt, and Cheryl Dileo. "Creative Approaches for Reducing Burnout in Medical Personnel." *The Arts in Psychotherapy*, vol. 37, no. 3, 2010, pp. 255–63.
Calhoun, Lawrence, and Richard Tedeschi. *Facilitating Posttraumatic Growth: A Clinician's Guide*. Mahwah, NJ: Lawrence Erlbaum Associates, 1999.
Dreison, Kimberly C., Lauren Luther, Kelsey Bonfils, Michael Sliter, John H. McGrew, and Michelle P. Salyers. "Job Burnout in Mental Health Providers: A Meta-analysis of 35 years of Intervention Research." *Journal of Occupational Health Psychology*, vol. 23, no. 1, 2018, pp. 18–30.
Felitti, Vincent, Robert Anda, Dale Nordenberg, David Williamson, Allison Spitz, Valerie Edwards, Mary Koss, and James Marks. "Relationship of Childhood Abuse and Household Dysfunction to Many of the Leading Causes of Death in Adults: The Adverse

Childhood Experiences Study." *American Journal of Preventive Medicine*, vol. 14, no. 4, 1998, pp. 245–58.
Goffman, Erving. *The Presentation of Self in Everyday Life*. Garden City, NJ: Doubleday, 1959.
Goleman, Daniel. *Emotional Intelligence: Why It Can Matter More Than IQ*. New York: Bantam Books, 1995.
Grandey, Alicia, and Robert Melloy. "The State of the Heart: Emotional Labor as Emotion Regulation Reflections and Revision." *Journal of Occupational Health Psychology*, vol. 22, no. 3, 2017, pp. 407–22.
Gross, James. "Emotion Regulation: Past, Present, Future." *Cognition & Emotion*, vol. 13, no. 5, 1999, pp. 551–73.
Halbesleben, Jonathan, and Matthew Bowler. "Emotional Exhaustion and Job Performance: The Mediating Role of Motivation." *Journal of Applied Psychology*, vol. 92, no. 1, 2007, pp. 93–106.
Hilliard, Russell. "The Effect of Music Therapy Sessions on Compassion Fatigue and Team Building of Professional Hospice Caregivers." *The Arts in Psychotherapy*, vol. 33, no. 5, 2006, pp. 395–401.
Hochschild, Arlie R. *The Managed Heart: Commercialization of Human Feeling*. Berkeley, CA: University of California Press, 1983.
Huet, Val, and Sue Holttum. "Art Therapy-based Groups for Work-related Stress with Staff in Health and Social Care: An Exploratory Study." *The Arts in Psychotherapy*, vol. 50, no. 1, 2016, pp. 46–57.
Kristensen, Tage, Marriane Borritz, Ebbe Villadsen, and Karl B. Chistensen. "The Copenhagen Burnout Inventory: A New Tool for the Assessment of Burnout." *Work and Stress*, vol. 19, no. 3, 2005, pp. 192–207.
Landy, Robert J. "Drama Therapy and Distancing: Reflections on Theory and Clinical Application." *The Arts in Psychotherapy*, vol. 23, no. 5, 1997, pp. 367–73.
Lorde, Audre. *Sister Outsider*. Berkeley, CA: Ten Speed Press, 1984.
Minnick, Michele. Personal communication with author, December 2016.
Mollica, Richard F. "The New H5 Model of Trauma and Recovery: A Summary."
NASMHPD.org. Harvard Program for Refugee Trauma, 2014. www.nasmhpd.org/sites/default/files/THE_NEW_H5_MODEL_TRAUMA_AND_RECOVERY.pdf. Accessed 31 January 2018.
Morse, Gary, Michelle Salyers, A. Rollins, Maria Monroe-DeVita, and C. Pfahler. "Burnout in Mental Health Services: A Review of the Problem and its Remediation." *Administration and Policy in Mental Health*, vol. 39, no. 5, 2012, pp. 341–52.
Mosek, Atalia, and Ben-Dori Gilboa. "Integrating Art in Psychodynamic-narrative group Work to Promote the Resilience of Caring Professionals." *The Arts in Psychotherapy*, vol. 51, no. 1, 2016, pp. 1–9.
Mühlhoff, Rainer. "Affective Resonance and Social Interaction." *Phenomenology and the Cognitive Sciences*, vol. 14, no. 4, 2015, pp. 1001–19.
Pandey, Jatin, and Manjari Singh. "Donning the Mask: Effects of Emotional Labour Strategies on Burnout and Job Satisfaction in Community Healthcare." *Health Policy and Planning* vol. 31, no. 5, 2016, pp. 551–62.
Reverby, Susan. *Ordered to Care: The Dilemma of American Nursing, 1850–1945*. Cambridge: Cambridge University Press, 1987.
Sajnani, Nisha. "Relational Aesthetics in the Performance of Personal Story." In *Autobiographical, Self-Revelatory, and Auto-Ethnographic Forms of Therapeutic Theatre*, edited by S. Pendzik, R. Emunah, and D. R. Johnson. London: Palgrave Macmillan, 2017, pp. 85–95.

Sajnani, Nisha, and Maitri Gopalakrishna. "Rasa: Exploring the Influence of Indian Performance Theory in Drama Therapy." *Drama Therapy Review*, vol. 3, no. 2, 2017, pp. 225–39.

Salovey, Peter, and John D. Mayer. "Emotional Intelligence." *Imagination, Cognition and Personality*, vol. 3, 1990, pp. 185–211.

Schechner, Richard. "Rasaesthetics." *TDR*, vol. 45, no. 3, 2001, pp. 27–50.

Scheff, Thomas. "The Distancing of Emotion in Psychotherapy." *Theory, Research, and Practice*, vol. 18, no. 1, 1981, pp. 46–53.

Wampold, Bruce E. "How Important Are the Common Factors In Psychotherapy? An Update." *World Psychiatry*, vol. 14, no. 3, 2015, pp. 270–77. Accessed 31 January 2018.

CHAPTER 12

Dancing on the Tongue[*]

ERIN B. MEE

Readers: this essay requires props. Please have on hand a piece of your favorite chocolate or hard candy. And please locate your favorite two-minute segment of Claude Debussy's "La Cathédrale Engloutie" in *Préludes*/Book 1 (L.117–10). Start the music, close your eyes, place the chocolate on your tongue, and let your tongue choreograph the dance of chocolate. When the dance is finished, begin reading the essay.

"Unwrap your chocolate, place it on your tongue, close your eyes, and let your tongue choreograph the dance of chocolate," instructed Alice B. Toklas as music wafted over the dinner guests in This Is Not A Theatre Company's[1] *A Serious Banquet* (New York, 2014 Judson Church and New York Theatre Workshop), which I conceived and directed. Many immersive and participatory performances include eating and/or drinking. In most cases, this is not simply an attempt to lower inhibitions (though it can serve that function too), but to create multisensory, multimodal, embodied engagement; it is an attempt to create theatre that can be tasted, smelled, and touched, as well as seen and heard. Strawberries taste sweeter when served on a white plate; brass instrumentation brings out the bitter notes in food; thus, theatricality affects taste.[2] Is the reverse also true? How does bringing something into the body to savor enhance a theatrical experience? What does it mean to "taste" theatre? Asking partakers to eat and drink during performances literalizes the Sanskrit aesthetic theory known as *rasa*. By asking partakers to ingest, relish, internalize, and personalize the event, engaging partakers as co-creators of the event, and focusing on affect, immersive and participatory productions are inherently rasic. When analyzed in terms of rasa, they emerge as genres that fundamentally shift the aesthetic goals and modes of engagement in contemporary theatre.

Rasa is, as the 10th-century aesthetic theorist Abhinavagupta—who commented extensively on the *Natyashastra*—puts it, an "*act* of *relishing*" (in Deshpande, emphasis mine). For Abhinavagupta, rasa is not a gift bestowed upon a passive spectator, but an attainment, an accomplishment; someone who wants to experience rasa has to be an active participant in the work. Movements of the mouth and tongue make flavor palpable, meaning taste is an active sense: one that requires activation, activity, and participation. Partakers of *A Serious Banquet*—a cubist dinner structured around the party Pablo Picasso threw for the painter Henri Rousseau in 1908 Paris that invited partakers to experience the world from many angles at once—were welcomed into Picasso's world by his overly perfumed and somewhat flustered mistress, Fernande Olivier. They were asked to deliver a rose to Gertrude Stein on behalf of Alice B. Toklas; they were invited to converse with a guitar programmed to respond to speech with music; they were asked to answer a phone that recited poetry; they were invited to listen to a still life (a bottle and vase that had a scene with each other); they entered a discussion with Georges Braque on Picasso's latest painting Demoiselles D'Avignon (played by three women set in a frame); they were asked to introduce Apollinaire (played by a glass of absinthe containing a speaker that recited his poems) to other guests; they stood in a room filled with the smells of garlic and rosemary to whet their appetite for dinner; and they were served wine and water in cups they decorated themselves. Partakers could not sit outside the event looking in; they entered the world and engaged with it—bringing parts of that world into their mouths.

Rasa posits the interactive partaker as co-creator of the event. In *A Serious Banquet*, after all the guests had arrived, and after they had participated in individual "salon" moments during which they painted with Picasso, were fed grapes and cheese by the three Demoiselles D'Avignon, composed a poem with Max Jacob, composed a song with Andre Salmon, and had Gertrude Stein paint a word-portrait of them, everyone sat down to dinner. Guests drew their own dinner plates on a paper tablecloth, and three-dimensional food was served on their two-dimensional plates. During dinner, characters offered their birthday gifts to Rousseau in the form of a sculpture made of posed dinner guests by Picasso; a silent dance by Ida Rubenstein; a cabaret song by the Demoiselles D'Avignon; and poetry by Max Jacob, Andre Salmon, and Gertrude Stein. Critic Colin McConnell described his experience co-creating the piece in this way:

> I was asked to discuss Picasso's latest painting, and to draw myself my dinner plate. . . . Often, I was asked to help create. My friend got to make miniature paintings while I listened for what I might find within a conversation between a vase and a bottle. . . . I was handed markers, and . . . convinced a painting to draw with me. I was invited to an evening of joy. . . . I was allowed . . . to play and grapple with the work, not as a spectator but as a creator myself—not from the outside peering in, but from within itself.
>
> (McConnell 2014)

Partakers and their experiences became an integral and essential part of the evening; in fact, they became what Gareth White calls "the work's aesthetic material" (White 2013, 9–10). Jacques Ranciere claims that the audience–performance relationship in conventional proscenium theatre is designed to bring audiences into "our" (playwrights, directors, actors, designers, dramaturgs) superior understanding (Ranciere 2009). The politics of a rasic experience are quite different: instead of having two distinct groups—one acting and another acted upon—everyone in participatory performance has agency to co-create the event, to make their own meaning, and to have their experiences and understandings matter. Production and reception are intertwined.

A production that privileges the taste of chocolate, the smell of garlic and rosemary, the touch of other people—the multisensory world of immersive and participatory theatre—privileges what Erin Hurley calls the "feeling body." Not only did the partakers' actions and experiences become "the work's aesthetic material" in *A Serious Banquet*, but their emotional responses also shaped and became the event: As Hurley claims, the "feeling body" is "the vehicle for [immersive and participatory] theatre's images and execution. The feeling body is both the basis and the means of theatre" (2010, 36). The feeling body is an affected and affecting body. Affect can be "found in those intensities that pass body to body . . . in those resonances that circulate" about and between bodies. These are also the affective interactions in which rasa can be found. Both affect and rasa "arise in the midst of in-between-ness [and] in the capacities to act and be acted upon." If "the capacity of a body is never defined by a body alone, but by . . . the context of its force-relations," and "affect is integral to a body's perpetual becoming" (Gregg and Seigworth 2010, 50, 51, 72), then rasa is a mechanism for privileging the constant becoming of the affected body. This positions immersive and participatory theatre as a force for affective change. The constant becoming of affected and affecting bodies interacting in the room allows for a fluid subjectivity that is "assembled and re-assembled through" encounters with others (and with different situations) during the course of the evening (White 2013:24).

Directors of immersive and participatory theatre often argue that the more active the participant, the stronger their emotional response to the work. While that is not always the case (spectators can have strong emotional responses to things they sit apart from and watch), the link between taste and emotion is both strong and physical: the amygdala, the area of the brain responsible for processing emotions, is also responsible for detecting the intensity of a flavor. Taste and emotion are wired together, and it is not a stretch to say that literally tasting parts of a production can "move" the partaker. This Is Not A Theatre Company's *Versailles* (2015), an immersive cocktail party focused on income inequality and various kinds of privilege, was set in an actual New York City apartment. Partygoers drank wine and ate hors d'oeuvres while being treated to scenes about gentrification in various rooms. In the kitchen, a woman discussed the kinds of food one can afford to consume as a member of the global 1%, in comparison with the kinds of food one can afford as a member of the 1% in the United States—while the listeners ate cake. Literalizing the phrase "let them eat cake" implicated partakers in a message about privilege by casting them in the play and asking them to engage bodily with the politics and emotions of the world they had entered.

If seeing "requires distance (objectivity) to reach understanding (to gain insight and to become a seer)," then "an aesthetic founded on the notion of ingesting, tasting, and relishing—rasa—is fundamentally different [. . .] than one founded on the '*theatron*,' the rationally ordered, analytically distanced panoptic" (Schechner 2015, 116). Highly Impractical Theatre's *Three Sisters* (New York 2014) offered several ways to experience Irina's birthday party. I went once as a serf, helping Anfisa pour "vodka" for the guests and serve food to the aristocrats at table. I went a second time as an aristocrat and, because I was allowed to wander around upstairs, saw scenes I had not seen the first time; sat in places I did not sit the first time (I never sat as a serf); ate the birthday dinner; and had a very different experience of Irina's party—I felt I had actually been invited. I have seen many productions of *Three Sisters*, but this is the first one that asked me to think so deeply about the class divisions in Chekhov's plays, because I had to embody them. My role dictated my status, which in turn dictated my behavior, the spaces I inhabited, the information I was privy to, what I ate and drank (or didn't), whom I spoke to, and how I viewed the action around me. My role dictated how I understood and felt about what happened around me. Admittedly, I had to re-read the play before I went—I would have been lost without brushing up on the plot and characters because I did not see "the whole play," I saw the parts of it my character had access to. I was not an "objective observer." I entered the world of the play. One of my students described his experience with the character Masha:

> She signaled that I should follow her [so I] trailed her through a maze of hallways and staircases that seemed to muffle her troubled life. . . . The sounds of the house . . . faded away, and after a few long moments, my guide held out her hand. "Masha," she said. "Sam," I said. "Look," and she pointed to the open skylight that I hadn't noticed above my head . . . Masha was quiet as she looked at the sky, and I sensed her deep sadness as voices called out her name from below, and she led me back downstairs. . . . In my time with Masha, I was allowed to live with her in a private moment of fear and confusion. I empathized with her. I understood her. . . . I was implicated in her personal drama, and lost my ability to remain [critically] removed from the play.
>
> (Silbiger 2014)

My student was bothered by the fact that he lost what he referred to as his "objectivity" and his "ability to remain [critically] removed from the play." But losing one's objectivity is in fact the point. Immersive and participatory theatre reveals the falseness in the very idea of objectivity (which is always already subjective) and revels in partial perceptions: unlike the proscenium, where the spectator believes she can see everything, immersive and participatory theatre are set up in such a way that the partaker cannot possibly see everything—and is aware of that. The partial view is celebrated. Objectivity is not the point. Subjectivity, in all aspects, is. Rasa allows us to understand—more fully than other aesthetic theories—the pleasures of immersive and participatory performance. Similarly, immersive and participatory performance allow us to see that rasa operates outside the context of Sanskrit drama.

Notes

* This is a shorter version of an article that appeared in *Performance Research*: Erin B. Mee "Dancing on the Tongue," *Performance Research*, 22:7, 29–34, 2017.
1 For more information, visit www.ThisIsNotATheatreCompany.com.
2 See Spence and Piqueras-Fiszman (2014).

Works Cited

Bharata. *The Natyasastra*. Translated by Adya Rangacharya. New Delhi: Munshiram Manoharlal Publishers Pvt. Ltd, 1996.
Deshpande, G. T. *Abhinavagupta*. New Delhi: The Sahitya Akademi, 1989.

Gregg, Melissa, and Gregory J. Seigworth, eds. *The Affect Theory Reader*, Kindle ed. Duke University Press Books, 2010.
Hurley, Erin. *Theatre & Feeling*. London: Palgrave Macmillan, 2010.
McConnell, Collin. "A Serious Banquet." *New York Theatre Now*, 10 June 2014. http://nytheaternow.com/2014/06/10/a-serious-banquet/. Accessed 5 January, 2016.
Ranciere, Jacques. *The Emancipated Spectator*. London: Verso, 2011 [2009].
Schechner, Richard. "Rasaesthetics." In *Performance Theory*, 2nd ed. London and New York: Routledge, 2001, pp. 333–67.
———. "Rasaesthetics." In *The Natyasastra and the Body in Performance*, edited by Sreenath Nair. Jefferson, US: McFarland, 2015, pp. 113–34.
Silbiger, Sam. "Analysis of Three Sisters for Drama in Performance Course," 2014.
Spence, Charles, and Betina Piqueras-Fiszman. *The Perfect Meal*. London: Wiley-Blackwell, 2014.
White, Gareth. *Audience Participation in Theatre: Aesthetics of the Invitation*. London: Palgrave Macmillan, 2013.

CHAPTER 13

Lights, Camera, Action!

Rasaboxes Training and Coaching for Brazilian Telenovelas

FERNANDA GUIMARÃES
TRANSLATED BY MICHELE MINNICK

I was trained as a theatre artist. While doing a pos-graduação[1] in movement for actors at Angel Vianna School of dance in Rio de Janeiro, Brazil, I began my first job preparing actors for network TV soap operas and mini-series. By 2014, I was coaching casts of nearly 500 television actors, using Rasaboxes as a core methodology for navigating the televisual language. I have continued training groups and coaching individuals in theatre, television, and cinema and have introduced Rasaboxes to hundreds of actors. What I describe here focuses on the ways Rasaboxes serves actors on the set of Brazilian telenovelas and other serial TV programming.

In Brazil, the telenovela, or soap opera, has a special role in the culture. They are broadcast during prime-time hours to a large audience and are one of the most popular forms of artistic expression in the country. Though they have a distinctly Brazilian quality and context, their appeal is widespread. More than 60 other countries broadcast Brazilian telenovelas, for a total of 60 million foreign viewers worldwide (Xavier 2007). Behind the scenes, the work of all involved in production requires a rigorous and ongoing attention to detail, a great deal of repetition, all during a long, fast-paced workday. Storytelling in the telenovela is accomplished through dialogue and a reliance on the close-up, which comprises the majority of shots. This puts even greater pressure on actors to be able to reproduce the subtleties of performance, as the camera will often capture only the actors' chest and face. It may seem as if Rasaboxes is not well suited for such work, but in fact, it is powerful preparation for the tasks most often required of telenovela actors.

The Fast-Paced Working Environment

In television, *time is money*. This constant pressure turns the gears in all the departments of television. Actors must repeat the same scene many times, and in a very short period of time, to achieve the desired result. An average of 20 scenes are recorded on a single day. There are many external factors not within actors' direct control that require them to repeat the same scene, including:

- Continuity errors that happen with costumes, characterization, the set, or even with the physical actions of the actor. For example, the actress should have been using the brown purse, not the black purse, because in the scene where she leaves the house (recorded on another day), she was given the brown one. Or, the actor had his left hand on his chin in the first take, and in the second, his right hand. Such errors can create problems when different takes are edited.
- Adjustments to sound and lighting equipment.
- Mistakes in camera movement. A complex sequence may require a precisely focused passage of the camera, for example, or minuscule framing adjustments.

There are also factors that actor training techniques such as Rasaboxes may improve:

- Lack of preparation or of focus on the part of an actor.
- Changes by the director to the scene, which can cause the actor to make mistakes.
- When recording scenes, the director moves quickly: "Action! Cut! Go Back! Neutralize! [Ressignifica!] Cut! From the top! Action! [Reestimula!]" This pace can challenge an actor's concentration, energy, and confidence, not to mention emotional connection and expressivity.

How can an actor achieve greater control, efficiency, and effectiveness in what can be a very stressful environment? Some questions are the same for theatre as they are for television, such as: how does one act a scene in which the character is at first very happy, but upon receiving terrible news, must enter into a desperate emotional state? What the television context adds is that one must act that scene multiple times without losing the quality, intensity, and freshness of the performance.

Immediacy, Intensity, and Transitions

Rasaboxes training offers ways to immediately activate and deactivate emotions, enabling actors to have greater dexterity and command within their performances during the demanding day-to-day work of recording. Working with eight basic rasas simplifies and clarifies the complexity of this psychophysical labor. It gives the actor a way of managing quick transitions between emotional states, or multiple repetitions of the same state, with agility and ease. Interestingly, the training does not make these emotional shifts seem artificial. Many actors have told me that this preparation allows the psychophysical memories formed during Rasaboxes training to come to the surface during recording. Most importantly, it offers them a sense of autonomy in shaping and reshaping their performances over many takes.

Scaling Emotional Intensity and Size of Expression

In the theatre, variations of physical and vocal expressivity can change according to the size of the theater and the number of people in the audience. In television, these intensities change with the different types of frames or shots. For example, in a theater that seats 1500 people, the actor communicates physically and vocally in a more expansive and energetic way than in a theater of 30 seats. By contrast, in Brazilian telenovelas, the actors communicate through wide and close-up shots against a realistic background most of the time. Rasaboxes trains actors' ability to dynamically vary the intensity and scale of their expression. It helps actors to use their entire body in order to communicate emotional expression in a wide shot (where the actor has the greatest liberty of movement in physical space), or to scale the size and intensity to serve a close-up shot—one in which a single step causes the actor to go out of frame, or the image to go out of focus. Television directors are usually quite meticulous about their framing, so the actor must not freeze up in the face of such attention to technical detail. For this reason, it is essential to stimulate the actor's vibrant inner life, to liberate the flow of breath and interior energies of the body, and to be able to modulate that flow. Included here are two exercises I have used consistently since my early years of training and coaching television actors. The first, *True Stories*, is one I devised as the final exercise culminating a workshop of four sessions or more, which would allow actors to delve deeply into fresh, text-based material, and to solo through the rasaboxes. The second, *Close-Up*, is one a workshop participant created for developing the skills of focus and containment necessary for close-up framing.

True Stories Exercise

Instructions

1. In pairs outside the rasaboxes grid, secretly relate to your partner an event from your life that had a strong emotional impact—positive, negative, or mixed.
2. After both people have shared, everyone surrounds the grid.
3. One at a time, you will have the opportunity to tell your partner's story, starting anywhere on the grid and moving through the boxes.
4. You can choose to enter any rasabox at any time. At certain points in the story, you may feel pulled or drawn to enter a particular rasa. Stay alert to these dynamics and allow yourself to play between the extremes of making deliberate choices and following where the story leads you.
5. When you are finished exploring your partner's story, exit the grid.

Options:

- You can tell the story in the first person, as a monologue, or you can narrate it in the third person, or a combination of both.
- The stories may be communicated physically without words, or with any combination of physical and verbal expression.

I introduce True Stories toward the end of a workshop, after at least three or four days of work in the rasaboxes. The stories people share are often intense, and intimate. They could be stories about a wedding day, or they could share experiences of abuse, or loss. They are often stories of a turning point in people's lives, and so have intrinsic dramatic qualities.

266 PART IV ▶ Notes From the Field

FIGURE 13.1 Daniel Siwek and Henrique Gottardo in Close-Up Rasaboxes exercise during rehearsals for TV Record's telenovela, "The Ten Commandments."

Source: Photo courtesy of Fernanda Guimarães.

There is anonymity in the performance of the stories, because people are telling their partner's story, not their own. This is usually the first opportunity I offer for participants to perform alone on the grid; most of the exercises before this point are for groups or pairs. At this point in our work together, the connection between the players, their ability to fully embody the rasas, and a facility with movement around the grid, allows the actors to integrate elements of technique into a mini solo performance that does what all acting must do: tell a meaningful and emotionally compelling story. Whereas True Stories tend to be about expanding the scale of performance, the next exercise focuses on limiting it by communicating only through the eyes, something that television and film acting requires.

Close-Up Exercise

The Close-Up exercise begins to train actors to use the work within the confines of the close-up, before they are on set (see Figure 13.1). Here, they have the liberty to use and move their bodies as they like, as long as they can maintain eye contact. In this way, they start to get a sense of both the full physicality necessary for acting on a small scale, and the degree to which they may have to contain and modulate the inner intensities of each rasa to enable them to focus on communicating with the eyes. The exercise can be adapted for smaller or larger groups: the minimal unit of people on the grid is two, with the guide outside the grid completing the trio; the maximum is eight inside the grid with four guides outside the grid.

Instructions

1. A pair of players starts in a corner of the grid, and then moves along a pathway through all the rasas, returning at the end to the starting rasabox.
2. The pair remain facing one another, one moving backward and one forward. The player moving backward initiates the movement to the next rasabox.

3. Each pair must maintain eye contact throughout the exercise, without looking where they are going. Communicate the rasa through the eyes, and the energy that flows from you, as if you are in close up.
4. A third player acts as a guide for the pair from outside the grid, informing them of the rasabox they are about to enter before they move into it.
5. All other forms of communication, gesture, touch, etcetera, are available, but players perform as if in close-up, imagining that their bodies are not visible to spectators.
6. When the pair hits the fifth rasabox, they change roles, turning around so that the person who had been moving backward now moves forward, and the person who had been following their partner moving forward, now leads the duo backward, through the remaining four rasaboxes.

Challenges and Resistance

Rasaboxes brings about great transformations in actors of different ages and different levels of personal and professional experience. The work has been most effective with those who need to deepen their work in the realm of self-discovery and self-awareness. More veteran actors have matured on the set itself, on which they have already trained their ability to manage their emotions through many years of experience acting for the camera. With these actors, I take a somewhat more intellectual and psychological approach, focusing more objectively on the character and script in question, looking for ways that other techniques may help them achieve the desired effects.

The most effective use of Rasaboxes occurs when the actors can pass through a progressive order of the exercises until arriving at work on character. With each new job, my decision to use Rasaboxes or not depends primarily on time. Before the beginning of filming on a telenovela or mini-series, the time for actor preparation is usually very short. In my view, Rasaboxes needs more time than other forms of training for actors to achieve an authentic psychophysical understanding. Nevertheless, in workshops and training periods with roughly 12 sessions, I usually offer at least six Rasaboxes encounters. Because of logistical issues such as changes to shooting schedules and release time for the actors, and due to the large numbers I am working with, even this can be a challenge. In anticipation of resistance that may arise, I advise participants to withhold judgment of the work until the third day of training. It is usually on day four that we begin to have any discussion of Rasaboxes as a methodology.

Conclusion

The television set can be considered an Olympic stadium for training emotional athleticism. Rasaboxes proves an excellent tool for accessing and modulating emotion, allowing the actor to manage her energy over the course of a day on set and to efficiently handle the diverse external and internal factors that challenge her performance. Rasaboxes helps to activate and deactivate, conserve, express, master, mix, and remix the taste of the emotions.

Note

1 The pos-graduação is a short program of focused study, usually about a year, that can be undertaken by a university graduate to investigate an area they wish to pursue in an MA or PhD, or to gain technical skills.—Trans.

Works Cited

Xavier, Nilson. *Almanaque da Telenovela Brasileira*. Brasil: Panda Editora, 2007.

CHAPTER 14

Character Building Through Rasaboxes

Staging Electra at Teatro Prometeo

FERNANDO CALZADILLA

I had been conducting Rasaboxes workshops at the Miami Theatre Center for two years when, in 2013, director Joann Yarrow invited me to conduct a workshop at Teatro Prometeo—Miami Dade College's 40-year-old Spanish-language theatre institution dedicated to promoting and educating theatre artists.[1] We scheduled a semester-long performance workshop, culminating in a public showing of my Spanish-language version of Sophocles' *Electra*. It was staged without sets, light changes, costumes, or props in order to highlight the importance of the psychophysical/vocal specificity of the acting we were aiming for in the workshop. The workshop included Rasaboxes configured specifically for our work on *Electra*. In addition to Rasaboxes, we used several other exercises from The Performance Workshop (TPW), including Entering the Space, Crossing the Line, One Sound One Movement (OSOM), and Crossings (see Chapter 4, pp. 89–116)—the latter being particularly relevant to the process of finding character through ensemble-oriented explorations.

For example, for one session I asked the actors to come prepared to dress as any one of the characters in the play. During our work in a Slow Motion Transformation exercise (see Chapter 4, pp. 128–135), I invited actors to encounter one another and exchange clothing/characters with another actor. The exercise revealed to us that inhabiting another actor's choices provided a different perspective on how a particular character might look and act. In another session during a Crossings exercise, I asked each actor to share a character's story with another actor, who would then inhabit that character as described, in the next crossing. This allowed them to see and reflect on how the story of the character they selected came across when reenacted by someone else. It gave them critical distance to analyze their choices and inform the options they had when playing a specific character.

Early in the *Electra* sessions,[2] I noticed resistance to physical contact within the group, a tendency for actors to work alone, or to drop their energy when not directly participating. We started using Contact Improvisation[3] in pairs, and then in small groups, until the whole group was working together. Next, I instructed them to gradually add sound, combining Contact Improvisation with One Sound One Movement. We practiced the exercise many times until the actors were comfortable

FIGURE 14.1 Rehearsal for *Electra* directed by Fernando Calzadilla at Teatro Prometeo, Miami, FL.

Source: Photo courtesy of Fernando Calzadilla, 2013.

with each other, overcoming resistance and building the stamina necessary to work with high energy levels for long periods of time. Next, I began to use this combination to stage the play. We called it "Running the Play in One Sound One Movement." First, I asked them to embody the play scene-by-scene, without words, moving in sync with one another and following the progression of the story. They pushed and pulled, fighting gravity and supporting each other's weight while they sustained sound and negotiated space and composition. When the group reached a climactic moment, they froze in a kind of tableau vivant, focusing on the main characters and key points in the action (see Figure 14.1). To accomplish this, the group had to sense one another, to pace themselves so as to complete and freeze the action together while simultaneously deciding who would play the characters in the scene—since we had not yet cast the play. The group had already been practicing Rasaboxes, but without incorporating text or character. While they improvised the play in OSOM, the rasas began to permeate their actions. After a while, I made the exercise more complex by adding rules so that they had many tasks to perform—and no time to think. For example, I provided instructions such as, "during a frozen climactic moment at least one person has to be off the ground," or "there should be two or more tones or rhythms in the sound at the same time." This eventually led them to perform an improvised version of the entire play. We would play in this form for about 90 minutes without interruption and then move on to working in Rasaboxes.

Casting Through Consensus

During the fourth week of the workshop, we began casting. I did not impose the casting; it emerged from the exercises exploring the story and characters. We had seven actors in the workshop, five women and two men. The play had seven characters, as well as a Chorus of Women. The actors self-selected their roles by exploring character building through Rasaboxes. The actors chose characters they identified with. We moved gradually from incorporating the text within a single rasabox to more complex variations by (1) finding a base or core rasa for each scene and character (see Chapter 4, pp. 171–176); (2) finding a character's physical attributes based on their backstory; or (3) mixing and layering rasas to add complexity the characters. Finally, we had two actors playing Electra—Maria Paula Cruz and Esther Gatica—and two playing Chrysothemis—Karen Almeida and Diana Vallejo. Pier Lendaro played the Tutor and Aegisthus. The other actors played one character each: Luis Fuentes as Orestes and Rosa Mendez as Clytemnestra. All the women formed the Chorus of Women. In hindsight, I would have cast it the same way if I had assigned the roles independently of the group's workshop process, because, as facilitator, I had observed the intensity and desire with which actors would gravitate toward a particular character. Once the casting was settled by consensus, I assigned scenes to those playing the same character.

Character Building Through Rasaboxes

When we began exploring the scenes in Rasaboxes, Orestes played the opening scene with his Tutor using a combination of vira and bhayanaka. Orestes had a duty to perform, a command from the oracle that came with a big responsibility and grave consequences: matricide. I also wanted to make clear that Orestes was young, probably in his late teens; that he had grown up in a foreign country (Phocis) so his speech was broken (in my version, Mycenaean was Spanish and Phocian was English); and that he had to conceal his identity to avoid being killed by Aegisthus' henchmen. Despite vira and bhayanaka being obvious and perhaps "correct" choices for the character and the scene, we were not happy with the results. We then tried an experiment: the actors played the scene in hasya. At first, they burst into laughter while they devised their plan to enter the city, but after the initial intensity of their reactions subsided, nuances of hasya began to emerge. For Orestes, the hasya/bhayanaka combination turned into a character trait: the nervous snicker of a frightened teenager. The snicker made him more human and less stereotypically hero-like, and more relatable. The actors sharing one character, Maria Paula and Esther (Electra) and Karen and Diana (Chrysothemis), had similar processes because they each played a different facet, a different trait of that character. They each identified a base rasa for their facet of the character and then built up layers of specific character detail from there.

We did a lot of work for the climactic scene of the play, Orestes' killing of Clytemnestra, because in addition to its intrinsic complexity (in our version Orestes strangled her on stage), the actors were a romantically involved couple in real life at the time. We began by exploring their shringara, first individually and then as a pair. We moved from sensual to idealized to condescending; from touching to staring to cuddling; and several combinations of them. It was important to keep a certain eroticism within the mother/son relationship. We then moved to layering shringara with bhayanaka, the other rasa they identified as the main component of the scene. We began in the simple mode, each actor in a different box, i.e., Orestes in bhayanaka and Clytemnestra in shringara, and moved from there until they were both in the same rasabox while using their first rasa as a base with which to mix and layer the second rasa. When they felt comfortable with the layering, we assigned quantities to get the right flavor: 70% shringara on the outside, 30% bhayanaka on the inside, for example. These percentages changed as the scene progressed. Clytemnestra struggled between shringara and bhayanaka with an internal trembling and an external languor. Of course, these were not the only rasas in the scene. Talking about that particular scene during an interview, Luis Fuentes (Orestes) said,

> That was some bhayanaka and shringara as a base, with raudra on top, and then some karuna. I started very strong, then I struggled and then I was crying after she died. I was totally destroyed when I came to the realization, "What have I done?" Intense, it was intense. The great thing about it is that, just like that [finger snap], nothing ever happened. Rosie and I were a couple—so pretty intense right there. It's so good being able to laugh, having accomplished those emotions.
>
> (Fuentes 2016)

Actor Reflections: Safety and Risk

Three years after the workshop, I had the opportunity to interview some of the actors. Most of them highlighted how Rasaboxes had allowed them to play the character without being emotionally afflicted in a personal way. Maria Paula Cruz (Electra) recounted how skeptical she was about Rasaboxes at the beginning of the process. The emotions felt fake to her and she couldn't relate to the rasaboxes—but she did not give up. She said,

> I was very reluctant at the beginning. I felt that everything I was doing was false, not organic. Then, when we started to work on *Electra*, everything started to fit together. During one exercise, when the Tutor gives Electra Oreste's funeral urn, a deep moan came out and I cried. Right after, I was like, what happened? I am not affected. How did I get out of it so quickly? It felt very real, yet I'm not affected. I don't want to keep crying; I don't feel the pressure on my chest that I felt a moment ago; my voice doesn't hurt. That's when I stopped doubting the process.
>
> (Cruz 2016)

Most of her previous acting training had used Emotion Memory, a Stanislavsky-based technique that asks the actor to recall memories of personal experiences to meet the emotional requirements needed for playing a role. As an only child, Maria Paula is very close to her mother. She worried about how she was going to play Electra—what memories could she use to relate to killing her own mother? She exclaimed,

> I love my mother, why would I want to kill her? And if I were in Elektra's situation, I would have sided with my mother, not my father. What memories could I use? I'm not a killer. I couldn't have done it without Rasaboxes, without the

daily playing with the emotions that we had—the constant exploration. We started without characters, then gradually added character and text. The layering of emotions showed me the complexity of the tools we had. The whole process revealed the amplitude that one can have as an actor, that you can be whatever you want without harm. Without Rasaboxes, I would have invented my own storms, created paranoias and at the end, it affects you, it affects you as a person.

(Cruz 2016)

Esther had the most distinctive moment in terms of changing quickly from one emotion to another. In a scene with Clytemnestra, Electra mocks her mother's fears about a dream she had about Agamemnon's death. Orestes' Tutor appears, in disguise, to bring news of his death in a chariot race. Electra's world is torn apart and she is consumed by tears of hopelessness. Esther's performance was so striking that the audience gasped with her—a true rasic moment. Esther said she had loved working in Rasaboxes; once she learned that there was no right or wrong, she felt free. In a 2016 email exchange about her experience with Rasaboxes in the *Electra* process she wrote:

Now, if I have the chance to talk to someone who doesn't know about Rasaboxes, the easiest way I can explain what I learned is that it's [not] an acting technique where you have to think of a sad memory to be sad, but that you actually evaluate your body's reaction to when you feel sad and observe your breath, your body's movement and tension, the sounds you make and overall the feeling of sadness. Therefore, it is giving you the opportunity to detach yourself from feeling sad night after night, to acknowledge that even though your character is sad it's just your body working, not your memory or personal feelings, making it easier to "snap" out of it once the play/performance is done. Because it is not about whether or not you *feel* it; it is about portraying it as clearly as possible for the audience to identify and relate to it emotionally.

(Gatica 2016)

All of the actors I interviewed afterward emphasized how safe and efficient it was to build and play a character through Rasaboxes exercises, and that they had incorporated what they learned into their own theatre practice. Luis Fuentes (Orestes) said:

Just being able to jump back in and then come back out, come back in, then come back out, and then, it got even better because we experienced that emotion with someone else from across the boxes, and then you made a jump to another box, another emotion, and we switch it up like that, and then we're joining and we're both experiencing the same emotion and it's like we're in sync, like harmony, yeah. That was pretty cool because I had never experienced anything like that; just being able to emit an emotion from nowhere, to bring it within me and just take it out. Every time I'm on set or have to create an emotion I think of Rasaboxes and I think of you Fernando because that's really one of the easiest methods and safe for your sanity. I mean you're not suffering.

(Fuentes 2016)

As the director, *Electra* was a rewarding experience in creating an ensemble with a common language, committing to process work rather than product, and building empathetic characters that were well rounded, complex, and relatable. In *Electra*'s final staging, the actors were in a circle onstage as the audience entered. They began an improvisation using Contact Improv with sound, which continued until the end of the play. They had a script to follow, they knew they had to get from A to B to C, etc., but the scenes happened as part of the long improvisation. How they got from point to point varied in each performance, as did their spatial and emotional relationships to each other within each scene. There were no costumes, props, sets, or light changes. We also broke the fourth wall by making eye contact and addressing the audience whenever the text allowed for it. This created a heightened sense of participation, a world in which the audience could not remain anonymous. *Electra*'s highly theatrical staging and use of Rasaboxes gave the actors the opportunity to create multi-dimensional characters, while revealing their own essential humanness. Both our journey and the audiences were enabled by our use of The Performance Workshop as the primary framework for developing character and shaping our creative process.

Notes

1. Joann Yarrow was familiar with TPW exercises through the work she had done with Richard Schechner during his staging of *Three Sisters* in 1997, in which she participated.
2. I call them "sessions" as opposed to rehearsals because, although we were working towards staging a play, we were still in the workshop process of exploring and playing with the elements in the story as opposed to rehearsing the play's text.
3. The first time I heard of Contact Improvisation (CI) was in 1976 when I arrived at NYU to study theatre design and audited Schechner's performance theory classes in the Drama Department. I did a one-week performance workshop with the Performance Group and Joan McIntosh in the summer of 1977. I saw Steve Paxton, the originator of CI, perform at Judson Memorial Church. But I would credit Marcia Moraes as my source for CI within the context of TPW with Michele Minnick and Paula Murray Cole. Moraes, a trained dancer, taught the basic principles of CI. We used it as a tool for exploration and then applied it to Rasaboxes. I have since used it in teaching and training of TPW and Rasaboxes.

Works Cited

Cruz, Maria Paula. Personal Interview. 2 May 2016.
Fuentes, Luis. Personal Interview. 28 April 2016.
Gatica, Esther. Personal email correspondence with the author. 24 May 2016.

CHAPTER 15

Experimenting with the Clown in Rasaboxes[1]

ANA ACHCAR
TRANSLATED BY MICHELE MINNICK

I have worked with Rasaboxes as a performer, director, and educator since being introduced to it in a pos-graduação[2] course with Michele Minnick at UNIRIO[3] in 2003. Since 2016, Rasaboxes has served as a key element in the medical clown training program, Enfermaria do Riso (The Laughter Ward) at UNIRIO. While this program trains performers for medical clowning, here I focus on the use of Rasaboxes as part of first-year students' training in clown techniques. We engage Rasaboxes to explore the comic body of the clown, and her physical dramaturgy in beginning clown work and in the composition of performance.

The clown is a transgressor. Her action is effective only when it subverts, surprises, and transforms. She is a poet of the flesh. Her scene is memorable only when she materializes it and makes it visible through the body. She moves us by seeing and showing us ourselves from the inside out, by communicating with something within us that we may not outwardly show, or even recognize in ourselves. Clown play works well with Rasaboxes because form, motivation, inspiration, feeling, and thought are integrated, rather than separated. Rasaboxes allows the clown to move from one emotional state to another through the body and through action without requiring explanation, a coherent trajectory, or transitions, and offers a specific palette of emotional colors and textures to shape the clown's dramaturgy.

Beginning the Work

When I introduced Rasaboxes to students of Enfermaria do Riso, I was asking myself questions like, "What are the conditions necessary for training the comic body?" "How do clowns use time and space in the construction of comic action?" Rasaboxes opens up innumerable possibilities for investigating these questions and for exploring the construction of clown play itself: the relationship of the clown with their own body, to objects, to other players, as well as the communication between the clown and the audience. As clown students, we learn that before pointing out the ridiculousness of the world, we must first seek to find the ridiculous in ourselves. This work is personally challenging because it requires us to stir our unexplored beliefs and habits, exposing and making vulnerable our networks of protection, and our personal defenses. The purpose of this research is to explore our own comic

FIGURE 15.1 Patrícia Ubeda doing clown work in karuna rasabox. Enfermaria do Riso, UNIRIO, Rio de Janeiro, Brazil.

Source: Photo courtesy of Ana Achcar.

nature, which inevitably leads—at the end of an extensive period of experimentation—to the formation of a unique clown for each performer. Playing on the rasaboxes grid gives us the chance to enjoy this process of accessing our vulnerability.

The Problem with Hasya

At first, we had a particular interest in hasya, the comic rasa, the locus of derision, jokes, irony, and play—which we imagined as the most likely "natural" home of the clown. But we quickly realized that the funniest moments emerged not in any one rasa, but rather, in the quick transitions from one rasa to another. It was the sudden change of movements and the shift in qualities of presence and rhythm that made us laugh. It was as if we were discovering the known mechanisms and laws of comedy: inversion, surprise, counterpoint, and the undermining of expectations. As we worked, we continued to struggle with hasya: it was everywhere, an attitude contaminating all the rasas to varying degrees. It took some time for us to realize that, in fact, we were trapped by the imposition of having to produce laughter, to make all of our explorations of emotion funny. What we were really doing was making it more and more impossible to experience the clown in Rasaboxes. In fact, this is one of the major problems that occupies us in our research and practice: to access the clown without the obligation of being funny. Rasaboxes made us confront hasya, what we thought had been the essence of the clown, only to discover that we needed to rethink our assumptions. It was via the route of relating to the other, through the fundamental technique of "triangulation," that we were able to overcome the limitation imposed by the apparent need to be funny.

Triangulation: Sharing the Clown's Discoveries With the Audience

In triangulation, the mask (of the clown, usually the red nose) organizes the action. It helps the clown to clarify its intention, affirm understanding, and confirm receptivity. It introduces a moment of suspension in the scene that authorizes its break, its inversion, a contrast, an opposition, repetition, and thus has comic effect.

Triangulation

Triangulation is a key technique in clown performance that involves three points of focus: 1) the self; 2) the other (whether the other is another performer or an object); and 3) the audience. As new content enters her game, she must share each discovery directly with the audience by using a series of "takes," which means looking directly at the other, then at the audience, then back at the other, then perhaps a moment of reflection or suspension with herself, and so on. This cycle, usually repeated many times, can involve people, objects, an idea, someone else entering the scene, anything *new*, which the clown must register and share with the other and with the audience.[4]

Rasaboxes makes triangulation even more challenging, because in addition to staying connected to whatever is happening onstage, as well as connecting to the audience, the clown must also maintain the rasa she is in while connecting with the spectator and be able to change rasas in the midst of her interaction with any part of the triangle. To combine triangulation with rasa, we distributed players around the grid, constructing an audience that could be directly addressed by the clowns working in the rasaboxes. We created a convention that the moment of changing the focus from the other to the audience, or from the audience to the other, would also be a good time to change from one rasabox to another. This introduced a previously unattainable agility to the game. In certain improvisations, the necessity for triangulation was so frequent that the clown barely stayed in any rasa for more than five seconds. It wasn't exactly a question of changing the quality of emotion we were working with in a certain rasa, but of exploring ways of interruption and of return, that is to say, of leaving and returning to a given box, in order to punctuate these comings and goings in the body. It was a decisive and liberating step for the clowns because they discovered that they could find humor in anger, for example, without necessarily laughing *at* it. And finally, we truly experienced the non-psychological nature of the game, the non-coherence of its logic.

Objects in the Rasaboxes

For the clown, an object is a partner, very much like an actor playing the scene with him. In clowning we say that the object is animated, that is to say, it takes on *anima*—it is alive. But animating an object is difficult if one is to respect its materiality without pretending or indicating. When we introduced objects into our play, the physicality of Rasaboxes reinforced the reality of each object explored by accentuating its form, affirming its significance, leaving us free to explore the meanings that the object would assume—often meanings and functions that were different from the original conventional uses. For example, a bouquet of plastic flowers in vira rasa would become a torch, in bibhatsa, a duster, in bhayanaka, a shield—without losing its identity as a bouquet.

Sensing Space, Making a Scene

Rasaboxes also allows the clown-in-training to visualize all their work spatially. They can see what they are constructing as they are working in one rasabox, and they can also see themselves working on the whole grid. It is empowering for the clown to envision their performance as they are creating it. We also explored how a performer might move through the particular three-dimensional space of a rasabox by working with numerous physical levels—the performer's relationship from floor to ceiling—and played with various densities of physical space from firm to soft—or as if moving through substances like mud, then syrup, then foam, then air bubbles. These explorations of space, form, and movement helped us to create work in an elemental yet dynamic field.

Questions Exercise

This exercise develops the capacity of the clown to solve one problem by creating another. First, we play the game off the grid. Players must establish a dialogue by means of questions:

1. One player asks a question.
2. The other player responds with another question, and so on.
3. If you are not able to answer a question with a question, you can perform a bodily expression, such as an action or a gesture, instead.

Then, we put the game on the grid. Each player begins in a different rasabox.

1. One player asks a question.
2. The other player must respond with another question, and so on.
3. If you are unable to ask a question, you must change to another rasabox.

Composing Performance

During our early explorations, we created our first clown show, *PalhaSOS*,[5] comprised of scenes constructed in part from material generated in Rasaboxes. In order to approach performance composition, we added the red nose to all our Rasaboxes explorations, such as those with triangulation and objects, and the exercises previously discussed. With the red nose, the clown seemed to gain an authorial potency, as if this small mask was a pen with which he could write his scene. Each clown constructed his own history or story in the passages between rasas. What is important here is that the *meaning* of a clown's history originated in and was given by the games played by the authors/clowns/players in Rasaboxes. In other words, we discovered that moving from one rasabox to another was a way of arriving at content: by way of the *how*, the clown accessed the *what*, and this finding of the what *via the how*—through embodied process rather than say, playwriting—became the dramaturgical process for constructing clown performance.

Conclusion

There is always something not quite right about the clown, something a little twisted, but this twistedness is liberating, because his creativity is pure play. Rasaboxes helped us to discover what it meant to construct a poetry of the flesh, through combining clown games, the red nose, and the rasas. The narrative elements emerged through the body, through emotions, and through relating to others and objects. The authorial role that Rasaboxes offers to the clown amplifies the reach of the laughter they produce and gives their performance even more autonomy and freedom. It is for this reason that we continue our research at the Enfermaria do Riso, learning and then going beyond the technical aspects of Rasaboxes training in order to arrive at the artistic development of the clown's dramaturgy.

Notes

1. The original in Portuguese was substantially restructured and edited by the editorial team.
2. The pos-graduação is a short program of focused study, usually about a year, that can be undertaken by a university graduate. It often is a way for people to investigate an area they wish to pursue in an MA or PhD, or to gain technical skills.—Trans.
3. UNIRIO is one of the Federal Universities of Brazil in Rio de Janeiro.—Trans.
4. This explanation of triangulation was added by the editors.
5. The title, *PalhaSOS*, is a play on words, using SOS—which means the same in Portuguese as it does in English—to substitute for the plural ending of the word "palhaços," which means "clowns."—Trans.

Works Cited

Cervantes, François. "Le Clown." In *Rencontres de Clowns*, edited by André Riot Sarcey. Bourg Saint Andeol, France: APIAC, 2001, pp. 29–31.

CHAPTER 16

Dramaturgy of the Emotions

The Performance Workshop and Rasaboxes in Directing Machinal

RACHEL BOWDITCH

Nervous anticipation fills the corridor outside the room where the ensemble gathers for their first rehearsal. Dressed in all-black movement clothing,[1] participants are instructed to enter the space in silence, remove their shoes, and place personal belongings against the back wall. After the group silently enters the darkened space, each performer brings their toes to meet a taped line across the length of the room. The ensemble is invited to observe the space and to imaginatively place themselves in it—to notice the textures, light, sound, and details of the open room before them. Once these details have been absorbed, they are invited to close their eyes and to consider how they want to enter the space—forwards, backward, sideways; walking, crawling, or rolling. Each member of the group crosses the line at the same moment—their first act as an ensemble.

Creating a Focused Work Environment

I highlight this daily ritual as a point of entry for how the structure, exercises, and ethos of The Performance Workshop (TPW) generate ensemble and dynamic, physically engaged performances in my work as a director. Crossing the line of tape on the floor (see Crossing the Line, pp. 90–92) has a significance beyond this first act—it helps to define how space will be used in rehearsals. Designating spaces for particular activities—the work space, the "green room," and outside social space—provides a productive working environment that fosters respect, focus, and concentration. I have found it to be exceptionally useful when working with undergraduate actors, who easily slip into casual conversation, disrupting the creative, focused space required in rehearsal.

Over time, I have developed a week-long movement intensive interweaving Lecoq training with TPW exercises such as Rasaboxes and Slow Motion Transformation. This physically intensive first week sets the tone for the rest of the rehearsal process and production and generates a shared physical vocabulary for the ensemble. What

CHAPTER 16 ▸ Dramaturgy of the Emotions

FIGURE 16.1 Katie Harroff as Mother and Caitlyn Conlin as Helen in *Machinal* by Sophie Treadwell directed by Rachel Bowditch at ASU.

Source: Photo courtesy of Rachel Bowditch, 2007.

follows is a detailed description of the first two weeks of a six-week rehearsal process—Monday through Saturday, five hours a day—focused on how TPW shaped my direction of Sophie Treadwell's *Machinal* at Arizona State University in 2007.[2] The production combined an ensemble of graduate and undergraduate actors representing a wide range of experience and ability. The 11 actors ranged in age from 19-year-old sophomores to third-year MFAs in their late 20s and 30s. TPW's exercises helped to level the playing field in this diverse group.

Machinal, which premiered on Broadway in 1928, fuses the haunting world of 1920s American Expressionism with a fast-paced, photojournalistic style. The story centers on a young woman, Helen Jones, who is caught up in a mechanized world and driven to the edge of sanity. As a springboard for the main character of the play, Treadwell[3] uses the sensational 1927 murder trial of Ruth Snyder, to speculate on what circumstances might drive a seemingly harmless stenographer to murder her husband. Snyder was the first woman in US history to be electrocuted. Audiences in 1928 would have been aware of Snyder's highly publicized case, in which both she and her accomplice, Judd Gray, were convicted and executed for murder at Sing-Sing prison. The real-life story and *Machinal* diverge: Treadwell all but dispenses with Judd, making Helen the sole protagonist and focus of the play. The playwright situates Helen amid a whirlwind of social forces beyond her control. In nine fast-paced episodes, she leads the spectators through Helen's harrowing journey from the frenzy of the office, memories of her childhood, the horrors of marrying and conceiving a child with a man she doesn't love, to meeting a lover who incites her to kill her husband. Helen goes through a grueling trial and is sent to the electric chair.

In my version of *Machinal*, the multi-level set inspired by Russian Constructivist set designer Lyubov Popova (1889–1924) allowed the actors to engage with the stage like a jungle gym. We used state-of-the-art media technology to embed nine surveillance cameras throughout the set, serving as a kind of multi-perspectival guard tower within a panopticon.[4] Helen was trapped in a world in which she was perpetually being watched and judged. My staging of *Machinal* was extremely stylized and physically demanding, also inspired by Constructivist aesthetics. The rigorous physical training of the week-long movement intensive enabled the actors to capture the mechanical clarity inspired by Taylorism,[5] the basis for American assembly-line efficiency.

Day 1: Warm-Up Ritual

Before any verbal introductions or discussion of the play occurs, I lead the cast through an hour-long series of stretches, somatic movement exercises, and a three-part yoga vinyasa sequence that departs significantly from Richard Schechner's yoga sequence.[6] After the yoga, I introduce the Clearing Breath (see p. 100), an exercise called Twelve Steps,[7] and Performative Introductions (see p. 93).

Entering the Space and Crossing the Line rituals are enacted at the first rehearsal, then become the frame for the entire rehearsal process. After the first day, the crossing line offers a moment to set intentions, return to the breath, and mindfully step into the workspace as an ensemble. After crossing the line, we form a circle and do the opening exercises mentioned earlier. As the director, I always participate in this warm-up ritual with the cast. This combination of exercises prepares us mentally, physically, and energetically for the work ahead. After a break, we do our first reading of the script. This is the last time we look at the script until our week-long movement intensive is complete. At the end of each rehearsal, we close with a single Clearing Breath.

Day 2: Neutral Mask

The second day of rehearsal begins with Crossing the Line, the Clearing Breath, Twelve Steps, yoga, and Crossings I (see pp. 108–110). Then, we work on Lecoq's neutral mask, starting with introductory exercises that focus on *pointe fixe* and the seven levels of tension.[8] I lead the ensemble through "The Fundamental Journey" of the neutral mask,[9] asking them to imagine moving through natural environments from the ocean, a forest, a cliff face, a slippery mountain slope, to crossing a river and into the desert to see the setting sun. The neutral mask is a crucial tool for the actor for opening the entire body and finding a sense of stage presence. The transformation for individual performers and for the ensemble is immediately noticeable, as the presence, energy, and focus in the room are heightened.

> In *The Moving Body: Teaching Creative Theatre*, Lecoq states, Essentially, the neutral mask opens up the actor to the space around [them]. It puts [them] in a state of discovery, of openness, of freedom to receive. It allows [them] to watch, to hear, to feel, to touch elementary things with the freshness of

beginnings.... A neutral mask puts the actor in a state of perfect balance and economy of movement.... Once [they] have achieved this freedom, the mask can be removed with no fear of falling back on artificial gestures. The neutral mask, in the end, unmasks!

(2002, 38)

For me, the most important moment in neutral mask work is at the end of the journey when the actor removes the mask and is in a heightened state of awareness and focus—being fully in the present moment. I see parallels between this moment and shanta in the rasaboxes (see Shanta as Witness, p. 159)—a state of pure presence and awareness. From this place of heightened presence, we can build anything.

Day 3: Exploration of Elements, Materials, and Animals

The third day begins with the warm-up ritual and Crossings II (see p. 112), followed by another day of Lecoq work—this time focusing on elements, materials, and animals. Lecoq's philosophy of "tout bouge" or "everything moves," which can be found throughout his pedagogy, means that the natural world—elements, materials, and animals—can be translated into movement, serving as theatrical inspiration and physical character development. I guide actors through a process that helps them find four baseline physical pillars of their character: a base element, a base material, a base animal, and a base rasa. To identify the character's base element, I lead the ensemble through an imaginary journey of the four elements—fire, air, earth, and water. Actors embody different aspects of water transforming from a drop of water into a trickle, a babbling brook, a stream, a river, a waterfall, the ocean, a sea storm, a wave evaporating into air; from a molecule of air, to a gentle breeze, to a gust, to a hurricane; into fire—a single candle flame to a blazing hearth, to a forest fire, to red coal, to ash, and finally resting as earth. Then, we experiment with humanizing each aspect of the four elements into characters. As we work through these explorations, I ask each actor to think about their character, to start "trying on" different elements. For example, Helen (played by Caitlyn Conlin) might experiment with different types of water—mist, fog, or rain. She seems to float or drift around the multi-leveled set—moving untethered within layers of surveillance.

Next, we explore materials—paper, plastic, metal, porcelain, elastic, and blood, among others—discovering the nuanced movement qualities of each material. Lecoq described materials as being inherently tragic—materials chip, tarnish, rust, crack, rip, erode—an idea ripe with potential for theatrical exploration. During these physical experimentations with the ensemble, each actor found a material and element that fit their character through trial and error. Katherine Harroff, the actor playing the Mother, chose iron as her dominant material. An iron-based Mother is a powerful force in Helen's life; however, over time her body, power, and agency are eroded, tarnished, rusted, and cracked—over a lifetime of hardship and struggle, her physical body is corroded and broken to the point of needing to use a cane for her limp.

I end the session with an exploration of animals—birds, cats, monkeys, giraffes, insects, and so on—finding the unique movement qualities and energies of each animal and then transforming that into human behavior while maintaining all of the characteristics and qualities of each animal. When I am teaching a devising class, we take a field trip to the zoo to observe animal movement and behavior, but during a rehearsal process, most often these explorations are done from memory or by watching videos. After these explorations, the actors determine a base animal for their character. These choices can shift and evolve as the actors get more in touch with their characters, but it is a starting point for physical exploration and building a shared vocabulary among cast members.

Day 4: Introduction to Rasaboxes

On day four, after the warm-up, I introduce Sounding with Resonators (see pp. 101–102), Scaling Intensity (see pp. 161–164), and Rasaboxes (see Chapter 4). As the actors explore the nine rasaboxes, the associations and drawings they produce for each rasabox become progressively more personal, gestural, and character specific. As the actors draw words, images, and associations in the rasaboxes, I ask them to respond in character. How does their character feel about each rasa? It is important to place the rasas in a new spatial configuration each time we prepare the grid to unsettle the relationship between the rasas to keep them fresh. To avoid the tendency for actors to fall into default patterns, after working in the rasaboxes for some time, I use the concept of "hatching" out of an egg or the "blossoming" of a flower. This is inspired by Lecoq's *éclosion*[10] exercise, of expansion and contraction—opening and closing to the environment, as found in nature.

Day 5: Objects, Base Rasas, and Rasic Chorus

On day five, once a basic understanding of Rasaboxes is established, we focus on Chorus Work (see pp. 167–169). First, I introduce Lecoq's tragic chorus exercise, referred to as the "balanced stage,"[11] by taping out a large box on the floor—these become the exterior gridlines of the rasaboxes later on. I ask the performers to imagine the taped box as a single surface balanced on a pin. Using their theatrical imaginations, the first actor enters the space and must balance the platform or it will tip over. Once the platform is stable, a second actor enters—renegotiating the sense of equilibrium. Stillness is not an option—the actors must keep moving. Then, a third actor enters, followed by a fourth—each time rebalancing the platform until the entire ensemble is on the platform. Then, imagining one performer's weight is equal to five performers, a protagonist and a tragic chorus is established. When the protagonist moves, the chorus must move in unison to balance the platform.

After this initial exploration, we tape out the rasaboxes grid, assign rasas to each box, then continue with the concept of Lecoq's tragic platform within the rasaboxes. If two performers are in the rasaboxes, they must be opposite each other and move around the rasaboxes accordingly. Then, repeating the protagonist/chorus work from earlier, we work with five actors being the same weight as one. The protagonist can introduce lines of text that their character speaks in the play and the chorus repeats those lines back. The protagonist might be in raudra (anger) and the chorus in bhayanaka (fear), creating a dynamic that fuels the protagonist to go deeper into raudra. Then, we work with a protagonist and an antagonist on the tragic platform, each with a chorus of three actors behind them. The three actors are in the same rasabox as the primary actor serving as their subconscious, supporting them emotionally and physically. At this stage in the rehearsal process, the focus is on the breath, the connection with the other actors, listening, and engaging with the rasa. Later in the rehearsal process, once lines are memorized, I repeat this exercise with scenes and monologues.

After the chorus work, we move onto objects. The actors bring in two objects that relate to their characters—one precious to them and one ordinary. We spend some time exploring objects in various rasaboxes and how their character interacts with these objects. The performers develop 15 seconds of behavior with one of their objects outside of the rasaboxes—a repeatable movement score. Then, they take their object and movement score into each rasabox—allowing their physical score to be affected by the rasa. Half the room observes while the other half explores; then we switch. Observations are discussed at the end of the exercise: *What did we see? What did we learn about the object or character? What relationships emerged with the object?* They repeat the exercise with their second object, using free form movement rather than a rehearsed movement score. Many interesting discoveries are made this way; for example, if the object is a cigarette and the character is a smoker—*what is their relationship to their cigarette? How do they hold it? Do they love it? Are they disgusted by it but still smoke?*

Next, I have them "try on" different base rasas for their characters. We experiment with at least three because often the first impulse is often not the best choice. Once they have selected a base rasa, we work with taking the base rasa through all the other rasas to explore all the combinations possible (see Mixing and Layering Rasas, pp. 171–176). Physical and emotional character discoveries are made at this stage, informing the rest of the rehearsal process.

To finish the day, the entire ensemble moves in character as a chorus through all eight rasas, responding to each other and the environment. This ends in shanta. I dim the lights in the rehearsal room and ask everyone to breathe. This is part of a de-roling process of calming the nervous system. I have them visualize that they are standing under a waterfall, allowing the water to wash away all the rasic energy that was stirred up—a kind of palette cleansing—coming back to a place of neutrality and stillness (see Shanta Waterfall, p. 180).

Day 6: Slow Motion Transformation

The last day of the week-long physical theatre intensive ends with Crossings V: Slow Motion Transformation (see pp. 128–135). I have found this to be one of the most effective psychophysical ensemble exercises for young actors. The slowness and presence required of this experience allows performers to enter into a deep state of "flow"[12] and mind–body connection with themselves and the ensemble. It allows the performers to engage somatically with the emotional lives of their characters and gain insight into their emotional complexity and the overall emotional arc of their characters in the production. On the first day of rehearsal, I ask the cast to think about costumes for their characters—not ones designed by the costume designer, but of their own creation. I encourage them to make their costumes out of found or recycled materials instead of purchasing something from a store. This prompt produces some highly imaginative and creative costumes. When I have given this prompt, I have seen some beautiful creations made out of Post-It notes, plastic bags, newspapers, cardboard boxes, and other found materials.[13]

In preparation for Slow Motion Transformation, we explore Crossings I and II earlier in the week. I also ask the performers to bring two recorded songs that they feel belong in the play or represent their character, an object that has significance for their character, a mobile light source, a handwritten biography of their character in the play, two rasic memories, and/or a recurring dream. The rasic memories and recurring dreams are from the performer's actual life—for example, the first time you remember feeling profound sadness or anger or a time when you first fell in love. The actor can also invent a rasic memory from their character's life and backstory. Self, persona, and character are interwoven throughout this exercise to create a complex, visceral web of connections (see pp. 128–129). This work feeds into the emotional life of the play in a textured, nuanced way.

After Crossing the Line and the yoga warm-up, the instructions for Slow Motion Transformation are given. We begin with the ensemble lining up on either side of the rasaboxes grid facing each other. I ask them to trace a physical score in their minds—a detailed path across the space from one side to the other, avoiding the middle box. For example, take three steps forward, turn around, get on your hands and knees, crawl at a diagonal to your left, lay on your back, stand up, take two steps sideways, pivot 90 degrees, walk two steps forward etc. Once they have a basic physical score in their mind's eye, they enact it several times in the space going at a regular speed. Then I say, "Freeze. Now begin moving in super slow motion at 2% velocity—so slowly that if I were to look at you, you would appear like a still photograph. That is how slowly you will be crossing the space." I emphasize that it isn't about getting to the other side but about the journey.

I customize the Slow Motion Transformation breakouts using specific prompts for each production I direct, incorporating the Lecoq work explored earlier in the week. Within the rasaboxes grid, a series of other boxes and spaces are taped out where various behaviors and breakouts can occur. I review these breakouts and allow time for questions and clarification on instructions as once the exercise begins, no more questions can be asked. Here is a sample set of customized breakouts for *Machinal*.

A. **Running and panting:** At any point during the crossing, a performer can break out of slow motion and run around the exterior of the rasaboxes counterclockwise panting in the "hah" resonator (see One Sound One Movement, pp. 106–107). This allows the performer to shake off any muscular tension that may be occurring in the slow motion. The performers can do this breakout as many times as needed during the exercise (A in Figure 16.2).

B. **Behavior breakouts:** On the inside of the taped rasaboxes grid of nine boxes, two corners are taped opposite each other, forming triangles. Inside these triangles three behaviors can occur (B in Figure 16.2):

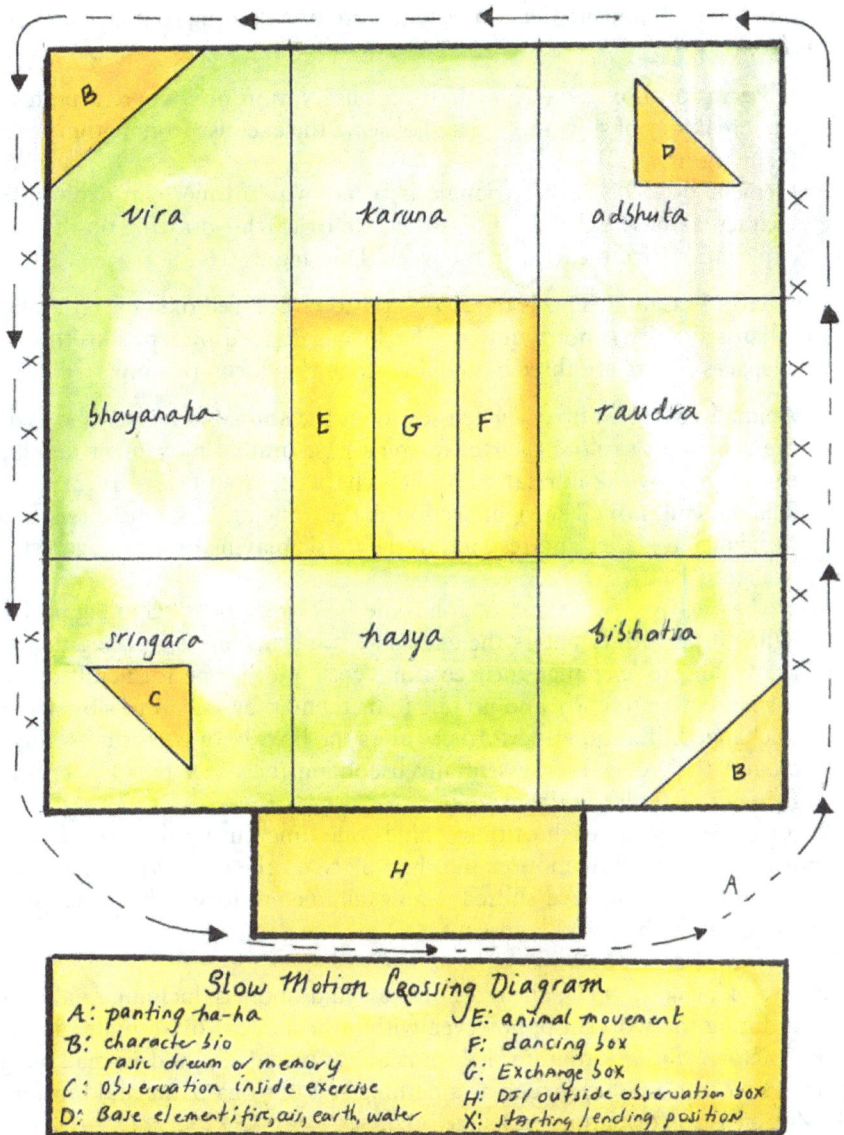

FIGURE 16.2 Slow Motion Transformation diagram for *Machinal* directed by Rachel Bowditch.

1. **Character biography:** The performer can read the character biography they created from the play and their imaginations.
2. **Rasic memory:** The performer can share a rasic memory from their life.
3. **Recurring dream:** The performer can share a recurring dream from their life.

Action boxes: Opposite the two triangles are two floating triangles within the rasaboxes.

C. **Observation box:** One triangle is an observation box where a performer can break out of slow motion and observe the exercise from within the grid (C in Figure 16.2).

D. **Element box:** The other triangle is where a performer can explore their character's base element—fire, water, air, or earth—drawing on the Lecoq explorations from earlier in the week (D in Figure 16.2).

The central rasabox: This is the *shanta* rasabox in Rasaboxes exercises. Here, the shanta quality is not required. This box is divided by tape into three distinct spaces. There are three possibilities for behavior in this box.

E. **Animal movement box:** The left section is the animal movement box where the actor can explore their character's base animal movement developed earlier in the week in relation to their character (E in Figure 16.2).

F. **The dancing box:** The right section is the dancing box where two actors can dance together and respond to the music playing or move against it (F in Figure 16.2).

G. **Exchange box:** The center section is the "exchange box" (G in Figure 16.2). When a performer enters the exchange box, they are signifying that they are willing to exchange their costume with another performer. If one performer enters the box and no one joins them, they return to slow motion, unchanged. If another performer enters the box, both performers fully exchange their costumes, essentially becoming the other person's character for the remainder of the exercise.

A performer can do each of these things one time during the exercise—each time returning to slow motion and their place on the grid. When they return, the performers will have shifted a few millimeters forward in their scores, creating a new theatrical landscape.

In the days of TPW at NYU, all states of dress and undress, including nakedness, occurred during the workshop; however, within the context of an undergraduate/graduate actor training program, I do not allow nakedness and instead suggest performers wear a base layer such as a bathing suit or yoga pants and top for the Slow Motion Transformation exchange box.

Once the instructions have been given, the actors place their costumes and objects in one of the four corners of the room and begin getting ready in silence (see Setting Up and Dressing Corners, pp. 129–130). The selected dressing corner determines your tribe, kin, or clan for the rest of the exercise. I provide a large mirror for each corner for performers to apply makeup and an area for privacy, should a performer require that when changing. While the performers are getting ready, I place a card in each box with a rasa on it. At any point, a performer can call out, "Going on a walk," at which point everyone in the room freezes mid-action and everyone in that performer's clan walks around the room and observes the others getting ready. Once they return to home base, the room unfreezes and getting ready continues. Once everyone in each corner is fully costumed, they form a still tableau and wait for the others to finish. Once all the performers are done getting ready, each performer moves in silence to their starting point on the crossing line and finds a still pose with their object. I review the placement of the rasas and ask the performers to begin to find the breath shape of their base rasa allowing that to inform their posture, attitude, and physical shape. I emphasize the journey—not the destination.

> Observe those across from you and to either side of you. Who are you drawn to? Who do you want to encounter on your journey? What occurs when you encounter another on your path inside a rasa moving in super slow motion at 2%? What happens? What discoveries are made? What exchanges do you want to have? Who do you want to give your object to? Is there an object that somebody has that you want?

I dim the lights, indicating that when the lights come on, the exercise will begin.

I ask performers to bring in music that resonates with their character or the play. During the exercise, I play the role of DJ, creating a sonic soundscape that informs the experience. The inclusion of recorded sound is a significant departure from what happens in TPW, as recorded sound is not typically used in this exercise; however, I feel it adds to the somatic journey of the exercise and helps performers to enter into the sonic world of the play. Often, we make discoveries that end up in the show. For me, the music is critically important for capturing the tone, mood, and emotional energy of the play. As DJ, I sit in the "watching box" to hold the space and be a witness to the exercise (see H in Figure 16.2). Performers can enter the box with me once during the exercise to observe from the outside and to document what they see using their cell phone camera (if the entire group has given consent in advance to allow photographs). Sometimes I invite designers to observe this exercise—which can help to inform costume and sound design choices.

The *Machinal* cast made many valuable discoveries in the Slow Motion Transformation exercise. At one point, the protagonist, Helen, encountered her husband, George Jones (played by Kane Anderson), in bibhatsa (disgust). This encounter deepened Helen's disgust for her husband. Later in the exercise, Helen meets her lover, Mr. Roe, in shringara (love). Helen's base rasa was bhayanaka (fear). Doing shringara and bhayanaka in the Slow Motion Crossing produced powerful discoveries—that there is both fear and excitement in falling in love for the first time. At different points during the exercise, I asked Helen to enter the center dancing box and then, at different times, to invite her mother, her husband, or her lover to dance with her. This allowed Helen to establish an emotional connection with each of these central characters in her life and to remain viscerally connected to them throughout the exercise and eventually, in the performance of the play.

For the final moment before the end of the exercise, I asked Helen to stand in the center box. Then I asked each character, one by one, to give Helen their object at a regular speed. The soundscape I used was the sound of church bells, such as one might hear at a funeral. Slowly, one by one each character gave Helen their objects—a watch, a pair of gloves, a hat, a book etc., until Helen had so many objects she could barely hold them. As this progressed, the actors/characters got more and more emotional, realizing that they were saying goodbye to Helen right before she was to be executed. There was not a dry eye among us. This exercise not

FIGURE 16.3 Shay Webster and Adriano Cabral in *The House of the Spirits* by Caridad Svich directed by Rachel Bowditch at ASU.

Source: Photo courtesy of Rachel Bowditch, 2012.

only emotionally bonded the group, it also gave us a tremendous amount of raw material to mine in scene work and added an emotional poignancy to the final execution scene.

Second Week of Rehearsal: Scene Work in the Rasaboxes

The second week of rehearsal was devoted to working on each scene in the rasaboxes grid. At first, we explored the scene in different rasaboxes to see what new discoveries could be unearthed. Each character moved between the rasaboxes—it could be one rasabox per line or per unit of action. For "Episode One: To Business," we returned to the rasic chorus exercise. Caitlyn Conlin, who played Helen, discovered bhayanaka as her base rasa. As Helen moved from rasabox to rasabox, the office workers formed a chorus, moving as one unit, mirroring her in an opposite rasa. The chorus discovered that the scene moved between hasya (mockery) and bibhatsa, helping the actors establish the tension and relationship between Helen and her office co-workers, who bombard her with a litany of rapid-fire questions about why she was late like a pack of wild hyenas. Helen combated their energy with a combination of bhayanaka and vira (courage). In the story, Helen fears losing her job, yet retains a sense of dignity and self-worth. Her sense of self erodes throughout the course of the play.

In "Episode Two: At Home," at first, I encouraged the performers to move freely between the rasaboxes, experimenting with different combinations until we discovered what worked. While exploring Helen's antagonistic relationship with her overprotective mother within the rasaboxes, we discovered that on the surface the mother appears to have a base rasa of raudra (anger), which is expressed in her harsh vocal tone and language. Her underlying emotion is bhayanaka because she is profoundly afraid that her daughter will abandon her. Helen reacts with growing frustration, building toward raudra tinged with bibhatsa, especially because it was her mother who had encouraged Helen to marry Mr. Jones, the rich boss of the company (see Figure 16.1). In "Episode Three: Honeymoon," Mr. Jones, filled with vira (here read as pride), treats Helen as a new acquisition. Helen's attitude toward Mr. Jones is tinged with bhayanaka and bibhatsa, yet she marries him and bears his child because she feels she has no other choice. Then, in "Episode Five: Prohibited" and "Episode Six: Intimate," Helen meets another man and they become lovers. Here, Helen is infused with bhayanaka, adbhuta (wonder), and shringara—terrified yet stimulated and excited because she is experiencing for the first time what she thinks is love. Her lover combined vira and shringara to create a smooth, sexually confident womanizer. For him, Helen is just another notch on his belt.

We made an interesting discovery while working on "Episode Eight: The Law." Helen is on trial for the murder of her husband. The actor playing her defense lawyer, John Caswell, at first used vira (in this case, pride) and raudra, drilling into Helen while supposedly defending her. However, after exploring the scene through several rasaboxes, the actor discovered the action played better with hasya (mockery) as the dominant base rasa. This gave his character a sarcastic, mocking edge, adding an entirely new reading of his relationship with Helen.

Finally, in "Episode Nine: A Machine," Helen is incarcerated and sent to the electric chair. The emotional climax was rooted in a complex cocktail of all the rasas she experienced throughout the arc of the play; bhayanaka mixed with karuna (sadness) when she realizes she is about to be executed; raudra fused with bibhatsa toward her mother and Mr. Jones; adbhuta (surprise) in response to the shock of being betrayed by her lover, who turned her in. Amid this emotional maelstrom, the actor discovered a sense of hasya (laughter), which bordered on insanity as well as a profound sense of vira (courage) and even shanta (peace) as she came to terms with her inevitable death.

This process was employed for all the characters in *Machinal*, creating a complex emotional score. This physical and emotional dramaturgical mapping was coupled with more traditional Stanislavsky-based acting involving objectives, actions, and obstacles. The exploration of the Rasaboxes within a rehearsal process trains actors' emotional intelligence, not only for their character development, but for themselves as performers. By combining the different emotional flavors of each character, a rasic "feast" was created for spectators to taste and enjoy the spectrum of emotion. As a director, the joy of developing the production using TPW and Rasaboxes exercises combined with the Lecoq exercises is in finding and exploring the unexpected. In each production, I continue to find new ways to refine, nuance, and open the performers to the world of the play and discover the emotional landscape of their characters. The combination of these techniques gives me indispensable tools for developing an ensemble and creating group synergy, leading to highly engaged, effective, and physically dynamic performances.

Notes

1 From 1998 to 1999, I attended Ecole de Jacques Lecoq in Paris, France, where I had the opportunity to work directly with Lecoq before he died in 1999, and with core Lecoq faculty Thomas Prattki, Norman Taylor, and Giovanni Fusetti. Lecoq's theatrical pedagogy is central to my work and vision as a theatre director. Wearing all-black neutral clothing is a tradition of Lecoq's training. It helps to quickly create a neutral visual palette for the ensemble.
2 A mainstage production of the School of Film, Dance, and Theatre (renamed the School of Music, Dance, and Theatre in 2020) in the Herberger Institute for Design and the Arts.
3 Sophie Treadwell (1885–1970) was an American playwright and journalist who wrote dozens of plays, mainly concerned with women's issues of her time, and is best known for *Machinal*.
4 The panopticon was proposed by Jeremy Bentham in 1791. This architectural semi-circular plan could be applied to asylums, hospitals, and prisons, where one guard tower could observe all the cells from a single vantage point. In *Machinal*, we adapted the concept to build a world in which Helen was under constant surveillance through cameras embedded throughout the set.
5 Taylorism was a system of management developed by Frederick W. Taylor as a way to analyze and streamline human movement and rest on the production line to maximize efficiency and productivity. Russian theatre director Vsevolod Meyerhold was inspired by Taylorism, evidenced in his system of actor training, Biomechanics.
6 Schechner learned a sequence of yoga asanas from Tirumalai Krishnamacharya in India (see Chapter 4, pp. 94–98) and integrated it into TPW. It is slow and methodical, whereas the more vigorous vinyasa yoga sequence I use is better suited for younger bodies.
7 Twelve Steps is an ensemble-building exercise that is seemingly simple, yet requires total focus, concentration, and presence for it to work. It brings the group into the present moment together. The group starts in a circle facing each other and takes 12 steps to the right, 11 to the left, 10 to the right, and so on, switching back and forth until the group reaches 1, facing center. I learned it in 1999 from Nereu Afonso, a classmate at Ecole de Jacques Lecoq.
8 Further information about the seven levels of tension, *pointe fixe*, and the neutral mask can be found in Lecoq's *Moving Body* (2002) and Simon Murray's *Jacques Lecoq* (2003). The neutral masks we use were created by Arizona-based master mask-maker Zarco Guerrero and are loosely modeled on Amleto Sartori's leather neutral masks designed specifically for Lecoq. Sartori (1915–1962) was a famous commedia dell'arte leather mask maker in Padua, Italy, who collaborated extensively with Lecoq at the Piccolo Teatro in Milan.
9 See Lecoq, "The Fundamental Journey," *The Moving Body* (41), for a description of the exercise.
10 Lecoq analyzes movements of the human body based on three movements in nature: undulation, inverse undulation, and éclosion (see *The Moving Body*, 71), which can best be described as "hatching."
11 A description of "The Balanced Stage" exercise and the tragic chorus can be found in *The Moving Body* (132–137).

12 For more on "flow," see Mihaly Csikszentmihalyi 1975.
13 This prompt arose from an experience while co-teaching TPW at NYU one summer. I did not have many belongings with me, so for this exercise I created a fancy hoop skirt, corset, and headdress—all constructed with tape and pages from the *New York Times*. This was a far more creative and interesting process than if I had bought something at a costume shop—and it cost me less than five dollars.

Works Cited

Csikszentmihalyi, Mihaly. *Beyond Boredom and Anxiety: Experiencing Flow in Work and Play*. San Francisco: Jossey-Bass, 1975.
Lecoq, Jacques. *The Moving Body: Teaching Creative Theatre*. London and New York: Routledge, 2002.
Murray, Simon. *Jacques Lecoq*. London and New York: Routledge, 2003.
Treadwell, Sophie. *Machinal*. London: Nick Hern Books, 1995.

INDEX

Note: Numbers in *italics* indicate a figure. Numbers in bold indicate a table. Page numbers followed by 'n' indicate an endnote on the corresponding page.

4/66 (Happening-like event) 14; *see also* happenings
6 Axioms for Environmental Theatre 15, 18, 23; *see also* Six Axioms

Abhinavagupta 50–1, 53n5, 56, 76n3; ninth rasa added by 61; rasa as understood by 260
abhinaya (acting) 49, 52, 58, 61–2; literal meaning of 74
Achcar, Ana 7, 275–9
Adams, Franklin 14, 194
Adishakti Theater Company, Pondicherry, India 236
adbhuta 49, 57, 61, 70, 72, converted into role types 239; experience of 152; experience of layering over karuna 173; experience of scaling intensity of 163–4; *Nutcracker* using concepts of 222; rasaboxes and 138, 254; Romeo as 73; sounds associated with 158; yellow associated with 78n16;
adbhuta rasabox 163; Minnick in *164*
aesthetic distance 236
Ajanta caves 64–5
Alexander, Frederick Matthias 228
Alexander Technique 4
allostasis 245–6; homeostasis and 245–6; Rasaboxes and 248–9; *see also* homeostasis
Almeida, Karen 271
Alternate Nostril Breathing (*nadi shodhana*) 98
American acting 62
American experimental performance scene 17
American Expressionism 281
AmeriKa 37
Animal Exercise 122–4
applause 120, *121*; Wait for It . . . Hold Your Applause (textbox) 93
Arie, Dana 6, 244–9
Arizona State University (ASU) 7; *House of the Spirits, The* (Svich) 290; *Machinal* (Treadwell) at 281; Slow Motion Crossing *127*

Around the World I 144–5
Around the World II 158; making a pose 71
Artaud, Antonin 198, 200; on actors as "athletes of the heart" 71, 78n15, 195, 242n8, 245
Aristotle: Greek theatre and 60; *Poetics* 47, 55–57; unity of time, space, and action 50
Aristotelian models: of performance 5; of tragedy 30, 60
asanas (yoga) 25; 94, 95–9, 292n6; *shavasana* 179
A Serious Banquet see Serious Banquet, A
Asia: cultural arts traditions of 69; medicines of 68; Schechner's engagement with 23–4, 26, 194; theatre traditions of 24; *see also* India; yoga
Asmat birth ritual 23
Association for Theater in Higher Education (ATHE) Conference: Schechner's 1992 keynote speech at 17
ASU *see* Arizona State University
audience participation 14–15, 21–22, 24, 38, 65; different types of 42n15
Austininan speech act 201
Athey, Ron 75
Ayurveda 68, 76n4; and rasa 140–1

Bacchae, The (Euripides) Schechner's essay on 13; *Dionysus in 69* and 21
Balasaraswati, T. ("Bala") 52–3
Banquet (exercise) 181–3
Barba, Eugenio 23, 233n7
Baroda critical edition of NS 76n3
Bateson, Gregory 207; "play frame" concept of 209n5
Baur-Worch, Arne 232n4, 233n7
Beckett, Samuel 194; *Waiting for Godot* 14
behavior: addictive 240; artistically performed

emotions and distinct kinds of 62; codes of 209n8; conventional social 92; emotional and psychological 176; exercise: performing rehearsed piece of 129, *130*; everyday 111; extra-daily 29; as performance 33, 111; playful 207; problems 219; repertoire 246–7; restored 117; "twice-behaved" 117; violence 222
behavioral: patterns 248
belly: brain in the belly 58, 65, 68, 138; mouth-to-belly-to-bowel 55, 140; snout-to-belly-to-bowel 55; tanden in the belly 68; visceral satisfaction in 63
Berliner Ensemble 194
B., Franko 75
Bharata-muni 66; *Natyashastra* 2, 5, 27, 47–53, 55–7, 58, 61, 76n3, 138, 142; rasa as conceived by 50–1, 138; sattvika states specified by 49; sons of 75n2
bharatanatyam 52, 53, 56, 73, 236
bhava 48–52; *anubhava* 49, 57; Bharata on 58; defining 49–50, 137; rasa and 57–8; rasa hoops exercise using 237; *sthayi* 48, 49, 57–8, 61–2, 68; *vibhava* 49, 57; *vyabhichari* 49, 57
bhayanaka 49, 57, 61, 70; black color associated with 78n16; Clara in *Nutcracker* 222; converted into role types 239; Helen in *Machinal* 290–1; Laura in *Glass Menagerie* 217, 218; Masha from *Three Sisters* 174; Nora from *A Doll's House* 173; Ofelia from *Hamlet* 174–5; Orestes in *Electra* 271–2
bhayanaka rasabox 72, 137; experience of 158; performer in *146*
bibhatsa 49, 57, 61, 70, 71, 72; Amanda in *Glass Menagerie* 217; Bowditch's first person

295

narrative of working with 172; blue color associated with 78n16; converted into role types 239; experience of 143, 152; *Machinal* 289; Ofelia in *Hamlet* 176; sounds associated with 157
bibhatsa rasabox 137; performer in 157
Blackburn, Jennifer 218
Black freedom struggle (the Movement) 13–14
Black Nationalism 14
Blakeslee, Sandra 66
Body-Mind Centering® 4, 226
Boliver, Rocio 75
borrowing (cultural) 11, 137; permission to borrow performance material in TPW 120; power differential implied by 41n2
Borst, Stephen 192
Bowditch, Rachel: *Machinal* and directing 7, 282–92; Rasaboxes development by 77; making a rasic persona172; Schechner interviewed by 190–6; as Schechner's student 4; as second wave teacher of TPW 3, 40; Slow Motion Crossings exercise, TPW at NYU 128; in *YokastaS* 38, 39
Brahma: creation of *Natyaveda* by 76n2, 77n8; creation of *Natyashastra* 47; fifth Veda of 75n2
Brahman, the 74
brain in the belly *see* belly; Gershon
Brazilian telenovela 263–8
Breath Work (exercises) 98–100; Clearing Breath 100; Humming and Clearing, *kapalabhati* (Skull Shining Breath) and in sets, *nadi shodhana* (Alternate Nostril Breathing), and *ujjayi* (Victorious Breath) 98–9
Brecht, Bertolt and Brechtian 128; "making strange" 138; *Mother Courage and Her Children* 26, 27, 35, 42n20; trained companies 194; *verfremdungseffekt* 74
Brook, Peter 198; trained companies 194
Burden, Chris 75

Cage, John 41–2n8
Caillois, Roger 94
Calzadilla, Fernando 3, 4, 40, 77n7, 95; *Electra* directed by 7, 269–74; yoga drawings by 95, 96, 97
Centre for Sensory Studies, Concordia 78n20; *see also* senses
Chaikin, Joseph 198
Chair Relaxation exercise 6, 228–9, 231–2
Chandra, Vikram 50
character: actor reflection on safety and risk while playing 272–4; actors who experience strong feelings but not the feelings of the character 62; "as if" of characters living out a narrative 74; backstory, creating 166; base element, exploring 288; building a character with Rasaboxes 174–6, 269–74; Chair Relaxation and Sense-Memory exercise and 231; disrobing while in character 207; doing, performing, non-matrixed, and matrixed acting 110, 128; Emo Lab/Rasaboxes course and 232; emotional and sensory life of 232; "emotional memory" in creation of 76n6, 116; finding 269; Jumping into New Roles 238; layering rasas and 173; layering over base rasa and 173–4; Lecoq on 283; of *Machinal* 281; Masha 261; music and 289; performer and, demarcating clear lines between 207; physical character development 283; psychological structure 175–6; Schechner's research on 26; Off the Grid exercise 166; performer as partaker 74; rasa and Rasaboxes folded into working on 124, 170, 174, 267; Rasaboxes, introduction into rehearsal and 284–6; Rasaboxes, scene work and 290; *rasika* or person responsive to feeling what a character feels 51; rehearsal scene work and 290; self-persona-character, continuum of 116; *Serious Banquet* 259, 261; Slow Motion Transformation and 128, 135, 286; "Spalding" 129; spectators' capacity to identify with 50; stock character 47; types 57; Zarrilli on 69, 227
character analysis and Rasamaps: rehearsal 217–8
character biography 287
character building through Rasaboxes 7, 269–74; *see also Electra*
characteristics of a play: Huizinga on 32
characterization 14; continuity errors 264
character journey: Macbeth 215; mapping 218
Chekhov, Anton 196; *Three Sisters* 37, *38*, 174
Chekhov, Michael 232n2
ch'i 68
Chorus Work in rasaboxes (exercises): 167; Chorus with One Sound One Movement 167–8; Chorus with Speaker and Listener 169; Chorus with Text 168–9, in *Electra* 269–74; Open Chorus 167; rasic chorus 284
Cieslak, Ryszard 19, 23, 62, 193
cisgendered 4
Claire, Elizabeth 176
Classen, Constance 78n20
Clearing Breath 100, 158, 178, 179, 184, 282
Close-Up 7, 263, 265, 266, 266–8
Closings 181, *see also* Banquet; Uncrossing the Line
clown: rasaboxes and 275–9; dramaturgy 275, 279; objects in Rasaboxes 275; the problem with hasya 276; red nose 277, 278, 279; triangulation 276, 277; *see also hasya*
Cole, Paula Murray 128–9, 198; "Building a Character with Rasaboxes" 174–76; as first wave teacher of TPW 3; member of ECA 38; role of workshop leader 197–209; Schechner interviewed by 190–6; Schechner as teacher of 4; Song of Self Notes from TPW Journal 1998 118–20; *Three Sisters* 38, 77n7; Wallin as mentee of 40; Yes and No 115–6
communitas *see* spontaneous communitas
Conlin, Caitlyn 283; in *Machinal* 281
Consent and Boundary Checks; establishing boundaries 83–4; "no touching others" rule while exploring 215; *see also* refusal

Index   297

Constructivism 282
Contact Improvisation (CI) 269, 274, 274n3
Cooldowns 179–80; Songs as 122; Tactics for Cooling Down 231; Waterfall exercises as 180
Coomaraswamy, Ananda K. 51
Corrigan, Robert W. 13, 18, 41n5
Crossings 6, 14, 38, 87, 106, 115, 136; conflict and drama arising out of desire in 125; early stages of 109; performing and watching roles in 111; Rasaboxes and 152; renaming exercise 110; silence 130; Slow Motion 125, 128, 135, 280; TPW's centering on 202; Crossings I: Encounters 108–11, 125, 282; exercise instructions 126; Crossings II: Display 112–13, 283; Crossings III: Desires 114–15, 125; Crossings IV: Slow Motion Crossing 125–8, 129, 130, 131; Crossings V: Slow Motion Transformation 128–35, *131*, *132*, *134*; 181, *287*; in Machinal rehearsal 285–90
Crossings Space, setting up 125–6
Crossing the Line 90–2
Crutcher, David 216–17
Cruz, Maria Paula 271, 272, 273
Csikszentmihalyi, Mihaly 107
Cultural and Intercultural Performance 32

Darwin, Charles 58, 138
Davis, Ossie: *Purlie Victorious* 14
deep acting 253
Decroux, Etienne 233n7
Dell'Arte International School of Physical Theatre 9, 81, *125*, *177*, *189*, *211*
Denzer, Ralph 37
Derby, Doris 13
Devin, Alexandra 236
dharma 77n8
Dharwadker, Vinay 58
Diderot, Denis 62, 72
Dionysus (Greek god) 64
Dionysus in 69 (play, TPG production) 20–3, 31, 42n15
disrobing 113; *see also* naked and nakedness
Doner-Tudanger, Gaye 236, 242n4
drama therapy: addiction 239–40; affective resonance 252–3; burnout 254; case study in Rasaboxes 247–49; clinical applications in 235–41; countertransference 206; deep and surface acting (Goffman) 253; de-role 240; developmental transformations (DvT) 251; drama therapists' training, Rasaboxes and 251–5; embodied narrative 247; emotional aesthetics 251–2; emotional intelligence 218–20, 223, 236, 251, 291; emotional labor 253; feedback and cooldown 240–1; Jumping into new Roles 238–40; rasaboxes and 244–49; over-distance and under distance 239, 249; performing care 253–4; Plotting Your Daily Life exercise 254; Rasa Hoops exercise 237–8
dramaturgical analogies 253
dramaturgs 259
dramaturgy: of the clown 275, 279; of the emotions in *Machinal* 7, 280–93
dressing *see* Nakedness, Crossings V: Slow Motion Transformation; Slow Motion Crossing in *Machinal*
Duberman, Martin: *In White America* 14, 41n6
Duerksen, Alyssa (in karuna rasabox) 160

East Coast Artists (ECA) 2, 3, 4, 25, 27, 36–40, 63, 76n7, 198, 225; *see also* Neuerburg
East End Players (EEP) 12, 14, 24, 194
Ekman, Paul: facial expression of emotion and 138–39; nine pathways to emotion 139; 186n4
Electra (Sophocles) 7, 269–74
Emo Lab 226–33
emotional: aesthetics 251–2; capabilities of performers 52; communication, centrality of 52; contact improvisation 205; containment skills 238; content, Rasabox as tool to discover 176; control 237; detachment 239; exhaustion 254; experience, Rasaboxes and 246; experience, "real" or "fake" 149; expressions, conveying 57; expressions, difficult 137; expressions, Ekman on 139; expressions in young performers 6, 212–23; extremes 236; flavors 137; intelligence 218–20, 223; intensity, scaling 264–7; labor 253; "memory" exercise 62, 76n6, 116; over-distance 239, 249; reactions 206; regulation 245; regulation, Rasaboxes as training for 246–7; state 58; states, impact of ayurveda and rasa on 141; states, memory as trigger of 230; states, using Rasaboxes to access 225, 227, 232, 245; under-distance 236, 239, 242n3, 249; vocabulary 248
emotions 245; acting of 61; addictions and 237, 240; "artistically performed" 62; in body, in story 6; Darwin on 138; dramaturgy of (Machinal) 280–293; six basic 139; ENS and 68; episodic nature of 163; facial expression of 138–9; in Indian aesthetic system 62; instruction of 52; mapping 218; mixed 73, 171–2; molecules of 149–50; performed 62, 238; performing of 27, 28, 56; psychophysical aspects of 138; rasaesthetics and 67, 74; rasa as flavor and 48, 76n4; rasa as savoring or tasting of 59, 61; Rasaboxes and 70, 139, 215, 218, 219, 246; rasic 174; recognizing 221; as rooted in the body 239; sphere of (Artaud) 78n15; subconscious 69; transient 49; why of 245; *see also bhava*
enteric nervous system (ENS) 5, 58, 65–69, 78n11; *see also* Gershon, Michael D.
Entering the Space (exercise) 89–90
environmental theatre 13–17; *Environmental Theater* by Schechner 2, 12, 13–17, 18, 22, 24, 26, 82, 197; Growtowski's exploration of 19, 197; immersive theater influenced by 23; "Participation" chapter of *Environmental Theater* (Schechner) 22; practical work of TPW influenced by 82, 199
Epstein, Paul 14, 194
Eucharist 77n9
Euripides: *Bacchae* 21
Evans, Mark 225

facial expression 142; base rasa and 173; case study (Michael) 247; of emotions, comparison of 186n5; "flavor" of rasa expressed and modulated through (Instruction) 171; Paul Ekman and facial expression of emotion 138–39; "personal fronts" (Goffman) 203; Sculpting in Partners (exercise) focusing on 145–7; separating elements of physicalization of rasas into 154–5; transitions in Rasaboxes, exercise focusing on facial expression 154–5
facial mask 158
facial muscles 150, 220
family dramas 194
Faust/gastronome 36–7, 37, 76n7
Feedback and Discussion Circles 84–5
Feuchtersleben, Ernst von: Lehrbuch der ärztlichen Seelenkunde 227
Finley, Karen 75
Finley, William 21
Flow, concept of 107, 293n12
Follow-No-Leader: One Sound 104; One Sound One Movement 106–7, 167; Rules of One Sound in Follow-No-Leader exercise 105
food: animal exercise and 122–3; ayurveda and 140–1; Banquet exercise 181–3; Dancing on the Tongue 258–60; eating of (slow motion exercise) 130; emotion and 76n4; Eucharist and 77n9; performance and 26, 48; orange exercise 139–41; prasad 64; Schechner's interest in 27; rasa and 57–9, 61, 142, 177; rasa of natya and 57; taste-rasa and 139; theatre akin to 51; traditional eating of food in India 74–5
found space 15, 26, 213
Forier Edie, Elise 6, 212–23
Four Phases of Performer Training (Schechner) 83
Freedom Summer 1964 14
Free Southern Theater (FST) 13–14, 17, 24, 41n7
Fuentes, Luis 271, 272, 273

Gaines, Andrew M. 6, 235–42
Gaines, Daphne: YokastaS Redux 39
Gaisseau, Pierre Dominque 24
Galileo 59

Garrick, David 72
Gatica, Esther 271, 273
Gennep, Arnold van 29, 209n5
Gershon, Michael D.: "brain in the belly" of 138; on the enteric nervous system (ENS) 66–68; Second Brain 66
Ghosh, Manomohan 27, 53n3, 77n8
Gillett, Cobina 1–8, 10–43
Glass Menagerie (Williams) 217, 218
Goffman, Erving 32, 242n3, 253; "personal fronts" of 203; Presentation of the Self in Everyday Life 17
Gopalakrishna, Maitri 236
gossiping (about TPW) 192
Gray, Spalding 32, 34–5, 42n13, Schechner on his performance persona 129
Greetings (exercises) 93–4
Grotowski, Jerzy 19, 24, 27, 32, 35, 194, 197–8; as guru 197–8; "association exercises" 20; Baur-Worch training with 233n7; Cieslak teaching workshop with 19, 62, 193; NYU and The Performance Group 18–23; plastiques 19, 20; Polish Laboratory Theatre of Opole 18, 19; "Poor Theater" concept of 19; resonators 101; Schechner, influence on ideas of 200; Schechner's publishing of articles by and about 19; Stanislavsky's influence on 18; Theatre of 13 Rows 18; Towards a Poor Theater 197;
Group Performances 124
Group Sound Work 102–7
guerrilla theatre protests (Schechner's), 1967, New York 15
Guerrero, Zarco 292n8
Guimarães, Fernanda 7, 263–68
guru 6, 63, 197–209

Hadhazy, Adam 67–8
Hall, Fitz Edward 76n3
Halprin, Anna 186n11
Happenings 14–17, 32; Kirby's theorization of 110–11; special issue of TDR 41n8
Harroff, Katie 281, 283
hastas 73; see also mudras
hasya 73; children and 220; character building with 272, 290–1; color associated with 78n16; converted into role types 239; definition or English translation of 49, 57,
61, 70; Doll's House base rasa for Nora 173; experience in 173; scaling intensity of 162; drama therapy client's experimentation with 249; Ofelia, experience of mixing with vira 171; mixed with raudra 176; problem with hasya (in clown work) 276; sthayi bhava, corresponding 49, 61; hasya rasabox 145
Harshbarger, Karl 12
Healey, Christopher: YokastaS Redux 39
Heymann or Haymann, Wilhelm 76n3
Hochschild, Arlie R. 253
holder of space 201–7; leader-as-holder 203
homeostasis 245–6; see also allostasis
Howes, David 78n20
Huizinga, Johan 31–32, 207
Humming and Clearing 98
Hurley, Erin 260
Hutchinson, Nick 216

Ibsen, Henrik A Doll's House 173; family drama 194; When We Dead Awaken 12
immersive theatre and performance 7, 23, 65, rasa and 258–61
improvisation: Contact Improvisation (CI) 269, 274n3; developmental transformations 255n1; of the workshop leader 205; performative response as 121; as basis of Rasaboxes training 138; sound in Rasaboxes 156, 163; rasic performers and 73–4; role-play 235; TPW and 82
improvisational theatre (see also Viola Spolin) 223n2
India: aesthetic performance system in 46–54, 62–4; Balasaraswati 52–3; Brecht in 26; 46–; classical dance styles of 73–4; Delhi 26; diaspora 28; eating style 59, 74–5; food metaphors and flavors of 48; gods 64, 77n9; importance of not exoticizing 137; Islam in 64; Kolkata 24, 26; language of theatre 52; Lucknow 26, 27; masala 10; Mumbai 26; performance 5; performance theory (Natyashastra) 55; performers 51–2; raga 74, 78n18; Schechner's trips to

and experiences of 23–9, 46; Sack's performances in 35; Sircar, Badal 24; theory and concept of rasa 46–54, 61, 137; *see also* Ayurveda; *Natyashastra*; yoga
Intensity Arc–On the Grid (exercise) 163–4
intercultural exchange, interculturalism 8, 11, 13, 18, 33, 37, 41n1; performance 5, 32
Introducing Each Rasa (exercise) 69–70, 142
In White America (Duberman) 14, 41n6
Ionesco, Eugène: Schechner's dissertation on 13; *Victims of Duty* 14
Islam 64
Ithaca College 3; Rasa Symposium in 2012 43n27; *see also* Cole, Paula Murray; Duerksen, Alyssa
Iyengar, B. K. S. student of Krishnamacharya 26; TPW yoga and 95, 98

Jacob, Max 259
Jackson, Phyllis: *YokastaS Redux* 39
James, William 245; Paul Ekman's research on emotion and 138
Jesus Christ Superstar (musical), Rasaboxes and 217
Jois, Patabi 26
Jones, Amelia 78n19

kalaripayattu 68
Kamasutra 64
Kapalabhati exercise 99 (*see* skull-shining breath)
Kaprow, Allan 15, 32, 75
karuna, Alyssa Duerksen exploring 160; definition and corresponding sthayi bhava 49, 57, 61, 70; Blanche Dubois character explored through 135, 173; Chekhov's *Three Sisters* explored through 174; clown work in Rasaboxes 276; Experiencing karuna as base rasa for Layering 173–4; *Glass Menagerie* explored according to 217–18; gray color associated with 78n16; Juliet (*of Romeo and Juliet*) as 72–3; *Macbeth* explored via 215; Ofelia (of *Hamlet*) explored through 175–6; young children's introduction to 220–1; working with high school students 215
karuna rasabox, 152, 276
kathak 56
kathakali 52, 56; Schechner's experience of 24, 26; Kathakali Kalamandalam in Kerala 23, 26
Kelley, Mike 75
Khajuraho 64
ki 68
Kirby, Michael 21, 32, 41–2n5 and 8; on acting and non-acting 110–11
Kirshenblatt-Gimblett, Barbara 33
Krishna (Lord) 50, 77n10
Krishnamacharya, Tirumalai 25–6, 95; Schechner looking at photo of 25; yoga 193, 209n3
Krishna Ni Bengane Baro (Balasaraswati) 52
kundalini 68, 74
kudiyattam 52, 56, 73, 236
kuchipudi 56

Laban, and Bartenieff approach 4; Effort Actions 226
Landy, Robert 235–6, 245; aesthetic distancing theory 242n3; taxonomy of roles 239
Lannoy, Richard 64–5
Layering Rasas (exercises) 172–6; Schechner on 73
Lecoq pedagogy and methods 4, 7, 226, 280, 282–3
LGBTQIA artists 159
lila (play) 64; *see also Maya-Lila*; *Ramlila*; *Raslila*
limen 29–30
liminality/liminal space 29–31, in TPW 74, 82, 129, holding of 201
liminoid 30, 129, 199–203
Lim, Jennifer: *YokastaS Redux* 39
Linklater, Kristin 37, 78n12, 100–1, 194
locograms 240
Lot's Daughters 12
Loukes, Rebecca 232

Mabou Mines 194
Macbeth (character) 215
Machinal (Treadwell) 7, 280–93; Slow Motion Transformation diagram 287
Making a Breath Phrase (exercise) 148–9; Schechner breath and sound in Rasaboxes 71
Mamallapuram 64

manipuri 56
Marshall, Thurgood 12
masking tape 89, to delineate areas of activity in TPW 90, 141, as neutral space in Rasaboxes 150, Uncrossing the Line 183
masks: emotional 72; *hee* sound and 102, 158; identity and 203; Mnouchekine mask work 226; neutral mask in rehearsal 282–3; *persona* as 116; pig snout 133; psychological distance achieved using 235; social 19, 60; sound-amplifying 60; surface acting using 253; red nose as 276, 277, 278–9
Maya-Lila 28, 29
Mayer, Emeran 67
McConnell, Colin 259
McCray, Porter 23–4
McCarthy, Paul 75
McFadden, Kelly 219, 222
McNamara, Brooks 32
Mee, Erin B. 7, 258–61
Meisner repetition exercises 226
Merlin, Bella 232n1
Meyerhold, Vsevolod 194, 292n5
Miller, Vernice 37
Minnick, Michele: in *adbhuta* rasabox 164; on actors as "athletes of the heart" 242n8; work with East Coast Artists 37; cool downs with 179; development of Rasaboxes with Schechner 77n7; drawing in rasaboxes 143; as first wave teacher of TPW 3; on "leader-as-holder" 203; on leader as "trickster" 207; Schechner interview with 190–6; "Shanta as Witness" 159; Slow Motion Crossing diagram by 126; Slow Motion Transformation diagram by 131; as student of Schechner 4; on "therapeutic" nature of Rasaboxes training 235; *Three Sisters* by Chekhov translated by 37; Wallin's interview of and workshops with 198–200, 202–3, 207, 209
Mixing Rasas (exercise) 171–2
mohiniyattam 56
Montano, Linda 75
Moraes, Marcia 3, 40, work with Schechner 77n7, Introduction of Contact Improvisation to TPW 274n3
Moreno, Jacob 240

Moroz, Mike 214–5, 219
Moscow Art Theatre 194
Moses, Gilbert 13
Mosse, Benjamin 36, 38, *39*
Mother Courage and Her Children (Brecht) 26, 27, Gray and Sack in Schechner's production 35; critical reception in India 42n20
mudras 64, 73, 75
murtis 64, 77n9

NAACP Legal Defense 12
nabhi mula 68
Nadi shodhana 98–9; *see also* Breath Work exercises
nakedness: in *Bacchae* 21; Schechner on 20; TPW and 113
Names (exercises) 92–4; with Crossings I 109–10; use of actors' names in Dionysus in 69 21
natya 47, 63; Brahma on 47; "first" 75n2; rasas of 48
Natyashastra (NS) (Bharata-muni) 46–54, 61; Abhinavagupta's commentary on 50, 258; bhava and rasa in 49; drama therapy and 235; editions of 56; Ghosh's translation of 27; history of English compilation of 76n3; interpreters of 56; introducing rasas in Rasaboxes 142; lack of direct access to 137; overlap with Ekman's work 139, *Poetics* (Aristotle) and 55–7; rasa theory adopted from 2, 5; rasa in 48; Schechner, influence on 27, 46; stagecraft outlined by 47; Veda status of 75n2; *see also* Abhinavagupta
Natyaveda (Brahma) 76n2, 77n8
Navigation Guide (for Part II) 87–8
Neuerburg, Ursula; at Concordia University 40; as first wave teacher of Rasaboxes 3, 77n7; founding member of ECA 37–40 psychophysical preparation for Rasaboxes 225–32; Rasaboxes used by 6, 40, 43n27,; as Schechner's student 4, 37, 40
neural crest 66
neurobiology 65
nervous system *see* "brain in the belly"; enteric nervous system (ENS)
New Orleans Group (NOG) 14, 194, 209n1

New York University (NYU) 3; Abe Burrows Theatre 199; Department of Graduate Drama 18, 32; Department of Performance Studies 4; Doner-Tanager's performance at 236; Drama Therapy Program 6; Grotowski's workshops and seminars at 19–20, 23, 193 197; Kirby at 110; Minnick's Rasaboxes workshop at 253; Schechner's retirement from 8, 41; Schechner's teaching and students at 32, 36–8, 40; School of the Arts 19; TPW at *105, 124, 128, 132, 134, 136, 143, 145, 153, 164, 168*; Steinhardt School 251; *see also* Landy
Noble, Adam consent practices 186n1
NOG *see* New Orleans Group
noh theatre 63, 68
NS *see* Natyashastra
NYU *see* New York University

Object Exercise 121–2
objects in Rasaboxes 277–8
Odin Teatret, Denmark 23, 37
odissi 52, 53n9, 56, 73
Oedipus Sack in Seneca's, directed by Schechner
Oedipus Tyrannus (Sophocles) 57
O'Neal, John 13
One Sound (exercise) 104–6, flow in 107; as preparation for Rasaboxes 136
One Sound One Movement (exercise) (OSOM) 106–7
Orange Exercise 139–40
Open Sound (exercise) 102–3, consent in 84; Schechner on 193
Orlan (artist) 75

Panting and Sounding with Resonators (exercises) 99–102
partaker 49, 61–3, 74–5, 137, 140, in Relating in Rasaboxes 152; in Rasaboxes rules for play 147; rasa received by, discussion regarding 149; *see also Serious Banquet, A*
performance: appreciation of 51; art 32, 34–5, 75; Asian 23–4, 68; composing (clown) 278–9; environment 16; experience in Greek theatre 64; experimental 13; four vectors of rasic performance 50; group 124;

genres of in performance studies 13; instruction in classical forms 52; manual (*see Natyashastra*); non-proscenium 27; objective of in *Natyashastra* 48; personal process of performer and 20; postmodern and rasic 65; principles 46; rasic 61–3; limen in ritual and aesthetic 30; Schechner's broad spectrum approach 17–18, 22; social roles (Goffman) 17; solo 34–5, 43n25; space 38; traditional Indian forms of 52; workshop leaders 197–209; *see also* rasa; TPW
Performance of Self and Persona 116–24; *see also* Performing the Self
performance theory 13, 17–8, course taught by Schechner at NYU 32; *Natyashastra* as 55, 57; rasic system of emotions 63
Performative Introductions (exercise) 93
Performative Responses 120–1
Performing the Self 32, 116–24
persona: base rasa and 174; objects and 122; self-persona-character, continuum of 116; Slow Motion Transformation and 128
Pert, Candace B. 149–50
Picasso, Pablo 258–9
Pillai, Shanti 5; 36, 46–53
Plato: neo-Platonism 77n9; Plato's cave 59
play Caillois theory of 94, event time and 85; Flow and 107; ritual, performance, performance studies and 29–34, Rasaboxes: Rules for 147; role-play 235; TPW: Rules for 88; and the Self (Winnicott) 120; vocal and physical in Rasaboxes with young children 220
"play frame" 209n5
play theory 31, 32, 94, playfulness in TPW 207; *see also* Caillois; Huizinga
Plessy v. Ferguson 12
Polish Theatre Laboratory 18, 19, actor training of 197
Pollock, Sheldon 53n1
Popova, Lyubov 282
prana 94
pranayama 94, 98, and stimulation of the vagus nerve 78n12

Index 301

prasad 64, 77n9, 86
psychophysical: accessing rasic flavors through 138; centering 68; embodiment of emotion in drama therapy 236; Stanislavsky and 18, Grotowski and 19; history and principles of 227–8; in transitions between rasaboxes 155
psychophysical acting 21; clearing breath following exercises in 100; nabhi mula, importance to 68; performer techniques 36; Schechner's Rasaboxes training 52
psychophysical-aesthetic exploration 20
psychophysical preparation for Rasaboxes 138, 225–32; *see also* Rasaboxes
Purlie Victorious (Davis) 14

queer 4
queer theory 33
Questions Exercise 278

raga 74, 78n18
Raghavan, Venkatarama 50
Rama 28
Ramanujan, A. K. 50
Ramcharitmanas (Tulsidas) 28
Ramlila of Ramnagar 28–9, 42n22, 63–5
Ranciere, Jacques 259
Rangacharya, Adya: English translation of *NS* 56, 76n3
rasa 61, 70; application to school curriculum 222; base 173–5, 218, 283–5; bhava and 57–8; colors of 73, 78n16, 159; defining and describing 46, 137–8; embodying 143–79; emotional intelligence and 218–19; Indian concepts of 5, 36, 46, 61, 138; introduction to each 142, 220–1; layering 173–4; mask 175, 176; mixing 171–172; music and 214; *raga* and 74, 78n18; scaling intensity of 162–3; syllables in names of 157–8; *see also Natyashastra*
Rasa≈Therapy 235–41; storytelling 238
Rasaboxes 136–79; Brazilian telenovelas and coaching using 263–7; building a character with 174–6; character building through 269–74; chorus work in 167–9; clown, experimenting with and 275–9; colors

of rasas 73, 78n16, 159; color palette, Rasaboxes as 171; directing undergrad and grad students using 280–93; drama therapists' training and 251–7; drama therapy and 235–250; Emo Lab 226–34; grid, setting up 69, 141–2; in K-3 219–24; middle and high school students 213–9; overview 136; introducing each rasa 142; resonators in 158; psychophysical preparation for 225–34; text in 72–3; (monologues) 166; training in TPW and 3–8, (development of) 36–41, *136, 143, 144, 145, 146, 153, 157, 164, 165, 168, 175,* writing and drawing in 69, 142–3; rasaesthetics, Schechner's essay on 27, 36, 47, 55–79
Rasa Bureau exercise 221
Rasa Collage exercise 221
rasa maps 217–18
Rasawalk: Site-Specific Explorations 177–9
rasic: chorus 284–5, 290; choices 166, 176; colors 159; "contamination" 154; experience 50, 58, 65; experience, politics of 259; expressiveness, facial expression 139; flavors 123; interpretation of performance 75, memory 286, 287; performance 61, performer 74; persona, creating 172; point of view 169, 218; sensation 165; space 148; system 62–5, 69
Raslila 64, 65
raudra: Blanche Dubois played with *raudra* as base rasa 173; chorus work in 167; cliché expression of 71; continuum of intensity of 161; converted into drama therapy role types 239; defining or translation into English of 49, 57, 61, 70; Juliet (of *Romeo and Juliet*) as 72–3; Ofelia (of *Hamlet*) with base rasa of 174–6; "no touching others" rule while exploring 215; red associated with 78n16; sounds associated with 158; sthayi bhava associated with 49, 61; youth groups exploring 215; *see also rauda* rasabox
raudra rasabox 137, 138, 168, 252; drawing in *144,* 150

regard, regarding: self-regarding 51, 74; showing and 149
refusal 83, 115, 125, 130; right of 115; Yes and No (Cole) 115–16
Relating in Rasaboxes for Two Players (exercise) 72, 152–4, *153*
Relating in Shanta (exercise) 159–60
Relating with Text: Scenework (exercise) 169–71
repertoire: bhava 49; behavior 246, 247; role 235, 240, 255; *see also bhava*
resonators *see* Panting and Sounding with Resonators
restoration of behavior 117
Reynaud or Regnaud, Paul 76
Richard's Lear 36
Richards, Thomas 19
Richmond, Farley 51
Rockefeller, John D. 23
role: role-play 94, 128, 235; repertoire 235, 240, 255
Romeo and Juliet (characters) 73
Rousseau, Henri 258–9
Rules, for Play 88; of Follow-No-Leader exercises 104; for moving on grid 69; in Rasaboxes 147

Sack, Leeny 34–5, 98, everything is content 111; witness in meditation and performance 159
Sahitya Darpana 51
Sajnani, Nisha 236; Bharatanatyam studied by 236; "Rasaboxes in Training of Drama Therapists" 6, 139, 251–5
Salmon, Andre 259
Sample Three-Week Workshop 184–5; *see also* The Performance Workshop (TPW)
Sartori, Amleto 292n8
Satabdi Theatre, Kolkata 24
sattriya 56
Scaling Intensity (exercises) 161–4
Schechner, Richard: 1980–1981 journal *34*; activism 11, 13–17; on actors as "athletes of the heart" 242n7; "Approaches to Theory/Criticism" 17–18; articles by 3; Asia and 23–9; *Between Theater and Anthropology* (1985) 5; brief biography of 2; environmental staging by 13–17; *Environmental*

Theater (1994 [1973]) 5, 83; *Faust/gastronome*, directed by 37; Grotowski, influence of 18–20, 23–4; hybridity in work of and 29–35; *Imagining O* directed by 39; interview, on principles of The Performance Workshop 6, 190–6; Krishnamacharya and 25; leftist views of 13; legacy and pedagogy of 35–41; "Magnitudes of Performance" chart, *Mother Courage* directed by 27; origins of The Performance Workshop and, 10–41; *Performance Studies, An Introduction* (2020) 5, 11; "performance theory" of 17; *Performance Theory* (1988) 5; "Performer" (chapter in *Environmental Theatre*) 20; retirement from NYU 8; as "Richard" 82–3; Schechner with an early sketch of Rasaboxes from his 1993 journal *191*; "selective inattention" 192, 196n1; Sircar and 24; TPG's *Commune* directed by 16; The Performance Group (TPG) and 2, *16*, 17–26, 27; The Performance Workshop (TPW) and 2, 4, 8, 10–41; *Three Sisters* directed by 38; Turner, influence of and association with 29–32; *workshop*, understanding of 20; yoga, introduction to 24; "Richard yoga" 95; *YokastaS* directed by 39
Schneemann, Carolee 75
Schneider, Rebecca 78n19
score: basic 109; concept of 118; performance 118, 124, 125; physical 91, 109, 131, 176; physical, creating (exercise) 166; set 94–5; slow motion physical (exercise) 182
Scott, John 98
Sculpting in Partners (exercise) 145–7
Seelenkunde 227
"selective inattention" 192, 196n1
self: Song of Self 35, 116; (exercise) 117; notes from Cole's 1998 journal entry 118–20; group performances 124; self and solo performance 34–5; *see also* Goffman; Performing the Self
self-consciousness 214, 222

self-disgust 172
self-feeding 75
self-judgment 115
self-knowledge 251
self-presentation 129
self-regard, self-regarding 51, 74
self-regulation 235, 237
self-revelatory theatre performance 236
self-training 163
self-who-is-observing 74
self-who-is-performing 74
Seneca's Oedipus 35
senses 60; animal exercise engaging 122–4; anthropology/aesthetics of 78n20; external environment as stimulus for 178; *Faust/gastronome* as feast for 36; Lannoy on 64; Linklater on 100–1; orange peel exercise involving 140; Pert on neuropeptide receptors and 149; rasa as flavor grounding world of 139; rasawalking exercise engaging 178; slow motion transformation variation engaging 135; snout and 59; watching (workshop) 111
Sense Memory and Rasaboxes (exercises) 6, 193, 229–31
Serious Banquet, A 7, 258–60
Setting Up the Rasaboxes Grid 141–2
"shadowing" 215–16, 223n2
shaman 200–2
shamanism 32
Shanghai Theatre Academy, China 3
shanta 73; Abhinavangupta's referencing of ninth rasa of 50, 61–2; converted into role types 239; definition or English translation of 49, 57, 61, 70; relating with 160; as state of detachment from other emotions 141–2; *sthayi bhava*, corresponding 49, 61; white associated with 78n16; as "white light" 152; as witness 159
shanta rasabox 70, 78n17, 137, 142, 150; as center box 70, 147, 238; exercise with 161; third player in 170
Shanta Rasabox: First Taste (exercise) 150
Shanta Waterfall (exercise) 180
shavasana 179; *see also* asanas
Shephard, William 21
Shopping for Rasas (exercise) 150–2

Showing and Regarding (exercise) 149
shringara: definition or English translation of 49, 57, 61, 70; erotic or physical 142; food associations 141; green color associated with 78n16; Juliet of *Romeo and Juliet* 73; Laura in *Glass Menagerie* 218; Masha from *Three Sisters* 174; Nora from *A Doll's House* 173; "no touching others" rule while exploring 215; Ofelia from *Hamlet* 175; sounds associated with 157, 158; relating with 160; as state of detachment from other emotions 142; *sthayi bhava*, corresponding 49, 61; transliterated as "sringara" 137; white associated with working with young people, potential issues with 220
shringara rasabox 70, 72, 137, 158, *165*, *175*
Silbiger, Sam 261
SITI Company 194
Sircar, Badal 24, 42n18
Six Axioms 18, 23
Skull Shining Breath 98–101; exercise 98–9; *see also kapalabhati*
Socha, David 236–7
somatic movement: exercises 282; therapy 4, 41
somatic practice and experience 35, 106, 179, 226, 227
somatic sensations 245, 248
somatic states 249
Song of Self 35, 116, 118–20; Cole on 118–20; exercise 117; Group Performances and 124; self and persona 116; TPW and 35, 116; in TPW journal entry 118–20, 124
songs: characters represented by, performers requested to bring recordings of songs they associated with 286; Cool Down, as activity 179–80; in Banquet exercise 182; Bridge and Holding Space, singing of 201; hand gestures and 74; in *Jesus Christ Superstar* 217; lyrics 168; sharing 184; Slow Motion Crossing, instruction to engage 126; Slow Motion Crossing, experience of 135; student exploration of Rasaboxes using 226; TPW

and sharing of 121; TPW and singing of 201
Sophocles: *Electra* 7, 269–74; *Oedipus Tyrannus* 57; *Philoctetes* 12
sound and sounding: Aiming and Passing Sound 103; Chorus work in Rasaboxes involving 167; of food 60; impulse as impetus for 101; masks to amplify 60; One Sound 84, 104–6, 111, 136; One Sound One Movement 94, 106–7, 133, 151, 167; One Sound One Movement exercise 122, 126, 178, 182; One Sound One Movement with Chorus 167; Open Sound 84, 102–3; painting with 101; Panting and Sounding with Resonators 99, 100–2; Rasabox exercises involving sound and/or absence of 69–73, 98; Rasabox exercises for Two Players involving 152; Rasabox soloing exercise using 158; sounding with resonators 102; Sound Sensation in Rasaboxes (exercises) 156–8; Sound Work, group 102–6; text as extension of 164–5
Spolin, Viola 215–16, 223n2
spontaneous communitas 29–30, 107
Sprinkle, Annie 75
Stanislavsky System of actor training 16, 76n6, 116, 186n10, 225, 232, 272, 290
Stanislavsky, Constantin 18, 62; "circle of attention" of 232; psychophysical approach of 227–8; undergraduate training using approaches to acting of 6, 225–32
Stanislavsky-Strasberg system 62–63
Stellarc 75
Strasberg, Lee: Actors Studio 76n6; chair relaxation exercise 228; emotional memory and 76n6; sense-memory practice of 229; undergraduate training using approaches to acting of 6, 225–32
Strasberg Method 225, 226, 232
Stebbins, Genevieve 227
Stein, Gertrude 259
Steinhardt School, NYU 251
stillness 284; Clearing Breath, completion of exercise using 100; Crossings I, ending

of exercise in 108; Group Clearing Breath, standing in for three cycles 100; intensity arc, listening in 164; Slow Motion Transformation 96, 131; Song of Self, Round #1 (Cole), sitting or standing in 118; yoga asanas 95
still pose 138; Banquet (exercise) 181, 182; embodiment of emotion in 248; Scaling Intensity of Rasa (exercise) 163; Sculpting in Partners 145–7, 148; Showing and Regarding 147–8; Slow Motion Crossing, Day Six rehearsal 289
Sun Huizhu (William Sun) 3
surface acting 253–4
"surface" rasa 174
Suzuki, Tadashi 4
svadhisthanam of yoga 68
Svitch, Caridad: *The House of the Spirits* 290

taboos 7, 29, 111, 115, 220; taboos in Rasaboxes with K-12 214–15
Tagore, Rabindranath 48
Taylorism 292n5
TDR (see *The Drama Review* and *The Tulane Drama Review*)
telenovela see Brazilian telenovela
theatre: Diderot on 62; environmental 12, 22, 23–4, 24, 65; experimental 13, 42n17; Greek 60, 64; group 34; guerilla theatre protests 15; immersive 6, 23, 65; Indian 63, 65, 73; Indian language of 52; racially integrated 13; musical 166; noh 68; orthodox western 74; protest 13; "theatre and its double" 74
Theatre Games 223n2
Theatre of Productions (Grotowski) 19
Theatre of Sources (Grotowski) 19
theatre studies 17
Teatro Prometeo: staging *Electra* at 269–74
Text in Rasaboxes (exercises) monologues 165; chorus with text 168–9; chorus with speaker and listener 169; scenework 169–71
The Performance Group (TPG) 2, 3, 20–2, 35, 194; *Commune* 16; Gray's and Sack's involvement with 35–6; *Mother Courage* 27, 35;

nakedness in context of 113; Schechner's departure from 42n13; see *Dionysus in 69*
The Performance Workshop (TPW) 1–8; applause held in 93, 120; breath work 98–9; communitas in 107; core principles of 32, 34; Crossings 14; *encounter* in 92; four resonators (vowels) 102; fundamental principles and practice 82–8; key principles of TPW according to Schechner 190–2; legacy and pedagogy since 1999 35–41; *Machinal* and undergraduate pedagogy 280–93; NYU and *105, 124, 128, 132, 136, 143, 145, 153, 164, 168*; permission to look in 109; physical nakedness in 113, 288; play theory and 94; Rasaboxes, expansion of 10; Sample Three-Week Workshop 184–5; Schechner and origins of 10–41, 113; "score" concept of 118; "Self" and performance of self in 116; serious play, as world of 31–2; Song of Self in 35, 122; space for dissent in 116; structure and practice of 184–5; structuring elements in 30; time in 85–6, 91–2; yoga in 95–8
The Performing Garage 16, 20, 21, 26, 38, 198
The Polish Theatre Laboratory of Opole 18
This is Not A Theatre Company 7, 258
time in TPW 85–6
TPW see The Performance Workshop
trance dancing 86
trance state 106
transitional object 60, 120, in Schechner's theory of double negativity 209
Transitions in Rasaboxes (exercise) 154–6
Treadwell, Sophie 281, *281*, 292n3
triangulation 276–7
trickster 200, 207–8, 239
True Stories (exercise) 265–6
truth(s) 47, 59, 116, 122
Tulane Drama Review (TDR) 13–14, 17–19, 209n1; history of 41n5
Tulane Drama Review: The Drama Review 18, 41

Turner, Victor 29–32, 107, 209n5
Twelve Steps exercise 282, 292n7

Ubeda, Patricia 276
Udbhata 56
Ujjayi (Victorious Breath) 98
Uncrossing the Line (exercise) 185

Vaghtangov, Yevgeni 225
vagus nerve 66; stimulation of 67–8, 78n12
Vail-Guevara, Maria 37
Vallejo, Diana 271
van Gennep, Arnold *see* Gennep, Arnold van
Vatsyayan, Kapila 51, 56, 76n3
Veda 75n2
verfremdungseffekt 74
Versailles (immersive cocktail party) 7, 260
Victims of Duty (Ionesco) 14
Victorious Breath (ujjayi) exercise 98
Vidal, Gore 13
Vietnam War 15; protests 22
Viewpoints (Mary Overlie and Anne Bogart) 4, 226
vihara (assembly hall) 64
vira 49, 57, 61, 70, 72; converted into role types 239; Michael's experimentation with 249; orange color associated with 78n16; rasa maps and 217–18; spicy or salty 140
vira rasabox 137, *168*, 171
Visit to a Small Planet (Vidal) 13

vismaya 49, 61
Visvakarman 76n2

Wallin, Scott 3, 4; Cole and Minnick as mentors of 40; first experience of the TPW 6, 197–209
Warm-ups: Physical and Vocal Training 94–102; *see also* Group Sound Work
Watching 111; Crossing the Line: being, doing and 7; Crossings IV: Slow Motion, involving 125; doing and watching of self 133; doing, showing, sharing and, in real time 83; jumping into new roles, using 240; by leader-as-holder 203; listening and, value of 190; nakedness and 113; others perform 31, 52; Presence and Absence, involving 83; seeing and 111; Showing and Regarding, involving 149; Schechner's thoughts on 205; by supervisor or workshop leader 202, 205; Tactics for Cooling Down 231; traditional Indian dance 73–4; of videos 284; watchers and 111, 202
watching box: Crossings V: Slow Motion, using 128; Crossings V: Slow Motion Transformation using 128; Setting up Crossing Space 125–6; Slow Motion Crossing Diagram for *Machinal*: box "H" 287, 288
Webster, Shay 127, *290*
White, Gareth 259
Whyman, Rose 227
Williams, Tennessee: *Streetcar Named Desire* 173; *see also Glass Menagerie*
Winnicott, D. W. 120, 209n5, 242n3
Wold, Kate 217–18
Wood, Frank 37, *38*
Woodstock 22
Wooster Group, The 34–5, 42n13, 194
Writing and Drawing in Rasaboxes (exercise) 69, 142–4

yoga: asanas 94, 95–9, 292n6; classical 68; drawings *96, 97*; ECA and 37; "Richard yoga" 95; Schechner's introduction to 23–5; TPW 6, *38*; Zarrilli's study of 36; Rising Up on the Toes 95–8; *see also* Iyengar; Krishnamacharya
YokastaS and *YokastaS Redux* 38–40, *39*

Zarrilli, Phillip 36, 43n26, 68–9, 227

For Product Safety Concerns and Information please contact our EU
representative GPSR@taylorandfrancis.com
Taylor & Francis Verlag GmbH, Kaufingerstraße 24, 80331 München, Germany

www.ingramcontent.com/pod-product-compliance
Lightning Source LLC
Chambersburg PA
CBHW051350290426
44108CB00015B/1951